The Convergence of Human and Artificial Intelligence on Clinical Care - Part I

The Convergence of Human and Artificial Intelligence on Clinical Care - Part I

Editor

Vida Abedi

MDPI • Basel • Beijing • Wuhan • Barcelona • Belgrade • Manchester • Tokyo • Cluj • Tianjin

Editor
Vida Abedi
Public Health Sciences
The Pennsylvania State University
Hershey
United States

Editorial Office
MDPI
St. Alban-Anlage 66
4052 Basel, Switzerland

This is a reprint of articles from the Special Issue published online in the open access journal *Journal of Clinical Medicine* (ISSN 2077-0383) (available at: www.mdpi.com/journal/jcm/special_issues/Artificial_Intelligence_on_Clinical_Care).

For citation purposes, cite each article independently as indicated on the article page online and as indicated below:

LastName, A.A.; LastName, B.B.; LastName, C.C. Article Title. *Journal Name* **Year**, *Volume Number*, Page Range.

ISBN 978-3-0365-3296-7 (Hbk)
ISBN 978-3-0365-3295-0 (PDF)

© 2022 by the authors. Articles in this book are Open Access and distributed under the Creative Commons Attribution (CC BY) license, which allows users to download, copy and build upon published articles, as long as the author and publisher are properly credited, which ensures maximum dissemination and a wider impact of our publications.

The book as a whole is distributed by MDPI under the terms and conditions of the Creative Commons license CC BY-NC-ND.

Contents

About the Editor vii

Preface to "The Convergence of Human and Artificial Intelligence on Clinical Care - Part I" . ix

Vida Abedi, Jiang Li, Manu K. Shivakumar, Venkatesh Avula, Durgesh P. Chaudhary and Matthew J. Shellenberger et al.
Increasing the Density of Laboratory Measures for Machine Learning Applications
Reprinted from: *J. Clin. Med.* **2020**, *10*, 103, doi:10.3390/jcm10010103 1

HyunBum Kim, Juhyeong Jeon, Yeon Jae Han, YoungHoon Joo, Jonghwan Lee and Seungchul Lee et al.
Convolutional Neural Network Classifies Pathological Voice Change in Laryngeal Cancer with High Accuracy
Reprinted from: *J. Clin. Med.* **2020**, *9*, 3415, doi:10.3390/jcm9113415 25

Debdipto Misra, Venkatesh Avula, Donna M. Wolk, Hosam A. Farag, Jiang Li and Yatin B. Mehta et al.
Early Detection of Septic Shock Onset Using Interpretable Machine Learners
Reprinted from: *J. Clin. Med.* **2021**, *10*, 301, doi:10.3390/jcm10020301 41

Mazen Osman, Zeynettin Akkus, Dragan Jevremovic, Phuong L. Nguyen, Dana Roh and Aref Al-Kali et al.
Classification of Monocytes, Promonocytes and Monoblasts Using Deep Neural Network Models: An Area of Unmet Need in Diagnostic Hematopathology
Reprinted from: *J. Clin. Med.* **2021**, *10*, 2264, doi:10.3390/jcm10112264 59

Yang Cao, Mustafa Raoof, Eva Szabo, Johan Ottosson and Ingmar Näslund
Using Bayesian Networks to Predict Long-Term Health-Related Quality of Life and Comorbidity after Bariatric Surgery: A Study Based on the Scandinavian Obesity Surgery Registry
Reprinted from: *J. Clin. Med.* **2020**, *9*, 1895, doi:10.3390/jcm9061895 71

Vida Abedi, Venkatesh Avula, Durgesh Chaudhary, Shima Shahjouei, Ayesha Khan and Christoph J Griessenauer et al.
Prediction of Long-Term Stroke Recurrence Using Machine Learning Models
Reprinted from: *J. Clin. Med.* **2021**, *10*, 1286, doi:10.3390/jcm10061286 83

Shima Shahjouei, Michelle Anyaehie, Eric Koza, Georgios Tsivgoulis, Soheil Naderi and Ashkan Mowla et al.
SARS-CoV-2 Is a Culprit for Some, but Not All Acute Ischemic Strokes: A Report from the Multinational COVID-19 Stroke Study Group
Reprinted from: *J. Clin. Med.* **2021**, *10*, 931, doi:10.3390/jcm10050931 99

Daisuke Kasugai, Masayuki Ozaki, Kazuki Nishida, Hiroaki Hiraiwa, Naruhiro Jingushi and Atsushi Numaguchi et al.
Usefulness of Respiratory Mechanics and Laboratory Parameter Trends as Markers of Early Treatment Success in Mechanically Ventilated Severe Coronavirus Disease: A Single-Center Pilot Study
Reprinted from: *J. Clin. Med.* **2021**, *10*, 2513, doi:10.3390/jcm10112513 113

Shima Shahjouei, Seyed Mohammad Ghodsi, Morteza Zangeneh Soroush, Saeed Ansari and Shahab Kamali-Ardakani
Artificial Neural Network for Predicting the Safe Temporary Artery Occlusion Time in Intracranial Aneurysmal Surgery
Reprinted from: *J. Clin. Med.* **2021**, *10*, 1464, doi:10.3390/jcm10071464 . . . . **125**

Miguel Angel Alvarez-Mon, Laura de Anta, Maria Llavero-Valero, Guillermo Lahera, Miguel A. Ortega and Cesar Soutullo et al.
Areas of Interest and Attitudes towards the Pharmacological Treatment of Attention Deficit Hyperactivity Disorder: Thematic and Quantitative Analysis Using Twitter
Reprinted from: *J. Clin. Med.* **2021**, *10*, 2668, doi:10.3390/jcm10122668 . . . . **135**

Massimo Micocci, Simone Borsci, Viral Thakerar, Simon Walne, Yasmine Manshadi and Finlay Edridge et al.
Attitudes towards Trusting Artificial Intelligence Insights and Factors to Prevent the Passive Adherence of GPs: A Pilot Study
Reprinted from: *J. Clin. Med.* **2021**, *10*, 3101, doi:10.3390/jcm10143101 . . . . **149**

Zeynettin Akkus, Yousof H. Aly, Itzhak Z. Attia, Francisco Lopez-Jimenez, Adelaide M. Arruda-Olson and Patricia A. Pellikka et al.
Artificial Intelligence (AI)-Empowered Echocardiography Interpretation: A State-of-the-Art Review
Reprinted from: *J. Clin. Med.* **2021**, *10*, 1391, doi:10.3390/jcm10071391 . . . . **161**

About the Editor

Vida Abedi

Dr. Abedi, Associate Professor at the Penn State College of Medicine, has a multidisciplinary background. Dr. Abedi has a Bachelor of Science in Biochemistry and a Bachelor's in Computer Engineering. She also has a Master's in Cellular and Molecular Medicine and a Master's in Bioinformatics. Dr. Abedi's Ph.D. degree is in Computer and Electrical Engineering. Given the years of experience and a unique fusion of expertise, Dr. Abedi has made a significant contribution to applied AI in healthcare. She is the AI lead on several funded studies aiming to bring predictive modeling to clinical settings to improve outcomes and reduce care gaps and health disparity.

Preface to "The Convergence of Human and Artificial Intelligence on Clinical Care - Part I"

Artificial intelligence is gradually becoming a go-to technology in clinical care, from diagnosing a wide range of diseases to predicting outcomes and selecting the best treatment at a personalized level. In the past few years, intelligent systems have contributed to building prediction models and identifying patients at higher risk of certain high-impact conditions such as heart failure, sepsis, and ischemic stroke. In this edited book, key areas that are pushing the forefront of innovation in healthcare are presented by leading experts. The studies showcase the power of technology, its limits, and the value of collaboration, all with a core mission of tackling healthcare's changing landscape using AI. This edited book contains twelve studies, large and pilots, in five main categories: (i) adaptive imputation to increase the density of clinical data for improving downstream modeling; (ii) machine-learning-empowered diagnosis models; (iii) machine learning models for outcome prediction; (iv) innovative use of AI to improve our understanding of the public view; and (v) understanding of the attitude of providers in trusting insights from AI for complex cases.

Overall, the studies used an array of data modalities, including data from electronic health records, imaging data, voice signals, resource utilization, Twitter data, and questionnaire, in addition to a wide range of modeling frameworks, designs, and algorithms. This edited book is an excellent example of how technology can add value in healthcare settings and hints at some of the pressing challenges in the field, including attitudes towards technology and the quality of the data used in predictive modeling. As we move toward implementing these tools in clinical settings, the experts from different fields need to work together to better understand the technological challenges, the needs of care providers and patients, and to ensure there are no unintended consequences which are introduced by integrating AI into the clinical workflow.

I believe that our future is in partnering with intelligent systems to solve complex multidimensional problems in many fields, including health care, and shifting from performance-driven outcomes to risk-sensitive model optimization, improved transparency, and better patient representation for more equitable healthcare for all.

Vida Abedi
Editor

Article

Increasing the Density of Laboratory Measures for Machine Learning Applications

Vida Abedi [1,2,*], Jiang Li [1], Manu K. Shivakumar [3], Venkatesh Avula [1], Durgesh P. Chaudhary [4], Matthew J. Shellenberger [5], Harshit S. Khara [5], Yanfei Zhang [6], Ming Ta Michael Lee [6], Donna M. Wolk [7], Mohammed Yeasin [8], Raquel Hontecillas [2,9], Josep Bassaganya-Riera [2,9] and Ramin Zand [4]

1 Department of Molecular and Functional Genomics, Geisinger Health System, Danville, PA 17822, USA; jli@geisinger.edu (J.L.); vavula1@geisinger.edu (V.A.)
2 NIMML Institute, Blacksburg, VA 24060, USA; rmagarzo@biotherapeuticsinc.com (R.H.); jbassaganya@biotherapeuticsinc.com (J.B.-R.)
3 Geisinger Medical Center, Biomedical Translational Informatics Institute, Danville, PA 17822, USA; manu.ksmanu@gmail.com
4 Geisinger Medical Center, Neuroscience Institute, Danville, PA 17822, USA; dpchaudhary@geisinger.edu (D.P.C.); rzand@geisinger.edu (R.Z.)
5 Geisinger Medical Center, Department of Gastroenterology and Hepatology, Danville, PA 17822, USA; mjshellenberger@geisinger.edu (M.J.S.); hskhara@geisinger.edu (H.S.K.)
6 Geisinger Medical Center, Genomic Medicine Institute, Danville, PA 17822, USA; yzhang1@geisinger.edu (Y.Z.); mlee2@geisinger.edu (M.T.M.L.)
7 Molecular and Microbial Diagnostics and Development, Geisinger Medical Center, Danville, PA 17822, USA; dmwolk@geisinger.edu
8 Department of Electrical and Computer Engineering, Memphis University, Memphis, TN 38152, USA; myeasin@memphis.edu
9 BioTherapeutics, Inc., Blacksburg, VA 24060, USA
* Correspondence: vidaabedi@gmail.com or vabedi@geisinger.edu

Abstract: Background. The imputation of missingness is a key step in Electronic Health Records (EHR) mining, as it can significantly affect the conclusions derived from the downstream analysis in translational medicine. The missingness of laboratory values in EHR is not at random, yet imputation techniques tend to disregard this key distinction. Consequently, the development of an adaptive imputation strategy designed specifically for EHR is an important step in improving the data imbalance and enhancing the predictive power of modeling tools for healthcare applications. Method. We analyzed the laboratory measures derived from Geisinger's EHR on patients in three distinct cohorts—patients tested for *Clostridioides difficile* (Cdiff) infection, patients with a diagnosis of inflammatory bowel disease (IBD), and patients with a diagnosis of hip or knee osteoarthritis (OA). We extracted Logical Observation Identifiers Names and Codes (LOINC) from which we excluded those with 75% or more missingness. The comorbidities, primary or secondary diagnosis, as well as active problem lists, were also extracted. The adaptive imputation strategy was designed based on a hybrid approach. The comorbidity patterns of patients were transformed into latent patterns and then clustered. Imputation was performed on a cluster of patients for each cohort independently to show the generalizability of the method. The results were compared with imputation applied to the complete dataset without incorporating the information from comorbidity patterns. Results. We analyzed a total of 67,445 patients (11,230 IBD patients, 10,000 OA patients, and 46,215 patients tested for *C. difficile* infection). We extracted 495 LOINC and 11,230 diagnosis codes for the IBD cohort, 8160 diagnosis codes for the Cdiff cohort, and 2042 diagnosis codes for the OA cohort based on the primary/secondary diagnosis and active problem list in the EHR. Overall, the most improvement from this strategy was observed when the laboratory measures had a higher level of missingness. The best root mean square error (RMSE) difference for each dataset was recorded as −35.5 for the Cdiff, −8.3 for the IBD, and −11.3 for the OA dataset. Conclusions. An adaptive imputation strategy designed specifically for EHR that uses complementary information from the clinical profile of the patient can be used to improve the imputation of missing laboratory values, especially when laboratory codes with high levels of missingness are included in the analysis.

Keywords: imputation; electronic health records; machine learning; EHR; laboratory measures; medical informatics; inflammatory bowel disease; *C. difficile* infection; osteoarthritis; complex diseases

1. Introduction

Given the complexity and high dimensionality of Electronic Health Records (EHR), the need for imputation is an inevitable aspect in any study that attempts to use such data for downstream analysis or building advanced machine learning models for decision support systems for clinical applications. The EHR or any other administrative dataset is not designed for research purposes, even though the breadth and depth of the information can be used to improve care at many levels [1]. Furthermore, the level and extent of the missing values in healthcare systems are typically not at random. Three main categories explain the missingness in clinical settings [2,3]—incompleteness, inconsistency, and inaccuracy—and these can capture a variety of situations, including the following: the patient could have been cared for outside of the healthcare system where the data are collected, the patient did not seek treatment, the health care provider did not enter the information, the patient expired, and the missing value was not needed.

Given the complexity of the clinical data and the advanced analytics that can be applied on such data, it is important to account for any sources of bias in the data that will be used to drive predictive models. Imputation is an example of data preprocessing that could lead to biased results. Furthermore, excluding variables or patients with a high-level of missingness can also introduce bias and reduce the scope of the study. From a recent review article, 85 out of 316 studies reported some form of missing data, and only 12 studies actively handled the missingness; as the authors showed, the majority of researchers exclude incomplete cases, causing biased outcomes [4]. Furthermore, imputation could boost the statistical power for data-poor patients who tend to be minorities and low-income patients with more restricted access to primary and specialty care and rehabilitation programs.

Imputation has been an ongoing solution in many fields, but only recently, the research has been focused on medical applications. Twelve different imputation techniques applied to laboratory measures from EHR were compared [5]. In general, the authors found that Multivariate Imputation by Chained Equations (MICE) and softImpute consistently imputed missing values with low error [5]; however, in that study, the analysis was restricted to 28 most commonly available variables. In another study, the authors assessed the different causes of missing data in the EHR data and identified these causes to be the source of unintentional bias [6]. A comparative analysis of three methods of imputation (a Singular Value Decomposition (SVD)-based method (SVDimpute), weighted K-nearest neighbors (KNNimpute), and row average for DNA microarrays showed that, in general, KNN and SVD methods surpass the commonly accepted solutions of filling missing values with zeros or row averages [7]. However, comparing imputation for clinical data with a DNA microarray can be misleading. The missingness in a DNA microarray is likely at random due to technical challenges unlike missingness in the EHR. In another study, fuzzy clustering was integrated with a neural network to enhance the imputation process [8].

Research has also been done to evaluate imputation methods for non-normal data [9]. Using simulated data from a range of non-normal distributions and a level of missingness of 50% (missing completely at random or missing at random), it was found that the linearity between variables could be used to determine the need for transformation for non-normal variables. In the case of a linear relationship, transformation can introduce bias, while the nonlinear relationship between variables may require adequate transformation to accurately capture the nonlinearity. Furthermore, many of the techniques are optimized for smaller levels of missingness (the most commonly available measurements), yet most clinical datasets (including the EHRs) have a significant level of missingness for many of their important variables that are routinely used for diagnosis purposes. To address this problem, machine learning methods have also been proposed [10]. There are more examples of imputation applied to simulated than real-life EHR data; however, few studies focused on imputing laboratory values. For instance, Ford E. and colleagues [11] proposed using logistic regression models with and without Bayesian priors representing the rates of misclassification in the data. However, in that study, the authors focused on misclassified diagnoses rather than laboratory values. The challenges of imputation for EHRs are unique, and if left unaddressed, the utility of the data becomes limited [12]. Consequently, even though, for smaller targeted studies, it could be possible to integrate additional modalities or perform an analytical evaluation through a chart review to determine a likely cause of missingness, for larger studies, this becomes infeasible. For example, the missingness level for very important variables, such as hemoglobin A1C or HbA1c (LOINC ID: 17856-6) levels, a common biomarker for diabetes can easily reach 50% or more in many realistic large datasets. At last, in a more recent study, the integration of genetic and clinical information was shown to improve the imputation of data missing from the Electronic Health Records [13]; however, genetic data integrated with the EHR is still scarce.

Finally, given the complexity and the scale of the problem, in many studies, MICE [14] remains the method of choice. The MICE fully conditional specification (FCS) algorithm imputes multivariate missing data on a variable-by-variable basis [15]. An imputation model is specified for each incomplete variable, and the imputation of missingness in one variable is conducted iteratively based on the other variables. There are also variations of MICE that have been proposed [16]; however, the need for imputation for data from EHR poses its challenges, especially when targeting less commonly measured variables. Nonetheless, given the high level of redundancy and the presence of highly correlated entities in the EHR, imputation by MICE still performs relatively well for large clinical datasets. A comprehensive overview of handling missing data in the EHR is presented in [12].

In this study, we created three unique cohorts from the EHR data, with varying sizes and heterogeneity, and developed a hybrid imputation strategy that we applied to these cohorts. We selected the inflammatory bowel disease cohort because of its heterogeneity and the fact that a clear understanding of IBD's risk factors is still lacking. We selected the *Clostridioides difficile*, because understanding of the recurrent infection is important, and the existing data from the EHR can help us identify clinical biomarkers; finally, we created the osteoarthritis (OA) cohort to test the limits of this model, as the OA diagnosis is not based on any laboratory measurements known today. Our imputation model was based on using comorbidity information to cluster patients prior to the imputation of their laboratory values.

2. Methods

In the following section, we will (1) describe our cohort definition and data extraction for the laboratory values and comorbidities from our EHR data warehouse and (2) outline our imputation design.

2.1. Study Cohort

The cohort in this study consisted of 67,445 patients from the Geisinger Health System with three different phenotypes. This study was exempted by the Geisinger Institutional Review Board for using deidentified information.

Clostridioides difficile (Cdiff) Infection case and control cohort: *Clostridioides difficile* (*C. difficile*) is an anaerobic, Gram-positive, and spore-forming bacterium and a major cause of intestinal infection and antibiotic-associated diarrhea. Toxins are the major virulence factors of *C. difficile* [17]. Toxins A (TcdA) and B (TcdB) are large, secreted glucosyltransferase proteins that target intestinal epithelia cells and disrupt the epithelial barrier, leading to secretory diarrhea. The diagnosis of *C. difficile* at Geisinger is captured and documented by Polymerase Chain Reaction (PCR) confirmation, which is highly sensitive. The latter is also considered the gold standard by the eMERGE algorithm for EHR mining [18]. We identified the *C. difficile* cohort, which includes patients tested for *C. difficile*, from the EHR of the Geisinger Health System. The cohort includes both cases and controls. Cases are defined as having laboratory positive PCR test results. Controls are patients tested for *C. difficile* with negative PCR test results. Case/control ratio is 1:8. We are interested in the combined case and control cohort, since patients tested for *C. difficile*, irrespective of their test results, share some of the signs and symptoms (such as diarrhea); furthermore, using a case and control combined cohort increases our sample size, an important factor for imputation, while providing a framework for building predictive models that can benefit from the integration of a large number of laboratory-based features.

Inflammatory Bowel Disease (IBD) cohort: We identified the IBD cohort from the EHR of the Geisinger Health System. Inclusion criteria of this cohort were based on the extraction of the patient population based on the diagnosis recorded for patients under their visits, admissions, and currently active problems listed based on the ICD9 and ICD10 codes for Crohn's disease (CD) and ulcerative colitis (UC) (see Table A1 in Appendix A). To have a higher fidelity regarding the diagnosis in the EHR, qualifying criteria included either two or more outpatient encounters, or one or more inpatient admissions, or an entry into the problem list with an active flag.

Osteoarthritis (OA) cohort: We identified an osteoarthritis (OA) cohort from the EHR of the Geisinger Health System; the cohort includes a knee or hip OA diagnosis, either primary or secondary diagnosis (see Table A1 in Appendix A for the OA diagnosis ICD codes).

2.2. Data Extraction

We extracted clinical laboratory measurements for this cohort using the Logical Observation Identifiers Names and Codes (LOINC) system. For comorbidities, we extracted all the diagnosis codes for all the patients based on the ICD9, as well as ICD10, codes. Comorbidity data included details from out-patient visits, in-patient admissions, and problem lists. The latter was used to capture conditions identified outside of the Geisinger Health System but discussed and assessed during the patient's care management. We excluded laboratory codes with more than 75% missingness. To further clarify, in this study, missingness is defined as the laboratory measure "not resulted". Therefore, if an order was placed but the results were not available (or not valid), we considered that as a missing value. We analyzed the data in three batches, including only laboratory measures that have, at most, (a) 25% missingness, (b) 50% missingness, and (c) 75% missingness.

2.3. Data Processing

Quality Control (QC) and outlier detection strategy: Geisinger has implemented a rigorous process to continuously extract, transform, organize, and store EHR data and remove erroneous entries for research purposes. For example, we currently have access to quality-controlled laboratory values with the reconciliation of units. Median laboratory values for each patient were calculated to be used for this study. It is important to mention that, especially for less common laboratory values, the frequency of measurements and the window between the first and last measurements per patient is relatively narrow. We analyzed the frequency patterns and reported the results in our descriptive section.

As part of the added data processing and outlier detection and removal, the distribution of each laboratory value was analyzed and fit to a tri-modal gaussian distribution model (see Equation (1)). The rationale for using this strategy, as opposed to the assumption of normality, is driven by the nature of the laboratory measures. Laboratory orders, especially those with a higher level of missingness, are typically missing not at random (MNAR), and there are mainly three groups of patients for whom there is a measurement recorded (those with higher or lower than average measures, as well as patients with average measurements). However, the average measurement is not necessarily associated with a larger group in all the cases, especially for laboratory measures that are specific to a phenotype, such as an iron-binding capacity. The latter is ordered for patients if the physician needs that information to make a diagnosis/management decision. Two cut-off values are created to filter outliers based on the three distributions model. The automated process to generate data-driven cut-off values is proposed for large-scale data mining, where limited manual curation is applied in the data preparation and preprocessing.

$$f = \mathcal{N}_1(\mu_1, \sigma_1^2) + \mathcal{N}_2(\mu_2, \sigma_2^2) + \mathcal{N}_3(\mu_3, \sigma_3^2) \tag{1}$$

where μ is the mean and σ is the standard deviation. The lowest boundary to filter out the outliers is set to c_low = max (min($\mu_1 - 3\sigma_1, \mu_2 - 3\sigma_2, \mu_3 - 3\sigma_3$), 0), and the highest boundary is set to c_high = max($\mu_1 + 3\sigma_1, \mu_2 + 3\sigma_2, \mu_3 + 3\sigma_3$).

Data processing of the comorbidity dataset was performed to remove noise by excluding the ICD9/10 codes that were recorded only once in the patient's chart (rule of 2). The resulting matrix was then converted to binary to represent the presence or absence of an ICD9/10 code for each patient. This is important, since the count does not necessarily correlate with the severity or duration of the condition. Therefore, a binary comorbidity matrix for each cohort was created for imputation modeling.

2.4. Data Abstraction and Imputation Strategy

The comorbidity dataset was used to compute an encoding matrix for each dataset (Cdiff, OA, and IBD) using singular value decomposition (Equation (2)).

$$A_{PT\_ICD\_cohort} = A_{PT \times ICD\_cohort} = USV^T \tag{2}$$

where $A_{PT\_ICD\_cohort}$ is the matrix encompassing all the ICD9/10 codes (presence of absence) for all the patients for each dataset, U is an *mxm* square matrix, S is an *mxn* diagonal matrix with m rows and n colums, and V is an *nxn* square matrix. The columns of V are eigenvectors of $A^T A$, and the columns of U are eigenvectors of AA^T. The diagonal elements of S are the square root of the eigenvalues of $A^T A$ or AA^T.

The encoding matrix was then used to create different levels of data abstraction by retaining only 100 or 1000 of the encoding using the dimensionality reduction technique (Equation (3)) for each dataset. We used these predefined cut-off values based on our preliminary assessment [19], as well as empirical studies [20,21]. For comparison, the full rank was also used in the modeling. Note that the approximation matrix is referred to as the data abstraction. The finalized output is referred to as latent comorbidities.

$$A_{PT\_ICD\_g} = U_{reduced} S_{reduced} V_{reduced}^T \tag{3}$$

where g is the level of abstraction (100 or 1000) corresponding to the level of reduced matrices. $A_{PT\_ICD\_cohort\_g}$ is an approximation of the initial matrix ($A_{PT\_ICD\_cohort}$).

As a final step in the data abstraction process, a baseline noise reduction is performed by removing the ICD codes if the sum of all the values for a given code in the latent comorbidity matrix is less than 1. This strategy reduces noise that is due to irrelevant (very rare) comorbidities in the model. The imputation method presented in this work is a hybrid method—that is, based upon concurrently applying dimensionality reduction and a clustering strategy—to efficiently capture relationships among the features (or variables) and reduce noise (through dimensionality reduction) while providing an adaptive mechanism to perform imputation for any complex phenotype or trait. Using latent comorbidity data, patients are clustered using the k-mean clustering technique with K set to 2, 4, 8, and 16 clusters, depending on the heterogeneity of the cohort.

Imputation was applied using the MICE fully conditional specification (FCS) algorithm [5], which imputes multivariate missing data on a variable-by-variable basis. An imputation model is specified to each incomplete variable, and the imputation of missingness in one variable is conducted in an iterative fashion using the Markov Chain Monte Carlo (MCMC) method. More specifically, we selected the predictive mean matching (pmm) algorithm, which is the default method of mice() for imputing continuous incomplete variables. For each missing value, pmm finds a set of observed values (default is 5) with the closest predicted mean as the missing one and imputes the missing value by a random draw from that set. In other words, pmm is restricted to the observed values. We also used Random Forest (rf), which is based on imputing missingness by recursively subdividing the data based on values of the predictor variables in the predictive model by a bootstrap aggregation of multiple regression trees to reduce the risk of overfitting and improve the predictions through a combination of prediction from many trees [22]. The latter does not rely on distributional assumptions and can better accommodate nonlinear relations and interactions.

Imputations using MICE-pmm and MICE-rf were applied to each subgroup independently to predict the missing values. The results were compared when MICE-pmm and MICE-rf were applied to estimate the missing in the laboratory values in three cohorts without any consideration of the comorbidity information. The reader is referred to the work [15] by S. van Buuren and K. Groothuis-Oudshoorn for more details about imputation by MICE.

2.5. Evaluation Strategy

Model evaluation is performed by randomly selecting variables and predicting them using the hybrid strategy. A total of 100 values from each laboratory measure was randomly withheld for testing. For example, for the Cdiff cohort, where we identified 48 laboratory codes with less than 75% missingness, we held out 100 values for each of the 48 laboratory codes and estimate these 10 times. The root mean square error (RMSE) was also calculated and averaged over the 10 runs. Comparison was based on calculating the difference between running imputation using the hybrid model and the standard MICE algorithm, without any consideration of the comorbidity information, using both the pmm and rf models implemented in the MICE package. The presented results were, therefore, the RMSE differences, where the negative values represent a reduction in the root mean square error.

3. Results

In the following section, we will (1) describe our cohorts, pattern of missingness, and frequency of available data for different levels of missingness and (2) present imputation results for the three datasets.

3.1. Description of Laboratory Values for the Three Cohorts

We identified a total of 67,445 patients in three different cohorts (Cdiff, OA, and IBD) from Geisinger's electronic data warehouse. Further, we identified 495 LOINC codes from this cohort. We selected the LOINC codes for which we had, at most, 75% missingness (i.e., the number of patients without any measurement divided by the total number of patients is less than or equal to 75%) in each of the three cohorts.

We identified a total of 46,215 patients tested for *C. difficile*. We extracted comorbidity and laboratory data from the EHR for this cohort. A total of 48 laboratory codes and 8160 ICD codes for comorbidities were used. Specifically, we identified a total of 48 of the laboratory codes from the 495 codes that had at least 25% of the 46,215 patients with at least one measurement in their records. It is important to highlight that many of the LOINC codes can be very specific (<1% of the patients have such measurements) or were used for a narrow period and may not be actively in use. The dimensionality reduction was set to 100 and 1000. The Cdiff cohort had high heterogeneity, since the dataset contained both cases (tested positive for *C. difficile*) and controls (tested negative for *C. difficile*). The number of clusters tested was 4, 8, and 16.

Similarly, we further identified 11,230 IBD patients with both comorbidity and laboratory data from the EHR. A total of 48 laboratory codes and 7916 ICD codes for comorbidities were identified. The dimensionality reduction was set to 100 and 1000. The number of clusters tested was two, four, and eight, given the smaller sample size of this cohort.

Finally, we identified 187,040 patients with a primary or secondary diagnosis of the knee or hip OA from which we randomly selected 10,000 patients for imputation modeling. A total of 44 laboratory codes and 2042 ICD codes for comorbidities were used. The OA cohort had high heterogeneity, since the dataset was large (almost 200,000 cases from the initial pool) and contained both hip and knee OA. We selected a random set of 10,000 patients, as it is impractical to use an extremely large cohort of patients for optimizing an imputation, as the optimization alone is a computationally extensive process. The number of clusters tested was 4, 8, and 16.

The distribution of missingness in the laboratory values was different for the different cohorts. Table A2 summarizes the percentage missing for the laboratory measures. Our results showed that the pattern and frequency of the laboratory measurements were dependent on the missingness level. Briefly, for laboratory values with high missingness, a larger percentage of patients (30–60%) had only one resulted value; therefore, the median that we calculated in our experiment was practically the exclusively reported value for the patient (see Figure 1A). We further observed that the laboratory values with a high level of missingness (when a patient had more than one value) tended to have an observation window of approximately two to six years (see Figure 1B) and a frequency that was below five measurements (see Figure 1C). However, for more common laboratory values, we observe a window of approximately 5 to 12 years and a frequency above 10 (see Figure 1C).

The outlier detection using a multimodal gaussian distribution function was applied to each laboratory measure for each cohort separately. Figure 2 highlights that, for laboratories with higher missingness levels, the distribution is different for the different cohorts, and therefore, the accepted range is adjusted accordingly. For more common laboratory measures (such as the example presented in Figure 3), the distributions are similar. The accepted range for these laboratory measures is within the calculated range. To further help the reader to better understand the pattern of laboratory data, we created distribution plots for all the laboratory values used in this study for the three cohorts (see Figure A1 and Table A2).

3.2. Imputation Applied to Laboratory Values

C. difficile (Cdiff) infection case and control cohort: Using adaptive imputation for the Cdiff cohort showed improved performance, especially for the high missingness group (laboratory measures that have, at most, 75% missingness). An average RMSE difference (comparing the proposed imputation with the standard imputation model, without any consideration of comorbidity information using MICE) was -31.47 for a level of abstraction $g = 1000$ and a cluster number $k = 4$. The average RMSE difference was -8.75 for $g = 100$ and $k = 4$, demonstrating that, at a high missingness level, additional information from the patient comorbidity information can play an important role in improving the accuracy of the imputation prediction. A total of 27 combinations (or nine combinations for each missingness threshold) were tested, and for each missingness level (Table 1), the tradeoff between the sample size and clustering approach resulted in one or two instances where clustering was associated with improved performance. Since the dataset is of fixed size, the higher number of clusters will reduce the power of the imputation method, especially when the number of clusters is increased to eight or beyond. However, as each dataset has its unique characteristics, the best set of parameters must be empirically determined prior to performing the imputation using the adaptive strategy. Using MICE and the random forest model (rf), the RMSE differences were negative for the majority of the combinations. The missingness group of <75% had seven out of the nine parameter combinations that were in favor of the novel method (See Table 1 and Figure 4).

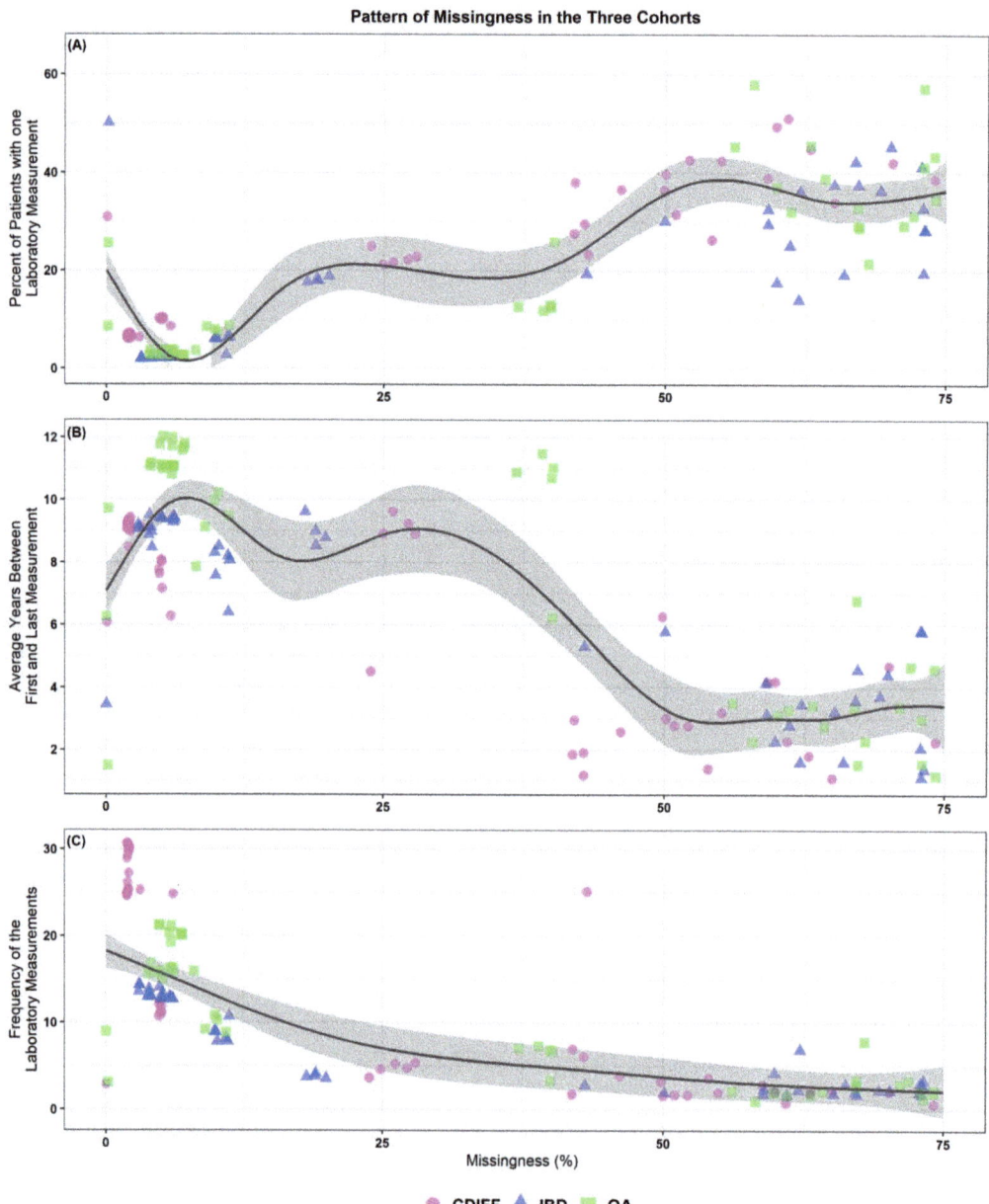

Figure 1. The pattern of missingness for the three cohorts. A generalized additive model was used for smoothing. The gray area around the smoothing curve represents a 95% confidence interval. (**A**) The percentage of patients with one laboratory measurement versus the missingness percentage for the three datasets. (**B**) The average number of years between the first and last laboratory measurements (calculated for patients with two or more measurements) versus the missingness percentage for the three datasets. (**C**) The frequency of the laboratory measurements calculated for patients with two or more measurements versus the missingness percentage for the three datasets. Cdiff: *Clostridioides difficile*, IBD: inflammatory bowel disease, and OA: osteoarthritis.

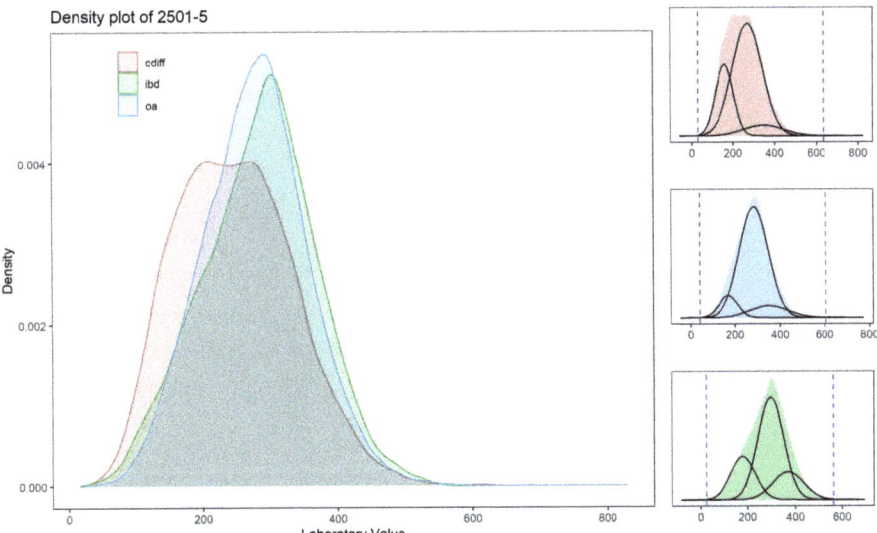

Figure 2. Distribution of laboratory values normalized for Logical Observation Identifiers Names and Codes (LOINC) 2501-5 (iron-binding capacity) for the three datasets (Cdiff in red, IBD in green, and OA in blue). The "ironbinding capacity" is missing at 52% in the Cdiff dataset, 65% in the IBD dataset, and 64% in the OA dataset. The subpanels represent the three modeled distributions to calculate the upper and lower boundaries. The dashed lines represent the upper and lower outlier boundaries (based on Equation (1)).

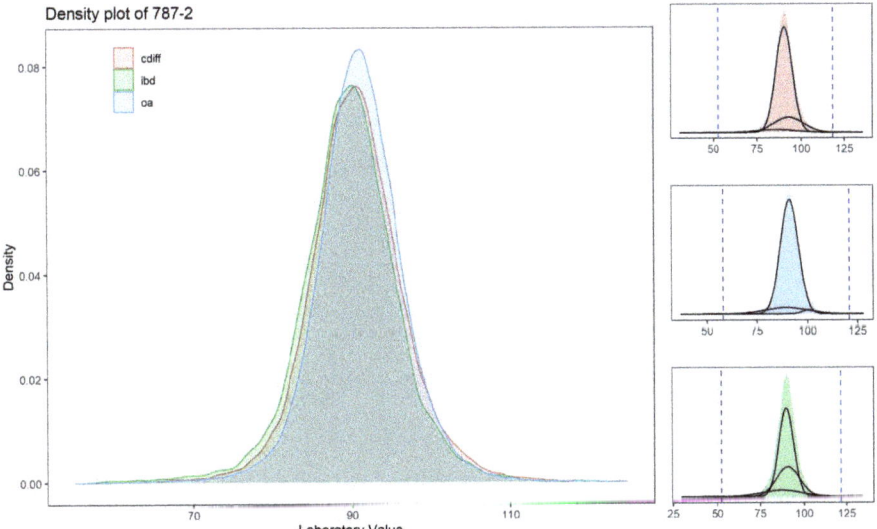

Figure 3. Distribution of laboratory values normalized for LOINC 787-2 (mean corpuscular volume or MCV) for the three datasets (Cdiff in red, IBD in green, and OA in blue). The "MCV" is missing at 2% in the Cdiff dataset, 5% in the IBD dataset, and 4% in the OA dataset. The subpanels represent the three modeled distributions to calculate the upper and lower boundaries. The dashed lines represent the upper and lower outlier boundaries (based on Equation (1)).

Table 1. The root mean square error (RMSE) difference from imputation is applied with and without the integration of comorbidity information for the three datasets. Negative RMSE correspond to improvements by the hybrid approach. The predictive mean matching (pmm) and Random Forest (rf) model in Multivariate Imputation by Chained Equations (MICE) were used in this study. The reader is referred to Tables A3–A5 for a more comprehensive results, with *p*-values reported from multiple runs.

		C. difficile (Cdiff) Infection							
		MICE-PMM					MICE-RF		
Cluster Number	Dimensionality Level (g)	Missingness < 25%	Missingness < 50%	Missingness < 75%	Cluster Number	Dimensionality Level (g)	Missingness < 25%	Missingness < 50%	Missingness < 75%
4	100	−0.77	7.12	−8.76	4	100	0.35	−1.47	−4.92
	1000	7.42	6.93	−31.47		1000	2.07	0.50	−12.72
	8160	−3.09	2.06	8.37		8160	−4.40	−3.28	0.49
8	100	0.11	9.19	12.39	8	100	1.40	11.06	−16.75
	1000	0.14	6.69	4.02		1000	1.24	4.04	9.73
	8160	4.63	10.09	6.99		8160	−0.88	−7.32	−5.11
16	100	−2.12	−3.00	5.03	16	100	−0.04	14.73	−2.36
	1000	5.92	16.21	23.33		1000	−0.19	5.98	−9.16
	8160	4.91	12.37	2.41		8160	0.63	−19.66	−9.50
		Inflammatory Bowel Disease (IBD)							
		MICE-PMM					MICE-RF		
Cluster Number	Dimensionality Level (g)	Missingness < 25%	Missingness< 50%	Missingness < 75%	Cluster Number	Dimensionality Level (g)	Missingness < 25%	Missingness < 50%	Missingness < 75%
2	100	0.94	0.22	−6.49	2	100	0.76	0.68	−3.19
	1000	1.28	0.08	5.44		1000	−1.14	0.23	−4.84
	7916	−0.89	1.97	0.24		7916	0.18	1.17	−8.35
4	100	1.26	0.17	−3.43	4	100	0.20	2.09	0.76
	1000	1.13	1.46	1.66		1000	−0.53	2.25	0.33
	7916	0.31	1.92	−4.15		7916	−0.91	1.97	−4.03
8	100	−0.36	2.85	6.60	8	100	0.97	−0.06	−4.16
	1000	−2.70	−0.74	−7.03		1000	1.08	2.15	1.17
	7916	0.01	4.40	3.76		7916	0.26	3.31	−8.24
		Osteoarthritis (OA)							
		MICE-PMM					MICE-RF		
Cluster Number	Dimensionality Level (g)	Missingness < 25%	Missingness < 50%	Missingness < 75%	Cluster Number	Dimensionality Level (g)	Missingness < 25%	Missingness < 50%	Missingness < 75%
4	100	0.04	0.08	−0.13	4	100	2.45	−4.23	6.83
	1000	0.03	0.11	−0.08		1000	3.35	10.16	−4.70
	2042	0.08	0.18	0.05		2042	1.70	−2.70	−0.75
8	100	−0.07	0.22	0.12	8	100	4.73	1.13	−0.10
	1000	−0.07	−0.07	0.16		1000	3.86	−1.27	−0.34
	2042	0.00	−0.01	−0.09		2042	4.42	−11.30	1.87
16	100	−0.02	0.10	0.20	16	100	−0.52	3.08	−2.33
	1000	0.08	0.15	−0.05		1000	1.41	−0.33	−6.45
	2042	−0.02	0.09	0.24		2042	1.60	3.23	10.93

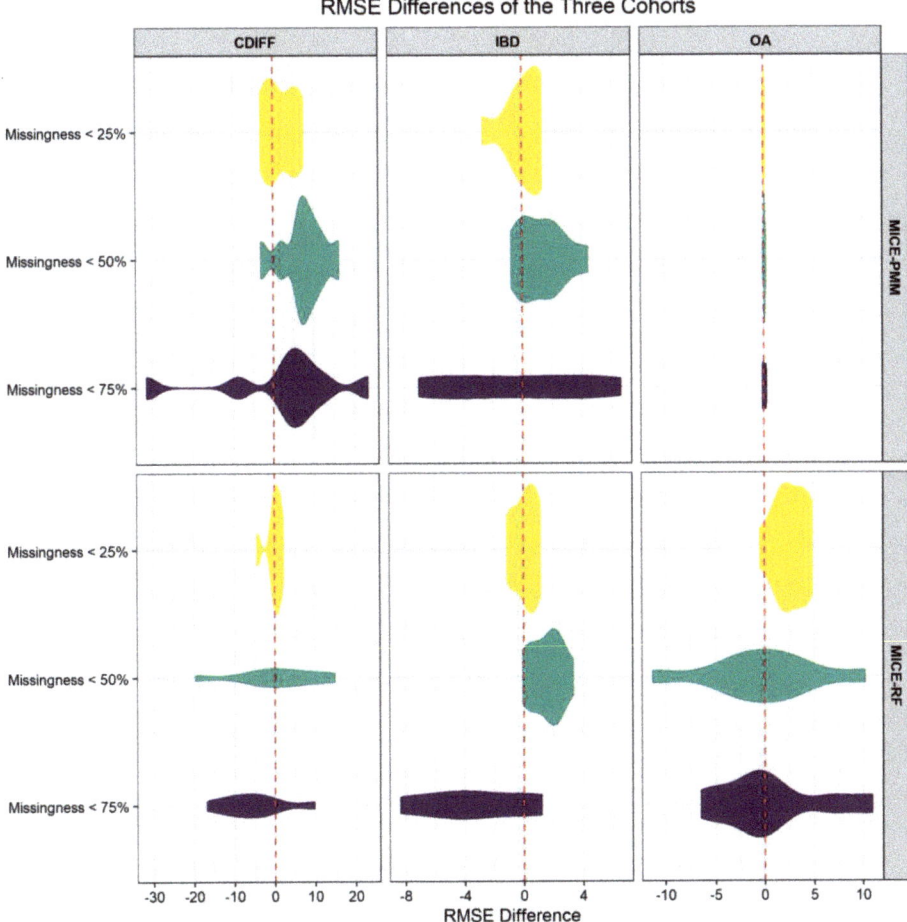

Figure 4. Violin plots representing the root mean square error (RMSE) differences—comparing the performance of Multivariate Imputation by Chained Equations (MICE) with and without the comorbidity information. Two algorithms, predictive mean matching (pmm) and Random Forest (rf), were compared. A Negative RMSE difference indicates a performance improvement when the comorbidity information is utilized.

Inflammatory Bowel Disease (IBD) cohort: Using adaptive imputation for the IBD cohort showed improved performance, especially for the high missingness group (laboratory measures that have, at most, 75% missingness). An average RMSE difference when compared to the standard model using MICE alone was −8.35 with no abstraction and cluster number $k = 2$. Similarly, an average RMSE difference when compared to the standard model using MICE alone was −8.24 for $k = 8$. The results highlighted that, at a high missingness level, additional information from the patient comorbidity data can play an important role in improving the accuracy of the imputation prediction, even as the sample size is significantly smaller (in this case, 11 K versus 46 K for the Cdiff cohort). A total of 27 combinations (or nine combinations for each missingness threshold) were tested. The tradeoff between the sample size and clustering approach resulted in parameter combinations that were associated with improved performance. Additional analyses were performed with the random forest model in MICE, and an RMSE difference of −2.70 was recorded for a missingness level of 25% (see Table 1 and Figure 4). Our results corroborate the value of parameter optimization on the dataset using various modeling frameworks. Thus, the best set of parameters should be empirically determined for each dataset.

Osteoarthritis (OA) cohort: Using adaptive imputation for the OA cohort showed that the best performance improvement was for missingness at 50% (Table 1 and Figure 4). The tradeoff between the sample size reduction, when clustering is utilized, and the use of additional information from comorbidities did show benefits even for this smaller and more heterogeneous dataset. The rf model in MICE was best fitted for this dataset.

4. Discussion

This study is a first step towards improving our many layers of data analytics and quality control pipelines to help enhance the quality of data extracted from the EHR that is ingested in machine learning applications for precision medicine. The use of heterogeneous and large-scale clinical datasets, such as EHRs, provides an avenue for the exploration of strategies to improve care at individualized levels, which include developing personalized models of responses to therapy and the prediction of disease onset, among others [1]. However, the data extracted from EHRs are noisy and have many missing values. In the majority of studies, variables suffering from missingness are excluded from models and analyses [4], even for some variables with high discriminative ability according to the clinical knowledge. As we showed in this work, it is not recommended to solely rely on the redundancy of EHR laboratory data to conduct imputation for realistic applications. That is because the majority of redundancy from laboratory measurements are associated with variables that are missing at high levels. However, laboratory data is highly associated with comorbidity, as the latter is based on laboratory values in realistic settings. For instance, besides the commonly ordered laboratory tests (20–30 laboratory measures), the remaining values are missing at very high rates, even in a healthcare system with a stable population (Geisinger is an integrated healthcare system with a drop-out rate <5%). However, the laboratory measures are highly correlated with comorbidities and diagnosis. Therefore, our intuitive modeling strategy is focused on using this redundancy to improve the imputation for laboratory values.

Furthermore, many diagnoses are based on laboratory values; however, due to the challenges associated with mining laboratory measures, many models ignore this important parameter or only include the ones that are not missing at high levels to reduce the noise and bias due to poor imputation predictions. We created three diverse datasets to test this intuitive strategy of imputation designed specifically for EHR laboratory data by including information from the comorbidities.

The IBD dataset was used, because IBD is a heterogeneous disease and a clear understanding of its risk factors is still lacking. Recent advances in the knowledge of IBD's pathogenesis have led to the implication of a complex interplay between metabolic reprogramming and immunity [23]. Furthermore, the response to treatment in IBD varies significantly among individuals and disease subtypes based on demographic characteristics, diet, comorbidities, underlying immunological factors, and genetic polymorphisms. Thus, there is an urgent unmet need to replace the current imputation approaches with personalized strategies that consider individual variability, diversity, and more balanced patient representation. Therefore, building predictive models for treatment outcomes for IBD is an important step in utilizing the available data on drug responses to provide better care for this patient population. Thus, the integration of laboratory measures in a predictive model for IBD has clinical value.

We created the Cdiff dataset, because the understanding of recurrent *C. difficile* infection is important, and the existing data from EHR can help us identify clinical biomarkers and help in building a decision support system for physicians to target the patients at a higher chance of recurrence for more targeted preventive care.

Finally, the OA dataset was added to test the limits of this model. An OA diagnosis is not based on any laboratory measure known today. An OA diagnosis is based on imaging alone. Therefore, we did not expect the OA cohort to have any special patterns in their laboratory profile, yet we observed that, even in this situation, the use of a comorbidity pattern can help in improving the imputation of laboratory values. The OA dataset was also the smallest dataset tested in this study.

Overall, our results showed that each dataset is unique, and a one-size-fits-all approach does not apply when selecting the imputation model. On simulated datasets with interactions between variables, the imputation of missing data using MICE with regression trees resulted in less biased parameter estimates than MICE with linear regression. [24] In the CALIBER study, MICE random forest showed more imputation efficiency with narrower confidence intervals for the error metric [25]. Through a simulation of a dataset in which the partially observed variable depended on the fully observed variables in a nonlinear way, MICE-RF showed less bias in parameter estimates and better confidence interval coverage. In our study, rf also performed well; however, the best performance was observed when pmm was used in the Cdiff cohort. Nonetheless, because the RMSEs were calculated across all laboratory variables, the improvement may be contributed by a few variables that were imputed better in perhaps some, but not all, cases. Further analysis will be needed to address this assumption.

The method presented here is an intuitive approach for any given complex disease where biosignatures or risk factors are only partially known and the relationship among the variables can be convoluted given the large dimensionality of the dataset. Even though the level of missingness can vary, the best results are typically obtained when the level of missingness is low or moderate. The improvement over conventional methods without the consideration of comorbidity information can be achieved when the missingness level is high. Our strategy was to ensure that (1) our experiment aligned with the current methodologies in practice and (2) others can easily adapt this modification to their work. In future directions, we will explore if advanced modeling frameworks such as the generative adversarial network [26] (GAN) or the newly proposed generative adversarial imputation nets (GAIN) framework [27] can be optimized for imputing laboratory values from EHRs.

Finally, our study provided a step in what we believe is a pipeline of data quality improvements for empowering machine learning models using EHRs. The main limitation of this approach is the need for large datasets. This is due to the nature of this approach, as the clustering step will reduce the sample size for the imputation, thus reducing its power. Therefore, this approach is ideal for machine learning applications where the sample size tends to be large and comprehensive. Our smallest cohort consisted of 10,000 OA patients. Our best prediction improvement was observed for the largest dataset of 46,215 patients. Another limitation of this study that we could not address is based on our masking strategy for the evaluation, which was done at random, even though we knew that the missingness in the EHR was not at random. However, given that we did not know *a priori* the reason for missingness for each patient, given the complex nature of the data, masking at random was the most sensible strategy in this case. As of now, we do not have a better strategy to simulate MNAR to withhold values. The contributing factors to MNAR are multifactorial and largely unknown.

This study had several other limitations. First, by converting the comorbidity information into binary, we may have lost important information. This study design can be enhanced further to answer a specific research question by optimizing the pattern of ICD codes recoded (both the frequency and time intervals) to capture the duration and severity of the conditions. Second, we withheld a relatively small number of values to evaluate our model. This is because we included laboratory codes with as high as 75% missingness and applied clustering prior to imputing; thus, withholding a higher level of laboratory values may further increase the sparsity of the dataset and introduce further bias. As a future direction, we plan on applying the algorithm several times to random subsamples of the data of size n/2 (n = number of samples). This repeated double randomization, similar to the concept of bagging and sub-bagging [28,29] algorithms, could further help optimize our strategy. Third, we are not limiting the window with respect to the diagnosis index event, as it should be for a carefully designed study [30,31]. However, the identification of pre-

and post-index windows should be thoroughly planned based on the research question, the sparsity of the data, the healthcare system, and the variables under consideration [30]. However, as this is a proof-of-concept study, we did not limit our observation window in order to help improve our data availability so that we could experiment with different levels of missingness. Even though this is a limitation of this study, we showed what, in many instances, were only a few laboratory values for each patient for the less commonly used laboratory codes. Fourth, as this was a pilot study, we wanted to corroborate the generalizability and scalability of the proposed strategy. Therefore, we did not exhaustively vary the abstraction level nor the size of the clusters; however, we applied the model on three different cohorts that were created specifically for this study. Finally, by combining the laboratory codes into three groups (<25% missing, <50% missing, and <75% missing), we were unable to determine if this improvement was due to one or a few laboratory variables. Further assessments will be needed to study the improvement of imputation for each laboratory on a case-by-case basis for more targeted evaluations and improvements.

To conclude, the advantages of imputing missingness are manifold; imputation can be used for increasing the data density, improving the representation of data-poor patients, thus reducing the implicit algorithmic bias. Patients with limited access to healthcare and specialty care may be prone to be less-represented in models, because their data footprint is lower. The inclusion of more laboratory values is important as a prediction of a diagnosis; if it is not at least partially based on laboratory information, it could be weak. Predicting a future disease by only focusing on past diagnoses (i.e., using only information based on the ICD codes) is not taking full advantage of the information in electronic health records. Laboratory measurements, similar to imaging and imaging reports, are at the core of diagnosis and care management. The novelty of this study is in its intuitive design and relatively simple implementation in incorporating information from a patient's comorbidity to improve the imputation of laboratory values.

As a future direction, we will investigate how best to impute longitudinal laboratory measures to better inform clinical studies. In addition, we will also explore integrating additional features, such as demographic information, age, gender, and medication usage, as well as genetic information when available, to further enhance the imputation outcome. Finally, we will evaluate various preprocessing and normalization strategies and evaluate if these manipulations can improve the outcome of our predictions, especially for variables with skewed distributions, and explore the impact of imputation on each laboratory value and further investigate any potential patterns or trends that can help improve predicting the missing values. To conclude, we optimized the level of abstraction needed to improve the imputation for three cohorts of varying sizes and complexities. This study demonstrates that the use of shared latent comorbidities can facilitate improvements in imputing laboratory measures from EHRs for downstream analysis and predictive modeling.

Author Contributions: Conceptualization, V.A. (Vida Abedi) and R.Z.; methodology, V.A. (Vida Abedi), J.L., M.K.S., V.A. (Venkatesh Avula); software, J.L., M.K.S., V.A. (Venkatesh Avula); validation, D.P.C., M.J.S., H.S.K., M.T.M.L., D.M.W., R.H., J.B.-R.; formal analysis, V.A. (Vida Abedi), J.L., V.A. (Venkatesh Avula); investigation, V.A. (Vida Abedi), J.L., R.Z.; resources, V.A. (Vida Abedi), R.Z.; data curation, D.P.C., Y.Z., J.L.; writing—original draft preparation, V.A. (Vida Abedi); writing—review and editing, V.A. (Vida Abedi), J.L., M.Y., R.Z.; visualization, V.A. (Venkatesh Avula); supervision, V.A. (Vida Abedi), R.Z.; project administration, V.A. (Vida Abedi); funding acquisition, V.A. (Vida Abedi), R.Z., R.H., J.B.-R. All authors have read and agreed to the published version of the manuscript.

Funding: This work was sponsored by funds from the Defense Threat Reduction Agency (DTRA) grant No. HDTRA1-18-1-0008 to J.B.-R., R.H. and V.A. (Vida Abedi) and funds from the National Institute of Health (NIH) grant No. R56HL116832 to V.A. (Vida Abedi), as well as funds from Geisinger Health Plan Quality to R.Z.

Institutional Review Board Statement: The study was reviewed and approved by the Geisinger Institutional Review Board to meet "Non-human subject research", for using de-identified information.

Informed Consent Statement: Not applicable.

Data Availability Statement: The data analyzed in this study is not publicly available due to privacy and security concerns. The data may be shared with a third party upon execution of data sharing agreement for reasonable requests, such requests should be addressed to V.A. (Vida Abedi) or R.Z.

Acknowledgments: The authors would like to thank the Phenomic Analytics and Clinical Data Core at Geisinger—more specifically, Joseph B. Leader, Monika Ahuja, and Amy Kolinovsky—for helping with data extraction and deidentification from the Electronic Health Records. Special thanks to Alvaro E. Ulloa Cerna for the insightful discussion.

Conflicts of Interest: Authors J.B.-R. and R.H. were employed by BioTherapeutics, Inc. The remaining authors declare that the research was conducted in the absence of any commercial or financial relationships that could be construed as a potential conflict of interests. The funders had no role in study design, data collection, and interpretation or the decision to submit the work for publication.

Appendix A

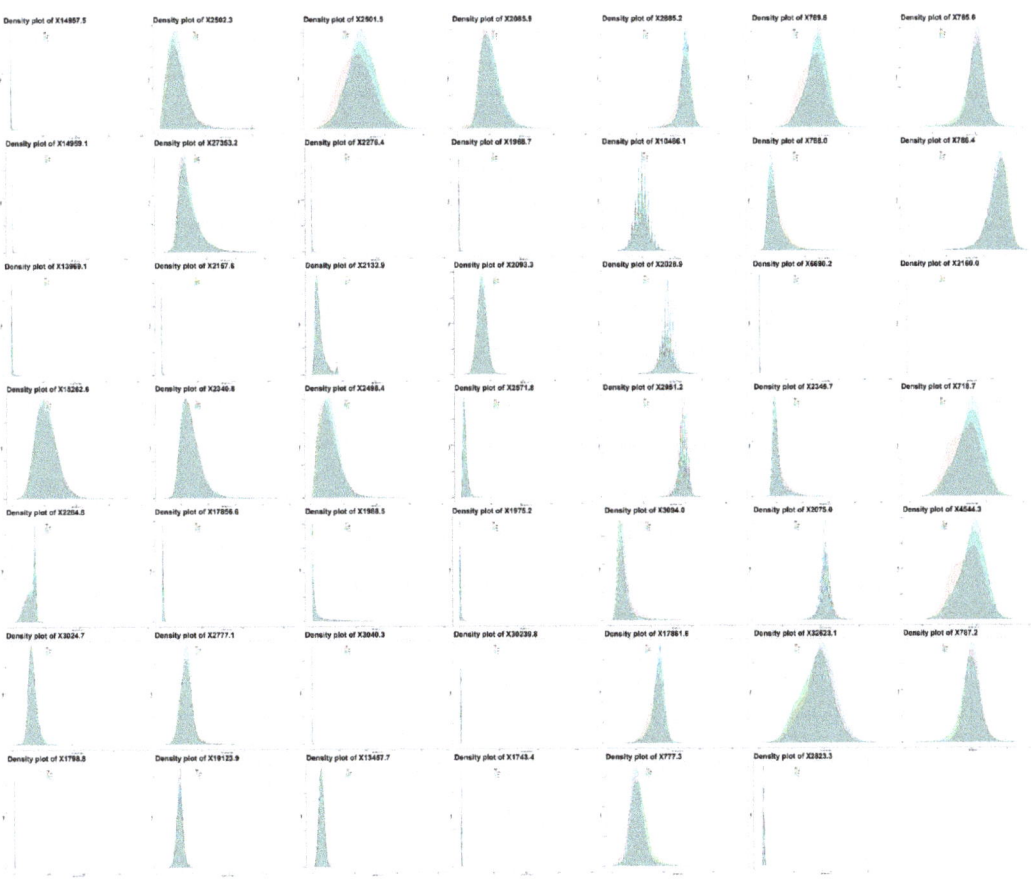

Figure A1. Distribution of the laboratory values normalized for all the LOINC included in this study.

Table A1. Diagnosis codes used for inflammatory bowel disease and osteoarthritis.

Diagnosis	Inclusion Criteria Using ICD Codes
ICD9 Diagnosis: Crohn's and Ulcerative Colitis	555, 55.0, 555.1, 555.2, 555.9, 556, 556.0, 556.1, 556.2, 556.3, 556.5, 556.6, 556.8, 556.9
ICD10 Diagnosis: Crohn's and Ulcerative Colitis	K50.00, K50.011, K50.012, K50.013, K50.014, K50.018, K50.019, K50.10, K50.111, K50.112, K50.113, K50.114, K50.118, K50.119, K50.80, K50.811, K50.812, K50.813, K50.814, K50.818, K50.819, K50.90, K50.911, K50.912, K50.913, K50.914, K50.918, K50.919, K51.80, K51.00, K51.011, K51.012, K51.014, K51.018, K51.019, K51.20, K51.211, K51.212, K51.213, K51.218, K51.219, K51.30, K51.311, K51.313, K51.314, K51.318, K51.319, K51.411, K51.414, K51.419, K51.50, K51.511, K51.513, K51.514, K51.518, K51.519, K51.80, K51.811, K51.812, K51.813, K51.814, K51.818, K51.819, K51.90, K51.911, K51.912, K51.913, K51.914, K51.918, K51.919
ICD9 Diagnosis: Osteoarthritis	715; 715.0; 715.00; 715.09; 715.1; 715.10; 715.15; 715.16; 715.30; 715.35; 715.36; 715.8; 715.80; 715.85; 715.86; 715.89; 715.9; 715.90; 715.95; 715.96;
ICD10 Diagnosis: Osteoarthritis	M15.0; M15.9; M16.0; M16.10; M16.11; M16.12; M16.2; M16.30; M16.31; M16.32; M16.9; M17.0; M17.10; M17.11; M17.12; M17.9; M19.91

Table A2. Various summary statistics for the laboratory variables included in this study. The empty cell represents a percentage missing that is higher than 75%.

LOINC ID	Short Description	Percentage Missing			Percent of Patient with 1 Lab Value			Average Number of Years between First and Last Laboratory Measurement, for Patient with 2 or More Measurements (in Years)												Frequency of the Laboratory Measurements Calculated for Patients with Two or More Measurements												
								Cdiff				IBD				OA				Cdiff				IBD				OA			
		Cdiff	IBD	OA	Cdiff	IBD	OA	Mean	Median	Q1	Q3	Mean	Median	Q1	Q3	Mean	Median	Q1	Q3	Mean	Median	Q1	Q3	Mean	Median	Q1	Q3	Mean	Median	Q1	Q3
14957-5	Microalbumin in Urine	75%	73%		31%	28%	26%	7.1	6.0	2.8	10.6	6.8	5.8	2.6	10.1	7.4	6.3	3.0	11.0	5	3	1	8	5	3	1	7	6	4	1	8
14959-1	Microalbumin/Creatinine in Urine		73%		31%	28%	25%	7.1	6.1	2.8	10.6	6.8	5.8	2.7	10.1	7.3	6.3	3.0	11.0	5	3	1	8	5	3	1	7	6	4	1	8
13969-1	Creatine kinase.MB in Serum/Plasma	54%	73%	74%	26%	20%	24%	3.6	1.4	0.0	5.9	3.6	1.1	0.0	6.0	3.9	1.5	0.0	6.7	7	4	2	9	6	3	1	7	6	3	2	7
18262-6	Cholesterol in LDL in Serum/Plasma (by direct assay)	70%	67%		42%	38%	35%	5.5	4.7	2.1	8.2	5.5	4.6	1.9	7.9	5.9	5.2	2.3	8.7	4	2	1	5	3	2	1	4	4	2	1	5
6768-6	Alkaline phosphatase in Serum/Plasma	5%	11%	9%	10%	6%	9%	8.5	7.8	3.1	13.4	8.9	8.2	3.5	13.7	10.1	9.7	4.9	15.1	18	11	5	22	14	8	3	18	14	9	4	17
2284-8	Folate in Serum/Plasma	65%	73%	74%	34%	33%	35%	3.2	1.1	0.0	5.1	3.5	1.4	0.0	5.6	3.4	1.2	0.0	5.5	3	2	1	3	3	2	1	3	3	2	1	3
3024-7	Thyroxine (T4) free in Serum/Plasma	60%	70%	74%	49%	45%	43%	5.7	4.2	1.4	8.9	6.0	4.4	1.7	9.4	6.3	4.6	1.8	9.8	3	2	1	4	3	2	1	3	4	2	1	4
1798-8	Amylase in Serum/Plasma	61%		73%	51%	50%	57%	3.9	2.3	0.2	6.5	4.5	3.1	0.8	7.2	4.5	3.0	0.4	7.7	3	1	1	3	3	1	1	3	2	1	1	2
2502-3	Iron saturation in Serum/Plasma	63%	73%	73%	45%	41%	41%	2.9	1.8	0.3	4.7	3.2	2.1	0.6	5.1	2.8	1.6	0.2	4.6	4	2	1	4	3	2	1	3	3	2	1	3
27353-2	Glucose mean value in Blood Estimated from glycated hemoglobin	59%	59%	72%	39%	33%	31%	4.6	4.2	1.8	7.2	4.5	4.1	1.8	7.3	4.9	4.7	2.1	7.8	7	3	1	9	6	2	1	7	7	3	1	10
2157-6	Creatine kinase in Serum/Plasma	46%	61%	71%	37%	25%	29%	4.4	2.6	0.1	7.3	4.5	2.8	0.2	7.5	4.9	3.4	0.2	8.0	7	4	1	8	5	2	1	5	5	3	1	6
2340-8	Glucose in Blood by Automated test strip	43%	62%	68%	23%	14%	22%	3.8	1.9	0.1	6.2	3.8	1.6	0.0	6.3	4.1	2.3	0.0	6.8	77	25	3	92	40	7	2	33	41	8	2	39
17856-6	A1c/Hemoglobin.total in Blood	50%	50%	67%	37%	30%	29%	7.5	6.3	2.7	11.4	7.1	5.8	2.4	10.8	7.8	6.8	3.0	11.8	9	3	1	12	8	2	1	8	10	3	1	13
2777-1	Phosphate in Serum/Plasma	42%	60%	67%	28%	18%	29%	4.0	1.9	0.1	6.4	4.4	2.3	0.1	7.2	5.2	3.3	0.5	8.2	14	7	2	17	10	4	1	10	8	3	1	8
19123-9	Magnesium in Serum/Plasma	43%	66%	67%	30%	19%	33%	3.0	1.2	0.1	4.5	3.6	1.6	0.1	5.6	3.4	1.5	0.0	5.3	13	6	2	16	10	3	1	10	7	3	1	7
2501-5	Iron binding capacity.unsaturated in Serum/Plasma	52%	65%	64%	43%	38%	39%	4.2	2.8	0.6	6.5	4.8	3.2	1.1	7.3	4.3	2.8	0.6	6.5	4	2	1	4	3	2	1	4	3	2	1	4
2276-4	Ferritin in Serum/Plasma	55%	67%	63%	42%	42%	46%	4.5	3.2	0.9	6.8	4.9	3.6	1.3	7.3	4.7	3.4	1.1	7.1	4	2	1	4	4	2	1	4	3	2	1	3
2132-9	Cobalamin (Vitamin B12) in Serum/Plasma	51%	59%	61%	31%	29%	32%	4.5	2.8	0.2	7.2	5.1	3.1	0.4	8.3	4.9	3.3	0.2	7.8	4	2	1	4	4	2	1	4	3	2	1	4

Table A2. Cont.

LOINC ID	Short Description	Percentage Missing				Percent of Patient with 1 Lab Value			Average Number of Years between First and Last Laboratory Measurement, for Patient with 2 or More Measurements (in Years)												Frequency of the Laboratory Measurements Calculated for Patients with Two or More Measurements												
									Cdiff				IBD				OA				Cdiff				IBD				OA			
		Cdiff	IBD	OA	Cdiff	IBD	OA	Mean	Median	Q1	Q3	Mean	Median	Q1	Q3	Mean	Median	Q1	Q3	Mean	Median	Q1	Q3	Mean	Median	Q1	Q3	Mean	Median	Q1	Q3
2498-4	Iron in Serum/Plasma	50%	62%	60%	40%	36%	37%	4.4	3.0	0.7	6.7	5.0	3.5	1.2	7.5	4.5	3.1	0.6	6.9	4	2	1	4	4	2	1	4	3	2	1	4
1988-5	C reactive protein in Serum/Plasma	74%		58%	39%	56%	58%	3.6	2.3	0.5	5.8	4.5	3.5	1.3	7.0	3.8	2.3	0.5	5.8	3	1	1	3	4	2	1	5	2	1	1	2
3040-3	Lipase in Serum/Plasma	42%	69%	56%	38%	36%	45%	4.5	3.0	0.6	7.1	5.1	3.7	1.2	7.9	5.0	3.5	0.9	8.0	4	2	1	4	4	2	1	4	3	2	1	3
13457-7	Cholesterol in LDL in Serum/Plasma (by calculation)	28%	20%	40%	23%	19%	13%	9.5	8.9	4.2	14.5	9.4	8.8	4.0	14.7	10.7	10.7	5.5	16.0	8	5	2	11	7	4	2	9	10	7	3	14
2085-9	Cholesterol in HDL in Serum/Plasma	27%	19%	40%	22%	18%	13%	9.6	9.2	4.3	14.8	9.6	9.0	4.1	15.0	11.0	11.0	5.7	16.3	8	5	2	12	7	4	2	10	10	7	3	14
1968-7	Bilirubin.direct in Serum/Plasma	24%	43%	40%	25%	19%	26%	6.0	4.5	1.0	9.8	6.6	5.3	1.8	10.4	7.2	6.2	2.1	11.6	8	4	2	9	7	3	2	8	6	3	1	7
2093-3	Cholesterol in Serum/Plasma	26%	18%	39%	22%	18%	12%	10.0	9.6	4.5	15.5	10.0	9.6	4.2	15.7	11.4	11.5	5.9	16.9	9	5	2	12	8	4	2	10	10	7	3	15
2571-8	Triglyceride in Serum/Plasma	25%	19%	37%	21%	18%	13%	9.4	8.9	4.1	14.6	9.2	8.5	3.5	14.7	10.8	10.9	5.6	16.2	8	5	2	12	7	4	2	10	10	7	3	14
1975-2	Bilirubin.total in Serum/Plasma	5%	11%	11%	10%	6%	9%	8.4	7.6	3.0	13.1	8.8	8.1	3.5	13.5	9.9	9.5	4.8	14.8	17	11	5	22	14	8	3	17	14	9	4	17
30239-8	Aspartate aminotransferase in Serum/Plasma	5%	10%	10%	10%	6%	8%	8.8	8.1	3.2	13.9	9.1	8.5	3.7	14.1	10.4	10.2	5.2	15.7	19	12	5	24	15	9	3	19	15	10	4	20
1743-4	Alanine aminotransferase in Serum/Plasma	5%	10%	10%	10%	6%	8%	8.6	8.0	3.2	13.5	9.0	8.3	3.8	13.8	10.2	10.0	5.2	15.2	19	12	5	25	15	9	4	20	16	11	5	22
2885-2	Protein in Serum/Plasma	5%	10%	9%	10%	6%	9%	7.9	7.2	2.9	12.4	8.3	7.6	3.3	12.8	9.3	9.1	4.6	14.0	17	11	5	22	14	8	3	17	14	9	4	17
10466-1	Anion gap 3 in Serum/Plasma	6%	11%	8%	9%	3%	4%	6.3	6.3	2.5	10.2	6.4	6.4	2.7	10.4	7.3	7.9	3.9	11.1	25	10	5	51	22	11	4	27	26	16	7	32
2028-9	Carbon dioxide, total in Serum/Plasma	2%	4%	7%	7%	2%	3%	9.6	9.2	3.8	15.1	9.5	8.9	3.7	15.0	11.3	11.6	6.0	16.9	45	29	12	59	26	13	5	31	31	20	9	40
2951-2	Sodium in Serum/Plasma	2%	4%	7%	7%	2%	3%	9.6	9.2	3.8	15.2	9.6	9.1	3.8	15.1	11.3	11.7	6.0	16.9	45	30	12	60	26	13	5	32	31	20	9	40
3094-0	Urea nitrogen in Serum/Plasma	2%	4%	7%	7%	2%	3%	9.7	9.3	3.9	15.3	9.6	9.1	3.7	15.2	11.4	11.8	6.1	17.1	45	30	12	60	26	13	5	32	32	20	9	41
17861-6	Calcium in Serum/Plasma	2%	4%	6%	7%	2%	3%	8.8	8.5	3.5	14.0	8.9	8.5	3.5	14.0	10.4	10.8	5.5	15.6	44	29	12	58	25	13	5	31	30	19	9	38
777-3	Platelets in Blood	2%	6%	6%	6%	2%	4%	9.5	9.1	3.7	15.1	9.8	9.4	3.9	15.4	11.0	11.1	5.6	16.6	40	25	11	52	25	13	5	31	27	16	7	33
789-8	Erythrocytes in Blood	2%	6%	6%	6%	2%	4%	9.5	9.1	3.7	15.1	9.8	9.4	3.9	15.4	11.0	11.1	5.6	16.7	40	25	11	52	25	13	5	31	27	16	7	33
788-0	Erythrocyte distribution width	3%	6%	6%	6%	2%	4%	9.5	9.1	3.7	15.0	9.8	9.4	3.9	15.4	11.0	11.1	5.6	16.6	40	25	11	52	25	13	5	31	27	16	7	33
6690-2	Leukocytes in Blood	2%	6%	6%	6%	2%	4%	9.5	9.1	3.7	15.1	9.8	9.4	3.9	15.4	11.0	11.1	5.6	16.7	41	25	11	53	25	13	5	31	27	16	7	33

Table A2. Cont.

LOINC ID	Short Description	Percentage Missing			Percent of Patient with 1 Lab Value			Average Number of Years between First and Last Laboratory Measurement, for Patient with 2 or More Measurements (in Years)												Frequency of the Laboratory Measurements Calculated for Patients with Two or More Measurements											
								Cdiff				IBD				OA				Cdiff				IBD				OA			
		Cdiff	IBD	OA	Cdiff	IBD	OA	Mean	Median	Q1	Q3	Mean	Median	Q1	Q3	Mean	Median	Q1	Q3	Mean	Median	Q1	Q3	Mean	Median	Q1	Q3	Mean	Median	Q1	Q3
2345-7	Glucose in Serum/Plasma	2%	3%	6%	7%	2%	3%	9.7	9.4	3.9	15.4	9.7	9.2	3.8	15.4	11.5	12.0	6.1	17.3	46	30	13	61	27	14	5	32	32	21	9	41
2075-0	Chloride in Serum/Plasma	2%	4%	6%	7%	2%	3%	9.6	9.2	3.8	15.1	9.5	9.0	3.7	15.0	11.3	11.7	6.0	16.9	45	30	12	59	26	13	5	31	31	20	9	40
32623-1	Platelet mean volume ir Blood	2%	6%	5%	7%	2%	4%	9.4	9.0	3.6	15.0	9.7	9.3	3.9	15.4	11.0	11.0	5.5	16.6	39	25	11	51	25	13	5	31	26	15	7	32
2823-3	Potassium in Serum/Plasma	2%	3%	5%	6%	2%	3%	9.7	9.3	3.9	15.4	9.6	9.1	3.7	15.2	11.5	11.8	6.1	17.2	47	31	13	62	27	14	5	33	32	21	9	41
785-6	MCH	2%	5%	5%	6%	2%	4%	9.5	9.1	3.7	15.0	9.8	9.4	3.9	15.4	11.0	11.1	5.6	16.6	40	25	11	52	25	13	5	31	27	16	7	33
786-4	MCHC	2%	5%	5%	6%	2%	4%	9.5	9.1	3.7	15.0	9.8	9.4	3.9	15.4	11.0	11.1	5.6	16.6	40	25	11	52	25	13	5	31	27	16	7	33
2160-0	Creatinine in Serum/Plasma	2%	3%	5%	6%	2%	3%	9.8	9.4	3.9	15.4	9.6	9.1	3.8	15.2	11.6	12.0	6.4	17.2	46	31	13	62	27	14	5	33	33	21	9	42
718-7	Hemoglobin in Blood	2%	4%	4%	6%	2%	3%	9.6	9.2	3.7	15.3	9.9	9.5	4.0	15.7	11.0	11.2	5.5	16.8	43	27	11	56	27	14	6	32	29	17	8	35
4544-3	Hematocrit of Blood by Automated count	2%	5%	4%	6%	2%	3%	9.5	9.2	3.7	15.2	9.8	9.4	3.9	15.5	11.0	11.1	5.5	16.7	42	26	11	55	26	14	5	32	28	16	8	34
787-2	Mean corpuscular voLume, or MCV	2%	5%	4%	6%	2%	4%	9.5	9.1	3.7	15.1	9.8	9.4	3.9	15.4	11.0	11.1	5.6	16.7	40	25	11	52	25	13	5	31	27	16	7	33

Table A3. The RMSE difference from imputation is applied with and without the integration of comorbidity information for the Cdiff dataset. Negative RMSE correspond to improvement by the hybrid approach. The pmm and rf models in MICE were used in this study. The p-value is reported based on 10 runs.

			Cdiff-PMM		Cdiff-RF	
Missingness Level	Dimensionality Level (g)	Cluster Number	RMSE Difference	p-Value	RMSE Difference	p-Value
25%	100	4	−0.774	0.376	0.349	0.625
25%	100	8	0.110	0.739	1.402	0.532
25%	100	16	−2.121	0.306	−0.189	0.629
25%	1000	4	7.417	0.456	2.066	0.391
25%	1000	8	0.141	0.584	1.238	0.581
25%	1000	16	5.916	0.139	−0.035	0.233
25%	8160	4	−3.088	0.419	−4.397	0.582
25%	8160	8	4.628	0.150	−0.882	0.868
25%	8160	16	4.910	0.493	0.631	0.594
50%	100	4	7.117	0.459	−1.470	0.789
50%	100	8	9.189	0.759	11.064	0.796
50%	100	16	−3.005	0.351	14.731	0.472
50%	1000	4	6.934	0.920	0.503	0.675
50%	1000	8	6.695	0.230	4.044	0.432
50%	1000	16	16.207	0.087	5.976	0.196
50%	8160	4	2.060	0.481	−3.279	0.865
50%	8160	8	10.087	0.435	−7.323	0.502
50%	8160	16	12.366	0.190	−19.655	0.476
75%	100	4	−8.756	0.386	−4.916	0.662
75%	100	8	12.386	0.174	−16.748	0.487
75%	100	16	5.026	0.392	−2.362	0.513
75%	1000	4	−31.468	0.017	−12.722	0.982
75%	1000	8	4.024	0.266	9.729	0.405
75%	1000	16	23.333	0.139	−9.162	0.258
75%	8160	4	8.368	0.569	0.488	0.787
75%	8160	8	6.993	0.515	−5.113	0.631
75%	8160	16	2.414	0.957	−9.496	0.979

Table A4. The RMSE difference from imputation is applied with and without the integration of comorbidity information for the IBD dataset. Negative RMSE correspond to improvement by the hybrid approach. The pmm and rf models in MICE were used in this study. The p-value is reported based on 10 runs.

			IBD-PMM		IBD-RF	
Missingness Level	Dimensionality Level (g)	Cluster Number	RMSE Difference	p-Value	RMSE Difference	p-Value
25%	100	2	0.938	0.565	0.756	0.759
25%	100	4	1.264	0.948	0.200	0.695
25%	100	8	−0.359	0.273	0.969	0.339
25%	1000	2	1.284	0.583	−1.145	0.425
25%	1000	4	1.134	0.234	−0.526	0.733
25%	1000	8	−2.696	0.196	1.083	0.132
25%	7916	2	−0.886	0.974	0.176	0.944
25%	7916	4	0.313	0.210	−0.906	0.249
25%	7916	8	0.005	0.307	0.264	0.177
50%	100	2	0.218	0.336	0.682	0.448
50%	100	4	0.168	0.196	2.094	0.281
50%	100	8	2.851	0.072	−0.057	0.428
50%	1000	2	0.080	0.411	0.230	0.561

Table A4. *Cont.*

			IBD-PMM		IBD-RF	
Missingness Level	Dimensionality Level (g)	Cluster Number	RMSE Difference	*p*-Value	RMSE Difference	*p*-Value
50%	1000	4	1.465	0.601	2.246	0.569
50%	1000	8	−0.745	0.609	2.145	0.604
50%	7916	2	1.973	0.338	1.165	0.912
50%	7916	4	1.922	0.188	1.973	0.676
50%	7916	8	4.401	0.078	3.309	0.288
75%	100	2	−6.485	0.256	−3.192	0.447
75%	100	4	−3.428	0.632	0.756	0.580
75%	100	8	6.598	0.825	−4.165	0.624
75%	1000	2	5.436	0.721	−4.835	0.306
75%	1000	4	1.664	0.511	0.329	0.584
75%	1000	8	−7.031	0.581	1.175	0.771
75%	7916	2	0.239	0.378	−8.353	0.175
75%	7916	4	−4.155	0.470	−4.033	0.689
75%	7916	8	3.760	0.468	−8.244	0.096

Table A5. The RMSE difference from imputation is applied with and without the integration of comorbidity information for the OA dataset. Negative RMSE correspond to improvement by the hybrid approach. The pmm and rf models in MICE were used in this study. The *p*-value is reported based on 10 runs.

			OA-PMM		OA-RF	
Missingness Level	Dimensionality Level (g)	Cluster Number	RMSE Difference	*p*-Value	RMSE Difference	*p*-Value
25%	100	4	0.035	0.317	2.449	0.245
25%	100	8	−0.074	0.444	4.734	0.385
25%	100	16	−0.017	0.375	−0.518	0.525
25%	1000	4	0.035	0.687	3.351	0.247
25%	1000	8	−0.066	0.363	3.859	0.183
25%	1000	16	0.085	0.706	1.414	0.172
25%	2042	4	0.081	0.889	1.705	0.161
25%	2042	8	0.004	0.595	4.417	0.460
25%	2042	16	−0.019	0.202	1.602	0.810
50%	100	4	0.081	0.700	−4.229	0.199
50%	100	8	0.218	0.079	1.132	0.970
50%	100	16	0.101	0.087	3.082	0.357
50%	1000	4	0.106	0.653	10.161	0.843
50%	1000	8	−0.066	0.577	−1.271	0.480
50%	1000	16	0.147	0.620	−0.328	0.891
50%	2042	4	0.178	0.252	−2.703	0.946
50%	2042	8	−0.013	0.216	−11.300	0.409
50%	2042	16	0.092	0.643	3.229	0.376
75%	100	4	−0.131	0.186	6.828	0.213
75%	100	8	0.118	0.507	−0.098	0.434
75%	100	16	0.197	0.142	−2.326	0.889
75%	1000	4	−0.077	0.092	4.702	0.222
75%	1000	8	0.157	0.428	−0.343	0.653
75%	1000	16	−0.053	0.508	−6.447	0.651
75%	2042	4	0.055	0.649	−0.749	0.430
75%	2042	8	−0.089	0.549	1.865	0.768
75%	2042	16	0.237	0.014	10.926	0.061

References

1. Noorbakhsh-Sabet, N.; Zand, R.; Zhang, Y.; Abedi, V. Artificial Intelligence Transforms the Future of Health Care. *Am. J. Med.* **2019**, *132*, 795–801. [CrossRef]
2. Botsis, T.; Hartvigsen, G.; Chen, F.; Weng, C. Secondary Use of EHR: Data Quality Issues and Informatics Opportunities. *AMIA Jt. Summits Transl. Sci.* **2010**, *1*, 1–5.
3. Sterne, J.; White, I.R.; Carlin, J.B.; Spratt, M.; Royston, P.; Kenward, M.G.; Wood, A.M.; Carpenter, J.R. Multiple imputation for missing data in epidemiological and clinical research: Potential and pitfalls. *BMJ* **2009**, *338*, b2393. [CrossRef]
4. Netten, A.P.; Dekker, F.W.; Rieffe, C.; Soede, W.; Briaire, J.J.; Frijns, J.H.M. Missing Data in the Field of Otorhinolaryngology and Head & Neck Surgery. *Ear Hear.* **2017**, *38*, 1–6. [CrossRef] [PubMed]
5. Beaulieu-Jones, B.K.; Lavage, D.R.; Snyder, J.W.; Moore, J.H.; Pendergrass, S.A.; Bauer, C.R. Characterizing and Managing Missing Structured Data in Electronic Health Records: Data Analysis. *JMIR Med. Inform.* **2018**, *6*, e11. [CrossRef] [PubMed]
6. Beaulieu-Jones, B.K.; Moore, J.H. Missing data imputation in the electronic health record using deeply learned autoencoders. *Biocomputing* **2017**, 207–218. [CrossRef]
7. Troyanskaya, O.G.; Cantor, M.; Sherlock, G.; Brown, P.O.; Hastie, T.; Tibshirani, R.; Botstein, D.; Altman, R.B. Missing value estimation methods for DNA microarrays. *Bioinformatics* **2001**, *17*, 520–525. [CrossRef]
8. Kuppusamy, V.; Paramasivam, I. Integrating WLI fuzzy clustering with grey neural network for missing data imputation. *Int. J. Intell. Enterp.* **2017**, *4*, 103. [CrossRef]
9. Lee, K.J.; Carlin, J.B. Multiple imputation in the presence of non-normal data. *Stat. Med.* **2017**, *36*, 606–617. [CrossRef]
10. Liu, Y.; Gopalakrishnan, V. An Overview and Evaluation of Recent Machine Learning Imputation Methods Using Cardiac Imaging Data. *Data* **2017**, *2*, 8. [CrossRef]
11. Ford, E.; Rooney, P.; Hurley, S.; Oliver, S.; Bremner, S.; Cassell, J. Can the Use of Bayesian Analysis Methods Correct for Incompleteness in Electronic Health Records Diagnosis Data? Development of a Novel Method Using Simulated and Real-Life Clinical Data. *Front. Public Health* **2020**, *8*. [CrossRef] [PubMed]
12. Wells, B.J.; Nowacki, A.S.; Chagin, K.M.; Kattan, M.W. Strategies for Handling Missing Data in Electronic Health Record Derived Data. *eGEMs Gener. Évid. Methods Improv. Patient Outcomes* **2013**, *1*, 1035. [CrossRef] [PubMed]
13. Li, R.; Chen, Y.; Moore, J.H. Integration of genetic and clinical information to improve imputation of data missing from electronic health records. *J. Am. Med. Inform. Assoc.* **2019**, *26*, 1056–1063. [CrossRef] [PubMed]
14. White, I.R.; Royston, P.; Wood, A.M. Multiple imputation using chained equations: Issues and guidance for practice. *Stat. Med.* **2010**, *30*, 377–399. [CrossRef] [PubMed]
15. van Buuren, S.; Groothuis-Oudshoorn, K. mice: Multivariate Imputation by Chained Equations in R. *J. Stat. Softw.* **2011**, *45*, 1–67. Available online: https://www.jstatsoft.org/v45/i03/ (accessed on 5 October 2020). [CrossRef]
16. Luo, Y.; Szolovits, P.; Dighe, A.S.; Baron, J.M. 3D-MICE: Integration of cross-sectional and longitudinal imputation for multi-analyte longitudinal clinical data. *J. Am. Med. Inform. Assoc.* **2017**, *25*, 645–653. [CrossRef]
17. Abt, M.C.; McKenney, P.T.; Pamer, E.G. Clostridium difficile colitis: Pathogenesis and host defence. *Nat. Rev. Genet.* **2016**, *14*, 609–620. [CrossRef]
18. Carrell, D.; Denny, J. Group Health and Vanderbilt. In *Clostridium Difficile Colitis*; PheKB: Nashville, TN, USA, 2012.
19. Abedi, V.; Shivakumar, M.K.; Lu, P.; Hontecillas, R.; Leber, A.; Ahuja, M.; Ulloa, A.E.; Shellenberger, M.J.; Bassaganya-Riera, J. Latent-Based Imputation of Laboratory Measures from Electronic Health Records: Case for Complex Diseas-es. *bioRxiv* **2018**, 275743. [CrossRef]
20. Landauer, T.K.; Dumais, S.T. A solution to Plato's problem: The latent semantic analysis theory of acquisition, induction, and representation of knowledge. *Psychol. Rev.* **1997**, *104*, 211–240. [CrossRef]
21. *Aspects of Automatic Text Analysis*; Mehler, A.; Köhler, R. (Eds.) Springer: Berlin/Heidelberg, Germany, 2006; Volume 209.
22. Breiman, L. *Manual on Setting Up, Using, and Understanding Random Forests v3.1*; Tech. Report; Statistics Department University of California Berkeley: Berkeley, CA, USA, 2002. Available online: https://www.stat.berkeley.edu/~{}breiman/Using_random_forests_V3.1.pdf (accessed on 29 December 2020).
23. Leber, A.; Hontecillas, R.; Tubau-Juni, N.; Zoccoli-Rodriguez, V.; Hulver, M.; McMillan, R.; Eden, K.; Allen, I.C.; Bassaganya-Riera, J. NLRX1 Regulates Effector and Metabolic Functions of CD4+ T Cells. *J. Immunol.* **2017**, *198*, 2260–2268. [CrossRef]
24. Burgette, L.F.; Reiter, J.P. Multiple Imputation for Missing Data via Sequential Regression Trees. *Am. J. Epidemiol.* **2010**, *172*, 1070–1076. [CrossRef] [PubMed]
25. Shah, A.D.; Bartlett, J.W.; Carpenter, J.; Nicholas, O.; Hemingway, H. Comparison of Random Forest and Parametric Imputation Models for Imputing Missing Data Using MICE: A CALIBER Study. *Am. J. Epidemiol.* **2014**, *179*, 764–774. [CrossRef] [PubMed]
26. Goodfellow, I.J.; Shlens, J.; Szegedy, C. Explaining and harnessing adversarial examples. *arXiv* **2014**, arXiv:1412.6572.
27. Yoon, J.; Jordon, J.; van der Schaar, M. GAIN: Missing data imputation using generative adversarial nets. *arXiv* **2018**, arXiv:1806.02920.
28. Breiman, L. Using Iterated Bagging to Debias Regressions. *Mach. Learn.* **2001**, *45*, 261–277. [CrossRef]
29. Bühlmann, P.; Yu, B. Analyzing bagging. *Ann. Stat.* **2002**, *30*, 927–961. [CrossRef]

30. Chen, R.; Stewart, W.F.; Sun, J.; Ng, K.; Yan, X. Recurrent Neural Networks for Early Detection of Heart Failure from Longitudinal Electronic Health Record Data: Implications for Temporal Modeling with Respect to Time Before Diagnosis, Data Density, Data Quantity, and Data Type. *Circ. Cardiovasc. Qual. Outcomes* **2019**, *12*, e005114. [CrossRef]
31. Ng, K.; Steinhubl, S.R.; Defilippi, C.; Dey, S.; Stewart, W.F. Early Detection of Heart Failure Using Electronic Health Records: Practical Implications for Time before Diagnosis, Data Diversity, Data Quantity, and Data Density. *Circ. Cardiovasc. Qual. Outcomes* **2016**, *9*, 649–658. [CrossRef]

Article

Convolutional Neural Network Classifies Pathological Voice Change in Laryngeal Cancer with High Accuracy

HyunBum Kim [1,†], Juhyeong Jeon [2,†], Yeon Jae Han [3], YoungHoon Joo [1], Jonghwan Lee [2], Seungchul Lee [2,4,*] and Sun Im [3,*]

1. Department of Otolaryngology-Head and Neck Surgery, Bucheon St. Mary's Hospital, College of Medicine, The Catholic University of Korea, Seoul 06591, Korea; goldgold11@hanmail.net (H.K.); joodoct@catholic.ac.kr (Y.J.)
2. Department of Mechanical Engineering, Pohang University of Science and Technology (POSTECH), Pohang 37673, Korea; jjeon@postech.ac.kr (J.J.); leejhd@postech.ac.kr (J.L.)
3. Department of Rehabilitation Medicine, Bucheon St. Mary's Hospital, College of Medicine, The Catholic University of Korea, Seoul 06591, Korea; duswohan@gmail.com
4. Graduate School of Artificial Intelligence, Pohang University of Science and Technology (POSTECH), Pohang 37673, Korea
*   Correspondence: seunglee@postech.ac.kr (S.L.); lafolia@catholic.ac.kr (S.I.)
†   These authors contributed equally to this work.

Received: 5 September 2020; Accepted: 22 October 2020; Published: 25 October 2020

Abstract: Voice changes may be the earliest signs in laryngeal cancer. We investigated whether automated voice signal analysis can be used to distinguish patients with laryngeal cancer from healthy subjects. We extracted features using the software package for speech analysis in phonetics (PRAAT) and calculated the Mel-frequency cepstral coefficients (MFCCs) from voice samples of a vowel sound of /a:/. The proposed method was tested with six algorithms: support vector machine (SVM), extreme gradient boosting (XGBoost), light gradient boosted machine (LGBM), artificial neural network (ANN), one-dimensional convolutional neural network (1D-CNN) and two-dimensional convolutional neural network (2D-CNN). Their performances were evaluated in terms of accuracy, sensitivity, and specificity. The result was compared with human performance. A total of four volunteers, two of whom were trained laryngologists, rated the same files. The 1D-CNN showed the highest accuracy of 85% and sensitivity and sensitivity and specificity levels of 78% and 93%. The two laryngologists achieved accuracy of 69.9% but sensitivity levels of 44%. Automated analysis of voice signals could differentiate subjects with laryngeal cancer from those of healthy subjects with higher diagnostic properties than those performed by the four volunteers.

Keywords: voice change; larynx cancer; machine learning; deep learning; voice pathology classification

1. Introduction

Laryngeal cancer is one of the most debilitating forms of malignancy, with an average incidence of 3.3 per 100,000 from 2012 to 2016 in the USA [1]. In 2019, there were 12,370 new cases diagnosed in the USA alone. Despite the rising incidence, early diagnosis remains challenging, resulting in delayed treatment [2,3]. With a delay of diagnosis, laryngeal cancer may lead to the most severe debilitating disabilities in phonation, swallowing [4] and overall quality of life. An automated voice analysis tool could advance the time of diagnosis regardless of patients' location, in line with the idea of telemedicine. Though voice changes can indicate the first clinical signs of disease, subjective perception of early voice changes can be listener dependent and subject to intrajudge variations [5].

Image analysis based on the use of computational algorithms in radiology is now expanding to signal processing in other fields such as electrodiagnosis [6]. Furthermore, the popularity of these new techniques has led to the use of automated detection of pathological voices using machine and deep learning algorithms. A voice pathology detection was reported successful using a deep learning model [7]. Algorithms based on feature extraction, such as the Mel-frequency cepstral coefficients (MFCCs) from the acoustic signals have been used for many years to detect vocal fold disorders and dysphonia [8–10]. For example, Chuang et al. [9] have used normalized MFCCs features and have shown that a deep neural network (DNN) can detect abnormal voice changes in voice disorders. Another study by Fang et al. [10], which included laryngeal cancer data, have reported that the results of a DNN were superior to other machine learning algorithms.

However, in past studies, the number of cancer patients was either too small [10,11] or often assessed as a single group together with other voice disorders. Most recent studies that investigated the role of automatic detection of voice disorders [8–10] were based on open voice databases such as the Massachusetts Eye and Ear Infirmary Database [12] or Saarbrucken Voice Database [13], and laryngeal cancer voices were rated together as one group in combination with other voice disorders. In addition, past algorithms have not been validated against the clinicians' judgement of voice change. Subjective perception of early voice changes can be difficult [5]. The possibility of an algorithm that can distinguish pathological voice changes at the early stages in laryngeal cancer from normal healthy voices with the potential to overcome the limitations imposed by inter-subject human perception remains to be explored.

Therefore, this study aims to investigate the role of computational algorithms including a support vector machine (SVM), extreme gradient boosting (XGBoost) and the recent popular convolutional neural network (CNN) in distinguishing voice signals of patients with laryngeal cancer against those obtained from healthy subjects. We also compared the performance levels of these algorithms to those obtained by four human raters who rated the same voice files.

2. Materials and Methods

2.1. Study Subjects

A retrospective review of medical records was performed at a single university center from July 2015 to June 2019. We identified patients who had undergone voice assessments at the time of laryngeal cancer diagnosis. Only the preoperative records were collected, whereas those obtained postoperatively or after radiotherapy were excluded.

Normal voice samples were acquired from otherwise healthy subjects who had undergone voice assessments for the evaluation of their vocal cords prior to general anesthesia for surgical procedures involving sites other than the head and neck region, such as the hands or legs. Any subject subsequently diagnosed with any benign laryngeal disease, sulcus vocalis, or one-sided vocal palsy were excluded from the data analysis of the healthy subjects. Any additional diagnosis of voice disorders was excluded by a detailed review of patients' medical records.

Patients' demographic information, including gender, age, and smoking history, were collected. In those diagnosed with laryngeal cancer, additional clinical information such as the TNM (Tumor Node Metastases Classification of Malignant Tumors) stage, a global standard for classifying the anatomical extent of tumor cancers, was recorded. The study protocols were approved by our institutional review board [HC19RES10098].

2.2. Datasets from Voice Files

The dataset comprises recordings of normal subjects and cancer patients. Voice samples were recorded with a Kay Computer Speech Lab (CSL) (Model 4150B; KayPENTAX, Lincoln Park, NJ, USA) supported by a personal computer, including a Shure-Prolog SM48 microphone with Shure digital amplifier, located at a distance of 10–15 cm from the mouth and an angle of 90°. Background noise was controlled below 45 dB. Analysis of a voice sample, directly recorded using digital technology and with a sampling frequency of 50,000 Hz, was carried out using MDVP 515 software (version 2.3). Patients phonated vowel sound /a:/ for over 4 s at a comfortable level of loudness (about 55–65 dB). The operator's experience dates back to 2011, and the voice testing protocol in the hospital was established in 2015.

2.3. Experimental Setups

The study used a NVIDIA GeForce RTX2080 Ti (11GB) graphic card. We examined the normal and cancer voice signal classification and tested the performance of the SVM, XGBoost, light gradient boosted machine (LightGBM), artificial neural network (ANN), one-dimensional convolutional neural network (1D-CNN), and 2D-CNN. The performance was evaluated via five-fold cross-validation. The accuracy, sensitivity, specificity, and area under the curve (AUC) values were used as performance metrics. This study strictly used male voice samples to exclude gender effects in that all laryngeal cancer cases were male and that male and female voices have different frequency range. Otherwise, some factors that are not directly related to cancerous voice can undermine the integrity of the study design.

2.4. Feature Extraction

In this study, two common features in speech analysis were selected. First, a term named after the word "talk" in Dutch, PRAAT is a speech analysis program (Paul Boersma and David Weenink, Institute for Phonetic Sciences, University of Amsterdam, The Netherlands) in phonetics designed to extract key features in the voice [14]. The raw voice input was 4 s of 50,000 Hz signal. The PRAAT features were extracted under a minimum value of 10 Hz and a maximum value of 8000 Hz to account for the spectral range of a human voice. Fourteen audio features include mean and standard deviation of the fundamental frequency, harmonic to noise ratio (HNR), and jitter and shimmer variants. The HNR denotes the degree of acoustic periodicity in the aspect of energy. The last two sets of features are measures of perturbation in acoustic analysis, where jitter demonstrates the frequency instability, whereas shimmer represents the amplitude instability of a signal. In other words, jitter refers to the frequency variation from cycle to cycle, and the shimmer represents the amplitude variation of the sound wave. Following is a description of the jitter and shimmer variants [14]. The localJitter is the average absolute difference between consecutive intervals, divided by the average interval, and localabsolutejitter uses absolute difference. The rapJitter is the relative average perturbation of itself and the two adjacent, and ppq5jitter accounts for four neighbors. Ddpjitter is the difference between differences of consecutive difference. In a similar fashion, six shimmer variants were defined: localshimmer, localdbshimmer, apq3shimmer, apq5shimmer, apq11shimmer, and ddashimmer.

Second, MFCCs, a collection of numerical values resulting from the transformation of time series data, were obtained [15]. The principle of MFCCs is based on a short-time Fourier transform and additional consideration for the distinct nature of a human voice in the lower frequency range, set by the biased bandpass filter design. Forty triangular bandpass filters were used. Initially, we down sampled the input signal to 16,000 Hz, accounting for the Nyquist frequency of the human voice range. As a result of the transformation, 200,000 data points of the input signal were converted to 64,000 points, and then into a 40 × 126-time spectral image. The graphic presentation of down sampling, normalization, and MFCCs transformation is shown in Figures 1 and 2. In addition, short time Fourier transform (STFT), another common time-spectral representation, was obtained for comparative evaluation. For this conversion, we down sampled the input signal to 4000 Hz and processed with a frame size of 0.02 without overlap, in order to match with the height size of the MFCCs. As a result, a 40 × 199-time spectral image was produced.

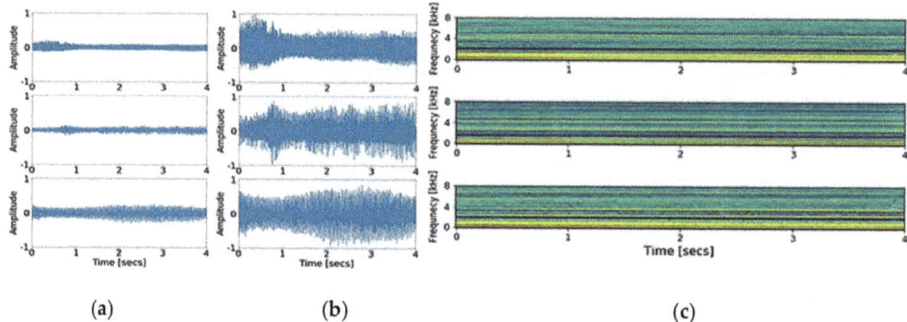

Figure 1. The graphic presentation of transformation from raw signal into Mel-frequency cepstral coefficients (MFCCs) image, a necessary process to comply with the two-dimensional convolutional neural network input shape. (**a**) Plot of signals down sampled to 16,000 Hz; (**b**) plot of signals normalized between −1 and 1; (**c**) image of signals after MFCCs transformation.

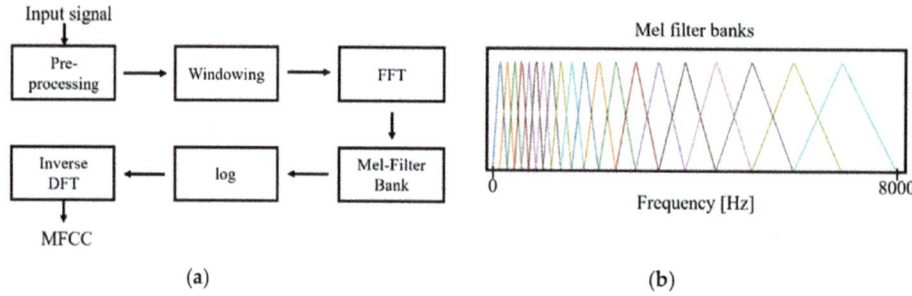

Figure 2. The flowchart of Mel-frequency cepstral coefficients (MFCCs) transformation. (**a**) and presentation of Mel filter banks (**b**). The triangular filter banks are densely located towards low frequency range, reflecting the distinctive nature of the human voice in that range. Abbreviations: FFT, fast Fourier transform; DFT, discrete Fourier transform.

2.5. Preprocessing

A series of preprocessing steps are introduced for the effective representation of the signal. The recordings represent continuous sounds. Normalization was performed to change the value of numerical voice signals to a common scale, because the magnitudes vary depending on the measuring distance of the record. Each signal was divided by the maximum absolute value of the recording per patient while taking account of the peak outliers.

For accurate validation, the data set was divided into two parts in each validation: one for training and another for testing. Performance metrics were only calculated with the testing dataset, the signals that the model did not process during its training. A five-fold validation method is used for reliable results, which divides the dataset into five subsets. For each validation fold, four subsets were used to train a model for appropriate representation and generalization power, and the model was validated with the remaining subset. Overall, five validations were conducted, and the performance matrix represented the average of all results. The process can be seen in Figure 3.

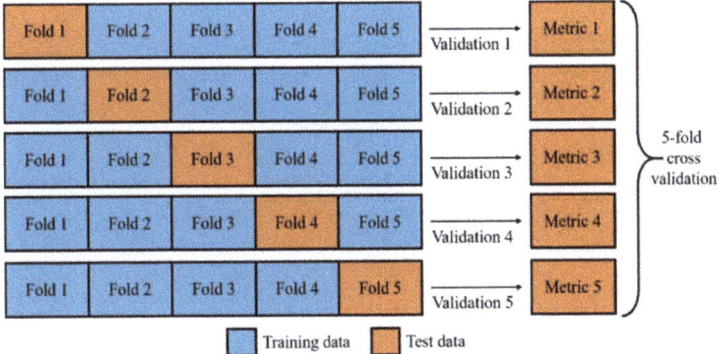

Figure 3. Illustration of five-fold validation. A given data set is split into five subsections where each fold is used as a testing set, a useful method to use all data where data is limited.

2.6. Machine Learning Algorithms

We tested three machine learning algorithms: SVM, XGBoost, LightGBM, and ANN. The SVM is the most frequently practiced method used in the classification task. The SVM resolves the classification task by drawing a decision boundary hyperplane that divides space with the maximum distance from each class. However, not all cases can be resolved similarly, as clusters often require a non-linear boundary. The kernel trick facilitates by warping spaces. In machine learning, the hyper-parameter is a high-level configurator empirically chosen to control complexity, conservativeness, and overfitting of a model before training the networks [16]. The governing decision-making equation and its classification decision is shown in the equations below, where ω_0 and ω represent bias and weights of the boundary.

$$\omega_0 + \omega^T x > 0 \rightarrow \text{x belongs to normal} \quad (1)$$

$$\omega_0 + \omega^T x < 0 \rightarrow \text{x belongs to pathological} \quad (2)$$

The LightGBM and XGBoost are classifiers derived from a decision tree family known to perform best in many practices. The decision tree is named after its shape comprising of a series of dividing rules. The model learns the optimal rules based on information gain and entropy. Information gain is a quantified value based on information generated by a certain event. Entropy is a relative degree of disorder [17]. Since a signal decision tree can easily overfit, a series of techniques are implemented to boost performance such as bagging, boosting, tree-pruning, and parallel processing. The techniques effectively combine predictions from multiple trees and multiple sequential models.

An ANN is a basic form of a DNN. A series of fully connected layers constitute an ANN. The model predicts the label of input data with trained weights and biases through a forward propagation. We consider this ANN model to be a machine learning model since the input is hand-crafted feature and the propagation mostly performs classification tasks only.

2.7. Deep Learning Algorithms

The human voice exhibits distinct characteristics in the lower frequency range, so biased filters are used in the MFCCs. Although a recent study has shown that MFCCs are consistent metric constraints [18], an inevitable information loss occurs at the conversion. Ten pieces of size 40 × 40 are randomly cropped per image to lower the computational cost and to elicit a data augmentation effect. In a similar fashion, ten pieces of size 40 × 40 segments from a STFT spectrogram are prepared from each signal.

Zero padding and down sampling are implemented for the 1D-CNN. Zero padding ensures stable frequency conversion and provides better resolution. Further, a recent study showed that the most contributive bands in both detection and classification ranged between 1000 and 8000 Hz [7]. Down sampling is set at 22,050 Hz for 1D-CNN and 16,000 for 2D-CNN preprocessing.

The 1D-CNN structure is composed of six convolution blocks and three fully connected layers (Figure 2). The number of kernels is 16, 32, 64, 128, and 256. A kernel is equivalent to a filter. For example, the first layer represents the filtered signals from 16 kernels. Max pooling sizes used are 8, 8, 8, 8, and 4 to compress the long signal, which choose the maximum single value from a given window size to progressively reduce the spatial size and to provide abstract representation. The dense layer is composed of 1536, 100, 50, and 2 nodes. Batch normalization and ReLU activation are used for faster and stable training [19]. The detailed structure of the algorithm is shown in Figure 4.

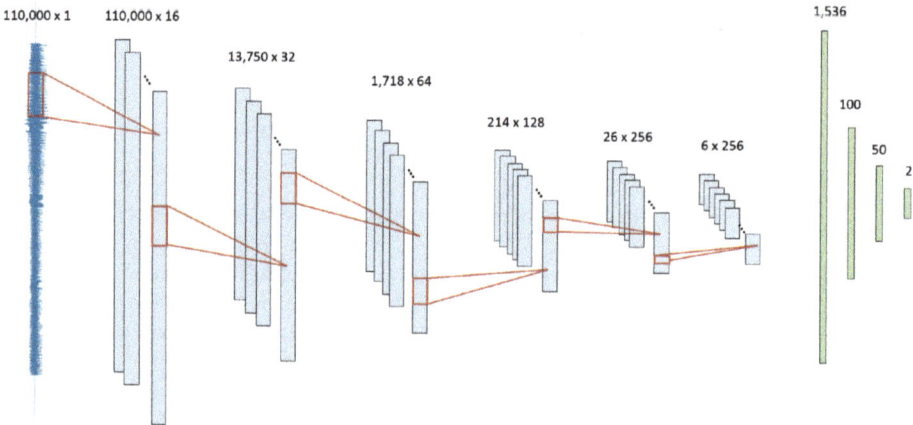

Figure 4. Illustration of one-dimensional convolutional neural network model structure.

The 2D-CNN structure is composed of three convolution blocks and three fully connected layers. The number of kernels is 64, 64, and 128. The dense layer is composed of 500, 50, and 2 nodes. A dropout of 0.3 is used twice at a dense layer to prevent overfitting. A Glorot uniform initializer and ReLU activations are used [20]. Maximum pooling is done conservatively, only once, because the input image is already small. The detailed structure of the algorithm is shown in Figure 5.

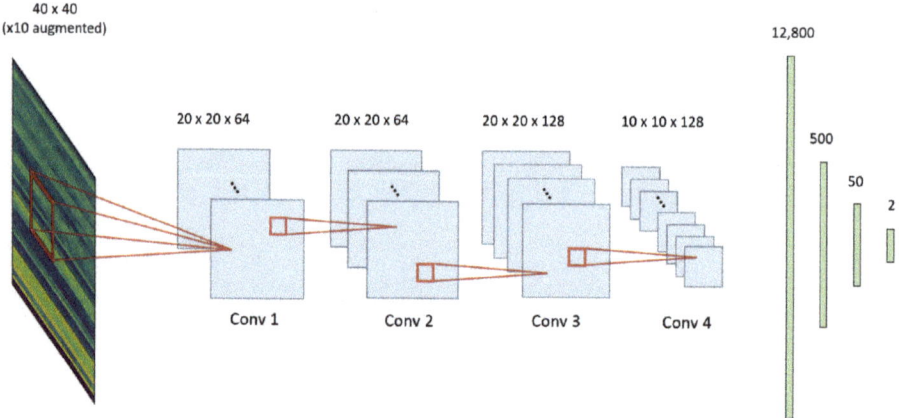

Figure 5. Illustration of two-dimensional convolutional neural network model structure.

2.8. Human Interpretation

Two laryngologists with 3–10 years of experience in laryngoscopy and laryngeal cancer were asked to listen to the same files and classify the voice sounds as either normal or abnormal. In addition, two volunteers with no medical background were asked to perform the same tasks. All volunteers were informed that abnormal voices are from laryngeal cancer patients, prior to the evaluation. No prior demographic information was provided. All volunteers were allowed to hear the voice files multiple times. The diagnostic parameters obtained from the four volunteers were calculated.

2.9. Statistical Analysis

Data are expressed as mean ± standard deviation for continuous data and as counts (%) for categorical data. Bivariate analyses were conducted using a two-tailed Student's *t*-test for continuous data and a two-tailed χ2 or Fisher's exact test for categorical data when appropriate.

All these statistical analyses were performed using IBM SPSS Statistics 20.0 (IBM Corp., Armonk, NY, USA), and *p*-values less than 0.05 were considered to indicate statistical significance.

Group differences between patients with cancer and healthy participants were determined using non-parametric tests. The AUC values, which reflect the diagnostic accuracy and predictive ability, were calculated for each parameter. The performance of laryngeal cancer classification was evaluated with an AUC of receiver operating characteristic (ROC) curves using roc_curve and auc functions of the Scikit-learn library and the matplotlib library in the Python 3.5.2. and R 2.15.3 package software (R Foundation for Statistical Computing, Vienna, Austria).

3. Results

3.1. Demographic Features

Using the medical records, we identified a total of 50 laryngeal cancer patients who had undergone voice analysis preoperatively. From the normal voices ($n = 180$), only the male voice data were selected ($n = 45$) and used for analysis. All cancer subjects were male. Laryngeal cancer included glottic (84%) and supraglottic (16%) types of cancer. The majority (84%) of patients were diagnosed at the T1–T2 stages when the voice recordings were performed. The characteristics of cancer and their staging are shown in Table 1. Compared with the healthy group, subjects with laryngeal cancer were significantly older, and showed higher smoking rates than the healthy subjects, as shown in Table 2.

Table 1. Clinicopathological characteristics of the cancer patients.

Characteristic		No. of Patients	[%]
Gender	Male	50	100
Primary site	Glottis	42	84
	Supraglottic	8	16
Differentiation	SCC	46	92
	Papillary SCC	2	4
	CIS	2	4
T classification	1	35	70
	2	7	14
	3	5	10
	4	3	6
N classification	0	42	84
	1	1	2
	2	4	8
	3	3	6
TNM stage	Early	39	78
	Advanced	11	22

Abbreviations: SCC; Squamous Cell Cancer, CIS; Carcinoma in Situ, TNM; Tumor Node Metastases Classification of Malignant Tumors.

Table 2. Demographic data from the 95 subjects, including the glottic cancer patients.

Clinical Variables		Normal Male ($n = 45$)	Larynx Cancer ($n = 50$)	*p*-Value *
Age (year)		49.7 ± 2.1 (24~83)	65.5 ± 1.3 (50~88)	<0.001
Smoking (yes)		12 (26.7)	37 (74.0)	<0.001 [†]
Smoking amount (packs per year)	<30	7 (58.3)	8 (21.6)	
	≥30	5 (41.7)	29 (78.4)	<0.001 [‡]

Values are presented in mean ± standard deviation (min~max) or number (%). * Group comparison between normal cases versus laryngeal cancer patients. [†] Hazards ratio: 14.8. [‡] Hazards ratio: 11.6.

3.2. Feature Selection

Figure 6 shows the contribution of each PRAAT 14 feature obtained from the XGBoost for the classification of voice changes. The HNR, standard deviation of F0, and apq11shimmer were major features in the classification of abnormal voices.

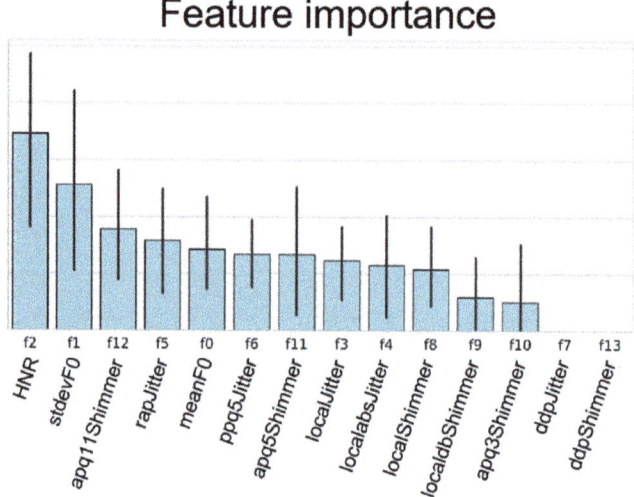

Figure 6. Feature importance analysis of XGBoost. The plot demonstrates the relative information gains based on the feature importance classification task of male voice samples.

3.3. Accuracy of the Automatic Detection in Male Voice Samples

We performed the analysis with no female data for two reasons. First, male and female voices are known to fall within different ranges of frequency [21]. Secondly, females rarely have larynx cancer, which is directly reflected in our data set that no female data exist in cancer class. Especially in East Asian countries, the proportion of female patients with laryngeal cancer is reported to be less than 10%. Therefore, voice signals comprising only the male dataset were analyzed. Among the algorithms, the 1D-CNN again showed good accuracy levels with sensitivity levels up to 85% (Table 3). Of interest was that five out of eight supraglottic cancer patients were correctly diagnosed with the 1D-CNN model.

The accuracy values and receiver operating characteristic (ROC) curves for a set of evaluations are demonstrated in Table 3 and Figure 7.

Table 3. Evaluation metrics table of only male voice samples for classification task of abnormal voice signals in laryngeal cancer (n = 50) from normal healthy subjects (n = 45).

Algorithms	Accuracy (%)	Sensitivity (%)	Specificity (%)	AUC
SVM	70.5 (67.9–73.0)	78.0 (75.6–80.3)	62.2 (58.0–66.3)	0.708
XGBoost	70.5 (68.2–72.8)	62.0 (58.5–65.4)	80.0 (77.3–82.6)	0.731
LightGBM	71.5 (68.2–74.8)	70.0 (66.6–73.3)	73.3 (69.9–76.6)	0.739
ANN	69.4 (67.6–71.2)	62.0 (60.4–63.5)	77.7 (75.3–80.2)	0.744
1D-CNN	85.2 (83.8–86.6)	78.0 (76.0–79.9)	93.3 (92.2–94.4)	0.852
2D-CNN * (MFCCs)	73.3 (72.0–74.7)	69.6 (66.9–72.2)	77.5 (74.2–80.8)	0.778
2D-CNN * (STFT)	67.1 (65.6–68.6)	58.6 (55.6–61.5)	76.6 (75.1–78.2)	0.707

Abbreviations: AUC, area under curve; SVM, support vector machine; XGBoost, extreme gradient boosting; LightGBM, light gradient boosted machine; ANN, artificial neural network; MFCCs, Mel-frequency cepstral coefficients; STFT, short-time Fourier transform. *: with 10 times augmented data.

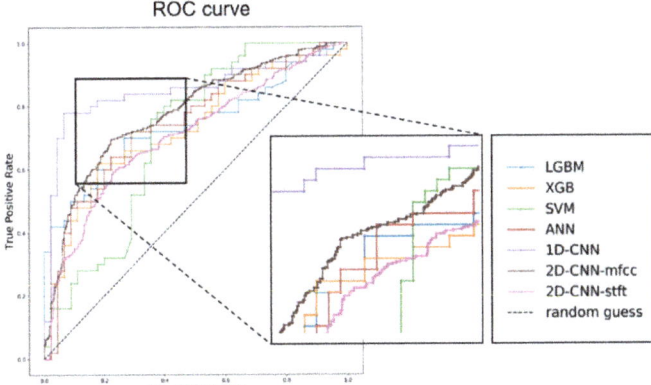

Figure 7. ROC (receiver operating characteristic) curve analysis of the different models for the classification of laryngeal cancer. ROC curves algorithms for classification task of only male voice samples. Abbreviations: LGBM, LightGBM; XGB, XGBoost; SVM, support vector machine; ANN, artificial neural network; 1D-CNN, one-dimensional convolutional neural network; 2D-CNN, two-dimensional convolutional neural network; MFCCs, Mel-frequency cepstral coefficients; STFT, short time Fourier transform.

3.4. Accuracy in Human Rating

Results show large variance in the sensitivity levels across the four raters with levels as low as 29% and the highest at 50%. The two experts showed higher accuracy levels than the two non-experts, but compared to the machine learning and deep learning algorithms, they showed low sensitivity and accuracy levels. Table 4 summarizes the result.

Table 4. Evaluation metrics table of only male voice samples for classification task of abnormal voice signals in laryngeal cancer (n = 50) from normal healthy subjects (n = 45).

Rater	Accuracy [%]	Sensitivity [%]	Specificity [%]	AUC
Non-expert 1	68.8 (58.3–78.2)	50.0 (35.5–64.7)	88.9 (75.9–96.3)	0.6944
Non-expert 2	56.7 (46.3–67.2)	29.1 (16.9–44.0)	86.6 (73.2–94.9)	0.5792
Expert 1	68.9 (58.7–78.0)	43.7 (29.4–58.8)	95.5 (84.8–99.4)	0.7930
Expert 2	70.9 (60.1–79.9)	43.7 (29.4–58.5)	100 (92.1–100)	0.7188
Experts Mean	69.9 (59.9–79.0)	43.7 (29.4–58.6)	97.7 (88.4–99.7)	0.7559

4. Discussion

The results of our study provide high accuracy levels of automated algorithms using machine learning and deep learning techniques that assess voice change in laryngeal cancer. The results are promising since the majority of the cancer subjects (84%) were at early stages of cancer. Among the algorithms, the 1D-CNN showed better performance than other algorithms, with accuracy levels of 85%. All the other computational algorithms showed promising levels of performance and some showed higher accuracy levels compared with the results obtained from two laryngologists, who showed sensitivity levels of 44%. To the best of our knowledge, this is one of the first studies that has compared the performance of automated algorithms against those performed by both clinicians and non-clinicians. Based on our results, automatic detection using the 1D-CNN and other computational algorithms may be considered as potential supplementary tools to distinguish abnormal voice changes in patients with laryngeal cancer.

Past studies have already used several machine learning techniques in attempts to distinguish pathological voice disorders in laryngeal cancer. Gavidia-Ceballos and Hansen [22] demonstrated accuracy levels of 88.7% in patients with vocal fold cancer, but their sample was limited to 20 glottic cancer and 10 healthy subjects. Previous studies employed an ANN in laryngeal cancer with accuracy levels of 92% [9]. However, their data included patients who were recovering from laryngeal cancer, mostly following surgery. The voice signals in the present study were obtained from laryngeal cancer patients preoperatively, and thus, our results are more appropriate for assistance in screening laryngeal cancer rather than detection of postoperative voice changes. The results are even more promising since our study also provided detailed clinical information about laryngeal cancer, mostly at the early stages.

Our results are also in accordance with previous studies that have suggested better performance of DNNs in some datasets compared with a SVM or Gaussian mixture model (GMM) in detecting pathological voice samples [9,10,23]. An unexpected finding was that the 1D-CNN showed better performance than the 2D-CNN, a more sophisticated algorithm. The processed signals contained 64,000 (4 [s] × 16000 [Hz]) data points representing acoustic information, whereas the MFCCs carried 15,640 (40 × 391) points. In addition, the 2D-CNN model has a limited scope of 40 by 40 kernel windows at a time. Through a series of feature conversion and windowing, the 2D-CNN method leads to unfortunate information loss. Thus, the 1D-CNN is associated with a higher resolution than the 2D-CNN in the presence of appropriate hyper parameters such as learning rate, kernel size, and the number of layers. Although the 1D-CNN is more difficult to optimize, higher resolution implies higher learning capacity. Although our results are consistent with recent studies that showed the superior performance of the 1D-CNN compared with the 2D-CNN in a heart sound classification study [24], one has to be conscious of the fact that performance of these algorithms may change depending on the nature of the data.

Laryngeal cancer is known to show a skewed gender distribution [25,26] with an approximately four- to six-fold higher risk in males [27] and poor prognosis compared with females [28]. Based on this gender difference, we assessed the performance levels of these algorithms when the analysis of voice features in laryngeal cancer was limited to males. In such gender-restricted analysis, the 1D-CNN showed good performance with accuracy levels of 85.2%. This phenomenon is discrepant to those observed by Fang et al. [10], who showed that the SVM outscored the GMM and ANN when the data were analyzed separately without the female subjects. Therefore, it was unexpected that the 1D-CNN performed well even with the limited sample of male voices. Despite our results favoring the 1D-CNN, due to the uneven gender distribution in laryngeal cancer, the gender composition of the data should be considered with caution when developing future deep learning algorithms since the female voice has broader distributions in cepstral domain analysis [29]. Furthermore, one has to be mindful that the performance of these algorithms may be different depending on the feature selection and amount of data, and therefore, caution is needed before making direct comparison of which algorithm is superior to the other.

In this study, among the many PRAAT features that played significant roles in helping to classify the voice changes, of interest, the HNR was shown to be an essential feature, followed by the F0 standard deviation and apq11shimmer from the XGBoost algorithms. Past studies [30,31] have shown changes in some acoustic parameters including the HNR, jitter, and shimmer in laryngeal cancer due to the structural effects on the vibration and wave movement of the vocal cord mucosa but have not shown which parameter contributes more than the other in the classification of laryngeal cancer. Abnormal HNR values reflect an asthenic voice and dysphonia [32], which may be expected with the mass effects. Controversies surrounding the role of fundamental frequencies exist, with some suggesting these values decrease in laryngeal cancer and smokers [31], compared to healthy groups [33]. Instead, this feature is a more prominent marker in voice change observed in smokers [34]. Of interest is that no study has yet emphasized the role of the apq11shimmer values in classifying these voice changes with high accuracy. The clinical implication of the apq11shimmer value in combination with changes of the F0 standard deviation, which reflects changes in voice tone, needs to be verified with future studies, including those related to other voice disorders.

Voice changes that do not improve within two weeks are known to be one of the earliest signs of laryngeal cancer and mandate a visit to the laryngologist. Our results indicated that the average time from onset of voice change to the first visit to the laryngologist was 16 weeks. Though most patients in our study were in the early stages of cancer, in reality, patients failed to consult with the laryngologist within the initial month when the voice changes develop. Subjective perception of voice change can be challenging and our results from the ratings by the four volunteers showed that half of the early stage cases could also be missed by the human ear, even by expert laryngologists. The diagnostic parameters from the four volunteers showed overall high specificity levels, which indicate good performance levels in discerning those with normal voices. However, the low sensitivity levels indicate that human perception of subtle voice changes within the short 4 s voice file may be insufficient to discern the initial voice changes in laryngeal cancer. Though the two experts showed better performance than the two non-experts, the low sensitivity levels of this latter group are of concern and reflect real-world situations where the patients may misjudge and miss the initial changes as normal. Voice change can be the only first symptom, and if not considered as a serious sign, it can inadvertently result in a delay when making the initial visit to the laryngologist. Automated algorithms may be used to alert the "non-expert" patients when these voice changes appear to seek medical advice. Higher sensitivity levels are ideal for screening tools. Therefore, the higher sensitivity levels from the deep learning algorithms may support the use of these automated voice algorithms in the detection of voice changes in early glottic cancer. Though based on a limited number of data, our results show the potential of future applications of these algorithms in digital health care and telemedicine.

One interesting point to consider is that the 1D-CNN showed good accuracy levels, even when most were at the early stages. In addition, the inclusion of these supraglottic cancer patients who usually remain asymptomatic in the early stages and are difficult to diagnose [35] may be clinically relevant. Voice changes in advanced laryngeal cancer stages can be evident because of the involvement of the vocal cord or thyroid cartilage. By contrast, in the T1 stage, these changes may be too subtle and may go unnoticed. The encouraging results of classifying those, even in the early laryngeal cancer stages, show the opportunity of automatic voice signal analysis to be used as part of future digital health tools for the noninvasive and objective detection of subtle voice changes at the early stages of laryngeal cancer. Future studies with more detailed separate analysis among the different tumor types and stages could be promising.

Significant new work has been reported recently using artificial intelligence techniques in the early detection of cancer, including skin and gastric cancer [36,37]. Similar attempts have also been made in oropharyngeal cancer with mixed results. A few studies have used features associated with hypernasalance in oropharyngeal cancer [38] and glottal flow in glottic cancer [39] and employed ANNs with mixed results. Recent studies have shown that the CNN can be used to predict the outcome automatically [40] or detect laryngeal cancer based on laryngoscope images with accuracy levels of

86% [41], which are similar to our accuracy levels of 85.2%. Our work differs from these past studies in that we employed voice signals rather than imaging data and compared the accuracy levels of the 1D-CNN to those rated by the human ear.

The algorithms presented in this study showed promising results. However, a few limitations remain to be addressed. First is the non-inclusion of other voice disorders such as those related to more common benign disorders, such as, vocal polyps or vocal fold palsies. The main objective was to determine the accuracy of various algorithms including the 1D-CNN against those performed by human raters. The use of these algorithms to classify other voice disorders may require rebuilding the algorithm structure based on additional hyper parameters. Ongoing studies by our research group are currently attempting to design new CNN algorithms that may be used to distinguish voice changes in cancer patients from other various voice disorders, such as those related to vocal palsy or polyps. Another factor to consider is the limited number of cancer cases. Machine learning requires a large amount of processed data, and its performance depends heavily on how well the feature is crafted. The limited number of data is a problem often encountered in medical data acquired from sources other than image files. It is even more challenging to obtain voice data from patients with laryngeal cancer during the preoperative period. However, the number of cancer patients was similar to past studies [9–11] that employed automated algorithms in voice pathologies. The voice, a signal carrying infinite information, can be represented in a simpler form by introducing digital signal processing tools such as PRAAT or MFCCs, which improves optimization potential despite the small datasets [15]. Second, the proposed algorithms performed well for datasets comprising only males. The inclusion of females in the analysis may inadvertently provide a clue to the model with all cancer data comprising male subjects and therefore excluded female data. Although our results supported the high-performance levels of the 1D-CNN, the model proposed in this study may lose its diagnostic power when female cancer patients are included. Therefore, our algorithms require re-validation when adequate data are collected from female patients in the future. Furthermore, prospective studies are needed for large-scale validation of our model. Third, since the cancer group showed more elderly males with a higher proportion of smokers, one could question whether our algorithm classified voice changes related to the presence of laryngeal cancer or related to smoking and old age. Smoking and old age are the cardinal risk factors of laryngeal cancer. However, these two conditions manifest in distinctive voice changes. For example, according to a recent meta-analysis study [34] voice changes in smoking are manifested mostly in the fundamental frequency (F0). Likewise, voice changes in elderly males are characterized by an increase of jitter values [42]. Had our algorithms classified based solely on senile and smoking changes, these two features would have been the two most important features. Instead, other features, which may reflect the tumor effects on the voice, played a more prominent role. Nevertheless, the skewed distribution of gender, age, and smoking status are important factors to consider in future studies that intend to employ artificial intelligence in voice disorders that include laryngeal cancer. Finally, our results are by no means intended to replace current diagnostic tools and future studies using voice signals as a supplementary screening tool in the age of telemedicine in conjunction with current laryngoscope studies in laryngeal cancer are warranted.

The results presented in our study demonstrate the ability of the proposed computational algorithms to distinguish voice changes in early laryngeal cancer from healthy voices in normal participants. However, this study did not include other voice disorders, which may be more common in clinical practice than laryngeal cancer patients. Therefore, a high degree of prudence is required in interpreting the results. Nevertheless, the application of voice signals to digital algorithms as alternative methods to assess patients at difficult times [43] when direct physical contact with the laryngologist is not feasible may have important social implications in the future.

5. Conclusions

This study has shown that automated voice detection based on both machine learning and deep learning algorithms facilitates detection of voice changes in laryngeal cancer in a noninvasive yet objective manner with accuracy levels that may surpass human performance. Future studies are warranted on techniques to implement and adopt these automated voice analyses using the 1D-CNN, as part of the digital health system [44].

Author Contributions: Conceptualization, J.J. and Y.J.H.; data curation, H.K., Y.J.H., and Y.J.; funding acquisition, S.L. and S.I.; investigation, S.L.; methodology, J.J., H.K., and Y.J.; project administration, S.L. and S.I.; software, J.L.; supervision, S.I.; validation, J.J. and J.L.; visualization, J.J.; writing—original draft, J.J. and H.K.; writing—review and editing, S.L. and S.I. All authors have read and agreed to the published version of the manuscript.

Funding: This work was supported by the Po-Ca Networking Groups funded by the Postech-Catholic Biomedical Engineering Institute (No. 5-2020-B0001-00050), National Research Foundation of Korea (NRF) grant funded by the Korea Government (MSIT) 2020R1F1A1065814 and 2020R1A2C1009744, and the Priority Research Centers Program funded by the Ministry of Education (2020R1A6A1A03047902).

Conflicts of Interest: The authors declare no conflict of interest.

Abbreviations

SCC	Squamous Cell Cancer
CIS	Carcinoma in Situ
TNM	Tumor Node Metastases Classification of Malignant Tumors
yr	Year
pyr	Pack Year
AUC	Area Under the Curve
SVM	Support Vector Machine
ANN	Artificial Neural Network
1D-CNN	One-Dimensional Convolutional Neural Network
2D-CNN	Two-Dimensional Convolutional Neural Network
MFCCs	Mel-Frequency Cepstral Coefficients
STFT	Short Time Fourier Transform

References

1. Siegel, R.L.; Miller, K.D.; Jemal, A. Cancer statistics. *CA Cancer J. Clin.* **2020**, *70*, 7–30. [CrossRef] [PubMed]
2. Nieminen, M.; Aro, K.; Jouhi, L.; Back, L.; Makitie, A.; Atula, T. Causes for delay before specialist consultation in head and neck cancer. *Acta Oncol.* **2018**, *57*, 1677–1686. [CrossRef] [PubMed]
3. Polesel, J.; Furlan, C.; Birri, S.; Giacomarra, V.; Vaccher, E.; Grando, G.; Gobitti, C.; Navarria, F.; Schioppa, O.; Minatel, E.; et al. The impact of time to treatment initiation on survival from head and neck cancer in north-eastern Italy. *Oral Oncol.* **2017**, *67*, 175–182. [CrossRef] [PubMed]
4. Aylward, A.; Park, J.; Abdelaziz, S.; Hunt, J.P.; Buchmann, L.O.; Cannon, R.B.; Rowe, K.; Snyder, J.; Deshmukh, V.; Newman, M.; et al. Individualized prediction of late-onset dysphagia in head and neck cancer survivors. *Head Neck* **2020**, *42*, 708–718. [CrossRef] [PubMed]
5. Balaguer, M.; Pommee, T.; Farinas, J.; Pinquier, J.; Woisard, V.; Speyer, R. Effects of oral and oropharyngeal cancer on speech intelligibility using acoustic analysis: Systematic review. *Head Neck* **2020**, *42*, 111–130. [CrossRef] [PubMed]
6. Jeon, J.; Han, Y.J.; Park, G.Y.; Sohn, D.G.; Lee, S.; Im, S. Artificial intelligence in the field of electrodiagnosis-a new threat or heralding a new era in electromyography? *Clin. Neurophysiol.* **2019**, *130*, 1995–1996. [CrossRef] [PubMed]
7. Mohammed, M.A.; Abdulkareem, K.H.; Mostafa, S.A.; Ghani, M.K.A.; Maashi, M.S.; Garcia-Zapirain, B.; Oleagordia, I.; Alhakami, H.; AL-Dhief, F.T. Voice pathology detection and classification using convolutional neural network model. *Appl. Sci.* **2020**, *10*, 3723. [CrossRef]
8. Al-Nasheri, A.; Muhammad, G.; Alsulaiman, M.; Ali, Z. Investigation of voice pathology detection and classification on different frequency regions using correlation functions. *J. Voice* **2017**, *31*, 3–15. [CrossRef]
9. Chuang, Z.Y.; Yu, X.T.; Chen, J.Y.; Hsu, Y.T.; Xu, Z.Z.; Wang, C.T.; Lin, F.C.; Fang, S.H. DNN-based approach to detect and classify pathological voice. In Proceedings of the 2018 IEEE International Conference on Big Data (Big Data), Seattle, WA, USA, 10–13 December 2018; pp. 5238–5241.

10. Fang, S.H.; Tsao, Y.; Hsiao, M.J.; Chen, J.Y.; Lai, Y.H.; Lin, F.C.; Wang, C.T. Detection of pathological voice using cepstrum vectors: A deep learning approach. *J. Voice* **2019**, *33*, 634–641. [CrossRef]
11. Godino-Llorente, J.I.; Gomez-Vilda, P. Automatic detection of voice impairments by means of short-term cepstral parameters and neural network based detectors. *IEEE Trans. Biomed. Eng.* **2004**, *51*, 380–384. [CrossRef]
12. Eye, M.; Infirmary, E. *Voice Disorders Database*; Kay Elemetrics Corporation: Lincoln Park, NJ, USA, 1984; Volume 1.03, [CD-ROM].
13. Saarbrucken Voice Database. Available online: http://www.stimmdatenbank.coli.uni-saarland.de/ (accessed on 30 January 2020).
14. Boersma, P.; Weenink, D. PRAAT, a system for doing phonetics by computer. *Glot. Int.* **2000**, *5*, 341–345.
15. Muda, L.; Begam, M.; Elamvazuthi, I. Voice recognition algorithms using mel frequency cepstral coefficient (MFCC) and dynamic time warping (DTW) techniques. *J. Comput.* **2010**, *2*, 138–143.
16. Huang, S.; Cai, N.; Pacheco, P.P.; Narrandes, S.; Wang, Y.; Xu, W. Applications of support vector machine (SVM) learning in cancer genomics. *Cancer Genom. Proteom.* **2018**, *15*, 41–51.
17. Tao, J.; Qin, C.; Li, W.; Liu, C. Intelligent fault diagnosis of diesel engines via extreme gradient boosting and high-accuracy time-frequency information of vibration signals. *Sensors* **2019**, *19*, 3280. [CrossRef]
18. Hao, X.; Bao, Y.; Guo, Y.; Yu, M.; Zhang, D.; Risacher, S.L.; Saykin, A.J.; Yao, X.; Shen, L.; Alzheimer's Disease Neuroimaging Initiative. Multi-modal neuroimaging feature selection with consistent metric constraint for diagnosis of Alzheimer's disease. *Med. Image Anal.* **2020**, *60*, 101625. [CrossRef] [PubMed]
19. Zeiler, M.D.; Ranzato, M.; Monga, R.; Mao, M.; Yang, K.; Le, Q.V.; Nguyen, P.; Senior, A.; Vanhoucke, V.; Dean, J.; et al. On rectified linear units for speech processing. In Proceedings of the 2013 IEEE International Conference on Acoustics, Speech and Signal Processing, Vancouver, BC, Canada, 26–31 May 2013; pp. 3517–3521.
20. Schmidt-Hieber, J. Nonparametric regression using deep neural networks with ReLU activation function. *Ann. Statist.* **2020**, *48*, 1875–1897. [CrossRef]
21. Titze, I.R. Physiologic and acoustic differences between male and female voices. *J. Acoust. Soc. Am.* **1989**, *85*, 1699–1707. [CrossRef]
22. Gavidia-Ceballos, L.; Hansen, J.H. Direct speech feature estimation using an iterative EM algorithm for vocal fold pathology detection. *IEEE Trans. Biomed. Eng.* **1996**, *43*, 373–383. [CrossRef]
23. Ritchings, R.T.; McGillion, M.; Moore, C.J. Pathological voice quality assessment using artificial neural networks. *Med. Eng. Phys.* **2002**, *24*, 561–564. [CrossRef]
24. Li, F.; Liu, M.; Zhao, Y.; Kong, L.; Dong, L.; Liu, X.; Hui, M. Feature extraction and classification of heart sound using 1D convolutional neural networks. *EURASIP J. Adv. Signal Process.* **2019**, *2019*, 59. [CrossRef]
25. Tang, J.A.; Lango, M.N. Diverging incidence trends for larynx and tonsil cancer in low socioeconomic regions of the USA. *Oral Oncol.* **2019**, *91*, 65–68. [CrossRef]
26. Louie, K.S.; Mehanna, H.; Sasieni, P. Trends in head and neck cancers in England from 1995 to 2011 and projections up to 2025. *Oral Oncol.* **2015**, *51*, 341–348. [CrossRef] [PubMed]
27. Cook, M.B.; McGlynn, K.A.; Devesa, S.S.; Freedman, N.D.; Anderson, W.F. Sex disparities in cancer mortality and survival. *Cancer Epidemiol. Biomark. Prev.* **2011**, *20*, 1629–1637. [CrossRef] [PubMed]
28. Chatenoud, L.; Garavello, W.; Pagan, E.; Bertuccio, P.; Gallus, S.; La Vecchia, C.; Negri, E.; Bosetti, C. Laryngeal cancer mortality trends in European countries. *Int. J. Cancer* **2016**, *138*, 833–842. [CrossRef]
29. Fraile, R.; Saenz-Lechon, N.; Godino-Llorente, J.I.; Osma-Ruiz, V.; Fredouille, C. Automatic detection of laryngeal pathologies in records of sustained vowels by means of mel-frequency cepstral coefficient parameters and differentiation of patients by sex. *Folia Phoniatr. Logop.* **2009**, *61*, 146–152. [CrossRef] [PubMed]
30. Skuk, V.G.; Schweinberger, S.R. Influences of fundamental frequency, formant frequencies, aperiodicity, and spectrum level on the perception of voice gender. *J. Speech Lang. Hear. Res.* **2014**, *57*, 285–296. [CrossRef]
31. Mekis, J.; Strojan, P.; Boltezar, I.H. Factors affecting voice quality in early glottic cancer before and after radiotherapy. *Radiol. Oncol.* **2019**, *53*, 459–464. [CrossRef]
32. Rabeh, H.; Salah, H.; Adnane, C. Voice pathology recognition and classification using noise related features. *Int. J. Adv. Comput. Sci. Appl.* **2018**, *9*, 82–87. [CrossRef]
33. Kinshuck, A.J.; Shenoy, A.; Jones, T.M. Voice outcomes for early laryngeal cancer. *Curr. Opin. Otolaryngol. Head Neck Surg.* **2017**, *25*, 211–216. [CrossRef]

34. Byeon, H.; Cha, S. Evaluating the effects of smoking on the voice and subjective voice problems using a meta-analysis approach. *Sci. Rep.* **2020**, *10*, 4720. [CrossRef]
35. Raitiola, H.; Pukander, J.; Laippala, P. Glottic and supraglottic laryngeal carcinoma: Differences in epidemiology, clinical characteristics and prognosis. *Acta Otolaryngol.* **1999**, *119*, 847–851.
36. Hirasawa, T.; Aoyama, K.; Tanimoto, T.; Ishihara, S.; Shichijo, S.; Ozawa, T.; Ohnishi, T.; Fujishiro, M.; Matsuo, K.; Fujisaki, J.; et al. Application of artificial intelligence using a convolutional neural network for detecting gastric cancer in endoscopic images. *Gastric Cancer* **2018**, *21*, 653–660. [CrossRef] [PubMed]
37. Esteva, A.; Kuprel, B.; Novoa, R.A.; Ko, J.; Swetter, S.M.; Blau, H.M.; Thrun, S. Dermatologist-level classification of skin cancer with deep neural networks. *Nature* **2017**, *542*, 115–118. [CrossRef] [PubMed]
38. de Bruijn, M.; ten Bosch, L.; Kuik, D.J.; Langendijk, J.A.; Leemans, C.R.; Leeuw, I.V.d. Artificial neural network analysis to assess hypernasality in patients treated for oral or oropharyngeal cancer. *Logoped. Phoniatr. Vocol.* **2011**, *36*, 168–174. [CrossRef] [PubMed]
39. Aicha, A.B.; Ezzine, K. Cancer larynx detection using glottal flow parameters and statistical tools. In Proceedings of the 2016 International Symposium on Signal, Image, Video and Communications (ISIVC), Tunis, Tunisia, 21–23 November 2016; pp. 65–70.
40. Diamant, A.; Chatterjee, A.; Vallieres, M.; Shenouda, G.; Seuntjens, J. Deep learning in head & neck cancer outcome prediction. *Sci. Rep.* **2019**, *9*, 2764. [CrossRef]
41. Xiong, H.; Lin, P.; Yu, J.G.; Ye, J.; Xiao, L.; Tao, Y.; Jiang, Z.; Lin, W.; Liu, M.; Xu, J.; et al. Computer-aided diagnosis of laryngeal cancer via deep learning based on laryngoscopic images. *EBioMedicine* **2019**, *48*, 92–99. [CrossRef]
42. Mueller, P.B. The aging voice. *Semin. Speech Lang.* **1997**, *18*, 159–168. [CrossRef] [PubMed]
43. Brody, R.M.; Albergotti, W.G.; Shimunov, D.; Nicolli, E.; Patel, U.A.; Harris, B.N.; Bur, A.M. Changes in head and neck oncologic practice during the COVID-19 pandemic. *Head Neck* **2020**, *42*, 1448–1453. [CrossRef] [PubMed]
44. Ali, Z.; Hossain, M.S.; Muhammad, G.; Sangaiah, A.K. An intelligent healthcare system for detection and classification to discriminate vocal fold disorders. *Future Gener. Comput. Syst.* **2018**, *85*, 19–28. [CrossRef]

Publisher's Note: MDPI stays neutral with regard to jurisdictional claims in published maps and institutional affiliations.

© 2020 by the authors. Licensee MDPI, Basel, Switzerland. This article is an open access article distributed under the terms and conditions of the Creative Commons Attribution (CC BY) license (http://creativecommons.org/licenses/by/4.0/).

Article

Early Detection of Septic Shock Onset Using Interpretable Machine Learners

Debdipto Misra [1], Venkatesh Avula [2], Donna M. Wolk [3], Hosam A. Farag [3], Jiang Li [2], Yatin B. Mehta [4], Ranjeet Sandhu [1], Bipin Karunakaran [1], Shravan Kethireddy [4], Ramin Zand [5] and Vida Abedi [2,*,†]

1. Steele Institute for Health Innovation, Geisinger Health System, Danville, PA 17822, USA; dmisra@geisinger.edu (D.M.); rs1444@scarletmail.rutgers.edu (R.S.); bkarunakaran@novanthealth.org (B.K.)
2. Department of Molecular and Functional Genomics, Geisinger Health System, Danville, PA 17822, USA; vavula1@geisinger.edu (V.A.); jli@geisinger.edu (J.L.)
3. Diagnostic Medicine Institute, Department of Laboratory Medicine, Geisinger Health System, Danville, PA 17822, USA; dmwolk@geisinger.edu (D.M.W.); hafarag@geisinger.edu (H.A.F.)
4. Critical Care Medicine, Geisinger Health System, Danville, PA 17822, USA; ybmehta@geisinger.edu (Y.B.M.); shravan.kethireddy@nghs.com (S.K.)
5. Neuroscience Institute, Geisinger Health System, Danville, PA 17822, USA; ramin.zand@gmail.com
* Correspondence: vidaabedi@gmail.com or vabedi@geisinger.edu
† Geisinger Health System, 100 N Academy Ave, Danville, PA 17822, USA.

Citation: Misra, D.; Avula, V.; Wolk, D.M.; Farag, H.A.; Li, J.; Mehta, Y.B.; Sandhu, R.; Karunakaran, B.; Kethireddy, S.; Zand, R.; et al. Early Detection of Septic Shock Onset Using Interpretable Machine Learners. *J. Clin. Med.* **2021**, *10*, 301. https://doi.org/10.3390/jcm10020301

Received: 12 November 2020
Accepted: 12 January 2021
Published: 15 January 2021

Publisher's Note: MDPI stays neutral with regard to jurisdictional claims in published maps and institutional affiliations.

Copyright: © 2021 by the authors. Licensee MDPI, Basel, Switzerland. This article is an open access article distributed under the terms and conditions of the Creative Commons Attribution (CC BY) license (https://creativecommons.org/licenses/by/4.0/).

Abstract: Background: Developing a decision support system based on advances in machine learning is one area for strategic innovation in healthcare. Predicting a patient's progression to septic shock is an active field of translational research. The goal of this study was to develop a working model of a clinical decision support system for predicting septic shock in an acute care setting for up to 6 h from the time of admission in an integrated healthcare setting. Method: Clinical data from Electronic Health Record (EHR), at encounter level, were used to build a predictive model for progression from sepsis to septic shock up to 6 h from the time of admission; that is, $T = 1, 3,$ and $6\ h$ from admission. Eight different machine learning algorithms (Random Forest, XGBoost, C5.0, Decision Trees, Boosted Logistic Regression, Support Vector Machine, Logistic Regression, Regularized Logistic, and Bayes Generalized Linear Model) were used for model development. Two adaptive sampling strategies were used to address the class imbalance. Data from two sources (clinical and billing codes) were used to define the case definition (septic shock) using the Centers for Medicare & Medicaid Services (CMS) Sepsis criteria. The model assessment was performed using Area under Receiving Operator Characteristics (AUROC), sensitivity, and specificity. Model predictions for each feature window (1, 3 and 6 h from admission) were consolidated. Results: Retrospective data from April 2005 to September 2018 were extracted from the EHR, Insurance Claims, Billing, and Laboratory Systems to create a dataset for septic shock detection. The clinical criteria and billing information were used to label patients into two classes-septic shock patients and sepsis patients at three different time points from admission, creating two different case-control cohorts. Data from 45,425 unique in-patient visits were used to build 96 prediction models comparing clinical-based definition versus billing-based information as the gold standard. Of the 24 consolidated models (based on eight machine learning algorithms and three feature windows), four models reached an AUROC greater than 0.9. Overall, all the consolidated models reached an AUROC of at least 0.8820 or higher. Based on the AUROC of 0.9483, the best model was based on Random Forest, with a sensitivity of 83.9% and specificity of 88.1%. The sepsis detection window at 6 h outperformed the 1 and 3-h windows. The sepsis definition based on clinical variables had improved performance when compared to the sepsis definition based on only billing information. Conclusion: This study corroborated that machine learning models can be developed to predict septic shock using clinical and administrative data. However, the use of clinical information to define septic shock outperformed models developed based on only administrative data. Intelligent decision support tools can be developed and integrated into the EHR and improve clinical outcomes and facilitate the optimization of resources in real-time.

Keywords: healthcare; artificial intelligence; machine learning; interpretable machine learning; explainable machine learning; septic shock; clinical decision support system; electronic health record

1. Introduction

Sepsis is a life-threatening condition that arises when the body's response to an infection injures its tissues and organs as defined by the 1991 consensus [1–3]. Sepsis is a complex syndrome that is difficult to identify early, as its symptoms, such as fever and low blood pressure, overlap with those of other common illnesses. Without timely treatment, sepsis can progress to septic shock, which has a hospital mortality rate greater than 40%. Identification of sepsis patients who are at high risk of septic shock will be helpful for clinicians to prioritize preventive care and improve the survival rate. Early diagnosis, prompt antibiotic, and supportive therapy are associated with improved outcomes [4–6]. Severe sepsis and septic shock are the leading causes of morbidity and mortality in the Intensive Care Unit (ICU) [7]. Septic shock is a subset of sepsis with significantly increased mortality due to severe circulation and/or cellular metabolism abnormalities. During septic shock, the heart and circulatory system begin to fail and blood pressure drops. Septic shock, the leading cause of morbidity and mortality in the Intensive Care Unit (ICU), is costing the United States' healthcare system more than $20 billion per year [8].

Translating recent advances in Artificial Intelligence (AI) to patient outcomes is an active area of research [9–11]. A few examples where AI has shown promise are interpreting chest radiographs [12], identifying malignancy in mammograms [10], and detecting incidental lung nodules analyzing computer tomography scans among others [13,14]. Leveraging data collected from the EHRs offers clinical insight, which can better augment favorable patient outcomes [15]. Data-driven AI models can also assign risk scores to transfer high-risk patients to intensive care units [16]. More and more advanced ML models are used to develop clinical decision systems, predicting in-hospital mortality, length of stay, readmission risk, and discharge diagnoses [17] and sepsis management [18,19]. In this study, we developed a working model for predicting septic shock in an acute care setting up to 6 h from the time of admission using real-time data. Predicting septic shock is challenging yet highly impactful, as timely diagnosis and prompt antibiotic and supportive therapy are associated with improved outcomes. This paper presents a practical working model for using ML to develop predictive models of septic shock in an Intensive Care Unit environment. The findings highlight how ML and large clinical and administrative data lakes can be leveraged to address practical challenges.

2. Related Works

Recent works have highlighted the unmet need for data-driven clinical decision systems for the identification of at-risk patients. For instance, in 2018, researchers [20] leveraged high-resolution time-series data to predict septic shock onset in the Intensive Care Unit, 4 to 12 h before the event. In 2019, it was demonstrated that [21] an expert AI system could outperform clinicians to predict sepsis onset. In 2020, Kim et al. [22] the possibility of predicting septic shock within 24 h using ML-based models was explored. Even though septic shock has higher mortality than sepsis [23], identification of both sepsis and septic shock patients in such a way to give the care providers more time (even a few hours) can lead to improved outcomes. Although there are many use cases of ML-based models of sepsis and septic shock, there is limited literature focusing on a working model in an integrated healthcare system focusing on scalability, real-time data access, and standardization of the sepsis and septic shock evolving phenotype definition. Previous works have focused on clinical models using various datasets and characteristics [24], focusing on the effect of ML algorithms on outcomes of sepsis patients.

This project was part of an initiative to build a translational and interpretable decision support system as an assistive technology for our providers. In particular, we aimed to develop a prediction model of sepsis and severe sepsis to septic shock by using clinical data and comparing the model performance when only billing data are used to define the cohort. Data extraction from administrative sources (such as billing codes), which are in a structured form, is easier compared to data extraction from unstructured clinical sources (such as notes for extraction of the source of infection). The latter requires more complex queries, including the integration of natural language processing pipelines. It was [25] reported that identifying sepsis or septic shock patients based on clinical data, as compared to administrative data, is more accurate; however, many studies still rely mainly on administrative data. For septic shock, administrative data can be inaccurate as the patient's progression to septic shock can occur at any time. While earlier works [26,27] have demonstrated moderate success using tree-based models for visit level prediction, recent works [26] leveraging temporal neural network-based models have shown promising results for predicting septic shock at visit and event levels. However, one of the challenges while defining cases and control revolves around the lack of consensus for defining sepsis and septic shock [7]. Cohort definition is the first and most important step of the modeling pipeline. In this study, we used clinical variables to map our cohort definition (cases: septic shock; controls: sepsis and severe sepsis [28]) with the Systemic Inflammatory Response Syndrome (SIRS) [29] criteria. The SIRS, as outlined by the Centers for Medicare & Medicaid Services [30], is outlined in Figure 1.

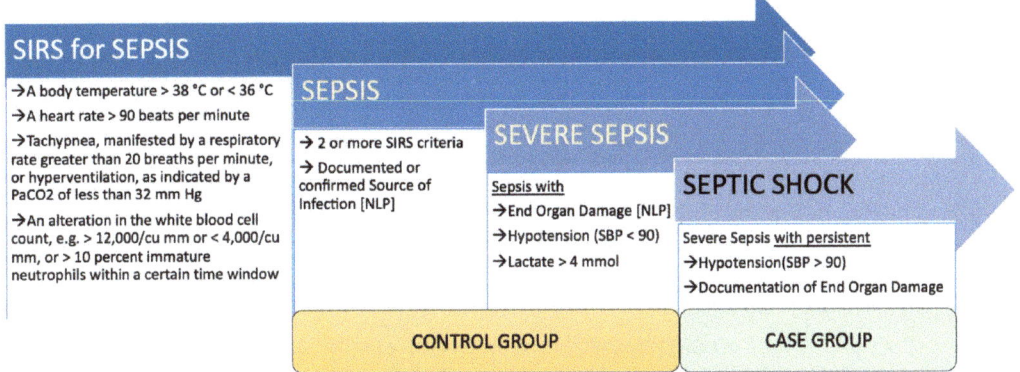

[NLP]: Data extracted using natural language processing applied to provider notes (unstructured sources)

Figure 1. Case and control definition based on the SIRS criteria and Centers for Medicare & Medicaid Services (CMS) definition.

3. Methods

3.1. Data Sources

This study was approved by the Geisinger Institutional Review Board (IRB). Geisinger, an integrated multi-site health system in North Eastern Pennsylvania with a catchment population of approximately 2.5 million citizens, has been known for being one of the most "wired" and innovative healthcare systems in the United States. Thirteen years of retrospective data between April 2005 to September 2018 from EHR (EPIC), Insurance Claims and Billing (AMISYS), and Laboratory Systems (Sunquest) were used to create a sepsis dataset for this study. The systemic inflammatory response syndrome (SIRS) [30] criteria, outlined by Centers for Medicare & Medicaid Services (CMS) [31], were used to assign patients into the case and control groups—septic shock patients (case group) and sepsis and severe sepsis patients (control group). In production, the system was designed to detect septic shock using real-time data to assist clinicians when treating high-risk sepsis patients in ICU. In addition to the EHR data, billing codes were utilized to ascertain the correct diagnosis for a patient at a given encounter for comparative assessment.

The initial assessment of clinical features, which was based on input from the clinicians and the literature, resulted in 65 features in six different categories from the structured sources. The features included during the first assessment were broadly in the following categories: demographics, vitals, pathology and laboratory measurements, medications, comorbidities, and procedures. Additional variables, which are critical in sepsis and septic shock, were also considered. In particular, (1) use of vasopressors was part of the criteria to define septic shock (persistent hypotension), (2) use of antibiotic administration was also included in the study (to suspect infection), and (3) creatinine level was utilized to evaluate kidney function since the use of urine output data, also an important parameter, was challenging; the latter is associated with a high error rate, given the needs for visual assessment and manual data recording.

Data from structured and unstructured sources were extracted and processed. Clinical notes (unstructured sources) were used to ascertain clinical states, including the source of infection, focused exam, documentation of septic shock, and severe sepsis documentation. Medical ontology from the Unified Medical Language System (UMLS) [31] meta-thesaurus, including SNOMED [32], LOINC [33] and ICD-9/ICD-10 [34] were used in the data model abstraction. Technical details of the natural language processing (NLP) pipeline are provided in the data extraction section.

3.2. Feature Assessment

The list of features was further evaluated for the clinical implementation to ensure clear workflow integration. Stakeholders from the data management, EHR vendor (EPIC), Laboratory Medicine, and clinicians reviewed the comprehensive feature list, and a decision was made to include actionable features with high clinical value. The final list included the following features: blood culture, diastolic and systolic blood pressure, creatinine, lactic acid, mean arterial pressure (MAP), platelet count, pulse, respiration, temperature, white blood cell count, age, gender, height, and weight. Association Rule Mining [35] was also performed as part of the feature exploration strategy to investigate the relationship between comorbidities using diagnosis codes. Results from this additional assessment are included in the Appendix A (Figure A1) for the interested reader.

3.3. Cohort Selection

Cohort definition involves establishing a reproducible process by which data elements from the EHR (both structured and unstructured) can be used to develop a longitudinal view of the patient. Deep phenotyping was performed to create different case and control cohorts based on structured and unstructured data sources. The Systemic Inflammatory Response Syndrome (SIRS) [30] criteria were used to group patients into the case (septic shock) and control (sepsis and severe sepsis) group (See Figure 1). Three different sets of case-control were also designed based on the adult patients (>18 years old) progressing from sepsis to septic shock at three different proceeding time frames from admission—$T = 1, 3$, and $6\ h$ from the time of admission to septic shock progression (visit level early diagnosis—based on a left-align design). Since vitals are extracted directly from sensors and fed into the system as they are generated, our data was time-stamped, which allowed us to collect data points preceding the observation window. For instance, if there were three data points at 0.5 h, 2.5 h, and 3.5 h for a patient, for $T = 3\ h$ window, data at 2.5 h was utilized, similarly, for the $T = 6\ h$, data point collected at 3.5 h was used and so forth.

3.4. Data Extraction

Analytics Infrastructure: Unified Data Architecture (UDA) is the Enterprise Data Lake providing core integration, storage, and user-specific access and retrieval information at Geisinger. It is an in-house 50-node cluster running with the capability to ingest, store, and transform big data using a combination of Apache Spark and Apache Hive on an Apache Hadoop cluster. Data from heterogeneous source systems and vendors (e.g., clinical, billing, radiology, laboratory) are ingested into an Enterprise Data Warehouse daily (EDW). The data model is used extensively for clinical reporting and advanced analytics. EDW was used as the source for the extraction of retrospective data and clinical features.

Data extraction from unstructured sources: Patient notes, specifically nursing notes, were used to determine the source of infection, chronic conditions, fluid bolus, and acute kidney disease. Apache cTAKES [36] was used as the natural language processing (NLP) engine. The NLP engine was modified to be utilized in a big data environment using the Apache Spark framework on Hadoop [37]. Concepts related to chronic conditions, fluid bolus, and acute kidney disease were identified from in-patient provider notes using entities from the UMLS meta-thesaurus. Notes with the relevant concepts were selected for downstream analysis. A custom regular expression-based NLP pipeline was applied to extract additional information for the three SIRS criteria, including the source of infection, chronic conditions, and fluid bolus.

Data extraction from structured sources: Various data elements, including vitals, flowsheets, and medications were processed, enhanced, and integrated into Geisinger's UDA platform. An Extract Transform Load (ETL) pipeline consolidated the data and aggregated clinical measures along with patients' encounters and demographic information. This data was aggregated with unstructured patient notes to determine various events such as SIRS and Organ Dysfunction (OD). Sepsis, severe sepsis, and septic shock classification are performed based on these medical events' chronology as defined by the CMS guidelines. The classified data was integrated with patients' additional historical data such as chronic conditions and medical history. Finally, a longitudinal chronological narrative of various clinical measures and medical events from the time of admission was generated and used for model development.

3.5. Data Processing

Various data processing, such as exploratory data analysis, imputation, and sampling, were performed before training and testing the various models.

3.5.1. Outlier Removal

The distribution of unique features was assessed to identify noise or outliers in the data. Units of the numeric variables and the bounds of lower and upper limits were applied (see Table A1). Furthermore, values identified outside of the six standard deviations were manually verified and removed if considered dubious.

3.5.2. Imputation

Variables with more than 40% missing were excluded from the analysis. The only exception is lactic acid, which had an overall higher missingness; however, given the importance of this variable, a decision was made to include this key variable. The MICE package in R with the random forest implementation was used to impute missingness [38]. Given the large dataset, a custom pipeline was implemented using Apache Spark [39] and optimized for scalability. The distribution of variables before and after imputation was assessed to ensure consistency.

3.5.3. Class Imbalance

Given that the percentage of patients with septic shock (cases) is significantly smaller than patients with sepsis and severe sepsis (controls), three sampling strategies were applied. Statistical techniques were applied in the following specific order. First, Edited Nearest Neighbors (ENN) [40] was used to smooth the data distribution by removing misclassified samples based on nearest neighbors from the majority class. The ENN was followed by the Synthetic Minority Over Sampling Technique (SMOTE) [41] to increase the size of the minority class. Two different variations of SMOTE (SMOTE and Synthetic Minority Over-sampling Technique for Nominal and Continuous (SMOTE-NC)) were used for numeric and categorical features. Finally, under-sampling was addressed by using a random under-sampling (RUS) algorithm, applied to balance the classes [42]. Up-sampling, synthetically increasing the sample size of the minority class, was performed separately for labels from the Billing and CMS-based cohorts.

3.6. Modeling Strategy

Geisinger's big data environment used for our modeling consisted of 34 physical nodes with 1140 vCores using 11.07 TB of memory. We also used the Yet Another Resource Negotiator (YARN) [37] cluster manager for jobs that are configured to use 200 executors with 5 GB memory container size. The technology stack used consisted of running spark jobs submitted to the YARN cluster resource manager.

As the list of features was limited to actionable features with the highest clinical utility, we did not perform data-driven feature selection; however, we used Pearson pairwise correlation analysis to corroborate that features in the cohort were not highly correlated. We split the data into training and testing (80/20 split) while retaining the proportion of classes. Model development was performed on 80% of the data, while model testing was performed on 20% of the data. During the model development (on the 80% of the data), 5-fold cross-validation was utilized. Furthermore, synthetic sampling was used only on the training data. Model performances were evaluated on the holdout test data set (20% of the data) using the area under the receiver operating characteristic curve (AUROC), specificity, and sensitivity. Consolidated metrics for 1, 3, and 6-h feature windows were also calculated. Thus, if the patient was assigned a septic shock label in any of the three time intervals, the consolidated prediction was selected as septic shock.

The models were derived from the two cohorts (cohort designed based on CMS criteria and billing information). Predicting the onset of septic shock in the proceeding T hours after admission was designed for $T = 1, 3$ and $6\ h$. Time-dependent features (dynamic features) were collected for each window, and the results of the model performance were compared.

A total of eight different algorithms were trained: Logistic Regression [43], Regularized Logistic Regression [44], Bayes General Linear Model [45], Boosted Logistic Regression [46], C5.0 [46], Decision Trees [47], Support Vector Machine (SVM) [48], and Random Forest [49]. Grid search [50] was used to tune the hyperparameters for the classification models. Twenty node cluster, running Apache Spark, was used for tuning the models in conjunction with sparkR and R [39].

4. Results

4.1. Patient Characteristics

This study includes a total of 46,651 distinct adult patient (>18 years old) visits, extracted from Geisinger's data warehouse between April 2005 and September 2018. Each record corresponds to a unique encounter. A set of 1226 records were excluded due to data quality and the excessive missing of static features such as height, gender, and age. The remaining 45,425 records met the inclusion criteria.

Sepsis data sets for 1, 3, and 6 h feature windows had labels from CMS and Billing, depending on the data extraction process. There was a total of 3179 encounters from CMS (7% of the cohort) while billing-based septic shock records accounted for 6127 encounters—14% of the total records analyzed. Among the 45,425 records, 5784 were identified as a septic shock while 30,192 were identified as sepsis and severe sepsis (control) within a $T = 1\ h$ window; similarly, 5845 cases were classified as septic shock (cases) while 31,668 records were identified as controls within a window of $T = 3\ h$. A total of 5852 records (cases) were septic shock while 32,329 records were sepsis (controls) within a $T = 6\ h$ window. Overall, 51% of all the cases and controls were men. The mean age was higher in the case group compared to the control group for the three case-control designs ($T = 1, 3,$ and $6\ h$ from admission). The same trend was observed for the average weight of the patients; however, the difference was marginal. Table 1 illustrates the cohort statistics for the $T = 1, 3$ and $6\ h$ prediction windows. This study was based on 15 features, including vitals, laboratory values, and baseline demographics.

Table 1. Cohort Statistics based on CMS criteria.

SEPSIS DATASET	1 H		3 H		6 H	
	Cases	Controls	Cases	Controls	Cases	Controls
PATIENTS, N	5784	30,192	5845	31,668	5852	32,329
ENCOUNTERS, N	6409	40,242	6475	42,475	6486	43,332
MALE, N(%)	3322(51)	18,468(51)	3355(51)	19,130(51)	3360(51)	17,984(49)
MEAN AGE(SD)	51(27)	48(29)	65(19)	62(21)	65(19)	62(21)
MEDIAN AGE(IQR)	56(11–101)	50(5–95)	67(44–90)	67(42–92)	69(46–92)	66(41–91)
MEAN WEIGHT(SD)	166.55(76.46)	158.13(81.50)	179.34(67.18)	178.75(71.28)	179.30(67.26)	178.51(71.51)
VITALS, MEAN(SD)						
DIASTOLIC BP	72.3(16.6)	73.8(16.9)	63.2(20.8)	67.4(17.9)	63.2(20.8)	67.3(17.9)
SYSTOLIC BP	129.8(26.3)	129.2(25.6)	111.0(29.4)	123.5(28.1)	110.9(29.5)	123.3(28.2)
PULSE	95.80(27.06)	101.54(28.30)	108.20(26.23)	100.89(24.65)	108.22(26.26)	100.83(24.69)
RESPIRATION	20.90(8.04)	21.92(9.08)	23.46(8.53)	21.64(7.85)	23.49(8.64)	21.65(7.93)
TEMPERATURE	98.59(1.91)	98.84(1.99)	99.32(2.94)	99.44(2.33)	99.29(2.93)	99.41(2.32)
MAP [1]	92.14(18.02)	92.55(17.73)	79.91(22.15)	86.59(19.20)	79.66(22.30)	85.96(19.58)
GCS [2]	4.93(0.40)	4.95(0.32)	4.76(0.76)	4.88(0.51)	4.75(0.77)	4.88(0.51)
LABORATORY MEASURES, MEAN(SD)						
CREATININE	1.446(1.445)	1.459(1.470)	1.912(1.637)	1.645(1.605)	1.914(1.650)	1.645(1.610)
LACTIC ACID	2.59(2.49)	2.07(1.38)	4.48(3.53)	2.15(1.50)	4.51(3.54)	2.12(1.46)
APTT [3]	35.17(12.56)	35.17(11.57)	37.24(13.86)	36.49(12.38)	37.45(14.09)	36.56(12.43)
PLATELET COUNT	231.20(101.84)	237.76(106.06)	221.66(126.62)	231.20(120.81)	220.82(126.11)	231.10(121.14)
PT/INR [4]	1.55(0.94)	1.53(0.90)	1.74(1.09)	1.61(0.95)	1.77(1.12)	1.61(0.96)
WBC	15.33(10.82)	13.98(9.34)	15.47(11.12)	13.99(9.93)	15.47(11.12)	13.95(9.93)

[1] Mean Arterial Pressure; [2] Glasgow Coma Score; [3] Activated Partial Thromboplastin Time; [4] Prothrombin Time Test.

Our data showed that the average levels of lactic acid and creatinine were lower as the feature window is reduced to $T = 3\ h$ and $T = 1\ h$. The average pulse followed the same trend (higher in the cases at $T = 6\ h$ versus $T = 1\ h$). The average blood pressure had an opposite pattern; septic shock patients had on average lower blood pressure (both diastolic and systolic) at $T = 6\ h$. The average temperature was lowest in the $T = 1\ h$ window for both case and control groups. Finally, the whole blood count (WBC) was lower in the case group compared to the control group for the three feature windows.

4.2. Machine Learning Models Can Be Trained for the Detection of Septic Shock Using Administrative Datasets

In this study, we used different case-control designs by focusing on different prediction windows, as well as labeling strategies—CMS versus billing information to label the cases. We also used a sampling technique to address the data imbalance. Overall, consolidated results demonstrated that clinical decision support systems can be developed for the detection of septic shock in ICU using administrative or clinical data. In the consolidated results, the final prediction label was determined based on whether at least one of the three case-control designs (based on the $T = 1, 3,$ or $6\ h$ windows) was able to detect septic shock (Table 2). Overall, four of the modeling algorithms resulted in an AUROC above 0.92, with an average AUROC of 0.91. The parameters for the grid search for the different models are also listed in Table 2. The average sensitivity and specificity of the consolidated results were 0.82 and 0.86 respectively. Finally, the best performance (AUROC of 0.943) was when Random Forest was used (Figure 2 and Table 2). The 95% confidence interval of the AUROC, sensitivity, and specificity are provided in Appendix A Figure A2.

Table 2. Performance metrics for the best model for each machine learning algorithm.

MODELS	AUROC	SENSITIVITY	SPECIFICITY	HYPER PARAMETERS	TUNED HP VALUES
RF	0.9483	0.8392	0.8814	mtry, maxTree, maxdepth	2, 1000, 4
C5.0	0.9474	0.8087	0.8944	Model, Winnowing, Boosting Iterations	Rules, False, 20
DT	0.9436	0.8553	0.8577	Complexity Parameter	0.000351617
BL	0.9239	0.8328	0.8448	Boosting Iterations	31
SVM	0.8962	0.8336	0.851	Sigma, Cost	0.01898621, 16
LR	0.8839	0.8304	0.8622		
RLR	0.8821	0.8288	0.8615	Cost, Loss Function, Epsilon	2, L1, 0.001
BGLM	0.882	0.828	0.8625		

RF: Random Forest, DT: Decision Trees, BL: Boosted Logistic, SVM: Support Vector Machine (Radial), LR: Logistic Regression, RLR: Regularized Logistic Regression, BGLM: Bayes Generalized Logistic Regression, HP: hyper-parameters.

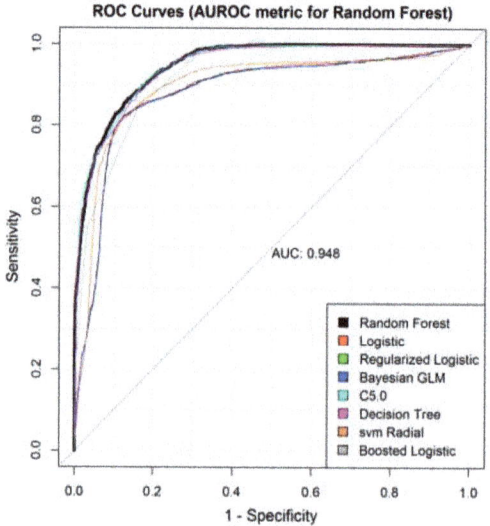

Figure 2. Receiver Operating Characteristic plots for the best machine learning algorithms.

4.3. Model Prediction Performance Improves as the Time from Admission Widens

Analysis of performance metrics, comparing the different case-control designs based on the feature window, demonstrated that the average model performance—in terms of AUROC, accuracy, sensitivity, and specificity—increased monotonically as time elapsed from admission increased from $T = 1\ h$ to 3 and 6 h (Figure 3). Furthermore, our results on the best performing model using Random Forest also corroborated that the models based on the longer time frame ($T = 6\ h$) consistently outperformed the others in terms of all performance metrics used in this study (Figure 3).

The prediction of models (at $T = 1, 3, 6\ h$) are aggregated, such that the final prediction is true even if only one of the models labels that as true. This strategy reduced false negatives at the cost of false positives. Model AUROC, Specificity, Sensitivity, are reported in Table 2. It is important to indicate that the aggregate models for the best performing model are presented in Table 2 and the model performance metrics, especially model sensitivity and specificity, are above 0.8 for all the models.

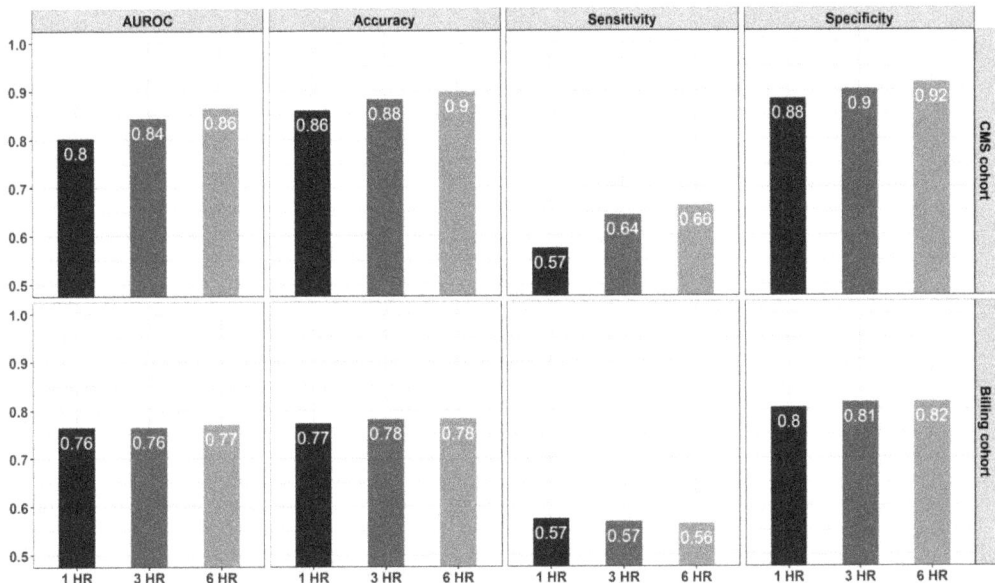

Figure 3. Consolidated Metrics, using Random Forest-based models, comparing CMS and Billing-based cohort as well as models based on the different windows, $T = 1, 3$, and $6 h$.

4.4. Models Based on CMS-Derived Information Have Better Detection Power

Our results highlight that the prediction models when used in conjunction with labeling rules that are derived from CMS information (clinical information), rather than billing data (administrative information), can improve the performance metrics in terms of model AUROC, model accuracy, sensitivity, and specificity. Figure 3 shows that on average, model AUROC, sensitivity, specificity, and accuracy were higher for the CMS-based cohort for all three different case-control designs ($T = 1, 3$ and $6 h$). Model AUROC had the highest improvement for the 6 h window, with CMS-cohort reaching an average of 0.87, while billing-cohort for the same time frame reached an average of 0.77. Similarly, average model accuracy was highest for the same $T = 6 h$ cohort when CMS information was used to define the cohort (0.90 versus 0.78 average accuracies). Model sensitivity and specificity were also higher with the CMS-based cohort (model sensitivity for $T = 6 h$ is 0.66 versus 0.56; model specificity for $T = 6$ is 0.92 versus 0.82). The same pattern was observed for the cohorts where the time from admission was defined as $T = 1$ and $T = 3 h$.

4.5. Important Clinical Markers of Septic Shock

Our results (Figure 4) demonstrated that the eight ML algorithms were able to identify lactic acid as the most important feature. Furthermore, there was a consensus in feature importance ranking in three out of the eight algorithms (logistic regression, regularized logistic regression, and Bayes generalized logistic regression). Overall, the dynamic features including laboratory features and vitals were important clinical markers for the majority of the algorithms. Demographic variables such as sex, age, and weight were the least discriminative variables by most of the models.

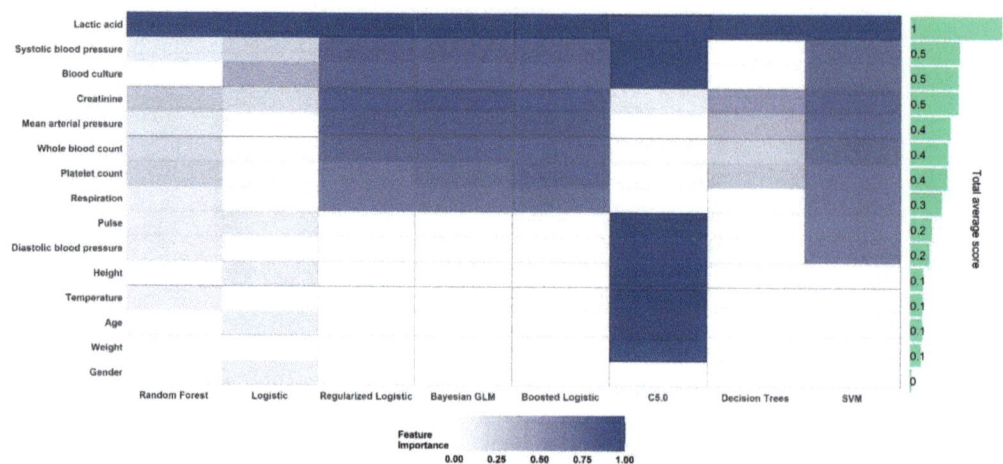

Figure 4. Feature Importance Profile for the eight machine learning models, based on aggregated measures.

5. Discussion

This study demonstrated that machine learning models can be used to predict septic shock within the first 6 h of admission. Furthermore, model performance can be improved by aggregating the temporal models from each prediction window. Even when the rate of septic shock was between 7–14% (depending on how the septic shock is defined), the presented pipeline achieved a good balance of sensitivity and specificity at 1, 3, and 6 h from the time of admission. The major contribution of this study, is the use of a well-established framework, big data analytics and solid infrastructure in building interpretable decision support systems that can be integrated into clinical workflow in EHR.

5.1. Design Consideration for Building a Clinical Decision Support System for Detection of Septic Shock Using Healthcare Data

Our findings highlighted the value of data density for building predictive models. As the time from admission increases from $T = 1\ h$ to 3 and 6 h, more clinical variables were available for each patient. The latter had an impact on model performance. This observation, even though expected, (a) can help design models with a balance between performance improvement versus how much time in advance a practitioner could be able to be notified of a patient's declining condition, (b) corroborated the value of advances in laboratory technologies that can reduce the turn-around time, which could eventually facilitate the development of models that could target narrower windows as the data becomes available.

Our findings also demonstrated that the cohort definition for a clinical application can benefit if clinical information is leveraged as opposed to relying only on administrative (billing) information. The latter might be counter-intuitive, as billing codes may be more robust, at least for some conditions. Administrative data tend to be considered in many studies as a gold standard since billing codes are entered after chart review and have legal implications. However, as our results corroborated, clinically derived criteria using data from structured and unstructured sources, such as SIRS criteria, can exhibit higher fidelity in identifying septic shock patients when compared to leveraging only diagnostic codes.

Besides a carefully-designed cohort definition and selection of the optimal prediction window (based on clinical workflow settings and turn-around time to have patient-level data for the model), we discussed important technical considerations for building a successful ML-enabled decision support system. One such consideration was to address the class imbalance between cases and controls. Our results denoted the value of applying robust sampling strategies to address the challenges due to the imbalanced nature of the dataset. Even though we did not compare our model performance with and without sampling as a pre-processing step, evidence suggests that this design strategy likely aided our model performance. Fleuren et al. [51], in their systematic review of ML-based models of sepsis, identified that some of the studies [51] potentially suffered from selection bias. In particular, to label septic shock patients, authors [5] used discharge ICD9 codes for acute infection to identify acute organ dysfunction and complemented that information with the need for vasopressors within 24 h of ICU transfer. In another study [27], authors used deep learning models to assess risk score 4 h before onset. In essence, since many patients present themselves in the Emergency Department with imminent or overt symptoms of septic shock, it is important that a decision support system, when integrated into the clinical workflow, can detect septic shock patients; therefore, in our design strategy, we ensured patients with imminent or overt septic shock were included to mimic a realistic situation. Finally, as EHR provides a valuable resource, it is important to leverage scalable analytical frameworks (such as pre-processing, data augmentation, use of ontologies, etc.) for providing assistive tools to providers in real-time.

5.2. Lactic Acid and Other Laboratory Measurements are Highly Important Indicators of Progression to Septic Shock

Epidemiological studies have established that the initial hypotension and lactic acid levels are important indicators of the progression of sepsis to septic shock [52,53]. Our results also highlighted that lactic acid is the most important indicator of septic shock followed by blood culture, creatinine level, and systolic blood pressure. However, it should be mentioned that lactic acid demonstrated higher than 40% overall sparsity, yet, it was decided to include this important variable in the model. In our dataset, lactic acid was not missing completely at random, as the missing level in the control group was higher; our data included 25,352 encounters out of 43,332 with lactic acid data available in the control group, versus 6037 encounters out of 6486 with lactic acid in the case group, for the 6-h window. Our team is leading comprehensive studies in the imputation of laboratory values [54] and we hope in the follow-up study we can better address this challenge.

Overall, other laboratory values were found to be relevant to the decision support system. Early warning scores do not consider laboratory values, however, in a recent meta-analysis of 28 studies [53] it was observed that overall laboratory values play an important role. Static features (age, sex, height, and weight) are the least important variables in the majority of the models used in this study. Furthermore, as different algorithms demonstrated different patterns (see Figure 4), it is imperative to not only rely on one modeling algorithm but an ensemble of models [55] when building prediction models based on a limited set of variables for time-critical conditions.

5.3. Strengths, Limitations, and Future Work

This study had several strengths and some limitations. Using a large dataset from an integrated healthcare system was a clear strength; however, Geisinger's patients' cohort were predominantly Caucasians, therefore, models developed in this study may not be generalizable to other healthcare systems without further fine-tuning and optimization. Furthermore, the use of large clinical data leads also to a study limitation. Data from the EHR tend to be noisy; however, with the proper data extraction pipeline and close collaboration with the clinical team, it is possible to augment data quality and reduce systemic bias. However, models developed using EHR-based data can be integrated and deployed into the same healthcare system more effectively, as ML models trained on the data specific to a particular healthcare system (and population) can provide better specificity and sensitivity.

Another strength and key contribution of this study is the development and comparison of two cohorts, based on administrative and clinical data, using billing information and clinical information based on CMS guidelines. Other studies have relied on using clinical markers such as lactic acid levels in combination with hypotension for determining septic shock [53]; however, the progression from sepsis to septic shock occurs on a spectrum and there are specific criteria that define this progression, from sepsis to severe sepsis and eventually to septic shock, the latter is clearly defined by the CMS guidelines [53,56]. Our results showed that the clinically derived cohort is more robust and leveraging guideline recommendations can improve the performance of the models. However, since the use of SIRS criteria may also lead to labeling bias (over-diagnosed cases), it is important to work closely with the clinical team and consider additional guidelines and metrics as needed. It is also important to perform a careful evaluation and comparative analysis (such as targeted chart review, etc.). Also, given the study limitation around the use of SIRS criteria, the strategy in this study was to align our decision support system with the contemporaneous roll-out of the CMS sepsis protocol, which did not include qSOFA or SOFA at the time this study was conceptualized. As in any healthcare system, with changing recommendations and guidelines, we are working on adapting our models with clinical workflow accordingly. Finally, since we use a multi-level approach in defining our cohort, our strategy is robust and can be updated relatively efficiently based on new guidelines. In particular, we use ICD codes as the first level, complemented with clinical data from notes and other sources of structured data. It is important to emphasize that diagnosis codes may have a systemic bias as they are intended for billing purposes. Furthermore, our case/control ratio had a significant imbalance, which typically leads to a reduction in model performance. However, as the field of machine learning is advancing at an unprecedented rate, we are exploring the use of novel strategies (such as the use of the generative adversarial network (GAN)) [57], which could be used to address data imbalance and to improve our models.

As future directions, our team is actively working on further refining our septic early detection models based on technical and clinical advances. In particular, (1) some of the important data elements such as SOFA score (and different variations of SOFA score) were not captured in our EHR routinely at the time of this study. Given the clinical utility of such data elements, our system is now capturing these important variables more consistently. Therefore, as part of future work, we will be integrating these new variables and assessing their predictive utility. (2) Certain variables, especially laboratory variables (such as blood cultures), have a higher turn-around time (sometimes ranging between 48 to 72 h). In this study, we used the presence of blood culture order as a binary variable; however, having the actual test results could improve the detection of septic shock. We are working on integrating more laboratory-based features as their turn-around time improves. Finally, (3) many other laboratory variables could be included in the model; however, laboratory values tend to suffer from non-at-random missing and at high rates, and imputing them is a challenging task. Our team is developing imputation modeling that is designed specifically for laboratory-based features [54]. We believe better imputation and more targeted hyperparameter tuning, including sensitivity-based analysis, could further improve model performance.

One of the main limitations of this study design is that some patients who progress to septic shock might be mislabeled as controls in the cohort. Even though this can be avoided by taking a large time window and leveraging pathology results, the technical and clinical steps needed to address this study limitation are manifold and beyond the scope of this study. Currently, the turnaround time for pathology reports makes it impractical for the integration of such data into a decision support system that is aimed at assisting ICU providers in real-time-few hours after the patient is admitted to ICU. Another potential source of noise is the intervention by care providers e.g., administration of fluid bolus based on capillary refill, which would suppress clinical markers e.g., SBP, lactate to baseline, thus misleading the model during training.

Furthermore, it is difficult to know the impact of antibiotics on the specific trajectory of an individual patient as infection types are different and outcomes of progression are predicated based on many dynamic variables. For instance, it has been shown that 30% of patients who received appropriate anti-infective before the onset of hypotension continued to develop septic shock [12]. Thus, more targeted research is needed to assess the impact of medication at a personalized level before such information can be used for practical and time-sensitive applications.

Finally, this study is unique as it operates directly on the multiple sources of clinical data to build an ML-based decision support system for the detection of septic shock. This study also demonstrated that high-resolution and large heterogeneous data sets from administrative sources can be used to develop assistive tools for time-sensitive conditions such as the progression of sepsis or severe sepsis to septic shock. Such technologies could be integrated into the electronic healthcare system to improve the detection of septic shock and enable optimization of resources. The models have the potential to improve clinical outcomes in real-time.

Author Contributions: Conceptualization, V.A. (Vida Abedi), D.M., B.K. and S.K.; methodology, V.A. (Vida Abedi), V.A. (Venkatesh Avula); D.M., R.S.; software, D.M., R.S., V.A. (Venkatesh Avula); validation, H.A.F., Y.B.M., S.K., D.M.W.; formal analysis, V.A. (Vida Abedi), V.A. (Venkatesh Avula); D.M.; investigation, V.A. (Vida Abedi), R.Z.; D.M., S.K.; resources, V.A. (Vida Abedi), R.Z., B.K., S.K.; data curation, D.M., R.S., V.A. (Venkatesh Avula); writing—original draft preparation, D.M., V.A. (Vida Abedi); writing—review and editing, V.A. (Vida Abedi), H.A.F., S.K., D.M.W., J.L., D.M.; visualization, D.M., V.A. (Venkatesh Avula); supervision, V.A. (Vida Abedi), S.K., B.K. All authors have read and agreed to the published version of the manuscript.

Funding: This research received no external funding.

Institutional Review Board Statement: This study was approved as a quality improvement project (IRB Number: 2020-0355) as well as exempt study (IRB Number: 2014-0242) by the institutional review board of Geisinger Health System.

Data Availability Statement: The data analyzed in this study is not publicly available due to privacy and security concerns. A GitHub link to the team's notebook with exploratory data analysis, additional meta-data and summary plots are compiled for reference: https://github.com/TheDecodeLab/early_sepsis_detection_2020.

Acknowledgments: The authors would like to thank Arjun Lingala, Data Engineer- Sr, William Wenrich, Technical Analyst- Sr, Jody Pensyl, Data Analyst-Sr, and Dhruv Mathrawala, Data Architect-Lead for their contribution in implementing the Geisinger Data Model and the Data Engineering pipeline. The authors would also like to thank Cheryl Fritzen (RNC, MSN), Quality Data and Reporting Coordinator for her assistance in validating the data for dubious entries and insightful discussions.

Conflicts of Interest: The authors declare no conflict of interest.

Appendix A

Table A1. Upper and lower limits on variables as part of the data pre-processing for variables that had outliers after considering six standard deviations.

MEASURE	LOWER_LIMIT	UPPER_LIMIT
Temperature	96.8	101
Heart rate (pulse)		90
Respiration		20
White blood cell count	4000	12,000
Systolic blood pressure (SBP)	90	
Mean arterial pressure	65	

Table A1. *Cont.*

MEASURE	LOWER_LIMIT	UPPER_LIMIT
SBP decrease	Baseline-40	
Creatinine		2
Urine output	0.5	
Bilirubin		2
Platelets	100,000	
INR [1]		1.5
APTT [2]		60
Lactate		2

[1] Prothrombin Time and International Normalized Ratio; [2] Activated Partial Thromboplastin Time.

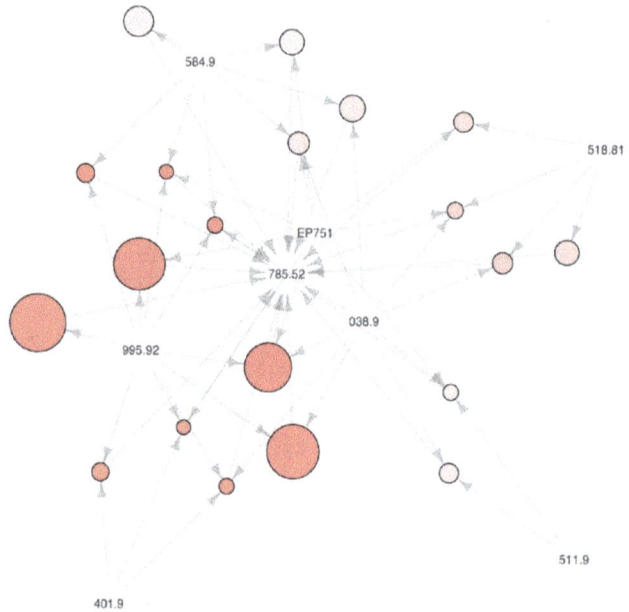

Figure A1. Graphical Representation of Association Rules with Septic Shock (ICD9 = 785.52) as a consequent. Diagnosis codes for the patients in the cohort were obtained and Association Rule Mining [35] was run to mine for relationships between comorbidities. In the study, "items" are diagnosis codes. Items are connected to rules using directional edges. For nodes representing rules, edges pointing from codes to rule vertices indicate antecedent items and an edge from a rule to an item indicates the consequent item. The reader is referred to [58] for more details about the visualization. 511.9: Unspecified pleural effusion; 401.9: Unspecified essential hypertension; 995.2: Severe sepsis; 038.9: Unspecified septicemia; 518.81: Acute respiratory failure; EP751: Other congenital anomalies of digestive system: 584.9: Acute kidney failure.

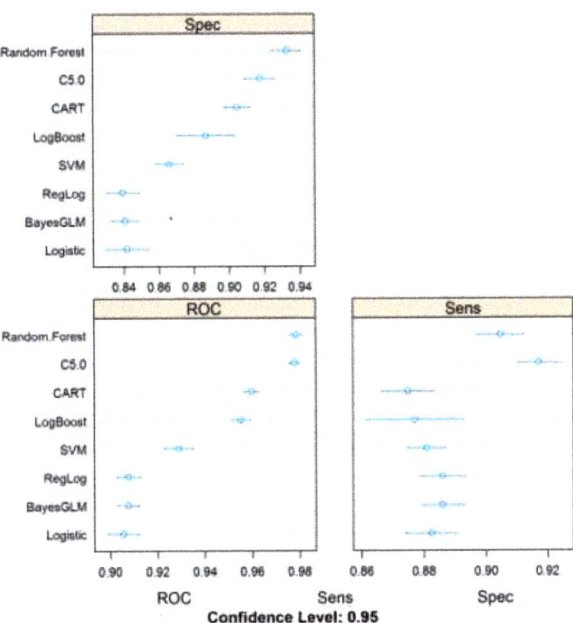

Figure A2. Comparison Performance Profiles based on aggregated data.

References

1. Bone, R.C.; Balk, R.A.; Cerra, F.B.; Dellinger, R.P.; Fein, A.M.; Knaus, W.A.; Schein, R.M.; Sibbald, W.J. Definitions for sepsis and organ failure and guidelines for the use of innovative therapies in sepsis. *Chest* **1992**, *101*, 1644–1655. [CrossRef] [PubMed]
2. Gul, F.; Arslantas, M.K.; Cinel, I.; Kumar, A. Changing Definitions of Sepsis. *Turk. J. Anesth. Reanim.* **2017**, *45*, 129–138. [CrossRef] [PubMed]
3. Marik, P.E.; Taeb, A.M. SIRS, qSOFA and new sepsis definition. *J. Thorac. Dis.* **2017**, *9*, 943–945. [CrossRef] [PubMed]
4. Kumar, A.; Roberts, D.; Wood, K.E.; Light, B.; Parrillo, J.E.; Sharma, S.; Suppes, R.; Feinstein, D.; Zanotti, S.; Taiberg, L.; et al. Duration of hypotension before initiation of effective antimicrobial therapy is the critical determinant of survival in human septic shock*. *Crit. Care Med.* **2006**, *34*, 1589–1596. [CrossRef] [PubMed]
5. Rivers, E.P.; Nguyen, B.; Havstad, S.; Ressler, J.; Muzzin, A.; Knoblich, B.; Peterson, E.; Tomlanovich, M. Early Goal-Directed Therapy in the Treatment of Severe Sepsis and Septic Shock. *N. Engl. J. Med.* **2001**, *345*, 1368–1377. [CrossRef] [PubMed]
6. Mayr, F.B.; Yende, S.; Angus, D.C. Epidemiology of severe sepsis. *Virulence* **2014**, *5*, 4–11. [CrossRef]
7. Ruokonen, E.; Takala, J.; Kari, A.; Alhava, E. Septic shock and multiple organ failure. *Crit. Care Med.* **1991**, *19*, 1146–1151. [CrossRef]
8. Paoli, C.J.; Reynolds, M.A.; Sinha, M.; Gitlin, M.; Crouser, E. Epidemiology and Costs of Sepsis in the United States—An Analysis Based on Timing of Diagnosis and Severity Level. *Crit. Care Med.* **2018**, *46*, 1889–1897. [CrossRef]
9. Nam, J.G.; Park, S.; Hwang, E.J.; Lee, J.H.; Jin, K.-N.; Lim, K.Y.; Vu, T.H.; Sohn, J.H.; Hwang, S.; Goo, J.M.; et al. Development and Validation of Deep Learning–based Automatic Detection Algorithm for Malignant Pulmonary Nodules on Chest Radiographs. *Radiology* **2019**, *290*, 218–228. [CrossRef]
10. Wu, N.; Phang, J.; Park, J.; Shen, Y.; Huang, Z.; Zorin, M.; Jastrzebski, S.; Fevry, T.; Katsnelson, J.; Kim, E.; et al. Deep Neural Networks Improve Radiologists' Performance in Breast Cancer Screening. *IEEE Trans. Med. Imaging* **2020**, *39*, 1184–1194. [CrossRef]
11. Noorbakhsh-Sabet, N.; Zand, R.; Zhang, Y.; Abedi, V. Artificial Intelligence Transforms the Future of Health Care. *Am. J. Med.* **2019**, *132*, 795–801. [CrossRef] [PubMed]
12. Singh, R.; Kalra, M.K.; Nitiwarangkul, C.; Patti, J.A.; Homayounieh, F.; Padole, A.; Rao, P.; Putha, P.; Muse, V.V.; Sharma, A.; et al. Deep learning in chest radiography: Detection of findings and presence of change. *PLoS ONE* **2018**, *13*, e0204155. [CrossRef] [PubMed]
13. Karunakaran, B.; Misra, D.; Marshall, K.; Mathrawala, D.; Kethireddy, S. Closing the loop—Finding lung cancer patients using NLP. In Proceedings of the 2017 IEEE International Conference on Big Data (Big Data), Boston, MA, USA, 11–14 December 2017; pp. 2452–2461.

14. Zheng, L.; Wang, Y.; Hao, S.; Sylvester, K.G.; Ling, X.B.; Shin, A.Y.; Jin, B.; Zhu, C.; Jin, H.; Dai, D.; et al. Risk prediction of stroke: A prospective statewide study on patients in Maine. In Proceedings of the 2015 IEEE International Conference on Bioinformatics and Biomedicine, BIBM, Washington, DC, USA, 9–12 November 2015; pp. 853–855. [CrossRef]
15. Escobar, G.J.; Turk, B.J.; Ragins, A.; Ha, J.; Hoberman, B.; LeVine, S.M.; Ballesca, M.A.; Liu, V.; Kipnis, P. Piloting electronic medical record—based early detection of inpatient deterioration in community hospitals. *J. Hosp. Med.* **2016**, *11*, S18–S24. [CrossRef] [PubMed]
16. Brun-Buisson, C.; Doyon, F.; Carlet, J.; Dellamonica, P.; Gouin, F.; Lepoutre, A.; Mercier, J.-C.; Offenstadt, G.; Régnier, B. Incidence, Risk Factors, and Outcome of Severe Sepsis and Septic Shock in Adults. *JAMA* **1995**, *274*, 968–974. [CrossRef] [PubMed]
17. Raghu, A.; Komorowski, M.; Ahmed, I.; Celi, L.; Szolovits, P.; Ghassemi, M. Deep reinforcement learning for sepsis treatment. *arXiv* **2017**, arXiv:1711.09602.
18. Lagu, T.; Rothberg, M.B.; Shieh, M.-S.; Pekow, P.S.; Steingrub, J.S.; Lindenauer, P.K. Hospitalizations, costs, and outcomes of severe sepsis in the United States 2003 to 2007. *Crit. Care Med.* **2012**, *40*, 754–761. [CrossRef]
19. Vogel, T.R.; Dombrovskiy, V.Y.; Lowry, S.F. Trends in Postoperative Sepsis: Are We Improving Outcomes? *Surg. Infect.* **2009**, *10*, 71–78. [CrossRef]
20. Nemati, S.; Holder, A.; Razmi, F.; Stanley, M.D.; Clifford, G.D.; Buchman, T.G. An Interpretable Machine Learning Model for Accurate Prediction of Sepsis in the ICU. *Crit. Care Med.* **2018**, *46*, 547–553. [CrossRef]
21. Giannini, H.M.; Ginestra, J.C.; Chivers, C.; Draugelis, M.; Hanish, A.; Schweickert, W.D.; Fuchs, B.D.; Meadows, L.R.; Lynch, M.; Donnelly, P.J.; et al. A machine learning algorithm to predict severe sepsis and septic shock: Development, implementation, and impact on clinical practice. *Read Online Crit. Care Med. Soc. Crit. Care Med.* **2019**, *47*, 1485–1492. [CrossRef]
22. Kim, J.; Chang, H.; Kim, D.; Jang, D.-H.; Park, I.; Kim, K. Machine learning for prediction of septic shock at initial triage in emergency department. *J. Crit. Care* **2020**, *55*, 163–170. [CrossRef]
23. Schoenberg, M.H.; Weiss, M.; Radermacher, P. Outcome of patients with sepsis and septic shock after ICU treatment. *Langenbeck's Arch. Surg.* **1998**, *383*, 44–48. [CrossRef] [PubMed]
24. Shimabukuro, D.W.; Barton, C.W.; Feldman, M.D.; Mataraso, S.J.; Das, R. Effect of a machine learning-based severe sepsis prediction algorithm on patient survival and hospital length of stay: A randomised clinical trial. *BMJ Open Respir. Res.* **2017**, *4*, e000234. [CrossRef] [PubMed]
25. Iwashyna, T.J.; Odden, A.; Rohde, J.; Bonham, C.; Kuhn, L.; Malani, P.; Chen, L.; Flanders, S. Identifying Patients With Severe Sepsis Using Administrative Claims. *Med. Care* **2014**, *52*, e39–e43. [CrossRef] [PubMed]
26. Khoshnevisan, F.; Ivy, J.; Capan, M.; Arnold, R.; Huddleston, J.; Chi, M. Recent Temporal Pattern Mining for Septic Shock Early Prediction. In Proceedings of the 2018 IEEE International Conference on Healthcare Informatics (ICHI), New York, NY, USA, 4–7 June 2018; pp. 229–240.
27. Lin, C.; Zhang, Y.; Ivy, J.; Capan, M.; Arnold, R.; Huddleston, J.M.; Chi, M. Early Diagnosis and Prediction of Sepsis Shock by Combining Static and Dynamic Information Using Convolutional-LSTM. In Proceedings of the 2018 IEEE International Conference on Healthcare Informatics (ICHI), New York, NY, USA, 4–7 June 2018; pp. 219–228.
28. Klompas, M.; Rhee, C. The CMS Sepsis Mandate: Right Disease, Wrong Measure. *Ann. Intern. Med.* **2016**, *165*, 517. [CrossRef] [PubMed]
29. Allison, M.G.; Schenkel, S.M. SEP-1: A Sepsis Measure in Need of Resuscitation? *Ann. Emerg. Med.* **2017**, *71*, 18–20. [CrossRef] [PubMed]
30. Davies, M.G.; Hagen, P.-O. Systemic inflammatory response syndrome. *BJS* **1997**, *84*, 920–935. [CrossRef] [PubMed]
31. Bodenreider, O. The Unified Medical Language System (UMLS): Integrating biomedical terminology. *Nucleic Acids Res.* **2004**, *32*, D267–D270. [CrossRef]
32. Spackman, K.A.; Campbell, K.E.; Côté, R.A. SNOMED RT: A reference terminology for health care. In Proceedings of the AMIA Annual fall Symposium, Nashville, TN, USA, 25–29 October 1997; p. 640.
33. McDonald, C.J.; Huff, S.M.; Suico, J.G.; Hill, G.; Leavelle, D.; Aller, R.; Forrey, A.; Mercer, K.; Demoor, G.; Hook, J.; et al. LOINC, a Universal Standard for Identifying Laboratory Observations: A 5-Year Update. *Clin. Chem.* **2003**, *49*, 624–633. [CrossRef]
34. World Health Organization. *Enth Revision of the International Classification of Diseases Chapter V (F: Mental, Behavioural and Developmental Disorders, Clinical Descriptions and Diagnostic Guidelines, Rev. 2 1988 Draft*; Verlag Hans Huber, Ed.; World Health Organization: Bern, Switzerland, 1991. Available online: https://apps.who.int/iris/handle/10665/61362 (accessed on 1 October 2020).
35. Agrawal, R.; Imieliński, T.; Swami, A. Mining association rules between sets of items in large databases. *ACM SIGMOD Rec.* **1993**, *22*, 207–216. [CrossRef]
36. Savova, G.K.; Masanz, J.J.; Ogren, P.V.; Zheng, J.; Sohn, S.; Kipper-Schuler, K.C.; Chute, C.G. Mayo clinical Text Analysis and Knowledge Extraction System (cTAKES): Architecture, component evaluation and applications. *J. Am. Med. Inform. Assoc.* **2010**, *17*, 507–513. [CrossRef]
37. Vavilapalli, V.K.; Murthy, A.C.; Douglas, C.; Agarwal, S.; Konar, M.; Evans, R.; Graves, T.; Lowe, J.; Shah, H.; Seth, S.; et al. Apache hadoop yarn: Yet another resource negotiator. In Proceedings of the 4th Annual Symposium on Cloud Computing; Association for Computing Machinery: Santa Clara, CA, USA, 2013; pp. 1–16.
38. Zhang, Z. Missing data imputation: Focusing on single imputation. *Ann. Transl. Med.* **2016**, *4*, 9. [PubMed]

39. Venkataraman, S.; Yang, Z.; Liu, D.; Liang, E.; Falaki, H.; Meng, X.; Xin, R.; Ghodsi, A.; Franklin, M.; Stoica, I.; et al. Sparkr: Scaling r programs with spark. In Proceedings of the 2016 International Conference on Management of Data; Association for Computing Machinery: San Francisco, CA, USA, 2016; pp. 1099–1104.
40. Wilson, D.L. Asymptotic Properties of Nearest Neighbor Rules Using Edited Data. *IEEE Trans. Syst. Man Cybern.* **1972**, SMC-2, 408–421. [CrossRef]
41. Chawla, N.V.; Bowyer, K.W.; Hall, L.O.; Kegelmeyer, W.P. SMOTE: Synthetic minority over-sampling technique. *J. Artif. Intell. Res.* **2002**, *16*, 321–357. [CrossRef]
42. Tahir, M.A.; Kittler, J.; Mikolajczyk, K.; Yan, F. A multiple expert approach to the class imbalance problem using inverse random under sampling. In *International Workshop on Multiple Classifier Systems*; Springer: Berlin/Heidelberg, Germany, 2009; pp. 82–91.
43. Abramson, N.; Braverman, D.; Sebestyen, G. Pattern recognition and machine learning. *IEEE Trans. Inf. Theory* **2004**, *9*, 257–261. [CrossRef]
44. Lee, S.-I.; Lee, H.; Abbeel, P.; Ng, A.Y. Efficient l~1 regularized logistic regression. *Aaai* **2006**, *6*, 401–408.
45. Friedman, J.; Hastie, T.; Tibshirani, R. *The Elements of Statistical Learning*; Springer: New York, NY, USA, 2001; Volume 1.
46. Pandya, R.; Pandya, J. C5. 0 Algorithm to Improved Decision Tree with Feature Selection and Reduced Error Pruning. *Int. J. Comput. Appl.* **2015**, *117*, 18–21. [CrossRef]
47. Quinlan, J. Decision trees and decision-making. *IEEE Trans. Syst. Man Cybern.* **1990**, *20*, 339–3460. [CrossRef]
48. Boser, B.E.; Guyon, I.M.; Vapnik, V.N. A training algorithm for optimal margin classifiers. In Proceedings of the Fifth Annual Workshop on Computational Learning Theory, Pittsburgh, PA, USA, 27–29 July 1992; pp. 144–152.
49. Ho, T.K. Random decision forests. Proceedings of 3rd International Conference on Document Analysis and Recognition, Montreal, QC, Canada, 14–16 August 1995; pp. 278–282.
50. Nasrabadi, N.M. Pattern recognition and machine learning. *J. Electron. Imaging* **2007**, *16*, 49801.
51. Thiel, S.W.; Rosini, J.M.; Shannon, W.; Doherty, J.A.; Micek, S.T.; Kollef, M.H. Early prediction of septic shock in hospitalized patients. *J. Hosp. Med.* **2010**, *5*, 19–25. [CrossRef]
52. Jones, M. NEWSDIG: The National Early Warning Score Development and Implementation Group. *Clin. Med.* **2012**, *12*, 501–503. [CrossRef]
53. Fleuren, L.M.; Klausch, T.L.T.; Zwager, C.L.; Schoonmade, L.J.; Guo, T.; Roggeveen, L.F.; Swart, E.L.; Girbes, A.R.J.; Thoral, P.; Ercole, A.; et al. Machine learning for the prediction of sepsis: A systematic review and meta-analysis of diagnostic test accuracy. *Intensiv. Care Med.* **2020**, *46*, 383–400. [CrossRef] [PubMed]
54. Abedi, V.; Li, J.; Shivakumar, M.K.; Avula, V.; Chaudhary, D.P.; Shellenberger, M.J.; Khara, H.S.; Zhang, Y.; Lee, M.T.M.; Wolk, D.M.; et al. Increasing the Density of Laboratory Measures for Machine Learning Applications. *J. Clin. Med.* **2020**, *10*, 103. [CrossRef] [PubMed]
55. Opitz, D.W.; Maclin, R. Popular Ensemble Methods: An Empirical Study. *J. Artif. Intell. Res.* **1999**, *11*, 169–198. [CrossRef]
56. Hiensch, R.; Poeran, J.; Saunders-Hao, P.; Adams, V.; Powell, C.A.; Glasser, A.; Mazumdar, M.; Patel, G. Impact of an electronic sepsis initiative on antibiotic use and health care facility–onset Clostridium difficile infection rates. *Am. J. Infect. Control.* **2017**, *45*, 1091–1100. [CrossRef]
57. Goodfellow, I.J.; Shlens, J.; Szegedy, C. Explaining and Harnessing Adversarial Examples. 2014. Available online: http://arxiv.org/abs/1412.6572 (accessed on 1 October 2020).
58. Hahsler, M.; Chelluboina, S. Visualizing association rules: Introduction to the R-extension package arulesViz. *R Project Module* **2011**, 223–238.

Article

Classification of Monocytes, Promonocytes and Monoblasts Using Deep Neural Network Models: An Area of Unmet Need in Diagnostic Hematopathology

Mazen Osman [1,*], Zeynettin Akkus [2,*], Dragan Jevremovic [3], Phuong L. Nguyen [3], Dana Roh [3], Aref Al-Kali [4], Mrinal M. Patnaik [4], Ahmad Nanaa [4], Samia Rizk [5] and Mohamed E. Salama [3,*]

1. Division of Anatomic and Clinical Pathology, Mayo Clinic, Rochester, MN 55905, USA
2. Division of Cardiovascular Diseases, Mayo Clinic, Rochester, MN 55905, USA
3. Division of Hematopathology, Mayo Clinic, Rochester, MN 55905, USA; jevremovic.dragan@mayo.edu (D.J.); nguyen.phuong@mayo.edu (P.L.N.); roh.dana@mayo.edu (D.R.)
4. Division of Hematology, Mayo Clinic, Rochester, MN 55905, USA; alkali.aref@mayo.edu (A.A.-K.); Patnaik.Mrinal@mayo.edu (M.M.P.); nanaa.ahmad@mayo.edu (A.N.)
5. Department of Clinical Pathology, Cairo University, 11562 Cairo, Egypt; rizksh@gmail.com
* Correspondence: osman.mazen@mayo.edu (M.O.); akkus.zeynettin@mayo.edu (Z.A.); Salama.Mohamed@mayo.edu (M.E.S.)

Citation: Osman, M.; Akkus, Z.; Jevremovic, D.; Nguyen, P.L.; Roh, D.; Al-Kali, A.; Patnaik, M.M.; Nanaa, A.; Rizk, S.; Salama, M.E. Classification of Monocytes, Promonocytes and Monoblasts Using Deep Neural Network Models: An Area of Unmet Need in Diagnostic Hematopathology. *J. Clin. Med.* **2021**, *10*, 2264. https://doi.org/10.3390/jcm10112264

Academic Editor: Vida Abedi

Received: 18 April 2021
Accepted: 19 May 2021
Published: 24 May 2021

Publisher's Note: MDPI stays neutral with regard to jurisdictional claims in published maps and institutional affiliations.

Copyright: © 2021 by the authors. Licensee MDPI, Basel, Switzerland. This article is an open access article distributed under the terms and conditions of the Creative Commons Attribution (CC BY) license (https://creativecommons.org/licenses/by/4.0/).

Abstract: The accurate diagnosis of chronic myelomonocytic leukemia (CMML) and acute myeloid leukemia (AML) subtypes with monocytic differentiation relies on the proper identification and quantitation of blast cells and blast-equivalent cells, including promonocytes. This distinction can be quite challenging given the cytomorphologic and immunophenotypic similarities among the monocytic cell precursors. The aim of this study was to assess the performance of convolutional neural networks (CNN) in separating monocytes from their precursors (i.e., promonocytes and monoblasts). We collected digital images of 935 monocytic cells that were blindly reviewed by five experienced morphologists and assigned into three subtypes: monocyte, promonocyte, and blast. The consensus between reviewers was considered as a ground truth reference label for each cell. In order to assess the performance of CNN models, we divided our data into training (70%), validation (10%), and test (20%) datasets, as well as applied fivefold cross validation. The CNN models did not perform well for predicting three monocytic subtypes, but their performance was significantly improved for two subtypes (monocyte vs. promonocytes + blasts). Our findings (1) support the concept that morphologic distinction between monocytic cells of various differentiation level is difficult; (2) suggest that combining blasts and promonocytes into a single category is desirable for improved accuracy; and (3) show that CNN models can reach accuracy comparable to human reviewers (0.78 ± 0.10 vs. 0.86 ± 0.05). As far as we know, this is the first study to separate monocytes from their precursors using CNN.

Keywords: digital imaging; artificial intelligence; improving diagnosis accuracy; monocytes; promonocytes and monoblasts; chronic myelomonocytic leukemia (CMML) and acute myeloid leukemia (AML) for acute monoblastic leukemia and acute monocytic leukemia; concordance between hematopathologists

1. Introduction

The classification of the monocytic subpopulations (monoblasts, promonocytes, and monocytes) is important for the proper diagnosis and classification of various monocytic-lineage leukemias, namely, chronic myelomonocytic leukemia (CMML) and acute myeloid leukemia (AML), including acute monoblastic leukemia and acute monocytic leukemia, and acute myelomonocytic leukemia [1].

To meet the World Health Organization (WHO) diagnostic criteria, the peripheral blood (PB) or bone marrow (BM) of patients with acute monoblastic and monocytic leukemia must have ≥20% blasts (including promonocytes), and ≥80% of the leukemic cells must be of monocytic lineage, including monoblasts, promonocytes, and monocytes. Differentiation between acute monoblastic leukemia and acute monocytic leukemia is based on the relative proportions of monoblasts and promonocytes. In acute monoblastic leukemia, the majority of the monocytic cells (≥80%) are monoblasts, whereas in acute monocytic leukemia, the predominant populations are mature monocytes and promonocytes [1–3].

The diagnostic criteria for CMML include PB monocytosis ($\geq 1 \times 10^9$/L), in which >10% of the PB leukocytes are monocytes. In addition, the PB and BM blast count of <20% of blasts and promonocytes (a blast equivalent cell) must be ascertained [4,5]. Beyond diagnosis, CMML can be stratified into three subcategories based on accurate enumeration of blasts and equivalents (i.e., promonocytes) in the PB and BM. CMML-0: <2% in PB and <5% in BM, CMML-1: 2–4% in PB or 5–9% in BM, CMML-2: 5–19% in PB and 10–19% in BM [2,6].

As seen from the diagnostic criteria listed above, distinction between CMML and AML, and the staging of CMML, depend on accurate differentiation between blast equivalents (monoblasts and promonocytes) and mature monocytes. WHO classification still uses cytomorphology as the gold standard for the definition of blasts. In many cases, the expression of immature marker CD34 is used to supplement the enumeration of blasts. However, monoblasts are frequently negative for CD34 [7], and there are no other reliable immunophenotypic markers to distinguish monoblasts and promonocytes from mature monocytes. As a result, the differential diagnosis in these cases relies solely on cytomorphology.

In general, monocytes are mature cells with minimal morphologic atypia. However, atypical monocytes can be present with abnormal cellular features such as unusually fine chromatin but with prominent nuclear folds or convolutions that partially overlap with more immature forms, including monoblasts and promonocytes [8,9]. This renders distinguishing them from the immature forms notoriously difficult and might lead to under- or overestimation of blast cell numbers [10].

In this article, we present the applicability of artificial intelligence using convolutional neural network architecture for separating monocytes from the spectrum of monocyte precursors (i.e., promonocytes and monoblasts) with reference labels generated based on experts' morphologic review consensus. Differentiating myeloblasts from monoblasts solely on optical cytology can be very difficult; therefore, we will refer to monoblasts as blasts (monoblasts and/or myeloblasts) in this manuscript.

2. Methods

We trained convolutional neural network (CNN) architecture on digital images of monocytes, promonocytes, and blasts to separate monocytes from monocyte precursors (i.e., promonocytes and monoblasts). We experimented and evaluated several data preprocessing configurations and assessed the performance of well-known CNN architecture in order to find the best-performing CNN model and preprocessing strategy for this classification task. The data were imbalanced; therefore, we used the weighted categorical cross entropy loss function (see Equation (1)) to penalize loss for each category during the training [11–13]. We used the Adam optimizer [14] and initialized the learning rate to 1×10^{-4}.

$$L = \frac{1}{n} \sum_{i=1}^{n} \sum_{j=1}^{m} -y_{ij} log(\hat{y}_{ij}) w_{ij} \qquad (1)$$

where n is number of samples, m is number of classes, y is the true labels, $\hat{y}$ is the predicted labels, and w_{ij} is the weighting for each sample of classes. $w_{ij} = max\{n_0 \ldots n_j\}/n_j$ is defined to balance the impact of each class in the loss function.

2.1. Data Collection

After approval by the Mayo Clinic institution review board (IRB protocol #19-001950), 935 consecutive monocytic cell images were acquired from the PB smear samples of 10 patients diagnosed with AML with monocytic differentiation and CMML using a 100× objective lens under immersion oil using an Olympus BX53 microscope with Olympus DP74 camera to obtain digital images. Each cell was manually cropped by an experienced hematopathologist (M.E.S.) into 200 × 200 pixel images using HyperSnap V7 software (Hyperionics Technology, Murrysville, PA, USA). In order to eliminate the impact of non-relevant background information that might include red blood cells, artifacts, and platelets, a manually segmented mask was provided for each monocytic cell. The cytoplasm and nucleus were labelled separately in each segmentation mask. All collected cells were split into 3 categories (i.e., monocyte, promonocyte, and blast) by 5 hematopathology experts. The consensus between the five experienced morphologists (four hematopathologists, D.J., P.L.N., S.R. and M.E.S., and an experienced pathologist assistant, D.R.) was considered as a ground truth reference label for each cell.

2.2. Experiments and Evaluations

We split the data into 70%, 10%, and 20% for training, validation, and testing purposes, respectively, and assessed the performance of five well-known CNNs architectures: InceptionV3 [15,16], Resnet50 [17], Inception_resnet [18], VGG16 [19], and Densenet121 [20]. The training set was used for learning about the data. The validation set was employed to establish the reliability of learning results, and the test set was used to assess the generalizability of a trained model on the data that were not seen by the model. Furthermore, we applied stratified 5-fold cross validation to the best-performing model configuration to further assess the generalization ability of the model. In the 5-fold cross validation, the data were divided randomly into 5 equal sized pieces and samples of each class were equally distributed to each piece. One piece was reserved for assessing the performance of a model, and the remaining 4 pieces were utilized for training models.

We generated five configurations based on pre-processing input data and assessed the impact of data pre-processing to select the best configuration for our classification task. In configuration 1, cell masks were applied to image patches to suppress the background (i.e., assigning zeros to non-cell pixels) and leave only the cell content in image patches. Afterwards, color normalization (i.e., RGB color channels values were normalized as a percentage of sum of RGB values) was applied to image patches and cells were centered and resized into 200 × 200 pixels. In configuration 2, cell masks were applied to image patches to suppress the background and leave only the cell content in image patches. Next, z-scoring, which is also called the standard score, was applied to image patches. In z-scoring, RGB image channel values were scaled with 0 mean and unit variation. Lastly, cells were centered and resized into 200 × 200 pixels. In configuration 3, image patches without suppressing background (i.e., whole image patched including all the background information) were used as the input data for CNN models. In configuration 4, cell masks were also applied to image patches to suppress the background, leaving only cell content (Figure 1). Lastly, in configuration 5, cell masks were applied to suppress the background as well as the cells of interest but excluding their nuclei, leaving only the nuclei content in image patches (Figure 1). We then centered and resized only the nuclei of each cell into 200 × 200 pixels and applied to them z-scaling to standardize RGB color distribution. For each configuration, we presented accuracy, precision, recall, and F1-score metrics. In addition, we also generated t-SNE plots using the features of the last convolution layer of the best model to show the separation of monocytic cells on the test dataset.

	Monoblast	Promonocyte	Monocyte
Cells without mask applied to background	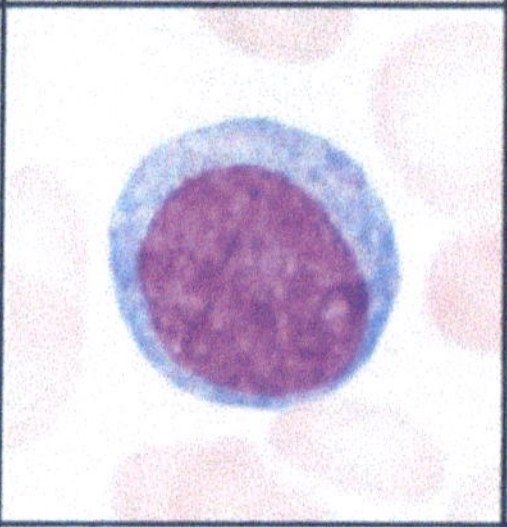	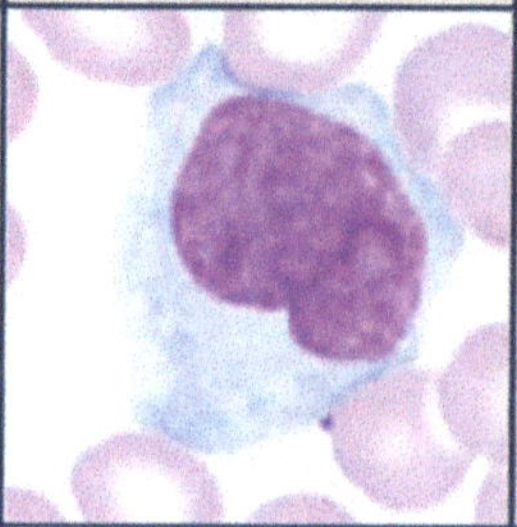	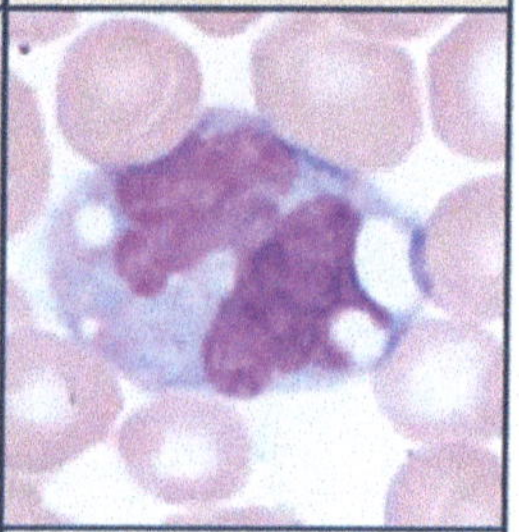
Cells with mask applied to background	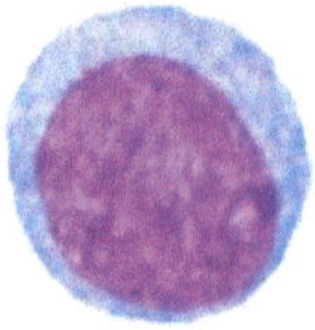	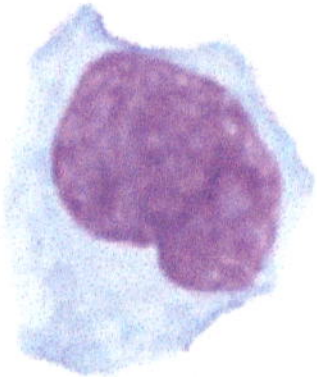	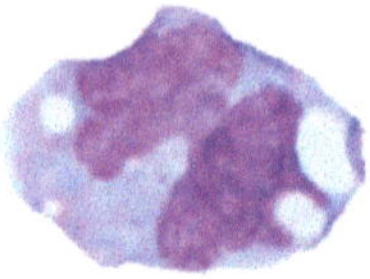
Nuclei only with applied mask	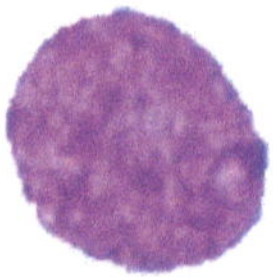	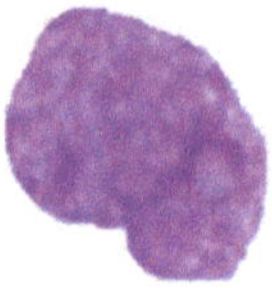	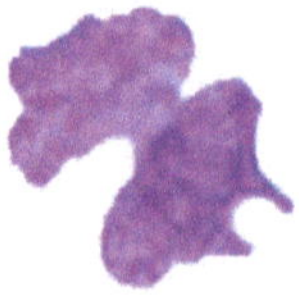
N:C ratio	7:1 to 3:1	7:1 to 3:1	4:1 to 2:1
Cell shape	Round to oval	Round to oval	Round with smooth edges, may have pseudopod-like extensions
Nuclear shape	Round, more regular	Indented or lobulated, more irregular than monoblast	Indented, often reniform or folded resembling three-pointed hat, but may be rounded, oval or lobulated
Nucleoli	1 or 2, distinct	1 or 2, less distinct than monoblast	Generally absent, but occasionally small and inconspicuous
Cytoplasm	Grey to cloudy blue, few red granules	Grey to cloudy blue, few red granules	Abundant grey or grey-blue, may contain fine azurophilic granules

Figure 1. Examples of monocytes, promonocytes, and monoblasts with criteria.

In order to assess the inter-reviewer variability (i.e., the variability between the five expert reviewers), we compared the labels of each reviewer to consensus labels and the average performance and standard deviation were presented. Similarly, to assess the intra-reviewer variability, reviewer 5 labeled the cells a second time (one month later) and a correlation matrix was calculated, as shown in the results section below.

3. Results

The performance of the five CNN models with different configurations and the resulting classification of the monocytic cells (i.e., monocyte, promonocyte, and blast) on the validation and test datasets are shown in Tables 1 and 2. Table 1 shows the results of CNN models with configurations 1–5 for the three-subcategory classification (monocyte vs. promonocyte vs. blast), while Table 2 shows results of CNN models with configurations 1–5 for the two-subcategory classification (monocyte vs. blast + promonocyte). Overall, the Inception_resnet model [18], which is a version of the inception model with residual connection, using configuration 2, gave the best performance in terms of accuracy, precision, recall, and F1-score in the validation and test datasets of both the two-subcategory and the three-subcategory classifications. Densenet121 using configuration 2 was the second-best performing model.

Using configuration 2, the accuracy of CNN models for predicting three subcategories (Table 1) on the test dataset ranged from 42% to 58%, while it ranged from 70% to 85% for predicting two subcategories (Table 2). In the three-subcategory classification (Table 1), the Inception_resnet model achieved 81% accuracy in the validation dataset, but its performance dropped to 53% in the test dataset. In the two-subcategory classification (Table 2), the accuracy of CNN models using configuration 2 ranged from 79% to 88% on the validation dataset. Inception_resnet using configuration 2 provided the most consistent performance in the two-subcategory classification as well in terms of accuracy, precision, recall, and F1-score in the validation and test datasets.

Color Key for Tables 1–5:

Relatively Lower Performance			Relatively Higher Performance

Table 1. Performance of CNN models using five pre-processing configurations on 3-subcategory (monocytes, promonocytes, and blasts) classification task.

CNN Models	Validation Dataset				Test Dataset			
	Accuracy	Precision	Recall	F1-Score	Accuracy	Precision	Recall	F1-Score
Configuration 1 (Centered and resized whole cell only and color normalization—cell mask applied)								
Inception_resnet	0.67	0.41	0.64	0.50	0.41	0.36	0.48	0.33
InceptionV3	0.33	0.43	0.41	0.30	0.49	0.46	0.53	0.39
Resnet50	0.62	0.69	0.52	0.50	0.55	0.47	0.49	0.42
VGG16	0.63	0.59	0.68	0.60	0.57	0.54	0.62	0.51
Densenet121	0.68	0.42	0.67	0.51	0.42	0.39	0.50	0.34
Configuration 2 (Centered and resized whole cell only and z-score pre-processing—cell mask applied)								
Inception_resnet	0.81	0.83	0.80	0.76	0.53	0.50	0.58	0.45
InceptionV3	0.63	0.73	0.62	0.48	0.42	0.36	0.47	0.33
Resnet50	0.63	0.55	0.65	0.56	0.49	0.53	0.56	0.44
VGG16	0.69	0.67	0.74	0.69	0.50	0.54	0.57	0.46
Densenet121	0.72	0.81	0.71	0.63	0.58	0.40	0.60	0.44
Configuration 3 (Image patch including monocytic cell and surrounding red blood cells—no cell mask applied)								
Inception_resnet	0.71	0.70	0.70	0.59	0.45	0.41	0.52	0.36
Configuration 4 (Only whole cell presented after applying cell mask)								
Inception_resnet	0.73	0.71	0.73	0.64	0.44	0.41	0.51	0.35
Configuration 5 (Centered and resized nucleus only and z-score pre-processing—mask applied excluding nucleus)								
Inception_resnet	0.74	0.73	0.76	0.74	0.66	0.65	0.70	0.62

Table 1 shows the Inception_resnet model using configuration 2 performing the best in terms of accuracy, precision, recall, and F1-score in the validation and test datasets of the 3-subcategory classification.

Table 2. Performance of CNN models using five pre-processing configurations on 2-subcategory (monocytes and promonocytes + blasts) classification task.

CNN Models	Validation Dataset				Test Dataset			
	Accuracy	Precision	Recall	F1-Score	Accuracy	Precision	Recall	F1-Score
Configuration 1 (Centered and resized whole cell only and color normalization—cell mask applied)								
Inception_resnet	0.84	0.88	0.83	0.83	0.70	0.75	0.71	0.69
InceptionV3	0.46	0.46	0.46	0.45	0.63	0.63	0.63	0.63
Resnet50	0.63	0.79	0.61	0.55	0.66	0.68	0.65	0.64
VGG16	0.76	0.76	0.76	0.76	0.79	0.82	0.80	0.79
Densenet121	0.87	0.90	0.87	0.87	0.72	0.79	0.73	0.71
Configuration 2 (Centered and resized whole cell only and z-score pre-processing—cell mask applied)								
Inception_resnet	0.88	0.91	0.88	0.88	0.80	0.83	0.81	0.80
InceptionV3	0.87	0.87	0.87	0.87	0.70	0.74	0.71	0.70
Resnet50	0.80	0.80	0.80	0.80	0.76	0.83	0.77	0.75
VGG16	0.79	0.79	0.79	0.79	0.76	0.83	0.77	0.75
Densenet121	0.79	0.86	0.78	0.77	0.85	0.85	0.85	0.85
Configuration 3 (Image patch including monocytic cell and surrounding red blood cells—no cell mask applied)								
Inception_resnet	0.87	0.89	0.87	0.87	0.77	0.84	0.78	0.76
Configuration 4 (Only whole cell presented after applying cell mask)								
Inception_resnet	0.91	0.92	0.91	0.91	0.76	0.83	0.77	0.75
Configuration 5 (Centered and resized nucleus only and z-score pre-processing—mask applied excluding nucleus)								
Inception_resnet	0.79	0.79	0.79	0.79	0.83	0.85	0.83	0.83

Table 2 shows the Inception_resnet model using configuration 2 performing the best in terms of accuracy, precision, recall, and F1-score in the validation and test datasets of the 2-subcategory classification.

In Tables 1 and 2, CNN models with configuration 1 showed less consistency between validation and test datasets and had worse performance compared to those with configuration 2. The Inception_resnet model using configurations 3 and 4 showed poor performance compared to the model using configuration 2 (Table 1). However, their performance improved with two-subcategory classification (Table 2). The overall performance of Inception_resnet using configuration 5, which included the nucleus only in image patches, was slightly lower than the performance of the best model in both the two-subcategory and three-subcategory classification tasks, as shown in Tables 1 and 2.

Figure 2 shows the t-SNE plots for the learned features of the last convolutional layer of the Inception_resnet model with configurations 1 and 2 that were generated from the test dataset. As shown in the t-SNE plot of the Inception_resnet model with configuration 1, all promonocytes demonstrated similar features to blasts, and some of monocytes were also not discernable from blasts. In the t-SNE plot of the model with configuration 2, promonocytes were distributed across monocyte and blast classes. There was a narrow band to differentiate promonocytes from both other classes.

The average performance of the fivefold cross validation using the best performing model, Inception_resnet, is shown in Table 3. The average accuracy of the model and its standard deviation across the fivefold cross validation were 0.66 ± 0.12 and 0.78 ± 0.10 for three-subcategory and two-subcategory classifications, respectively. The performances in the first two iterations, were the lowest while the performance in iteration three was the highest. In the two-subcategory classification, the average performance of the fivefold cross validation (Table 3) was slightly lower than the performance of the Inception_resnet model (Table 2) on the test dataset (78% vs. 80%, respectively).

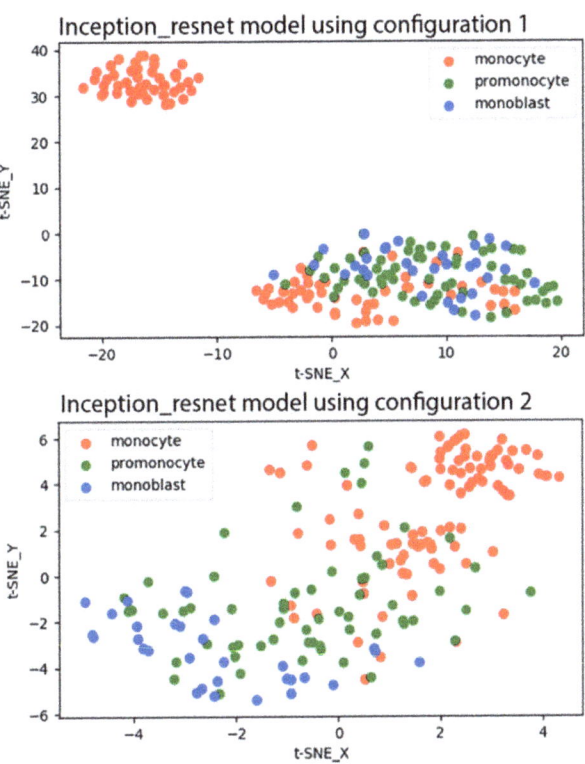

Figure 2. t-SNE plots for the performance of the Inception_resnet model using configurations 1 and 2 on the test. In the configuration 1 plot, all promonocytes demonstrated similar features to blasts and some of monocytes were also not discernable from blasts. In the configuration 2 plot, promonocytes were distributed across monocyte and blast classes.

Table 3. Overall performance of fivefold cross validation using the Inception_resnet CNN model.

5-Fold Cross Validation	3-Subcategory (Monocytes vs. Promonocytes vs. Blasts)				2-Subcategory (Monocytes vs. Promonocytes + Blasts)			
	Accuracy	Precision	Recall	F1-Score	Accuracy	Precision	Recall	F1-Score
Iteration 1	0.56	0.60	0.46	0.47	0.67	0.67	0.67	0.67
Iteration 2	0.57	0.55	0.45	0.45	0.68	0.72	0.67	0.66
Iteration 3	0.81	0.79	0.78	0.77	0.89	0.90	0.88	0.89
Iteration 4	0.77	0.75	0.78	0.77	0.83	0.83	0.83	0.83
Iteration 5	0.58	0.56	0.62	0.53	0.81	0.84	0.82	0.81
Mean ± STD	0.66 ± 0.12	0.65 ± 0.11	0.62 ± 0.16	0.60 ± 0.16	0.78 ± 0.10	0.79 ± 0.09	0.77 ± 0.10	0.77 ± 0.10

The performance of the five human expert reviewers compared to the consensus reference labels is shown in Table 4. The mean and standard deviation of the performance of the reviewers were 0.81 ± 0.07 and 0.86 ± 0.05 for the three-subcategory and two-subcategory classifications, respectively. Apart from reviewers 3 and 5, there was a strong consensus between the other three reviewers. The performance of reviewer 3 was 72% accurate, which was the lowest performance among the other reviewers. As seen in Table 4, human performance could be as low as 72% and 80% accurate for the three-subcategory and two-subcategory classifications, respectively. The overall results in the fivefold cross validation test (Table 3) were slightly lower than the human reviewers' performance in the two-subcategory classification task (0.78 ± 0.10 vs. 0.86 ± 0.05).

Table 4. Performance of human experts compared to consensus reference labels.

	Reviewers vs. Consensus Reference							
	3-Subcategory (Monocytes vs. Promonocytes vs. Blasts)				2-Subcategory (Monocytes vs. Promonocytes + Blasts)			
	Accuracy	Precision	Recall	F1-Score	Accuracy	Precision	Recall	F1-Score
Reviewer 1	0.86	0.83	0.88	0.85	0.90	0.90	0.90	0.90
Reviewer 2	0.86	0.87	0.84	0.85	0.89	0.89	0.89	0.89
Reviewer 3	0.72	0.77	0.64	0.67	0.80	0.81	0.79	0.79
Reviewer 4	0.86	0.86	0.85	0.85	0.89	0.89	0.88	0.89
Reviewer 5	0.76	0.75	0.80	0.76	0.80	0.82	0.81	0.80
Mean ± STD	0.81 ± 0.07	0.82 ± 0.05	0.80 ± 0.10	0.80 ± 0.08	0.86 ± 0.05	0.86 ± 0.04	0.86 ± 0.05	0.85 ± 0.05

A Pearson's correlation matrix between reviewers and consensus reference labels is displayed in Table 5. The Pearson's correlation between the five reviewers ranged from 0.5 to 0.75. The correlation between reviewers and consensus reference labels ranged from 0.67 to 0.86. The correlation between the two labels of reviewer 5 (reviewer 5 vs. reviewer 5R) is 0.92 and represents the intra-reviewer variability.

Table 5. Pearson's correlation matrix between reviewers. Reference: consensus of 5 reviewers. Reviewer 5R: second repetition of reviewer 5.

	Reviewer 1	Reviewer 2	Reviewer 3	Reviewer 4	Reviewer 5	Reviewer 5R	Reference
Reviewer 1	1	0.73	0.58	0.75	0.74	0.76	0.86
Reviewer 2	0.73	1	0.61	0.73	0.65	0.66	0.84
Reviewer 3	0.58	0.61	1	0.58	0.5	0.49	0.67
Reviewer 4	0.75	0.73	0.58	1	0.62	0.63	0.86
Reviewer 5	0.74	0.65	0.5	0.62	1	0.92	0.73
Reviewer 5R	0.76	0.66	0.49	0.63	0.92	1	0.73
Reference	0.86	0.84	0.67	0.86	0.73	0.73	1

4. Discussion

Monocyte assessment is frequently used in day-to-day practice to differentiate neoplastic processes from reactive monocytosis such as infections. According to the WHO criteria, the diagnosis of monocytic neoplasms is dependent on quantitating monoblasts, promonocytes, and monocytes [2]. Specifically, for the accurate recognition and quantification of the two subtypes (promonocytes and monoblasts) most characteristic of acute leukemia, we are required to distinguish between the subtypes of AML with monocytic differentiation and CMML [2,21]. In addition, quantification of monoblasts is necessary for CMML staging, and quantification of monocytes is important for the differential diagnosis of other chronic myeloid neoplasms, including atypical CML [22].

Microscopic evaluation and enumeration of monoblasts, promonocytes, and monocytes by an experienced hematopathologist remains to be the only accepted gold standard; however, morphologic assessment alone can be difficult and subject to significant inter- and intra-observer variability. In fact, monocytes and monocytic precursors are the most difficult cells to identify and classify with confidence in the peripheral blood or in the bone marrow [8]. Other modalities such as multiparameter flow cytometry have been attempted to determine whether immunophenotypic expressions such as anti-CD14 antibodies, which recognize the MO2 and MY4 epitopes, can identify monoblasts, promonocytes, and monocytes [23]. However, the adoption of alternatives to morphology requires technical expertise and remains limited in terms of widespread applicability.

It is imperative that diagnoses distinguish accurately between CMML, including the correct subcategory, and AML with monocytic differentiation, because incorrect diagnosis has significant therapeutic ramifications. For instance, management of CMML is guided by risk categories (high or low risk) based on a CMML-specific scoring system [24] that incorporates the percentage of PB and BM blasts as an important factor determining survival and prognosis [25]. Accordingly, high-risk groups are more subject to hematopoietic cell transplantation—which is associated with significant morbidity and mortality—than the low-risk groups, which are more subject to symptom-directed therapy (e.g., hydroxyurea, hypomethylating agents, and/or supportive care) [26]. Likewise, patients with AML have a different therapeutic approach, because their treatment regimen usually begins with intensive remission–induction chemotherapy, which generally includes a seven-day continuous infusion of cytarabine along with anthracycline treatment on days 1–3 (the so-called "7 + 3" regimen) [27]. This induction therapy can be highly toxic and typically entails hospitalization for several weeks. Hence, precise identification and detailed characterization of monocytic cells is of major relevance not only for diagnosis, but also for treatment. Other neoplastic myeloid conditions have been associated with monocytic abnormalities including juvenile myelomonocytic leukemia, chronic myeloid leukemia with p190 fusion, and myeloid neoplasm with rearrangements of PDGFRA, PDGFRB, FGFR1 and PCM1-JAK2. In addition, monocytosis could be a sign of progression of Philadelphia-negative myeloproliferative neoplasms [28].

The evolution of digital imaging and AI application provides a promising potential in cell-based classification. As such, we thought to evaluate the applicability in monocytic cell-type classification. In this study, we assessed the performance of five well-known CNN architectures for separating monocytes from the spectrum of monocyte precursors (i.e., promonocytes and monoblasts). As mentioned before, ground truth reference labels to train these models were generated based on the consensus of five expert reviewers. Table 4 shows that the percentage of agreement between expert reviewers ranged from 72% to 86% for the three-subcategory classification task, which is a good concordance for such a difficult task. These results were in line with previously reported concordance rates in the literature (76.6%) between expert hematopathologists [8,10]. This agreement was further improved when monocyte precursors were combined. Importantly, consensus on the classification of cells, which is used as the gold standard, was achieved by individual classification of each cell by each one of the evaluators. This is a higher standard than applied in a regular clinical practice, where there are other parameters which could be helpful in reaching the correct percentage of blast-equivalents (for example: similarity between individual cells, bone marrow cellularity, absence of other hematopoietic lineages).

The performance of CNN models did not reach the level of the performance of human experts in separating monocytic cells in the three-subcategory classification, while their performance was significantly improved in the three-subcategory classification, and hence more comparable to the performance of human experts. The improvements in the inter-observer agreement and CNN model support the practice of combining blasts/promonocytes into a single subcategory. As shown in our experiment in the three-subcategory classification (Table 1)—to find the best model and preprocessing approach—we conclude that Inception_resnet using configuration 2 provides the best overall results in validation and test datasets. However, the performance of the other models and configurations, apart from configuration 1, was comparable with small differences in the two-subcategory classification, as shown in Table 2. Even though the results are comparable, configurations using cell masking to suppress the impact of irrelevant background information on the prediction outcome are more reliable. Configuration 5 using nucleus only data also showed consistent results of cross-validation and test datasets, both in the two-subcategory and three-subcategory classifications (Tables 1 and 2). The impact of the cytoplasm and nucleus on predicting monocytic cells could be further investigated in a larger study to validate our preliminary findings.

The scope of this study was limited to the applicability of monocytic classification based on the morphologic assessment by our expert hematopathology reviewers. Other cell types, immunohistochemical, or flow cytometric immunophenotyping features were not collected to address the reproducibility of the results presented in this article and its direct impact on the diagnosis. Even though we obtained promising results in the identification of monocytes and its precursors using CNNs, these results still need to be validated with a larger study population. We used high-resolution cell images which required the manual acquisition of images. Both image acquisition and cell classification posed challenges that limited the number of cells used in our study.

A larger study with higher numbers of cells could also help further improve the performance of CNN models and obtain a better generalization ability. A larger cohort will likely improve training of the CNN models and could possibly provide an improved ground truth reference. Furthermore, additional work is needed to explore the clinical applicability and clinical validity of such CNN models. Finally, our results underline the fact that monocytic cell differentiation is a difficult task, with relatively low concordance between expert reviewers.

5. Conclusions

In summary, we present that CNN models could perform almost as well as human experts in separating monocytes from their precursor cells. To the best of our knowledge, this is the first study to separate monocytes from their precursors using deep learning. Our promising results demonstrate that CNN models could be adopted for this task and further improved with a larger study population.

Author Contributions: Conceptualization, M.E.S., A.N. and M.M.P.; methodology, M.E.S., M.O. and Z.A.; software, Z.A.; validation, M.E.S., M.O., Z.A., D.J., P.L.N., D.R. and S.R.; formal analysis, M.E.S., M.O. and Z.A.; investigation, M.E.S., M.O. and Z.A.; resources, M.E.S., M.O. and Z.A.; data curation, M.E.S., M.O., D.J., P.L.N., D.R. and S.R.; writing— original draft preparation, M.E.S., M.O. and Z.A.; writing—review and editing, M.E.S., M.O., Z.A., D.J., P.L.N., D.R., S.R., A.A.-K., M.M.P. and A.N.; visualization, M.E.S. and M.O.; supervision, M.E.S.; project administration, M.E.S.; funding acquisition, M.E.S. All authors have read and agreed to the published version of the manuscript.

Funding: This study was supported by the division of hematopathology research funds at Mayo Clinic, Rochester, MN, USA.

Institutional Review Board Statement: The study was conducted according to the guidelines of the Declaration of Helsinki, and approved by the Institutional Review Board of Mayo Clinic (IRB protocol #19-001950).

Informed Consent Statement: Informed consent was waived per (IRB protocol #19-001950).

Data Availability Statement: The data presented in this study are contained within this article.

Conflicts of Interest: Mohamed Salama serves on the Board of Directors and has stock option at Techcyte Inc.

References

1. Arber, D.A.; Orazi, A.; Hasserjian, R.; Thiele, J.; Borowitz, M.J.; Le Beau, M.M.; Bloomfield, C.D.; Cazzola, M.; Vardiman, J.W. The 2016 revision to the World Health Organization classification of myeloid neoplasms and acute leukemia. *Blood* **2016**, *127*, 2391–2405. [CrossRef] [PubMed]
2. Campo, E.; Harris, N.L.; Pileri, S.A.; Jaffe, E.S.; Stein, H.; Thiele, J. *WHO Classification of Tumours of Haematopoietic and Lymphoid Tissues*; IARC Who Classification of Tum: Lyon, France, 2017; ISBN 9789283244943.
3. Arber, D.A. Acute myeloid leukaemia, not otherwise specified. In *World Health Organization Classification of Tumours of Haematopoietic and Lymphoid Tissues*, Revised 4th ed.; Campo, E., Harris, N.L., Jaffe, E.S., Pileri, S.A., Stein, H., Thiele, J., Eds.; IARC Press: Lyon, France, 2017; pp. 156–166.
4. Arber, D.A.; Orazi, A. Update on the pathologic diagnosis of chronic myelomonocytic leukemia. *Mod. Pathol.* **2019**, *32*, 732–740. [CrossRef] [PubMed]
5. Bain, B.; Bain, B.J.; Matutes, E. *Chronic Myeloid Leukaemias*; Clinical Publishing, Atlas Medical Pub Ltd.: New York, NY, USA, 2012; ISBN 9781846920943.
6. Orazi, A.; Bennett, J.M.; Germing, U.; Brunning, R.D.; Bain, B.J.; Cazzola, M. Chronic myelomonocytic leukemia. In *WHO Classification of Tumours of Haematopoietic and Lymphoid Tissues*, 4th ed.; Campo, E., Jaffe, E.S., Stein, H., Thiele, J., Harris, N.L., Pileri, S.A., Eds.; International Agency for Research on Cancer: Lyon, France, 2017; pp. 82–86.
7. Naeim, F.; Rao, P.N. Chapter 11—Acute Myeloid Leukemia. In *Hematopathology*; Naeim, F., Rao, P.N., Grody, W.W., Eds.; Academic Press: Oxford, UK, 2008; pp. 207–255, ISBN 9780123706072.
8. Goasguen, J.E.; Bennett, J.M.; Bain, B.J.; Vallespi, T.; Brunning, R.; Mufti, G.J. International Working Group on Morphology of Myelodysplastic Syndrome Morphological evaluation of monocytes and their precursors. *Haematologica* **2009**, *94*, 994–997. [CrossRef] [PubMed]

9. Lynch, D.T.; Hall, J.; Foucar, K. How I investigate monocytosis. *Int. J. Lab. Hematol.* **2018**, *40*, 107–114. [CrossRef] [PubMed]
10. Foucar, K.; Hsi, E.D.; Wang, S.A.; Rogers, H.J.; Hasserjian, R.P.; Bagg, A.; George, T.I.; Bassett, R.L., Jr.; Peterson, L.C.; Morice, W.G., 2nd; et al. Concordance among hematopathologists in classifying blasts plus promonocytes: A bone marrow pathology group study. *Int. J. Lab. Hematol.* **2020**, *42*, 418–422. [CrossRef] [PubMed]
11. Akkus, Z.; Galimzianova, A.; Hoogi, A.; Rubin, D.L.; Erickson, B.J. Deep Learning for Brain MRI Segmentation: State of the Art and Future Directions. *J. Digit. Imaging* **2017**, *30*, 449–459. [CrossRef] [PubMed]
12. Akkus, Z.; Kostandy, P.; Philbrick, K.A.; Erickson, B.J. Robust brain extraction tool for CT head images. *Neurocomputing* **2020**, *392*, 189–195. [CrossRef]
13. Akkus, Z.; Kim, B.H.; Nayak, R.; Gregory, A.; Alizad, A.; Fatemi, M. Fully Automated Segmentation of Bladder Sac and Measurement of Detrusor Wall Thickness from Transabdominal Ultrasound Images. *Sensors* **2020**, *20*, 4175. [CrossRef] [PubMed]
14. Kingma, D.P.; Ba, J. Adam: A method for stochastic optimization. In Proceedings of the International Conference Learn. Represent. (ICLR), San Diego, CA, USA, 5–8 May 2015.
15. Szegedy, C.; Liu, W.; Jia, Y.; Sermanet, P.; Reed, S.; Anguelov, D.; Erhan, D.; Vanhoucke, V.; Rabinovich, A. Going Deeper with Convolutions. In Proceedings of the 2015 IEEE Conference on Computer Vision and Pattern Recognition (CVPR), Boston, MA, USA, 7–12 June 2015; pp. 1–9.
16. Szegedy, C.; Vanhoucke, V.; Ioffe, S.; Shlens, J.; Wojna, Z. Rethinking the inception architecture for computer vision. *Conf. Proc.* **2016**, 2818–2826. [CrossRef]
17. He, K.; Zhang, X.; Ren, S.; Sun, J. Deep residual learning for image recognition. In Proceedings of the IEEE Conference on Computer Vision and Pattern Recognition, Las Vegas, NV, USA, 27–30 June 2016; pp. 770–778.
18. Szegedy, C.; Ioffe, S.; Vanhoucke, V.; Alemi, A.A. Inception-v4, inception-resnet and the impact of residual connections on learning. In Proceedings of the Thirty-First AAAI Conference on Artificial Intelligence, San Francisco, CA, USA, 4–9 February 2017.
19. Simonyan, K.; Zisserman, A. Very deep convolutional networks for large-scale image recognition. *arXiv* **2014**, arXiv:1409.1556.
20. Huang, G.; Liu, Z.; Van Der Maaten, L.; Weinberger, K.Q. Densely Connected Convolutional Networks. In Proceedings of the IEEE Conference on Computer Vision and Pattern Recognition (CVPR), Honolulu, HI, USA, 21–26 July 2017; pp. 4700–4708.
21. International Agency for Research on Cancer. *World Health Organization WHO Classification of Tumours of Haematopoietic and Lymphoid Tissues*; World Health Organization: Geneva, Switzerland, 2008.
22. Xubo, G.; Xingguo, L.; Xianguo, W.; Rongzhen, X.; Xibin, X.; Lin, W.; Lei, Z.; Xiaohong, Z.; Genbo, X.; Xiaoying, Z. The role of peripheral blood, bone marrow aspirate and especially bone marrow trephine biopsy in distinguishing atypical chronic myeloid leukemia from chronic granulocytic leukemia and chronic myelomonocytic leukemia. *Eur. J. Haematol.* **2009**, *83*, 292–301. [CrossRef] [PubMed]
23. Yang, D.T.; Greenwood, J.H.; Hartung, L.; Hill, S.; Perkins, S.L.; Bahler, D.W. Flow cytometric analysis of different CD14 epitopes can help identify immature monocytic populations. *Am. J. Clin. Pathol.* **2005**, *124*, 930–936. [CrossRef] [PubMed]
24. Elena, C.; Gallì, A.; Such, E.; Meggendorfer, M.; Germing, U.; Rizzo, E.; Cervera, J.; Molteni, E.; Fasan, A.; Schuler, E.; et al. Integrating clinical features and genetic lesions in the risk assessment of patients with chronic myelomonocytic leukemia. *Blood* **2016**, *128*, 1408–1417. [CrossRef] [PubMed]
25. Such, E.; Germing, U.; Malcovati, L.; Cervera, J.; Kuendgen, A.; Della Porta, M.G.; Nomdedeu, B.; Arenillas, L.; Luño, E.; Xicoy, B.; et al. Development and validation of a prognostic scoring system for patients with chronic myelomonocytic leukemia. *Blood* **2013**, *121*, 3005–3015. [CrossRef] [PubMed]
26. Patnaik, M.M.; Tefferi, A. Chronic myelomonocytic leukemia: 2018 update on diagnosis, risk stratification and management. *Am. J. Hematol.* **2018**, *93*, 824–840. [CrossRef] [PubMed]
27. Dombret, H.; Gardin, C. An update of current treatments for adult acute myeloid leukemia. *Blood* **2016**, *127*, 53–61. [CrossRef] [PubMed]
28. Bain, B.J.; Horny, H.-P.; Arber, D.A.; Tefferi, A.; Hasserjian, R.P. Myeloid/lymphoid neoplasms with eosinophilia and rearrangement of PDGFRA, PDGFRB or FGFR1, or with PCM1-JAK2. In *WHO Classification of Tumours of Haematopoietic and Lymphoid Tissues*, 4th ed.; Campo, E., Jaffe, E.S., Stein, H., Thiele, J., Harris, N.L., Pileri, S.A., Eds.; International Agency for Research on Cancer: Lyon, France, 2017; pp. 71–78.

Article

Using Bayesian Networks to Predict Long-Term Health-Related Quality of Life and Comorbidity after Bariatric Surgery: A Study Based on the Scandinavian Obesity Surgery Registry

Yang Cao [1,*], Mustafa Raoof [2], Eva Szabo [2], Johan Ottosson [2] and Ingmar Näslund [2]

1. Clinical Epidemiology and Biostatistics, School of Medical Sciences, Örebro University, 70182 Örebro, Sweden
2. Department of Surgery, Faculty of Medicine and Health, Örebro University, 70182 Örebro, Sweden; mustafa.raoof@regionorebrolan.se (M.R.); eva.szabo@regionorebrolan.se (E.S.); johan.ottosson@regionorebrolan.se (J.O.); ingmar.naslund@regionorebrolan.se (I.N.)
* Correspondence: yang.cao@oru.se; Tel.: +46-19-602-6236

Received: 27 May 2020; Accepted: 15 June 2020; Published: 17 June 2020

Abstract: Previously published literature has identified a few predictors of health-related quality of life (HRQoL) after bariatric surgery. However, performance of the predictive models was not evaluated rigorously using real world data. To find better methods for predicting prognosis in patients after bariatric surgery, we examined performance of the Bayesian networks (BN) method in predicting long-term postoperative HRQoL and compared it with the convolution neural network (CNN) and multivariable logistic regression (MLR). The patients registered in the Scandinavian Obesity Surgery Registry (SOReg) were used for the current study. In total, 6542 patients registered in the SOReg between 2008 and 2012 with complete demographic and preoperative comorbidity information, and preoperative and postoperative 5-year HROoL scores and comorbidities were included in the study. HRQoL was measured using the RAND-SF-36 and the obesity-related problems scale. Thirty-five variables were used for analyses, including 19 predictors and 16 outcome variables. The Gaussian BN (GBN), CNN, and a traditional linear regression model were used for predicting 5-year HRQoL scores, and multinomial discrete BN (DBN) and MLR were used for 5-year comorbidities. Eighty percent of the patients were randomly selected as a training dataset and 20% as a validation dataset. The GBN presented a better performance than the CNN and the linear regression model; it had smaller mean squared errors (MSEs) than those from the CNN and the linear regression model. The MSE of the summary physical scale was only 0.0196 for GBN compared to the 0.0333 seen in the CNN. The DBN showed excellent predictive ability for 5-year type 2 diabetes and dyslipidemia (area under curve (AUC) = 0.942 and 0.917, respectively), good ability for 5-year hypertension and sleep apnea syndrome (AUC = 0.891 and 0.834, respectively), and fair ability for 5-year depression (AUC = 0.750). Bayesian networks provide useful tools for predicting long-term HRQoL and comorbidities in patients after bariatric surgery. The hybrid network that may involve variables from different probability distribution families deserves investigation in the future.

Keywords: machine learning-enabled decision support system; improving diagnosis accuracy; Bayesian network; bariatric surgery; health-related quality of life; comorbidity

1. Introduction

Over the past two decades, obesity has been continuously increasing worldwide, which has become a major health issue worldwide and raised public concern across the globe [1]. Severe obesity, defined as body mass index (BMI) over 35 kg/m^2 with obesity-related comorbidities, or BMI > 40 kg/m^2, has been associated with impaired health-related quality of life (HRQoL) and multiple comorbidities, including type 2 diabetes (T2D), hypertension, and cancer [2–4]. Gastric bypass and other weight-loss surgeries, known collectively as bariatric surgery, are currently considered the most effective treatment options for morbid obesity to help severe obese patients to lose excess weight and reduce potentially life-threatening risk of weight-related health problems, such as heart disease and stroke, hypertension, T2D, nonalcoholic fatty liver disease, and sleep apnea [5,6].

Based on the findings from several long-term (follow-up time ranging between 5 and 10 years) prospective studies, bariatric surgery patients' HRQoL improved considerably after surgery and much of the initial HRQoL improvement was maintained over the long term [7]. While bariatric surgery can offer many benefits, all forms of weight-loss surgery are major procedures that can pose serious risks and side effects, including acid reflux, chronic nausea and vomiting, infection, obstruction of stomach, failure to lose weight, low blood sugar, malnutrition, and hernias, which in turn may have adverse impacts on HRQoL of the patients with morbid obesity after surgery [8–10].

Previously published literature has identified a few predictors of HRQoL after bariatric surgery, including baseline demographic data and depression severity score [11–14]. However, none of these studies evaluated the models' performances or the predictors' predictive abilities rigorously using real world data. In our previous study, we have examined the performance of the convolution neural network (CNN) for predicting 5-year HRQoL after bariatric surgery based on the available preoperative information from the Scandinavian Obesity Surgery Registry (SOReg) [15]. We found that, although the CNN is better than the traditional multivariate linear regression model at predicting long-term HRQoL after bariatric surgery, the overfitting issue is still apparent and needs to be mitigated [15]. In the two recently published studies, using the same database, we found that patients with postoperative complications had significantly less improvements in all aspects of HRQoL compared to those without any form of postoperative complication [16], and the ability of multilayer perceptron and CNN for predicting the postoperative serious complications after bariatric surgery is limited [17].

To find better methods for predicting prognosis and provide evidence for patient management after bariatric surgery, in this study, we examined the performance of the Bayesian networks (BN) method in predicting long-term postoperative HRQoL and compared it with the CNN and multivariable linear regression. At the same time, we also evaluated the performance of the BN in predicting postoperative comorbidities and compared it with multivariable logistic regression (MLR) model.

2. Materials and Methods

2.1. Subjects and Variables

The patients registered in the Scandinavian Obesity Surgery Registry (SOReg) were used for the current study. The registry was launched in 2007 and covers 98% of bariatric surgery in Sweden since 2009. It is validated regularly and shows high data quality [18–21]. In total, 6542 patients registered in the SOReg between 2008 and 2012, operated with primary Roux-en-Y gastric bypass, with complete demographic and preoperative comorbidity information; and preoperative and postoperative 5-year HROoL scores and comorbidities were included in the study. HRQoL was measured using the RAND-SF-36 [22] and the obesity-related problems (OP) scale [23] for the patients. In the present study, 35 variables were used for analyses, including 19 predictors (i.e., sex, and preoperative age, BMI, physical functioning (PF), role physical (RP), bodily pain (BP), general health (GH), vitality (VT), social functioning (SF), role emotional (RE), mental health (MH) scale, summary physical scale (PCS), summary mental scale (MCS), OP, sleep apnea syndrome (SAS), hypertension, pharmaceutically treated T2D, depression, and dyslipidemia) and 16 outcome variables (i.e., postoperative 5-year PF, RP, BP, GH, VT, SF, RE, MH, PCS, MCS, OP, SAS, hypertension, T2D, depression, and dyslipidemia). All scale scores ranged from 0 to 100, with higher scores indicating better health status, except for OP, for which low values represent good health; comorbidity variables are binary, with 1 indicating yes and 0 no.

The characteristics of the patients are shown in Table 1. Briefly, the average age and body mass index (BMI) of the patients were 42.7 years and 42.3 kg/m^2, respectively. More than three quarters (78.8%) were female and 45% had at least one of the five comorbidities before bariatric surgery. Prevalence for all the comorbidities was reduced except for depression, and all the HRQoL scores were improved except for MCS after five years of bariatric surgery (Table 1).

Table 1. Characteristics of the patients (n = 6542) included in the study, mean ± SD or n (%).

	Preoperative	5-Year Postoperative
Age (year)	42.7 ± 11.0	47.7 ± 11.0
BMI (kg/m^2)	42.3 ± 5.2	30.3 ± 5.2
Female	5154 (78.8%)	5154 (78.8%)
SAS	668 (10.2%)	188 (2.9%)
Hypertension	1817 (27.8%))	1420 (21.7%)
T2D	973 (14.9%)	452 (6.9%)
Depression	855 (13.1%)	1162 (17.8%)
Dyslipidemia	732 (11.2%)	429 (6.6%)
PF	61.7 ± 21.9	84.2 ± 20.7
RP	60.3 ± 38.9	77.9 ± 36.5
BP	56.0 ± 26.9	65.2 ± 30.7
GH	58.2 ± 21.4	68.1 ± 24.7
VT	47.4 ± 23.0	54.5 ± 26.9
SF	74.9 ± 26.1	79.6 ± 26.4
RE	76.0 ± 36.2	76.9 ± 37.8
MH	71.5 ± 19.4	72.0 ± 23.0
PCS	38.3 ± 10.7	47.6 ± 11.1
MCS	46.8 ± 11.7	44.6 ± 13.8
OP	61.0 ± 26.4	25.6 ± 27.4

SD, standard deviation; BMI, body mass index; SAS, sleep apnea syndrome; T2D, type 2 diabetes; PF, physical functioning; RP, role-physical; BP, bodily pain; GH, general health; VT, vitality; SF, social functioning; RE, role-emotional; MH, mental health; PCS, summary physical scale; MCS, summary mental scale; OP, obesity-related problems.

The study was approved by the Regional Ethics Review Committee in Stockholm (approval number: 2013/535-31/5). The data that support the study are not publicly available because they contain information that could compromise research subjects' privacy and confidentiality. However, the data may be available upon reasonable request and with permission of the Committee of Scandinavian Obesity Surgery Registry in Örebro, Sweden.

2.2. Statistical Methods

A BN is a probabilistic directed acyclic graphical model that represents a set of variables and their conditional dependencies via a directed acyclic graph (DAG). In particular, each node in the DAG represents a random variable, while the edges between the nodes represent probabilistic dependencies among the corresponding random variables. A BN takes an event that occurred and predicts the likelihood that any one of its parent nodes was the possibly contributing factor [24]. Applications of BN have multiplied in recent years, spanning such different topics as systems biology, economics, social sciences, and medical informatics [25,26].

In the current study, prediction for 5-year HRQoL scores was conducted using a Gaussian BN (GBN) because it follows or approximates a normal distribution [25]. GBN is a specially directed graphical model, which offers algorithms for prediction and inference when all variables could be defined by a Gaussian prior distribution or a Gaussian conditional distribution [27,28]. Binary predictors were transformed into continuous propensity scores using MLR before they entered the GBN [29]. Performance factors of the GBN were all compared with those from the previous CNN [15] and a traditional linear regression model.

Prediction for 5-year comorbidities was conducted using both multinomial discrete BN (DBN) and MLR, and the results from the two methods were compared. Before entering the DBN, the continuous predictors were discretized into ten categories using the information-preserving discretization method introduced by Hartemink [30]. Although at the cost of losing some information, the discretization may accommodate skewness of the variables and nonlinear relationships between them, and speed up the computation substantially [25,31].

2.3. Model Training and Validation

In total, 80% of the patients were randomly selected as a training dataset for learning the structure of the GBN and the DBN. When learning the structure of the networks, only a black list was used to block the edges directing from the postoperative variables to the preoperative variables, and no other constraints were used. The hill-climbing (HC) algorithm was used to learn the structure of the networks, which starts from a network with no edges, and then adds, removes, and reverses one edge at a time and picks the change that increases the network's Bayesian information criterion score the most [25].

The remaining 20% of the patients were used as the validation dataset to evaluate the performance of the Bayesian networks, CNN, multivariable linear, and logistic regression models. Performance of the GBN was evaluated using the mean squared error (MSE) in view of the existence of zero values in the outcome variables [32]. MSE from the min-max normalized scores (between 0 and 1) was used to compare the results from the GBN and those from the previous multivariable linear regression and the CNN [33]. Performance of the DBN and MLR was evaluated using accuracy, sensitivity, specificity, and area under the receiver operating characteristic (ROC) curve. Terminology and derivations of the metrics were given in detail elsewhere [33]. A successful prediction model for comorbidities was defined as with an area under the ROC curve (AUC) greater than 0.7 [33–35].

2.4. Software and Hardware

The descriptive statistical analyses were performed using Stata 16.0 (StataCorp LLC, College Station, TX, USA). The Bayesian networks were constructed using package *bnlearn* [25,36] in software R version 3.62 (R Foundation for Statistical Computing, Vienna, Austria), and the multiple linear and logistic regression models were achieved in R as well.

All of the computation was conducted in a computer with a 64-bit Windows 7 Enterprise operation system (Service Pack 1), Intel® Core TM i5-4210U CPU @ 2.40 GHz, and 16.0 GB random access memory.

3. Results

3.1. Structure of the GBN

The structure of the GBN for predicting the postoperative 5-year HRQoL is shown using the DAG in Figure 1. It shows all the edges based on the HC algorithm. The DAG looks complicated and messy because it indicates all the contributors to each postoperative 5-year variable at the same time. For example, the possible direct contributors for the 5-year OP are preoperative T2D, BMI, age, OP, and PCS, and 5-year GH, PCS, SF, PF, and MH. The conditional distribution of the 5-year OP, therefore, can be presented as:

$$OP\_5y \big| \big(age_p = x_1, BMI_p = x_2, DM_p = x_3, OP_p = x_4, PCS_p = x_5, GH_{5y} = x_6,$$
$$PCS_{5y} = x_7, SF_{5y} = x_8, PF_{5y} = x_9, MH_{5y} = x_{10}\big) \sim N(\beta_0 + \beta_1 x_1 +$$
$$\beta_2 x_2 + \beta_3 x_3 + \beta_4 x_4 + \beta_5 x_5 + \beta_6 x_6 + \beta_7 x_7 + \beta_8 x_8 + \beta_9 x_9 + \beta_{10} x_{10}, \varepsilon^2\big)$$

where N means a normal distribution with a variance ε^2.

The probability distribution above is just one of the conditional Gaussian distributions proposed by the DAG in Figure 1, and we can construct the conditional distribution for any one of the eleven postoperative 5-year HRQoL scores based on the edges pointing to them.

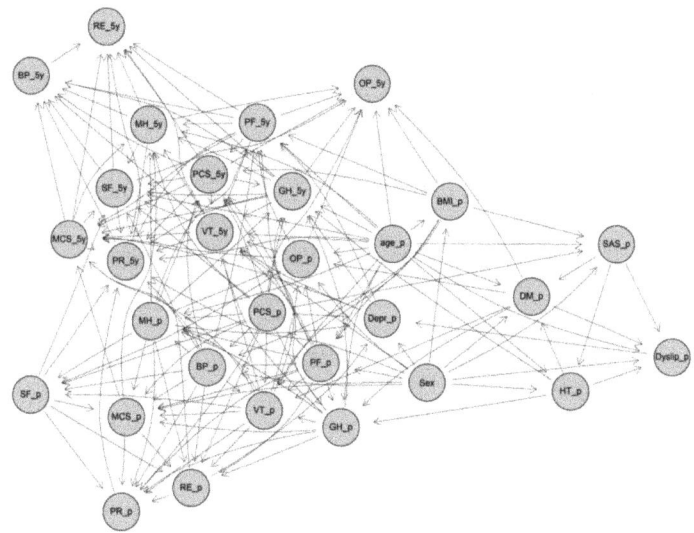

Figure 1. The directed acyclic graph (DAG) of the GBN for predicting postoperative 5-year HRQoL scores. DAG, directed acyclic graph; GBN Gaussian Bayesian network; PF, physical functioning; RP, role physical; BP, bodily pain; GH, general health; VT, vitality; SF, social functioning; RE, role emotional; MH, mental health; PCS, summary physical scale; MCS, summary mental scale; OP, obesity-related problems; BMI, body mass index; SAS, sleep apnea syndrome; HT, hypertension; DM, diabetes; Depr, depression; Dyslip, dyslipidemia; _p, preoperation; _5y, 5-year.

3.2. Performance of the GBN in the Validation Dataset

When the models were evaluated using the validation data that were not seen previously by the GBN, in general, the GBN presented a better performance than the CNN and the linear regression model (Table 2); all MSEs were smaller than those from the CNN and eight of eleven MSEs were smaller than those from the linear regression model (Table 2). For example, MSE of PCS was only 0.0196 for GBN compared to the 0.0333 seen in the CNN (Table 2), which means the average prediction error of the GBN accounted for less than 3% of the normalized mean of the postoperative 5-year PCS (which is 0.653). In general, the GBN could provide better prediction for postoperative 5-year HRQoL than the CNN and multivariable linear regression did.

Table 2. Mean squared errors of the GBN, the CNN, and the multivariable linear regression model.

HRQoL Scores	GBN	CNN	Linear Regression
PF	0.0335	0.0350	0.0343
RP	0.1166	0.1324	0.1211
BP	0.0813	0.0898	0.0772
GH	0.0499	0.0618	0.0508
VT	0.0590	0.0914	0.0625
SF	0.0599	0.0995	0.0588
RE	0.1230	0.2118	0.1269
MH	0.0436	0.0807	0.0416
PCS	0.0196	0.0333	0.0219
MCS	0.0356	0.0584	0.0305
OP	0.0597	0.0750	0.0608

GBN, Gaussian Bayesian network; CNN, convolutional neural network; PF, physical functioning; RP, role physical; BP, bodily pain; GH, general health; VT, vitality; SF, social functioning; RE, role emotional; MH, mental health; PCS, summary physical scale; MCS, summary mental scale; OP, obesity-related problems.

3.3. Structure of the DBN

The structure of DBN for predicting postoperative 5-year comorbidities is shown using the DAG in Figure 2, which is much simpler than the GBN. The comorbidities might be predicted using much less preoperative variables. For example, the conditional probability of 5-year depression (Depr_5y) depended only on sex and preoperative depression (Depr_p), which could be predicted by conditional probability tables between preoperative and postoperative depression for men or women separately. The conditional probability tables needed for men and women were estimated in a Bayesian setting in the DBN. When a comorbidity involved more predictors, such as 5-year dyslipidemia, there were more conditional probability tables to be referred to for prediction. Interestingly, preoperative BMI was not involved in any potential causal relationships in the network regarding the postoperative 5-year comorbidities (Figure 2).

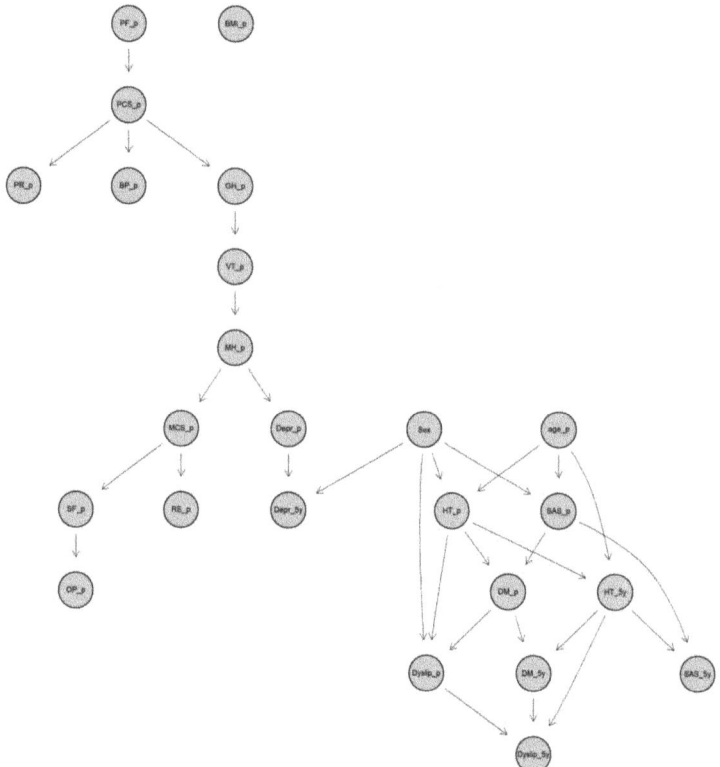

Figure 2. The DAG of the DBN for predicting postoperative 5-year comorbidities. DAG, directed acyclic graph; DBN, discrete Bayesian network; PF, physical functioning; RP, role physical; BP, bodily pain; GH, general health; VT, vitality; SF, social functioning; RE, role emotional; MH, mental health; PCS, summary physical scale; MCS, summary mental scale; OP, obesity-related problems; BMI, body mass index; SAS: sleep apnea syndrome; HT, hypertension; DM, diabetes; Depr, depression; Dyslip, dyslipidemia; _p, preoperation; _5y, 5-year.

3.4. Performance of the DBN in the Validation Dataset

The DBN showed excellent predictive ability for 5-year T2D and dyslipidemia (AUC = 0.942 and 0.917, respectively), good ability for 5-year hypertension and SAS (AUC = 0.891 and 0.834, respectively), and fair ability for 5-year depression (AUC = 0.750) (Figure 3).

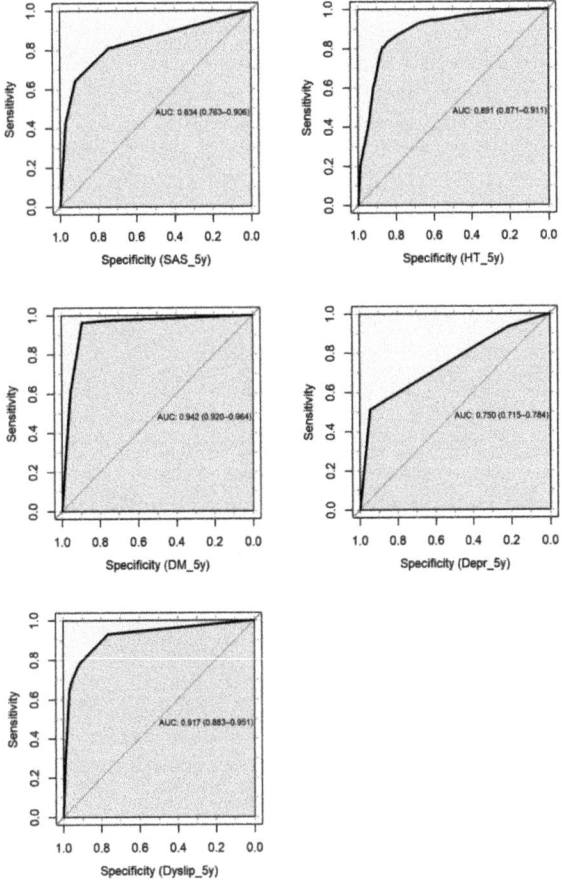

Figure 3. Receiver operating characteristic (ROC) curve of the discrete Bayesian network (DBN) for predicting 5-year comorbidity after bariatric surgery.

Compared with the results from the MLR, the DBN presented significant improvement in predicting 5-year comorbidities. All the AUCs from the DBN were larger than those from the MLR, and the differences were statistically significant ($p < 0.05$), except for SAS (Table 3). The sensitivity and specificity of the DBN in predicting postoperative 5-year T2D could be as high as 0.96 and 0.89, in contrast to the 0.78 and 0.68 of the MLR, respectively (Table 3).

Table 3. Performance metrics of the DBN and MLR model for predicting the 5-year comorbidities.

Comorbidity	DBN				MLR			
	Sen	Spe	Acc	AUC (95% CI)	Sen	Spe	Acc	AUC (95% CI)
SAS	0.64	0.92	0.91	0.83 (0.76, 0.91)	0.90	0.73	0.73	0.90 (0.86, 0.94)
Hypertension	0.83	0.83	0.84	0.89 (0.87, 0.91)	0.73	0.67	0.68	0.76 (0.73, 0.79)
T2D	0.96	0.89	0.90	0.94 (0.92, 0.96)	0.78	0.68	0.69	0.76 (0.72, 0.81)
Depression	0.51	0.95	0.87	0.75 (0.72, 0.78)	0.66	0.55	0.57	0.61 (0.67, 0.65)
Dyslipidemia	0.78	0.91	0.90	0.92 (0.88, 0.95)	0.76	0.67	0.68	0.77 (0.74, 0.82)

DBN, discrete Bayesian network; MLR, multivariable logistic regression; Sen, sensitivity; Spe, specificity; Acc, accuracy; AUC, area under the ROC curve; CI, confidence interval; SAS: sleep apnea syndrome; T2D, type 2 diabetes.

4. Discussion

In this study, we explored application of Bayesian networks for predicting long-term outcomes after bariatric surgery in a national registry. They showed promising predictive ability for both continuous and binary outcomes. For predicting the postoperative 5-year HRQoL, the GBN had smaller MSEs than those seen from the CNN for all scores and from the traditional multivariable linear regression for most scores. The most accurate predictions from the GBN were seen for PCS, and followed by PF and MCS; average prediction errors were lower than 3%, 4%, and 6% of their normalized means, respectively. For predicting the postoperative 5-year comorbidity, the DBN showed statistically significantly better performance compared with the MLR. It showed good and even excellent predictive ability for four of the five comorbidities, with an AUC as high as 0.942 in postoperative T2D.

Bayesian networks use Bayesian inference to model conditional dependence, and therefore causation, via a DAG. They are ideal for taking an event that occurred and predicting the likelihood that any one of several possible known causes was the contributing factor. Experience has shown that Bayesian networks and associated methods are geared to reasoning with uncertainty in a way closely resembling physicians [37–39]. Physicians who aim to develop computer-assisted systems for making clinical decisions are frequently confronted by the complexity and uncertainty in the models and prediction. In many cases, the situation is even worse, as many of the processes in medicine are only partly known [38]. During the past decade, Bayesian networks have become important tools for building decision-support systems in medical sciences and are now steadily becoming mainstream in some areas [40]. However, we should notice that DAGs are not designed to capture cyclic patterns, such as depression causing increased BMI [41]. Potential cyclic causal relationships may be explored using cyclic structural equation models [42] or Markov networks [43].

Many methods have been applied to predict the outcomes in patients after bariatric surgery, including stepwise multivariable linear regression [44,45], MLR [46], and machine learning methods such as the decision tree [47] and CNN [15,33]. Although an intelligent decision-making support system involving Bayesian networks has been reported for the nutrition diagnosis of bariatric surgery patients [48], according to our literature search, there is no study that has used the method for predicting outcomes after bariatric surgery. In our previous study, we illustrated that CNN might be a useful tool to predict long-term HRQoL after bariatric surgery; however, its overfitting on external validation dataset was still noticeable. To further mitigate the overfitting issue commonly seen in the machine learning field, we explored the application and performance of Bayesian networks in the current study and achieved desired results.

A significant advantage of the study in clinical sense is that it provides a solution with which to predict outcomes as far as 5 years after bariatric surgery. To give realistic and relevant information about the long-term prognosis of bariatric surgery is currently challenging. This type of knowledge can be used in clinical practice when it comes to giving scientifically-based preoperative information to patients considering the surgery. The knowledge can also be helpful in giving scientifically-based information to policy makers in health care to explain the expected positive effects of bariatric surgery. This information can also be used to customize the follow-ups of the individual patients. However, we would also note that this kind of prediction should not be used to exclude individual patients, who otherwise fulfil criteria for surgery, from having an operation. Meanwhile, while limited by the relatively small sample size compared to those usually recommended in statistical learning studies, it would be premature to use the models presented in the study in clinical decision-making right now.

There are several advantages in Bayesian networks. First, commonly used methods in epidemiological studies such as logistic regression and related methods do not take account of causal relationships that may exist between the covariates. Causal relationships between some of the risk factors may be already known, or may be regarded as plausible on biological grounds [49,50]. However, such information was incorporated into our BN models to reveal the potential relationships between the health or disease status and the associated risk factors [51]. Second, high correlation among predictors has long been an annoyance in regression analysis. The crux of the problem is that the linear regression model assumes each predictor has an independent effect on the response that can be encapsulated in the predictor's regression coefficient. As opposed to creating problems of multicollinearity, the associations between candidate predictor variables are naturally accounted for when defining a BN's conditional probability distributions. The HC algorithm used in the study may search a structure starting from either an empty, full, or possibly random DAG, or an initial DAG chosen according to existing knowledge. The main loop then consists of attempting every possible single-edge addition, removal, or reversal relative to the current candidate network. The change that increases the score the most then becomes the next candidate. The process iterates until a change in a single-edge no longer increases the score. By gradually taking into account the relationships between the variables, the problem of multicollinearity, therefore, can be reduced in a BN analysis [52]. Third, the DAG proposed by the BN method captures the dependence structure of multiple variables, and used appropriately, allows more robust conclusions about the direction of causation. BN analysis revealed a richer structure of relationships than could be inferred using the traditional multivariable regression methods, such as logistic regression, and highlight a potential pathway unseen previously for further investigation [53]. Fourth, compared with the deep learning method CNN used in our previous study for predicting HRQoL scores, the GBN provided much faster computing, better performance, and interpretable results. Finding the final DAG with the HC algorithm using 35 variables and 6542 observations only took 2 min in GBN analysis, in contrast to about 10 min in CNN analysis [33]. Except for the output HRQoL scores, the contributions of and relationships between the variables could not be explained or were hard to explain in the CNN analysis. In contrast, the GBN showed us all the potential causal relationships between the variables and estimated the strength of the relationships using liner regression coefficients.

However, there are limitations in our study. Our dataset includes both continuous and binary variables. To reduce the complexity of the networks and computing time, we converted the binary variables to continuous propensity scores for the GBN analysis, and discretized the HRQoL scores to categorical variables for the DBN analysis, which may involve tortuous information or lose some information in the analyses. A better solution would be a hybrid BN with use of Markov chain Monte Carlo techniques [25]. Although limited by the software packages available and adopting the compromising methods so far, we would like to explore the hybrid BN in the future and see whether it could improve the performance of prediction further. Besides, even though HRQoL and comorbidities are of importance, we have not tested hard endpoints, such as survival, heart attack, stroke, and cancer, which warrants a subsequent study when more detailed data are available. We should also notice that this study only included patients from Roux-en-Y gastric bypass, since this was almost the only operation method used in Sweden during the study period. Whether the results could be applied to other methods, such as sleeve gastrectomy, is not known yet. However, we will be able to investigate this in the future, since SOReg has contained a large number of sleeve gastrectomy patients in recent years. Besides, there are many more females than males in the database (80% vs. 20%). The generalizability of the BN models might be limited by the gender imbalance. Meanwhile, the menopausal transition can be an important factor related to HRQol in women [54]. In view of the average age with a wide standard deviation at 5 years after surgery, which is right around the menopause of women, this issue deserves clarification and assessment by incorporating with the menopause information in women. Therefore, the applicability and validity of the models need be further explored using a larger representative dataset with more covariates and longer follow-up.

5. Conclusions

Bayesian networks provide useful tools for predicting long-term HRQoL and comorbidities in patients after bariatric surgery, based on their preoperative health and disease status. The GBN and DBN used in our study outperformed the deep learning method CNN and multivariable logistic regression. However, the hybrid network that may involve variables from different probability distribution families deserves investigation in the future.

Author Contributions: All authors have read and agree to the published version of the manuscript. Conceptualization, Y.C.; data curation, M.R.; formal analysis, Y.C.; funding acquisition, Y.C.; investigation, M.R., E.S., J.O., and I.N.; methodology, Y.C.; project administration, J.O., and I.N.; resources, E.S., J.O., and I.N.; software, Y.C.; validation, Y.C.; visualization, Y.C.; writing—original draft, Y.C. and J.O.; writing—review and editing, Y.C., M.R., E.S., J.O., and I.N.

Funding: Yang Cao's work was supported by Örebro Region County Council (OLL-864441). The funders had no role in study design, data collection and analysis, decision to publish, or preparation of the manuscript.

Conflicts of Interest: The authors declare no conflict of interest.

References

1. Arroyo-Johnson, C.; Mincey, K.D. Obesity Epidemiology Worldwide. *Gastroenterol. Clin. N. Am.* **2016**, *45*, 571–579. [CrossRef] [PubMed]
2. Chang, C.Y.; Hung, C.K.; Chang, Y.Y.; Tai, C.M.; Lin, J.T.; Wang, J.D. Health-related quality of life in adult patients with morbid obesity coming for bariatric surgery. *Obes. Surg.* **2010**, *20*, 1121–1127. [CrossRef] [PubMed]
3. Kolotkin, R.L.; Crosby, R.D.; Williams, G.R. Health-related quality of life varies among obese subgroups. *Obes. Res.* **2002**, *10*, 748–756. [CrossRef] [PubMed]
4. White, M.A.; O'Neil, P.M.; Kolotkin, R.L.; Byrne, T.K. Gender, race, and obesity-related quality of life at extreme levels of obesity. *Obes. Res.* **2004**, *12*, 949–955. [CrossRef] [PubMed]
5. Angrisani, L.; Santonicola, A.; Iovino, P.; Formisano, G.; Buchwald, H.; Scopinaro, N. Bariatric Surgery Worldwide 2013. *Obes. Surg.* **2015**, *25*, 1822–1832. [CrossRef] [PubMed]
6. Welbourn, R.; Pournaras, D.J.; Dixon, J.; Higa, K.; Kinsman, R.; Ottosson, J.; Ramos, A.; van Wagensveld, B.; Walton, P.; Weiner, R.; et al. Bariatric Surgery Worldwide: Baseline Demographic Description and One-Year Outcomes from the Second IFSO Global Registry Report 2013-2015. *Obes. Surg.* **2018**, *28*, 313–322. [CrossRef] [PubMed]
7. Andersen, J.R.; Aasprang, A.; Karlsen, T.I.; Natvig, G.K.; Vage, V.; Kolotkin, R.L. Health-related quality of life after bariatric surgery: A systematic review of prospective long-term studies. *Surg. Obes. Relat. Dis.* **2015**, *11*, 466–473. [CrossRef] [PubMed]
8. Kalarchian, M.A.; Marcus, M.D.; Courcoulas, A.P.; Cheng, Y.; Levine, M.D. Self-report of gastrointestinal side effects after bariatric surgery. *Surg. Obes. Relat. Dis.* **2014**, *10*, 1202–1207. [CrossRef]
9. O'Brien, P.E. Bariatric surgery: Mechanisms, indications and outcomes. *J. Gastroenterol. Hepatol.* **2010**, *25*, 1358–1365. [CrossRef]
10. Balsiger, B.M.; Murr, M.M.; Poggio, J.L.; Sarr, M.G. Bariatric surgery. Surgery for weight control in patients with morbid obesity. *Med. Clin. N. Am.* **2000**, *84*, 477–489. [CrossRef]
11. Peterhansel, C.; Nagl, M.; Wagner, B.; Dietrich, A.; Kersting, A. Predictors of Changes in Health-Related Quality of Life 6 and 12 months After a Bariatric Procedure. *Obes. Surg.* **2017**, *27*, 2120–2128. [CrossRef] [PubMed]
12. Khandalavala, B.N.; Geske, J.; Nirmalraj, M.; Koran-Scholl, J.B.; Neumann-Potash, L.; McBride, C.L. Predictors of Health-Related Quality of Life After Bariatric Surgery. *Obes. Surg.* **2015**, *25*, 2302–2305. [CrossRef] [PubMed]
13. Wimmelmann, C.L.; Dela, F.; Mortensen, E.L. Psychological predictors of mental health and health-related quality of life after bariatric surgery: A review of the recent research. *Obes. Res. Clin. Pract.* **2014**, *8*, e314–e324. [CrossRef] [PubMed]
14. Janik, M.R.; Rogula, T.; Bielecka, I.; Kwiatkowski, A.; Pasnik, K. Quality of Life and Bariatric Surgery: Cross-Sectional Study and Analysis of Factors Influencing Outcome. *Obes. Surg.* **2016**, *26*, 2849–2855. [CrossRef]
15. Cao, Y.; Raoof, M.; Montgomery, S.; Ottosson, J.; Naslund, I. Predicting Long-Term Health-Related Quality of Life after Bariatric Surgery Using a Conventional Neural Network: A Study Based on the Scandinavian Obesity Surgery Registry. *J. Clin. Med.* **2019**, *8*, 2149. [CrossRef]
16. Raoof, M.; Szabo, E.; Karlsson, J.; Näslund, E.; Cao, Y.; Näslund, I. Improvements of health-related quality of life five years after gastric bypass. What is important besides weight loss? A study from Scandinavian Obesity Surgery Register. *Surg. Obes. Relat. Dis.* **2020**, in press. [CrossRef]

17. Cao, Y.; Montgomery, S.; Ottosson, J.; Naslund, E.; Stenberg, E. Deep Learning Neural Networks to Predict Serious Complications After Bariatric Surgery: Analysis of Scandinavian Obesity Surgery Registry Data. *JMIR Med. Inform.* **2020**, *8*, e15992. [CrossRef]
18. Hedenbro, J.L.; Naslund, E.; Boman, L.; Lundegardh, G.; Bylund, A.; Ekelund, M.; Laurenius, A.; Moller, P.; Olbers, T.; Sundbom, M.; et al. Formation of the Scandinavian Obesity Surgery Registry, SOReg. *Obes. Surg.* **2015**, *25*, 1893–1900. [CrossRef]
19. Gerber, P.; Anderin, C.; Szabo, E.; Naslund, I.; Thorell, A. Impact of age on risk of complications after gastric bypass: A cohort study from the Scandinavian Obesity Surgery Registry (SOReg). *Surg. Obes. Relat. Dis.* **2018**, *14*, 437–442. [CrossRef] [PubMed]
20. Stenberg, E.; Cao, Y.; Szabo, E.; Naslund, E.; Naslund, I.; Ottosson, J. Risk Prediction Model for Severe Postoperative Complication in Bariatric Surgery. *Obes. Surg.* **2018**. [CrossRef] [PubMed]
21. Tao, W.; Holmberg, D.; Naslund, E.; Naslund, I.; Mattsson, F.; Lagergren, J.; Ljung, R. Validation of Obesity Surgery Data in the Swedish National Patient Registry and Scandinavian Obesity Registry (SOReg). *Obes. Surg.* **2016**, *26*, 1750–1756. [CrossRef]
22. Hays, R.D.; Morales, L.S. The RAND-36 measure of health-related quality of life. *Ann. Med.* **2001**, *33*, 350–357. [CrossRef]
23. Karlsson, J.; Taft, C.; Sjostrom, L.; Torgerson, J.S.; Sullivan, M. Psychosocial functioning in the obese before and after weight reduction: Construct validity and responsiveness of the Obesity-related Problems scale. *Int. J. Obes.* **2003**, *27*, 617–630. [CrossRef] [PubMed]
24. Ben-Gal, I. *Bayesian Networks*; John Wiley & Sons, Ltd.: Hoboken, NJ, USA, 2008; Volume 1.
25. Scutari, M.; Denis, J.-B. *Bayesian Networks: With Examples in R*; Chapman and Hall/CRC: Boca Raton, FL, USA, 2014.
26. Nagarajan, R.; Scutari, M.; Lèbre, S. *Bayesian Networks in r: With Applications in Systems Biology*; Springer: London, UK, 2013; Volume 48.
27. Grzegorczyk, M. An introduction to Gaussian Bayesian networks. *Methods Mol. Biol.* **2010**, *662*, 121–147. [CrossRef] [PubMed]
28. Pozzi, M.; Der Kiureghian, A. Gaussian Bayesian network for reliability analysis of a system of bridges. In Proceedings of the 11th International Conference on Structural Safety and Reliability, New York, NY, USA, 16 June 2013.
29. Weitzen, S.; Lapane, K.L.; Toledano, A.Y.; Hume, A.L.; Mor, V. Principles for modeling propensity scores in medical research: A systematic literature review. *Pharmacoepidemiol. Drug Saf.* **2004**, *13*, 841–853. [CrossRef] [PubMed]
30. Hartemink, A.J. *Principled Computational Methods for the Validation Discovery of Genetic Regulatory Networks*; Massachusetts Institute of Technology: Cambridge, MA, USA, 2001.
31. Sachs, K.; Perez, O.; Pe'er, D.; Lauffenburger, D.A.; Nolan, G.P. Causal protein-signaling networks derived from multiparameter single-cell data. *Science* **2005**, *308*, 523–529. [CrossRef]
32. Caruana, R.; Niculescu-Mizil, A. Data mining in metric space: An empirical analysis of supervised learning performance criteria. In Proceedings of the Tenth ACM SIGKDD International Conference on Knowledge Discovery and Data Mining, Seattle, WA, USA, 22–25 August 2004; pp. 69–78.
33. Cao, Y.; Fang, X.; Ottosson, J.; Naslund, E.; Stenberg, E. A Comparative Study of Machine Learning Algorithms in Predicting Severe Complications after Bariatric Surgery. *J. Clin. Med.* **2019**, *8*, 668. [CrossRef]
34. Mandrekar, J.N. Receiver operating characteristic curve in diagnostic test assessment. *J. Thorac. Oncol.* **2010**, *5*, 1315–1316. [CrossRef]
35. Marzban, C. The ROC curve and the area under it as performance measures. *Weather Forecast.* **2004**, *19*, 1106–1114. [CrossRef]
36. Scutari, M. Learning Bayesian Networks with the bnlearn R Package. *J. Stat. Softw* **2010**, *35*, 1–22. [CrossRef]
37. Kammerdiner, A.R.; Gupal, A.M.; Pardalos, P.M. Application of Bayesian networks and data mining to biomedical problems. *AIP Conf. Proc.* **2007**, *953*, 132.
38. Lucas, P.J. Biomedical applications of Bayesian networks. In *Advances in Probabilistic Graphical Models*; Springer: Berlin/Heidelberg, Germany, 2007; pp. 333–358.
39. Pearl, J. *Probabilistic Reasoning in Intelligent Systems: Networks of Plausible Inference*; Elsevier: Amsterdam, The Netherlands, 2014.

40. Mani, S.; Valtorta, M.; McDermott, S. Building Bayesian network models in medicine: The MENTOR experience. *Appl. Intell.* **2005**, *22*, 93–108. [CrossRef]
41. Blaine, B. Does depression cause obesity? A meta-analysis of longitudinal studies of depression and weight control. *J. Health Psychol.* **2008**, *13*, 1190–1197. [CrossRef]
42. Hyttinen, A.; Eberhardt, F.; Hoyer, P.O. Learning linear cyclic causal models with latent variables. *J. Mach. Learn. Res.* **2012**, *13*, 3387–3439.
43. Neville, J.; Jensen, D. Relational dependency networks. *J. Mach. Learn. Res.* **2007**, *8*, 653–692.
44. Pontiroli, A.E.; Fossati, A.; Vedani, P.; Fiorilli, M.; Folli, F.; Paganelli, M.; Marchi, M.; Maffei, C. Post-surgery adherence to scheduled visits and compliance, more than personality disorders, predict outcome of bariatric restrictive surgery in morbidly obese patients. *Obes. Surg.* **2007**, *17*, 1492–1497. [CrossRef]
45. Tsushima, W.T.; Bridenstine, M.P.; Balfour, J.F. MMPI-2 scores in the outcome prediction of gastric bypass surgery. *Obes. Surg.* **2004**, *14*, 528–532. [CrossRef]
46. Finks, J.F.; Kole, K.L.; Yenumula, P.R.; English, W.J.; Krause, K.R.; Carlin, A.M.; Genaw, J.A.; Banerjee, M.; Birkmeyer, J.D.; Birkmeyer, N.J.; et al. Predicting risk for serious complications with bariatric surgery: Results from the Michigan Bariatric Surgery Collaborative. *Ann. Surg.* **2011**, *254*, 633–640. [CrossRef]
47. Hayes, M.T.; Hunt, L.A.; Foo, J.; Tychinskaya, Y.; Stubbs, R.S. A model for predicting the resolution of type 2 diabetes in severely obese subjects following Roux-en Y gastric bypass surgery. *Obes. Surg.* **2011**, *21*, 910–916. [CrossRef] [PubMed]
48. Cruz, M.R.; Martins, C.; Dias, J.; Pinto, J.S. A validation of an intelligent decision-making support system for the nutrition diagnosis of bariatric surgery patients. *JMIR Med. Inform.* **2014**, *2*, e8. [CrossRef]
49. Susser, M. What Is a Cause and How Do We Know One-a Grammar for Pragmatic Epidemiology. *Am. J. Epidemiol.* **1991**, *133*, 635–648. [CrossRef]
50. Karhausen, L.R. On the Logic of Causal Inference. *Am. J. Epidemiol.* **1987**, *126*, 556–557. [CrossRef] [PubMed]
51. Li, J.; Shi, J.J.; Satz, D. Modeling and analysis of disease and risk factors through learning Bayesian networks from observational data. *Qual. Reliab. Eng. Int.* **2008**, *24*, 291–302. [CrossRef]
52. Nguefack-Tsague, G. Using bayesian networks to model hierarchical relationships in epidemiological studies. *Epidemiol. Health* **2011**, *33*, e2011006. [CrossRef]
53. Moffa, G.; Catone, G.; Kuipers, J.; Kuipers, E.; Freeman, D.; Marwaha, S.; Lennox, B.R.; Broome, M.R.; Bebbington, P. Using Directed Acyclic Graphs in Epidemiological Research in Psychosis: An Analysis of the Role of Bullying in Psychosis. *Schizophr. Bull.* **2017**, *43*, 1273–1279. [CrossRef] [PubMed]
54. Hess, R.; Thurston, R.C.; Hays, R.D.; Chang, C.C.; Dillon, S.N.; Ness, R.B.; Bryce, C.L.; Kapoor, W.N.; Matthews, K.A. The impact of menopause on health-related quality of life: Results from the STRIDE longitudinal study. *Qual. Life Res.* **2012**, *21*, 535–544. [CrossRef] [PubMed]

© 2020 by the authors. Licensee MDPI, Basel, Switzerland. This article is an open access article distributed under the terms and conditions of the Creative Commons Attribution (CC BY) license (http://creativecommons.org/licenses/by/4.0/).

Article

Prediction of Long-Term Stroke Recurrence Using Machine Learning Models

Vida Abedi [1,2], Venkatesh Avula [1], Durgesh Chaudhary [3], Shima Shahjouei [3], Ayesha Khan [3], Christoph J Griessenauer [3,4], Jiang Li [1] and Ramin Zand [3,*]

1. Department of Molecular and Functional Genomics, Geisinger Health System, Danville, PA 17822, USA; vidaabedi@gmail.com (V.A.); vavula1@geisinger.edu (V.A.); jli@geisinger.edu (J.L.)
2. Biocomplexity Institute, Virginia Tech, Blacksburg, VA 24061, USA
3. Geisinger Neuroscience Institute, Geisinger Health System, Danville, PA 17822, USA; dpchaudhary@geisinger.edu (D.C.); sshahjouei@geisinger.edu (S.S.); akhan2@geisinger.edu (A.K.); cgriessenauer@geisinger.edu (C.J.G.)
4. Research Institute of Neurointervention, Paracelsus Medical University, 5020 Salzburg, Austria
* Correspondence: ramin.zand@gmail.com or rzand@geisinger.edu

Citation: Abedi, V.; Avula, V.; Chaudhary, D.; Shahjouei, S.; Khan, A.; Griessenauer, C.J; Li, J.; Zand, R. Prediction of Long-Term Stroke Recurrence Using Machine Learning Models. *J. Clin. Med.* **2021**, *10*, 1286. https://doi.org/10.3390/jcm10061286

Academic Editor: Nandu Goswami

Received: 30 January 2021
Accepted: 16 March 2021
Published: 20 March 2021

Publisher's Note: MDPI stays neutral with regard to jurisdictional claims in published maps and institutional affiliations.

Copyright: © 2021 by the authors. Licensee MDPI, Basel, Switzerland. This article is an open access article distributed under the terms and conditions of the Creative Commons Attribution (CC BY) license (https://creativecommons.org/licenses/by/4.0/).

Abstract: Background: The long-term risk of recurrent ischemic stroke, estimated to be between 17% and 30%, cannot be reliably assessed at an individual level. Our goal was to study whether machine-learning can be trained to predict stroke recurrence and identify key clinical variables and assess whether performance metrics can be optimized. Methods: We used patient-level data from electronic health records, six interpretable algorithms (Logistic Regression, Extreme Gradient Boosting, Gradient Boosting Machine, Random Forest, Support Vector Machine, Decision Tree), four feature selection strategies, five prediction windows, and two sampling strategies to develop 288 models for up to 5-year stroke recurrence prediction. We further identified important clinical features and different optimization strategies. Results: We included 2091 ischemic stroke patients. Model area under the receiver operating characteristic (AUROC) curve was stable for prediction windows of 1, 2, 3, 4, and 5 years, with the highest score for the 1-year (0.79) and the lowest score for the 5-year prediction window (0.69). A total of 21 (7%) models reached an AUROC above 0.73 while 110 (38%) models reached an AUROC greater than 0.7. Among the 53 features analyzed, age, body mass index, and laboratory-based features (such as high-density lipoprotein, hemoglobin A1c, and creatinine) had the highest overall importance scores. The balance between specificity and sensitivity improved through sampling strategies. Conclusion: All of the selected six algorithms could be trained to predict the long-term stroke recurrence and laboratory-based variables were highly associated with stroke recurrence. The latter could be targeted for personalized interventions. Model performance metrics could be optimized, and models can be implemented in the same healthcare system as intelligent decision support for targeted intervention.

Keywords: healthcare; artificial intelligence; machine learning; interpretable machine learning; explainable machine learning; ischemic stroke; clinical decision support system; electronic health record; outcome prediction; recurrent stroke

1. Introduction

Predictive modeling of stroke, the leading cause of death and long-term disability [1], is crucial due to high individual and societal impact. Each year, about 800,000 people experience a new or recurrent stroke in the United States [2]. It has been estimated that the 5-year risk of stroke recurrence is between 17% and 30% [3,4]. Recurrent stroke has a higher rate of death and disability [5]. Therefore, the identification of patients who are at a higher risk of recurrence can help the care-providers prioritize and define more vigorous secondary prevention plans for those at risk, especially when there are limited resources.

To date several predictive models of recurrent stroke, using regression or other statistical methods, have been developed; however, the clinical utility of these models tends to be limited due to the narrow scope of variables used in these models [6]. In a recent study, multivariable logistic models of 1-year stroke recurrence, developed based on 332 patients, using clinical and retinal characteristics (using 20 variables) have shown promising results with an area under the receiver operating characteristic (AUROC) curve of 0.71–0.74 [7]. Large real-world patient-level data from electronic health records (EHR) and machine learning (ML) methods can be leveraged to capture a greater number of features to help build better prediction models [8]. In a recent study of 2604 patients, ML has been successfully used to predict the favorable outcome following an acute stroke at three months [9]. We also showed that ML can be used for flagging stroke patients in the emergency setting [10–12].

The present study aimed at using rich longitudinal data from EHR to construct an ML-enabled model of long-term (up to 5-years) recurrent stroke. We evaluated Extreme Gradient Boosting (XGBoost), Gradient Boosting Machine (GBM), Random Forest (RF), Support Vector Machine (SVM), and Decision Tree (DT), and benchmarked these algorithms' performance against Logistic Regression (LR) as these are interpretable models and feature importance can be extracted for further validation and assessment by care providers. We hypothesized that (1) all of the modeling algorithms can be trained to predict long-term stroke recurrence, (2) A wide range of clinical features associated with stroke recurrence can be identified, and (3) performance metrics can be improved through sampling processes.

2. Methods

All of the relevant codes developed as well as summary data generated for this project can be found at https://github.com/TheDecodeLab/GNSIS_v1.0/tree/master/ModelingStrokeRecurrence (accessed on 19 March 2021).

2.1. Data Source

Database description and processing: this study was based on the extracted data from the Geisinger EHR system, Geisinger Quality database, and the Social Security Death database to build a stroke database called "Geisinger Neuroscience Ischemic Stroke (GNSIS)" [13]. GNSIS includes demographic, clinical, laboratory data from ischemic stroke patients from September 2003 to May 2019. The study was reviewed and approved by the Geisinger Institutional Review Board to meet "non-human subject research", for using de-identified information.

The GNSIS database was created based on a high-fidelity and data-driven phenotype definition for ischemic stroke developed by our team. The patients were included if they had a primary hospital discharge diagnosis of ischemic stroke; a brain magnetic resonance imaging (MRI) during the same encounter to confirm the diagnosis; and, an overnight stay in the hospital. The diagnoses were based on International Classification of Diseases, Ninth/Tenth Revision, Clinical Modification (ICD-9-CM/ICD-10-CM) codes. For each index stroke, the following data elements were recorded: (1) date of the event, (2) age of the patient at the index stroke, (3) encounter type, (4) ICD code and corresponding primary diagnosis of index stroke, (5) presence or absence (and date) of recurrent stroke, and (6) ICD code and corresponding primary diagnosis for the recurrent stroke. Other data elements include sex, birth date, death date, last medical visit within the Geisinger system, presence or absence of comorbidities, presence or absence of a family history of heart disorders or stroke, and smoking status. In the case of multiple encounters due to recurrent cerebral infarcts, the first hospital encounter was considered as the index (first-time) stroke. To improve the accuracy of comorbidity information based on ICD-9-CM/ICD-10-CM diagnosis, either two outpatient visits or one in-patient visit were used to assign a diagnosis code to a patient. Our database interfaces with the Social Security Death Index on a biweekly basis to reflect updated information on the vital status. The manual validation of a random set of patients, including reviewing the MRI, to ensure all patients in the GNSIS database had a correct diagnosis of acute ischemic stroke indicated a specificity of 100%.

Data pre-processing: Units were verified and reconciled if needed and distributions of variables were assessed over time to ensure data stability. The range for the variables was defined according to expert knowledge and available literature—and outliers were assessed and removed. To ensure that patients were active, the last encounter of patients was recorded.

2.2. Study Population

For this study, we excluded patients with recurrent stroke within 24 days of the index stroke. We organized the included patients into six groups. One control group and five case groups. The control group consisted of patients who did not have a stroke recurrence during the 5-year follow-up. Case groups 1, 2, 3, 4, and 5 comprised of patients who had a recurrent stroke between 24 days and 1, 2, 3, 4, and 5-years, respectively. The 24 day cut-off was selected to ensure that the recurrent stroke was independent of the index stroke; as our data demonstrate, the number of stroke recurrences stabilizes after approximately 24 days (Figure 1A). Nevertheless, we repeated the analysis by including the patients with a stroke recurrence within the 24 days for comparison. Patients with stroke-related or other vascular death might be excluded from this study if they did not meet the inclusion/exclusion criteria stated above.

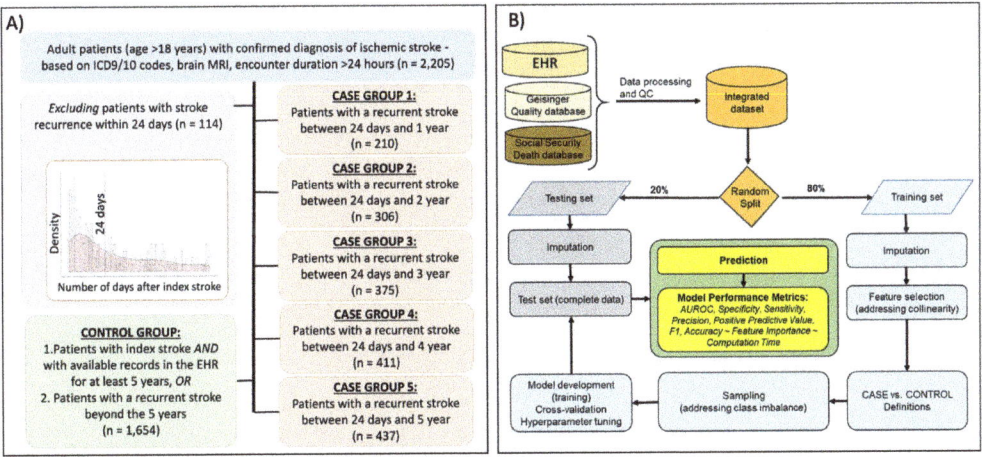

Figure 1. (**A**) Flow-chart of inclusion-exclusion of subjects in cases and control group in the study. Patients in the control group had available records in the electronic health record for at least 5 years and no documented stroke recurrence within 5 years. Distribution panel shows the number of recurrences over time. At 24 days, the number of recurrent cases can be seen to approach a plateau. (**B**) The design strategy for predicting stroke recurrence using electronic health records (EHR), Geisinger Quality database as well as Social Security Death database.

2.3. Data Processing, Feature Extraction, and Sampling

Training-testing set: Each of the cases and control groups was randomly split into 80:20 training and testing sets.

Imputation: A total of 53 features were used. Table 1 includes data on the missingness. Imputation of the missing values was performed separately on training and testing sets using Multivariate Imputation by Chained Equations (MICE) package [14]. The quality of the imputations was examined using t-test, summary statistics, as well as strip and density plots of the missing features to ensure distribution of the variables was comparable before and after imputation. Only four variables suffered from missingness at relatively higher levels.

Table 1. Patient demographics, past medical and family history in different groups. Detailed description of the variables is provided in the Geisinger Neuroscience Ischemic Stroke (GNSIS) study [13]. IQR: interquartile range; HDL: high-density lipoprotein; LDL: low-density lipoprotein.

Patient Characteristics	% Missing	Statistics (All Patients)	Control Group	Case Group 1	Case Group 2	Case Group 3	Case Group 4	Case Group 5
Total number of patients	-	2091	1654	210	306	375	411	437
Age in years, mean (SD)	-	67 (13)	66 (13)	71 (14)	71 (13)	71 (13)	71 (13)	71 (13)
Age in years, median (IQR)	-	68 (58–77)	67 (57–76)	73 (62–83)	72 (63–81)	73 (63–81)	73 (63–81)	73 (63–81)
Male, n (%)	-	1079 (52%)	53%	47%	46%	46%	47%	47%
Body mass index (BMI) in kg/m^2, mean (SD)	2.63%	30 (7)	30 (7)	29 (6)	29 (6)	29 (6)	29 (7)	29 (6)
Body mass index (BMI) in kg/m^2, median [IQR]	2.63%	29 (26–33)	29 (26–33)	28 (24–32)	28 (25–32)	28 (25–32)	28 (25–32)	28 (25–32)
Diastolic Blood Pressure, mean (SD)	31.90%	76 (12)	76 (12)	75 (13)	75 (12)	75 (12)	75 (12)	74 (12)
Systolic Blood Pressure, mean (SD)	31.90%	137 (22)	136 (22)	139 (26)	139 (25)	140 (24)	139 (24)	139 (24)
Hemoglobin (Unit: g/dL), mean (SD)	1.82%	14 (2)	14 (2)	13 (2)	14 (2)	14 (2)	14 (2)	14 (2)
Hemoglobin A1c (Unit: %), mean (SD)	25.11%	7 (2)	7 (2)	7 (2)	7 (2)	7 (2)	7 (2)	7 (2)
HDL (Unit: mg/dL), mean (SD)	5.40%	47 (15)	47 (15)	45 (13)	45 (14)	45 (14)	45 (14)	45 (14)
LDL (Unit: mg/dL), mean (SD)	5.79%	102 (40)	103 (40)	103 (44)	100 (43)	101 (42)	101 (41)	100 (41)
Platelet (Unit: 10^3/uL), mean (SD)	1.82%	232 (77)	233 (76)	227 (70)	229 (73)	231 (80)	230 (78)	229 (78)
White blood cell (Unit: 10^3/uL), mean (SD)	1.82%	9 (3)	9 (3)	8 (3)	8 (3)	9 (3)	9 (3)	9 (3)
Creatinine (Unit: mg/dL), mean (SD)	2.58%	1 (1)	1 (0.5)	1 (1)	1 (1)	1 (1)	1 (1)	1 (1)
Current smoker, n (%)	-	288 (14%)	14 (1)	12 (6)	12 (4)	13 (3)	13 (3)	13 (3)
Difference in days between Last outpatient visit prior to index date and index date, mean (SD)	26.16%	347 (726)	345 (691)	371 (882)	354 (846)	369 (855)	352 (826)	354 (840)
MEDICAL HISTORY, n (%)								
Atrial flutter		41 (2%)	28 (2%)	4 (2%)	9 (3%)	11 (3%)	13 (3%)	13 (3%)
Atrial fibrillation		319 (15%)	230 (14%)	35 (17%)	55 (18%)	72 (19%)	82 (20%)	89 (20%)
Atrial fibrillation/flutter		324 (15%)	233 (14%)	36 (17%)	56 (18%)	74 (20%)	84 (20%)	91 (21%)
Chronic Heart failure (CHF)		159 (8%)	103 (6%)	33 (16%)	42 (14%)	49 (13%)	53 (13%)	56 (13%)

Table 1. Cont.

Patient Characteristics	% Missing	Statistics (All Patients)	Control Group	Case Group 1	Case Group 2	Case Group 3	Case Group 4	Case Group 5
Chronic kidney disease		223 (11%)	142 (9%)	55 (26%)	68 (22%)	74 (20%)	78 (19%)	81 (19%)
Chronic liver disease		35 (2%)	23 (1%)	2 (1%)	7 (2%)	10 (3%)	11 (3%)	12 (3%)
Chronic liver disease (mild)		33 (2%)	21 (1%)	2 (1%)	7 (2%)	10 (3%)	11 (3%)	12 (3%)
Chronic liver disease (moderate to severe)		7 (0.3%)	5 (0.3%)	0 (0%)	1 (0.3%)	1 (0.3%)	2 (0.5%)	2 (0.5%)
Chronic lung diseases		391 (19%)	296 (18%)	51 (24%)	70 (23%)	83 (22%)	92 (22%)	95 (22%)
Diabetes		615 (29%)	439 (27%)	86 (41%)	122 (40%)	151 (40%)	165 (40%)	176 (40%)
Dyslipidemia		1298 (62%)	994 (60%)	142 (68%)	211 (69%)	258 (69%)	285 (69%)	304 (70%)
Hypertension		1495 (72%)	1150 (70%)	168 (80%)	240 (78%)	293 (78%)	327 (80%)	345 (79%)
Myocardial infarction		215 (10%)	159 (10%)	30 (14%)	43 (14%)	51 (14%)	53 (13%)	56 (13%)
Neoplasm		284 (14%)	211 (13%)	35 (17%)	49 (16%)	61 (16%)	65 (16%)	73 (17%)
Hypercoagulable		29 (1%)	24 (1%)	4 (2%)	4 (1%)	5 (1%)	5 (1%)	5 (1%)
Peripheral vascular disease		313 (15%)	219 (13%)	46 (22%)	65 (21%)	75 (20%)	88 (21%)	94 (22%)
Patent Foramen Ovale		241 (12%)	184 (11%)	30 (14%)	41 (13%)	47 (13%)	53 (13%)	57 (13%)
Rheumatic diseases		76 (4%)	53 (3%)	11 (5%)	14 (5%)	18 (5%)	21 (5%)	23 (5%)
FAMILY HISTORY								
Heart disorder		943 (45%)	747 (45%)	85 (40%)	130 (42%)	165 (44%)	182 (44%)	196 (45%)
Stroke		361 (17%)	279 (17%)	39 (19%)	60 (20%)	72 (19%)	77 (19%)	82 (19%)

Feature selection: We performed feature selection using different strategies. The feature sets were: Set 1: all features; Set 2: all features except medication history; Set 3: features selected by at least two data-driven strategies; and Set 4: minimum set, obtained as the intersect of Set 2 and Set 3 (Table S1). The full set of features (Sets 1, 2) were selected based on clinical expertise and previous studies [6,15]. Feature selection (Sets 3, 4) was performed based on three data-driven approaches for each set of case-control.

The data-driven approaches were: (1) filter-based methods including Pearson correlation [16] and univariate filtering; (2) embedded methods including RF [17] and Lasso Regression [18]; and (3) wrapper methods including the Boruta algorithm [19] and recursive feature elimination. Feature importance scores were scaled between zero and 100, with higher scores representing higher variable contributions. Using the reduced set of features will ensure variables with high collinearity are removed.

Sampling: The training dataset after applying the case-control definition was imbalanced. Many of the classification models trained on class-imbalanced data are biased towards the majority class. To avoid poor performance of minority class (recurrent stroke) compared with the dominant class, we balanced out the number of cases and controls by up-sampling and down-sampling methods. We applied the up-sampling method to the prediction window with the lowest and median rate of stroke recurrence and down-sampling to the prediction window with the median rate of stroke recurrence. In the up-sampling, we used the Synthetic Minority Over-sampling Technique (SMOTE) [19]. In the down-sampling, we randomly selected patients from the control group.

2.4. Model Development and Testing

We used six interpretable ML algorithms and four feature sets to develop a classification model for 1, 2, 3, 4, and 5-year recurrence prediction window. We developed 24 models for each prediction window. The ML algorithms included LR [20], XGBoost [21], GBM [22], RF [17], SVM [23], and DT [24]. We included SVM, LR, and DT as these could provide benchmarking metrics as well as better flexibility in terms of implementation into cloud-based EHR vendors. Therefore, simpler and faster models could provide strategic alternatives for future implementation if the results from this study indicate, similar to other studies [25], that by including a large number of features, models can reach convergence to the point of algorithm indifference (or marginal improvements). A parameter grid was built to train the model with 10-fold repeated CV with 10 repeats. Furthermore, 5-fold repeated CV for the prediction window with the median rate of stroke recurrence was also performed. Model tuning was performed by an automatic grid search with 10 different values to try for each algorithm parameter randomly. For each model, we used 20% of the data for model testing and calculated specificity, recall (sensitivity), precision (positive predictive value, PPV), AUROC, F1 score, accuracy, and computation time for model training. The modeling pipeline is summarized in Figure 1B.

3. Results

All of the detailed summary results with comprehensive performance metrics, feature importance and computation time for the 288 models this project are provided as Supplementary Information (see Tables S1–S3).

3.1. Patient Population and Characteristics

A total of 2091 adult patients met the inclusion criteria; 114 patients had a recurrent stroke within 24 days from their index stroke and were excluded from the analysis (Figure 1A). Out of 2091 patients, 51.6% were men. The median age was 68.1 years (IQR (interquartile range) = 58–77). The three most common comorbidities were hypertension (72%), dyslipidemia (62%), and diabetes (29%). Table 1 includes the patients' demographics and past medical history. The rate of stroke recurrence was 11%, 16%, 18%, 20%, and 21% at 1, 2, 3, 4, and 5-year window, respectively.

This study was based on 53 features. Table S1 summarizes the results from the feature selection process. Age, sex, BMI, systolic blood pressure, hemoglobin, high-density lipoprotein (HDL), creatinine, smoking status, chronic heart failure, chronic kidney disease, diabetes, hypertension, and peripheral vascular disease were selected by all of the different data-driven approaches for the five different case-control designs.

3.2. Models Can Be Trained to Predict the Long-Term Stroke Recurrence

Model AUROC was stable for the five case-control designs with the highest score for the 1-year prediction window and the lowest score for the 5-year window (Figure 2, Table S2). The best AUROC for the 1-year prediction window was 0.79 (Table S2, model#63). The top ten models (AUROC: 0.79–0.74) were from the 1-year prediction window. The best AUROC for the 2, 3, 4 and 5-year prediction windows were 0.70, 0.73, 0.73, and 0.69 respectively. Furthermore, when comparing features included in the models, the AUROC was highest when all of the features were used. The variation in AUROC was higher across the various study window and feature sets for DT, while the score variance was lowest for RF. The ROC curve for the different models is shown in Figure 3 for the 1-year prediction window.

Based on the accuracy, RF (RF, mtry = 14) model, using 26 features (Set3), had the best performance for a 1-year prediction window (accuracy: 90% (95% CI: 86%–92%), PPV: 80%, specificity: 100%). The average accuracy by using the six models and four sets of features was 88% (Table S2, model numbers 1–24). The prediction accuracy decreased as the prediction window widened to 2-years (average accuracy: 85%) with the best accuracy score reached by LR (86%, 95% CI: 82%–89%) and PPV of 80% with a specificity of 99%, Table S2 model number 79. The average accuracy of the 3-year prediction window was 82% for the 4-year prediction window. The average accuracy of the 5-year prediction window was 78%.

Out of the 24 models for the 1-year prediction window, one model reached a perfect PPV, while 11 models reached a 100% specificity. For the 2-year prediction window, 7 out of the 24 models reached a PPV of 100% while 9 reached a specificity of 100%. Overall, models based on all features had higher PPV. Model sensitivity and specificity had the best tradeoff when GBM was used. The highest model sensitivity was achieved using both DT and GBM, while the best specificity was achieved using RF, SVM, and XGBoost. When we compared the 3-year prediction window with and without the 24 days cut-off, the average AUROC, sensitivity, and specificity were unaffected; however, the average model accuracy was reduced by 5% when excluding the 24 days interval. Detailed performance metrics for the 288 models are presented in Table S2.

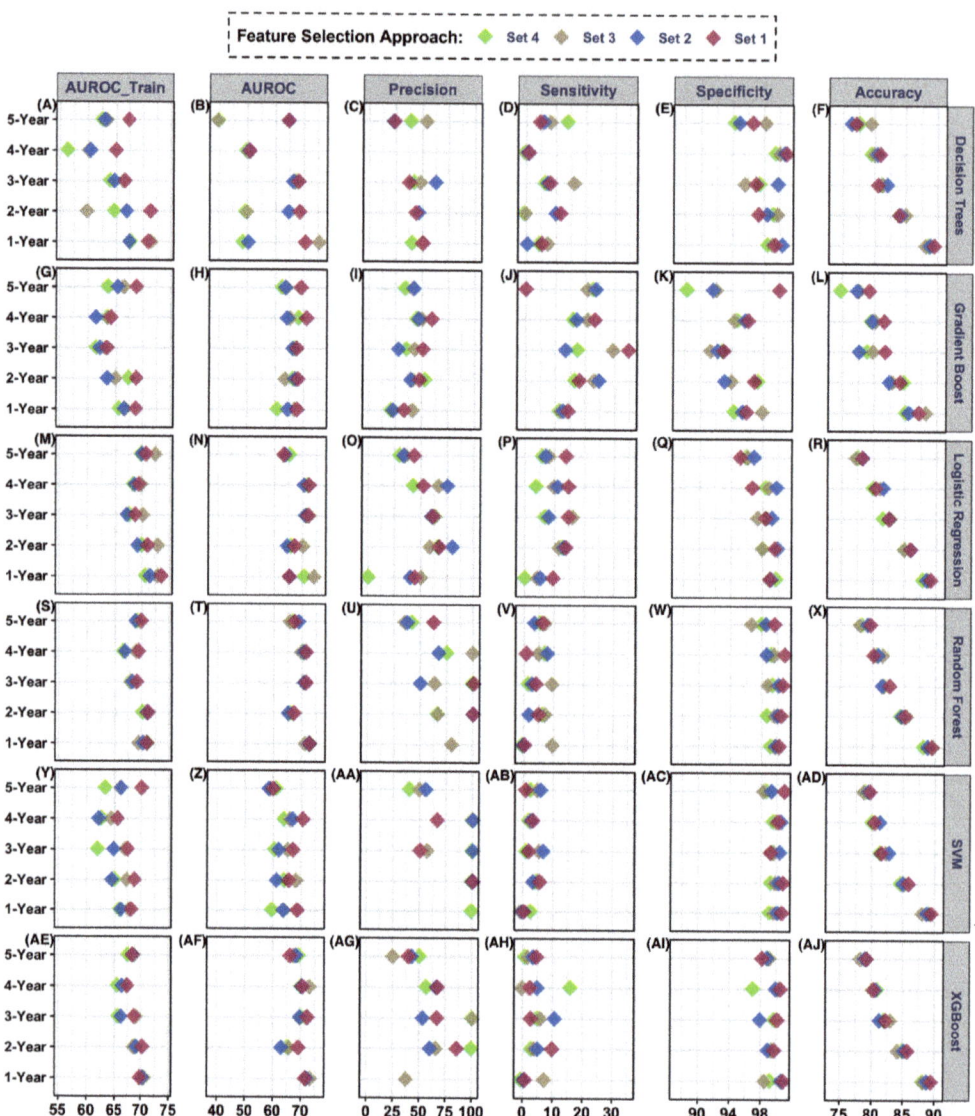

Figure 2. Model performance summaries for the five different prediction windows, six different classifiers, and four feature selection approaches. Performance metrics for (**A–F**) Decision tree, (**G–L**) Gradient Boost, (**M–R**) Logistic Regression, (**S–X**) Random Forest, (**Y–AD**) SVM, and (**AE–AJ**) XGBoost.

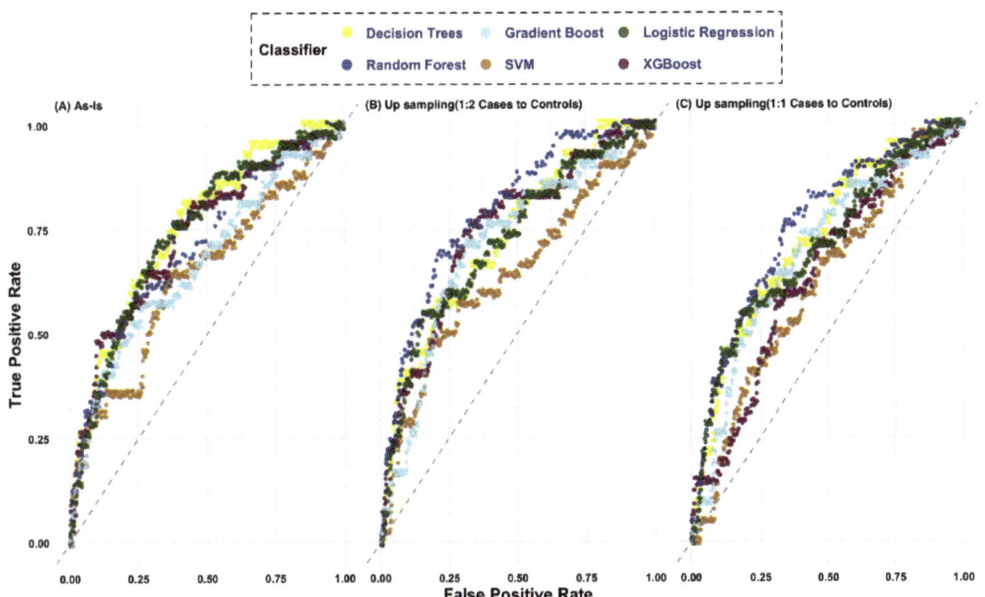

Figure 3. Area under the receiver operating characteristic (AROC) curve using six classifiers for the 1-year prediction window. The feature Set 3 is used for this figure. (**A**) Model without sampling; (**B**) Model with up-sampling at a 1:2 ratio; (**C**) Model with up-sampling at a 1:1 ratio. The best performer model (AUROC of 0.79) is when up-sampling is used with Random Forest algorithm (panel B).

3.3. Age, BMI, and Laboratory Values Highly Associated with Stroke Recurrence

Age and BMI had the highest overall feature importance at 90% ± 5% and 58 ± 10%, respectively. Laboratory values specifically LDL, HDL, platelets, hemoglobin A1c, creatinine, white blood cell, and hemoglobin were highly ranked in our different modeling frameworks. The feature importance of laboratory-based features ranged from 49% ± 10% to 39% ± 11% for HDL and platelet, respectively. Laboratory values had an average feature importance score of 44%, the highest among the different feature categories. Medications (statin, antihypertensive, warfarin, and antiplatelet), were also important features. Figure 4 (and Table S3) includes the feature importance of different models and the overall average feature importance across the models and different prediction windows. The difference in days between the last outpatient visit before the index date and index date (45% ± 12%) and certain comorbidities were other important features for the recurrence models.

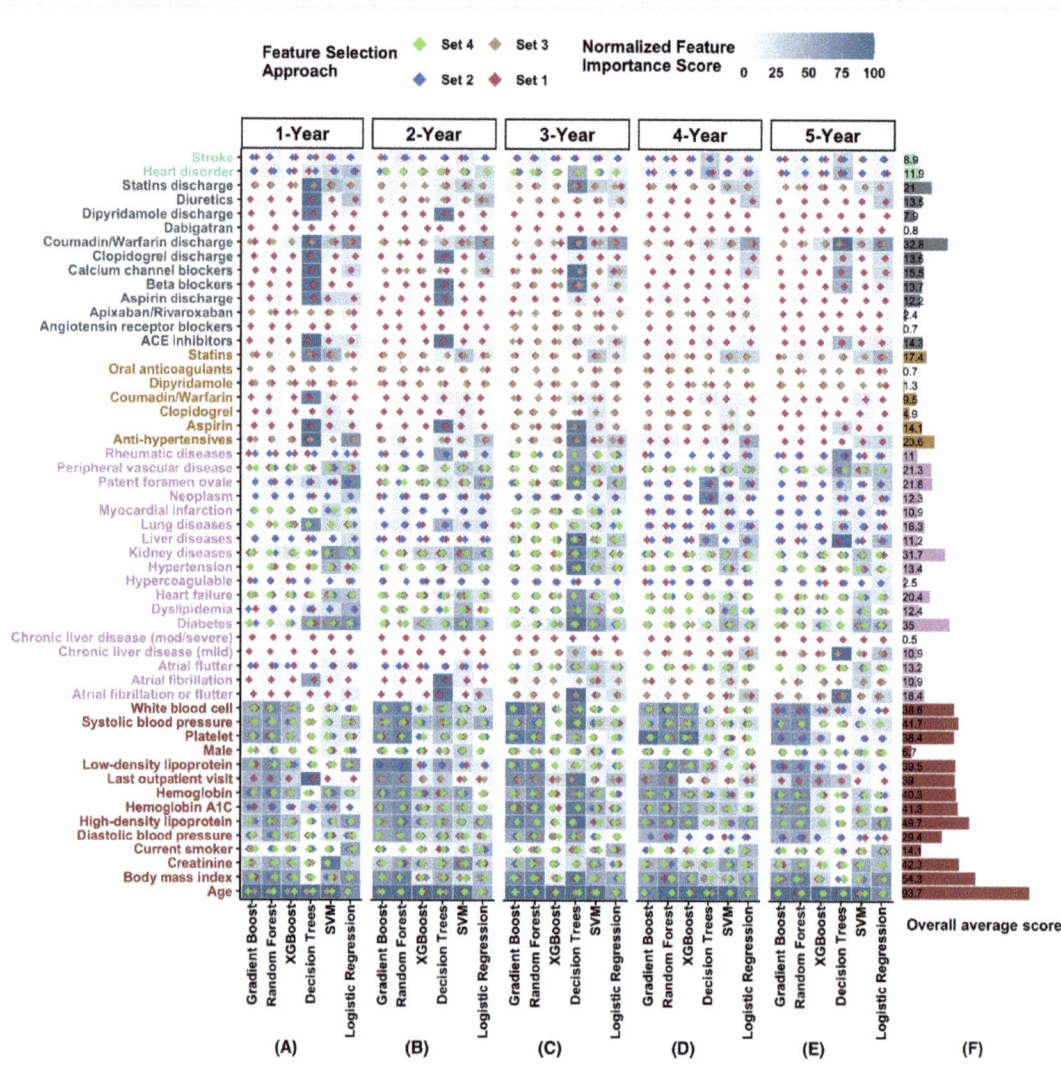

Figure 4. Feature importance based on the different trained models. (**A–E**) Six different classifiers (Gradient Boost, Random Forest, Extreme Gradient Boosting (XGBoost), Decision Trees, Support Vector Machine (SVM), and Logistic Regression) and five different prediction windows were used. (**F**) Average feature importance score across the different models and prediction windows.

3.4. Models' Performance Metrics Improved through Sampling Strategies

Given the low prevalence of recurrent stroke in our dataset (11–21%), we applied up- and down-sampling to the training dataset for the prediction window prior to the model training.

The application of up-sampling the minority class using 1:2 and 1:1 ratio for the 1-year prediction window improved the sensitivity to 55% while only slightly affecting the specificity to 91%. The model AUROC averaged 0.67 before up-sampling to 0.68 after up-sampling with five of the models reaching an AUROC above 0.75. The AUROC of the test set for the 3-year prediction window remained at 0.69 while the AUROC of the training set improved as expected with up-sampling (Figure 5, Table S2).

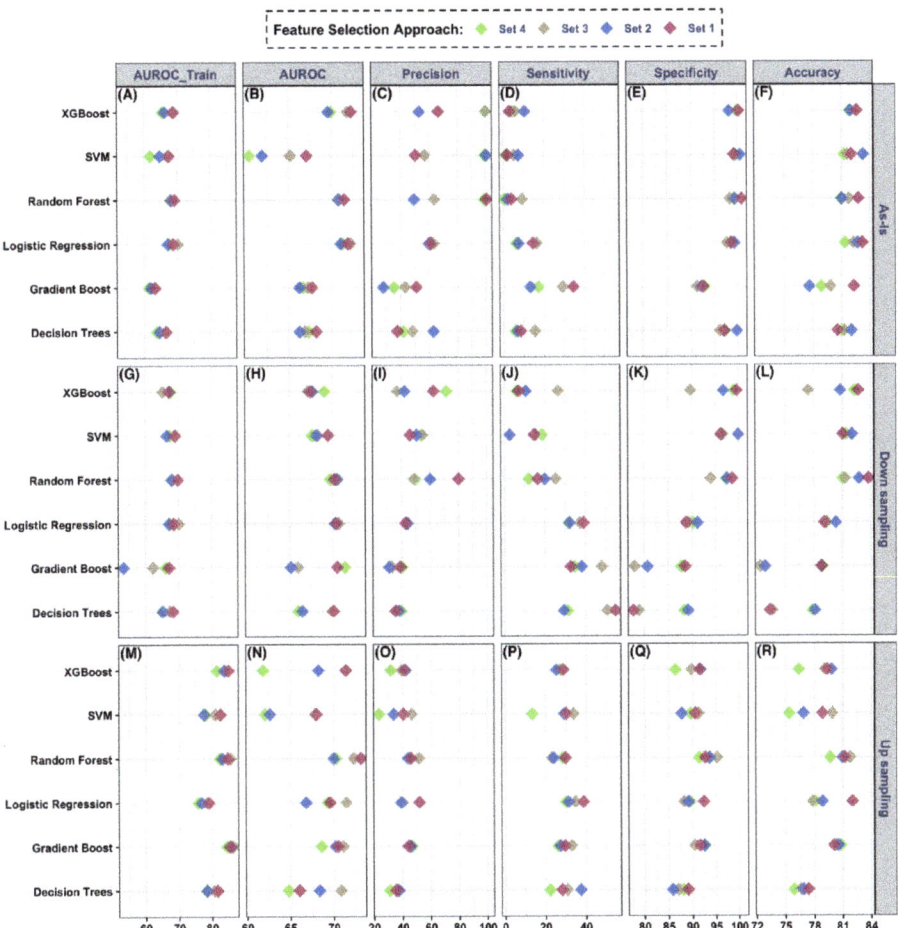

Figure 5. Model Performance summaries with sampling-based optimization for the 1 and 3-year prediction window. Up-sampling using was performed using the Synthetic Minority Over-sampling Technique (SMOTE). The feature Set 3 is used for this figure. (**A–F**) Model without sampling; (**G–L**) Model with down-sampling; (**M–R**) Model with up-sampling.

4. Discussion

We have taken a comprehensive approach to develop and optimize interpretable models of long-term stroke recurrence. We have shown that (1) the six algorithms used could be trained to predict the long-term stroke recurrence, (2) many of the clinical features that were highly associated with stroke recurrence could be actionable, and (3) model performance metrics could be optimized.

There have been multiple clinical scores developed for predicting recurrence after cerebral ischemia with limited clinical utility [6]. Among all, only Stroke Prognostic Instrument (SPI-II) [26] and Essen Stroke Risk Score (ESRS) [27] were designed to predict the long-term (up to 2-years) risk of recurrence after an ischemic stroke. SPI-II can be applied to patients with transient ischemic attack (TIA) and minor strokes; yet, ESRS application focuses on stroke. The main limitations of SPI-II are focusing on patients with suspected carotid TIA or minor stroke, developed using a cohort of 142 patients. The ESRS, derived from the stroke subgroup of the clopidogrel versus aspirin among patients at risk of ischemic events (CAPRIE) trial, includes only eight parameters. In a validation study, the PPV for each tool were low, raising questions about their utility [28–30]. Previous validation studies of SPI-II demonstrated a c-statistic of 0.62 to 0.65, which can be judged as only fair [26,31,32]. In addition, SPI-II has poor performance in stratifying recurrent stroke in isolation as compared with the composite of recurrent stroke and death. The above demonstrates that the SPI-II score's performance is driven mostly by its ability to predict mortality not a recurrence. There is an unmet need for better predictive measures of long-term prediction given the high rate and devastating consequences of a recurrent stroke. Other studies over the past few years have shown the power of ML in predicting short and long-term outcomes in various complex diseases [8,9,25].

4.1. Models Could Be Trained to Predict the Long-Term Stroke Recurrence

Our results showed that a high-quality training dataset with a rich set of variables can be utilized to develop models of recurrent stroke. Among the 288 models, prediction of stroke recurrence within a 1-year prediction window had an AUROC of 0.79, an accuracy of 88% (95% CI: 84%–91%), PPV of 42%, and specificity of 96% using RF with up-sampling the training dataset (Table S2, model number 63). The LR-based models have similar results when compared to more complex algorithms such as XGBoost or RF. Our results showed that 21 (7%) models reached an AUROC above 0.73 while 110 (38%) models reached an AUROC above 0.7. Furthermore, the AUROC for the training and testing dataset were within a similar range which corroborates that models were not suffering from over-fitting. As expected, a model based on LR took a fraction of the time for training when compared to XGBoost, RF, or SVM (Table S2).

We tested the prediction window for up to 5-years. Our results showed that the average model accuracy declined from 85% for the 1-year window to 78% for the 5-year window. However, the shorter prediction window provided the lowest rate of recurrence and therefore highest data imbalance, affecting model performance. The average model sensitivity increased as the prediction window widened, likely due to the increase in sample size and recurrent stroke rate. The optimal prediction window could depend on the richness of longitudinal data used for model training, in our dataset, that was between 2 and 4-years.

4.2. Clinical Features Highly Associated with Stroke Recurrence

In this study, 53 features were used as the full set (set1), followed by a subset of features excluding medication history (Set 2, 31 features). We also applied feature selection and created data-driven features (Set 3) and a minimum set of features (Set 4) for comparison. In most of the experiments more comprehensive feature set led to higher model performance, even though some features had some level of collinearity. In general, baseline clinical features, such as age, BMI, and laboratory values were among the most important features. Our results also highlighted that the last outpatient visit before the index stroke was important for the prediction of recurrence; patients in the control group had the lowest average number of days when compared to the five different case groups.

Analyzing the feature importance revealed that in general laboratory values were highly influential in the prediction models. The pattern of the importance of features was similar when considering different prediction windows, with many comorbidities and medications having the lowest relative impact. Laboratory values (LDL, HDL, platelets, HbA1c, creatinine, and hemoglobin), and blood pressure have shown to be high-ranking for all of the five different prediction windows and all of the different modeling framework with few exceptions. This finding highlights the fact that these potentially actionable features (e.g., HbA1c) may have more importance when compared to the corresponding comorbidities in the patient's chart. The binary nature of medical history without the corresponding measures may have limited power in predicting recurrence. However, one of the main limitations of using more comprehensive laboratory values is missingness, especially when the missing is not completely at random.

4.3. Model Performance Metrics Optimized Based on the Target Goals

We have also shown that model performance metrics, such as specificity and sensitivity can be optimized based on the availability of resources and institutional priorities. We were able to improve the sensitivity of the models for the 1 and 3-year prediction window by sampling the training dataset to address the data imbalance. The tradeoff between specificity and sensitivity was of special interest given that different healthcare systems likely have different constraints, availability of resources, and infrastructures to implement preventive strategies to reduce stroke burden. Some of the resources may include, the number of providers needed to schedule follow up appointments or to discuss medication plans and ensure that the patient is compliant; or availability of resources to provide home-care or telehealth for patients needing those services for continuity of care. Thus, optimizing sensitivity and specificity should be aligned with the institution's priorities. Here we demonstrated that sampling strategies could be useful tools in achieving optimal tradeoffs by increasing the sensitivity of the models up to 55% even with a low rate of stroke recurrence.

4.4. Study Strengths, Limitations, and Future Directions

The EHR data used in model development was longitudinally rich. However, that also leads to some of the study limitations. There is an inherent noise associated with the use of administrative datasets such as EHR, including biased patient selection and lack of information regarding stroke severity captured for approximately half of the patients. However, separate logistic regression models were employed to study the association of NIHSS with one-year stroke recurrence and did not show any association (OR: 1.01, 95% CI: 0.97–1.05, p = 0.625). Our phenotype definition to extract patients with stroke was strict, leading to 100% specificity on a randomly selected sample, which also means that our criteria likely missed some of the cases (for instance, if the patient had some MRI contraindication). Nevertheless, MRI is part of our stroke order-set and is performed for every stroke patient unless the patient refuses or has a contraindication (e.g., non-compatible pacemaker, etc.). We also did not include transient ischemic attacks since it is associated with significant misdiagnosis [33].

As future directions, we are expanding this study at two different levels by including additional layers of data and improving the model and model optimization. We are expanding the GNSIS dataset by incorporating a larger number of laboratory-based features; unstructured data from clinical notes such as signs and symptoms during the initial phases of patient evaluation; information about stroke subtypes; and genetic information from a subset of patients enrolled in the MyCode initiative [34]. We are also expanding our modeling strategies by (1) improving the imputation for laboratory values for EHR mining [35,36], which could improve patient representation and reduce algorithmic bias; (2) applying natural language processing to expand the feature set from clinical notes; (3) developing polygenic risk score [37] using genetic information from a subset of our GNSIS cohort; (4) improving model parameter optimization using sensitivity analysis (SA)-based approaches [38–41]; and (5) expanding the study by incorporating more advanced methodologies, including deep learning models to compare with binary classification developed in this study. Finally, we are planning on developing models that account for the competing risk of death and other major vascular events in addition to ischemic stroke.

In conclusion, predicting long term stroke recurrence is an unmet need with high clinical impact for improved outcomes. Using rich longitudinal data from EHR and optimized ML models, we have been able to develop models of stroke recurrence for different prediction windows. Model performance metrics could be optimized and implemented in the same healthcare system as an intelligent decision support system to improve outcomes. Even though validating the model in patients recruited at a later time point could be done within the Geisinger system, external validation will be necessary to predict how the model predictions may be affected with regard to other health care systems and patient demographics. External validation to assess generalizability and identify potential biases will be an important next step of this study as well. Finally, based on our findings, we recommend that studies aimed at using ML for the prediction of stroke recurrence should leverage more than one modeling framework, ideally including also logistic regression as benchmarking framework for comparison.

Supplementary Materials: The following are available online at https://www.mdpi.com/2077-0383/10/6/1286/s1, Table S1. Feature selection applied to cases and controls based on four criteria. Set 1: all features; Set 2: all features except medication history; Set 3: features selected by at least two data-driven strategies; Set 4: minimum set, obtained as the intersect of Set 2 and Set 3; Table S2. Comprehensive model performance measures for the 288 prediction models. https://www.dropbox.com/s/4h4qr6ivi1z9bt9/Final_Table_A2.xlsx?dl=0 (accessed on 19 March 2021). The file is too large for a word document. The file can be added to the GitHub folder if it cannot be added as an Excel supplemental document; Table S3. Feature importance ranking for the different modeling frameworks.

Author Contributions: Conception and design of the study: V.A. (Vida Abedi) and R.Z. Acquisition and analysis of data: V.A. (Vida Abedi), V.A. (Venkatesh Avula), D.C., A.K., and R.Z. Interpretation of the findings: V.A. (Vida Abedi), V.A. (Venkatesh Avula), D.C., J.L., S.S., C.J.G., and R.Z. Drafting a significant portion of the manuscript or figures: V.A. (Vida Abedi), V.A. (Venkatesh Avula), and R.Z. Resources and Supervision: V.A. (Vida Abedi) and R.Z. All authors have read and agreed to the published version of the manuscript.

Funding: This study had no specific funding. Vida Abedi had financial support from the Defense Threat Reduction Agency (DTRA) grant No. HDTRA1-18-1-0008 and funds from the National Institute of Health (NIH) grant No. R56HL116832 during the study period. Ramin Zand had financial research support from Bucknell University Initiative Program, ROCHE–Genentech Biotechnology Company, the Geisinger Health Plan Quality fund, and receives institutional support from Geisinger Health System during the study period.

Institutional Review Board Statement: The study was reviewed and approved by the Geisinger Institutional Review Board to meet "non-human subject research", for using de-identified information.

Informed Consent Statement: The study was reviewed and approved by the Geisinger Institutional Review Board to meet "non-human subject research", for using de-identified information. Informed consent was not required.

Data Availability Statement: The data analyzed in this study are not publicly available due to privacy and security concerns. The data may be shared with a third party upon execution of data sharing agreement for reasonable requests; such requests should be addressed to Vida Abedi or Ramin Zand. Codes and additional meta-data, summary plots, and information can be found at https://github.com/TheDecodeLab/GNSIS_v1.0/tree/master/ModelingStrokeRecurrence (accessed on 19 March 2021).

Conflicts of Interest: The authors declare no conflict of interest.

Abbreviations

AUROC	Area Under the Receiver Operating Characteristic Curve
CI	Confidence Interval
CV	Cross-Validation
DT	Decision Tree
EHR	Electronic Health Records
ESRS	Essen Stroke Risk Score
GBM	Gradient Boosting Machine
GNSIS	Geisinger Neuroscience Ischemic Stroke
HbA1c	Hemoglobin A1c

HDL	High-Density Lipoprotein
ICD-9/10-CM	International Classification of Diseases, Ninth/Tenth Revision, Clinical Modification
IQR	Interquartile Range
LDL	Low-Density Lipoprotein
LR	Logistic Regression
MICE	Multivariate Imputation by Chained Equations
ML	Machine Learning
MRI	Magnetic Resonance Imaging
NIHSS	National Institutes of Health Stroke Scale
OR	Odds Ratios
PPV	Positive Predictive Value
RF	Random Forest
SA	Sensitivity Analysis
SMOTE	Synthetic Minority Over-sampling Technique
SPI-II	Stroke Prognostic Instrument
SVM	Support Vector Machines
XGBoost	Extreme Gradient Boosting

References

1. Katan, M.; Luft, A. Global Burden of Stroke. *Semin. Neurol.* **2018**, *38*, 208–211. [CrossRef] [PubMed]
2. Benjamin, E.J.; Blaha, M.J.; Chiuve, S.E.; Cushman, M.; Das, S.R.; de Ferranti, S.D.; Floyd, J.; Fornage, M.; Gillespie, C.; Isasi, C.R.; et al. Heart disease and stroke statistics—2017 update a report from the American heart association. *Circulation* **2017**, *135*, e146–e603. [CrossRef] [PubMed]
3. Burn, J.; Dennis, M.; Bamford, J.; Sandercock, P.; Wade, D.; Warlow, C. Long-term risk of recurrent stroke after a first-ever stroke. The Oxfordshire Community Stroke Project. *Stroke* **1994**, *25*, 333–337. [CrossRef] [PubMed]
4. Hillen, T.; Coshall, C.; Tilling, K.; Rudd, A.G.; McGovern, R.; Wolfe, C.D. Cause of Stroke Recurrence Is Multifactorial. *Stroke* **2003**, *34*, 1457–1463. [CrossRef] [PubMed]
5. Samsa, G.P.; Bian, J.; Lipscomb, J.; Matchar, D.B. Epidemiology of Recurrent Cerebral Infarction. *Stroke* **1999**, *30*, 338–349. [CrossRef]
6. Chaudhary, D.; Abedi, V.; Li, J.; Schirmer, C.M.; Griessenauer, C.J.; Zand, R. Clinical Risk Score for Predicting Recurrence Following a Cerebral Ischemic Event. *Front. Neurol.* **2019**, *10*, 1106. [CrossRef] [PubMed]
7. Yuanyuan, Z.; Jiaman, W.; Yimin, Q.; Haibo, Y.; Weiqu, Y.; Zhuoxin, Y. Comparison of Prediction Models based on Risk Factors and Retinal Characteristics Associated with Recurrence One Year after Ischemic Stroke. *J. Stroke Cerebrovasc. Dis.* **2020**, *29*, 104581. [CrossRef] [PubMed]
8. Noorbakhsh-Sabet, N.; Zand, R.; Zhang, Y.; Abedi, V. Artificial Intelligence Transforms the Future of Health Care. *Am. J. Med.* **2019**, *132*, 795–801. [CrossRef]
9. Heo, J.; Yoon, J.G.; Park, H.; Kim, Y.D.; Nam, H.S.; Heo, J.H. Machine Learning–Based Model for Prediction of Outcomes in Acute Stroke. *Stroke* **2019**, *50*, 1263–1265. [CrossRef]
10. Abedi, V.; Goyal, N.; Tsivgoulis, G.; Hosseinichimeh, N.; Hontecillas, R.; Bassaganya-Riera, J.; Elijovich, L.; Metter, J.E.; Alexandrov, A.W.; Liebeskind, D.S.; et al. Novel Screening Tool for Stroke Using Artificial Neural Network. *Stroke* **2017**, *48*, 1678–1681. [CrossRef]
11. Stanciu, A.; Banciu, M.; Sadighi, A.; Marshall, K.A.; Holland, N.R.; Abedi, V.; Zand, R. A predictive analytics model for differentiating between transient ischemic attacks (TIA) and its mimics. *BMC Med. Infor. Decis. Mak.* **2020**, *20*, 112. [CrossRef]
12. Abedi, V.; Khan, A.; Chaudhary, D.; Misra, D.; Avula, V.; Mathrawala, D.; Kraus, C.; Marshall, K.A.; Chaudhary, N.; Li, X.; et al. Using artificial intelligence for improving stroke diagnosis in emergency departments: A practical framework. *Ther. Adv. Neurol. Disord.* **2020**, *13*, 1–8. [CrossRef] [PubMed]
13. Chaudhary, D.; Khan, A.; Shahjouei, S.; Gupta, M.; Lambert, C.; Avula, V.; Schirmer, C.M.; Holland, N.; Griessenauer, C.J.; Azarpazhooh, M.R.; et al. Trends in ischemic stroke outcomes in a rural population in the United States. *J. Neurol. Sci.* **2021**, *422*, 117339. [CrossRef] [PubMed]
14. Van Buuren, S.; Groothuis-Oudshoorn, K. mice. Multivariate Imputation by Chained Equations in R. *J. Stat. Softw.* **2011**, *45*, 1–67. Available online: https://www.jstatsoft.org/v45/i03/ (accessed on 19 March 2021). [CrossRef]
15. Kernan, W.N.; Ovbiagele, B.; Black, H.R.; Bravata, D.M.; Chimowitz, M.I.; Ezekowitz, M.D.; Fang, M.C.; Fisher, M.; Furie, K.L.; Heck, D.V.; et al. Guidelines for the Prevention of Stroke in Patients with Stroke and Transient Ischemic Attack: A Guideline for Healthcare Professionals from the American Heart Association/American Stroke Association. *Stroke* **2014**, *45*, 2160–2236. [CrossRef]
16. R Core Team. *R: A Language and Environment for Statistical Computing*; R Foundation for Statistical Computing: Vienna, Austria, 2018; Available online: https://www.R-project.org (accessed on 19 March 2021).
17. Liaw, A.; Wiener, M. Classification and Regression by randomForest. *R News* **2002**, *2*, 18–22.

18. Friedman, J.H.; Hastie, T.; Tibshirani, R. Regularization Paths for Generalized Linear Models via Coordinate Descent. *J. Stat. Softw.* **2010**, *33*, 1–22. [CrossRef]
19. Chawla, N.V.; Bowyer, K.W.; Hall, L.O.; Kegelmeyer, W.P. SMOTE: Synthetic minority over-sampling technique. *J. Artif. Intell. Res.* **2002**, *16*, 321–357. [CrossRef]
20. Kuhn, M. Caret: Classification and Regression Training. R package Version 6.0-86. 2020. Available online: https://cran.r-project.org/package=caret (accessed on 19 March 2021).
21. Chen, T.; He, T.; Benesty, M.; Khotilovich, V.; Tang, Y.; Cho, H. Xgboost: Extreme Gradient Boosting. R Package Version 1.1.1.1. 2020. Available online: https://cran.r-project.org/package=xgboost (accessed on 19 March 2021).
22. Greenwell, B.; Boehmke, B.; Cunningham, J.; Developers, G. GBM: Generalized Boosted Regression Models. R package version 2.1.5. 2019. Available online: https://cran.r-project.org/package=gbm (accessed on 19 March 2021).
23. Karatzoglou, A.; Smola, A.; Hornik, K.; Zeileis, A. kernlab—AnS4Package for Kernel Methods inR. *J. Stat. Softw.* **2004**, *11*, 1–20. [CrossRef]
24. Kuhn, M.; Quinlan, R. C50: C5.0 Decision Trees and Rule-Based Models. R package version 0.1.3.1. 2020. Available online: https://cran.r-project.org/package=C50 (accessed on 19 March 2021).
25. Wallert, J.; Tomasoni, M.; Madison, G.; Held, C. Predicting two-year survival versus non-survival after first myocardial infarction using machine learning and Swedish national register data. *BMC Med Inform. Decis. Mak.* **2017**, *17*, 1–11. [CrossRef]
26. Kernan, W.N.; Viscoli, C.M.; Brass, L.M.; Makuch, R.W.; Sarrel, P.M.; Roberts, R.S.; Gent, M.; Rothwell, P.; Sacco, R.L.; Liu, R.C.; et al. The stroke prognosis instrument II (SPI-II): A clinical prediction instrument for patients with transient ischemia and nondisabling ischemic stroke. *Stroke* **2000**, *31*, 456–462. [CrossRef] [PubMed]
27. Weimar, C.; Diener, H.-C.; Alberts, M.J.; Steg, P.G.; Bhatt, D.L.; Wilson, P.W.; Mas, J.-L.; Röther, J. The Essen Stroke Risk Score Predicts Recurrent Cardiovascular Events. *Stroke* **2009**, *40*, 350–354. [CrossRef]
28. Chandratheva, A.; Geraghty, O.C.; Rothwell, P.M. Poor Performance of Current Prognostic Scores for Early Risk of Recurrence After Minor Stroke. *Stroke* **2011**, *42*, 632–637. [CrossRef]
29. Andersen, S.D.; Gorst-Rasmussen, A.; Lip, G.Y.; Bach, F.W.; Larsen, T.B. Recurrent Stroke. *Stroke* **2015**, *46*, 2491–2497. [CrossRef]
30. Liu, Y.; Wang, Y.; Li, W.A.; Yan, A.; Wang, Y. Validation of the Essen Stroke Risk Score in different subtypes of ischemic stroke. *Neurol. Res.* **2017**, *39*, 504–508. [CrossRef]
31. Weimar, C.; Benemann, J.; Michalski, D.; Müller, M.; Luckner, K.; Katsarava, Z.; Weber, R.; Diener, H.-C. Prediction of Recurrent Stroke and Vascular Death in Patients with Transient Ischemic Attack or Nondisabling Stroke. *Stroke* **2010**, *41*, 487–493. [CrossRef]
32. Navi, B.B.; Kamel, H.; Sidney, S.; Klingman, J.G.; Nguyen-Huynh, M.N.; Johnston, S.C. Validation of the Stroke Prognostic Instrument-II in a Large, Modern, Community-Based Cohort of Ischemic Stroke Survivors. *Stroke* **2011**, *42*, 3392–3396. [CrossRef]
33. Sadighi, A.; Stanciu, A.; Banciu, M.; Abedi, V.; el Andary, N.; Holland, N.; Zand, R. Rate and associated factors of transient ischemic attack misdiagnosis. *eNeurological. Sci.* **2019**, *15*, 100193. [CrossRef]
34. Carey, D.J.; Fetterolf, S.N.; Davis, F.D.; Faucett, W.A.; Kirchner, H.L.; Mirshahi, U.; Murray, M.F.; Smelser, D.T.; Gerhard, G.S.; Ledbetter, D.H. The Geisinger MyCode community health initiative: An electronic health record–linked biobank for precision medicine research. *Genet. Med.* **2016**, *18*, 906–913. [CrossRef] [PubMed]
35. Abedi, V.; Shivakumar, M.K.; Lu, P.; Hontecillas, R.; Leber, A.; Ahuja, M.; Ulloa, A.E.; Shellenberger, M.J.; Bassaganya-Riera, J. Latent-Based Imputation of Laboratory Measures from Electronic Health Records: Case for Complex Diseases. *BioRxiv* **2018**, 275743. [CrossRef]
36. Abedi, V.; Li, J.; Shivakumar, M.K.; Avula, V.; Chaudhary, D.P.; Shellenberger, M.J.; Khara, H.S.; Zhang, Y.; Lee, M.T.M.; Wolk, D.M.; et al. Increasing the Density of Laboratory Measures for Machine Learning Applications. *J. Clin. Med.* **2020**, *10*, 103. [CrossRef] [PubMed]
37. Li, J.; Chaudhary, D.P.; Khan, A.; Griessenauer, C.; Carey, D.J.; Zand, R.; Abedi, V. Polygenic Risk Scores Augment Stroke Subtyping. *Neurol. Genet.* **2021**, *7*, e560. [CrossRef]
38. Alam, M.; Deng, X.; Philipson, C.; Bassaganya-Riera, J.; Bisset, K.; Carbo, A.; Eubank, S.; Hontecillas, R.; Hoops, S.; Mei, Y.; et al. Sensitivity Analysis of an ENteric Immunity SImulator (ENISI)-Based Model of Immune Responses to Helicobacter pylori Infection. *PLoS ONE* **2015**, *10*, e0136139. [CrossRef] [PubMed]
39. Chen, X.; Wang, W.; Xie, G.; Hontecillas, R.; Verma, M.; Leber, A.; Bassaganya-Riera, J.; Abedi, V. Multi-Resolution Sensitivity Analysis of Model of Immune Response to Helicobacter pylori Infection via Spatio-Temporal Metamodeling. *Front. Appl. Math. Stat.* **2019**, *5*. [CrossRef]
40. Available online: https://github.com/wwvt/bioSA (accessed on 19 March 2021).
41. Verma, M.; Bassaganya-Riera, J.; Leber, A.; Tubau-Juni, N.; Hoops, S.; Abedi, V.; Chen, X.; Hontecillas, R. High-resolution computational modeling of immune responses in the gut. *GigaScience* **2019**, *8*. [CrossRef] [PubMed]

Article

SARS-CoV-2 Is a Culprit for Some, but Not All Acute Ischemic Strokes: A Report from the Multinational COVID-19 Stroke Study Group

Shima Shahjouei [1], Michelle Anyaehie [1], Eric Koza [2], Georgios Tsivgoulis [3], Soheil Naderi [4], Ashkan Mowla [1,5], Venkatesh Avula [1], Alireza Vafaei Sadr [6], Durgesh Chaudhary [1], Ghasem Farahmand [7], Christoph Griessenauer [1,8], Mahmoud Reza Azarpazhooh [9], Debdipto Misra [10], Jiang Li [11], Vida Abedi [11,12], Ramin Zand [1,*] and the Multinational COVID- Stroke Study Group [†]

1 Neurology Department, Neuroscience Institute, Geisinger Health System, Danville, PA 17822, USA; sshahjouei@geisinger.edu (S.S.); MAnyaehie@som.geisinger.edu (M.A.); mowla@usc.edu (A.M.); vavula1@geisinger.edu (V.A.); dpchaudhary@geisinger.edu (D.C.); cgriessenauer@geisinger.edu (C.G.)
2 Neuroscience Institute, Geisinger Commonwealth School of Medicine, Scranton, PA 18510, USA; EKoza@som.geisinger.edu
3 Second Department of Neurology, "Attikon" University Hospital, National and Kapodistrian University of Athens, School of Medicine, 12462 Athens, Greece; tsivgoulisgiorg@yahoo.gr
4 Department of Neurosurgery, Tehran University of Medical Sciences, Tehran 14155-6559, Iran; soheilnaaderi@gmail.com
5 Division of Stroke and Endovascular Neurosurgery, Department of Neurological Surgery, Keck School of Medicine, University of Southern California, Los Angeles, CA 90033, USA
6 Department de Physique Theorique and Center for Astroparticle Physics, University Geneva, 1211 Geneva, Switzerland; vafaei.sadr@gmail.com
7 Iranian Center of Neurological Research, Neuroscience Institute, Tehran University of Medical Sciences, Tehran 14155-6559, Iran; Ghasem.farahmand89@gmail.com
8 Research Institute of Neurointervention, Paracelsus Medical University, 5020 Salzburg, Austria
9 Department of Clinical Neurological Sciences, Western University, London, ON N6A 3K7, Canada; azarpazhoohr@gmail.com
10 Steele Institute of Health and Innovation, Geisinger Health System, Danville, PA 17822, USA; dmisra@geisinger.edu
11 Department of Molecular and Functional Genomics, Geisinger Health System, Danville, PA 17822, USA; jli@geisinger.edu (J.L.); vabedi@geisinger.edu (V.A.)
12 Biocomplexity Institute, Virginia Tech, Blacksburg, VA 24060, USA
* Correspondence: rzand@geisinger.edu
† Please see the supplemental material.

Citation: Shahjouei, S.; Anyaehie, M.; Koza, E.; Tsivgoulis, G.; Naderi, S.; Mowla, A.; Avula, V.; Vafaei Sadr, A.; Chaudhary, D.; Farahmand, G.; et al. SARS-CoV-2 Is a Culprit for Some, but Not All Acute Ischemic Strokes: A Report from the Multinational COVID-19 Stroke Study Group. *J. Clin. Med.* **2021**, *10*, 931. https://doi.org/10.3390/jcm10050931

Academic Editor: Hugues Chabriat

Received: 16 January 2021
Accepted: 16 February 2021
Published: 1 March 2021

Publisher's Note: MDPI stays neutral with regard to jurisdictional claims in published maps and institutional affiliations.

Copyright: © 2021 by the authors. Licensee MDPI, Basel, Switzerland. This article is an open access article distributed under the terms and conditions of the Creative Commons Attribution (CC BY) license (https://creativecommons.org/licenses/by/4.0/).

Abstract: Background. SARS-CoV-2 infected patients are suggested to have a higher incidence of thrombotic events such as acute ischemic strokes (AIS). This study aimed at exploring vascular comorbidity patterns among SARS-CoV-2 infected patients with subsequent stroke. We also investigated whether the comorbidities and their frequencies under each subclass of TOAST criteria were similar to the AIS population studies prior to the pandemic. Methods. This is a report from the Multinational COVID-19 Stroke Study Group. We present an original dataset of SASR-CoV-2 infected patients who had a subsequent stroke recorded through our multicenter prospective study. In addition, we built a dataset of previously reported patients by conducting a systematic literature review. We demonstrated distinct subgroups by clinical risk scoring models and unsupervised machine learning algorithms, including hierarchical K-Means (ML-K) and Spectral clustering (ML-S). Results. This study included 323 AIS patients from 71 centers in 17 countries from the original dataset and 145 patients reported in the literature. The unsupervised clustering methods suggest a distinct cohort of patients (ML-K: 36% and ML-S: 42%) with no or few comorbidities. These patients were more than 6 years younger than other subgroups and more likely were men (ML-K: 59% and ML-S: 60%). The majority of patients in this subgroup suffered from an embolic-appearing stroke on imaging (ML-K: 83% and ML-S: 85%) and had about 50% risk of large vessel occlusions (ML-K: 50% and ML-S: 53%). In addition, there were two cohorts of patients with large-artery atherosclerosis (ML-K: 30% and ML-S: 43% of patients) and cardioembolic strokes (ML-K: 34% and ML-S: 15%) with consistent comorbidity and imaging patterns. Binominal logistic regression demonstrated that ischemic heart disease (odds ratio (OR), 4.9; 95% confidence interval (CI), 1.6–14.7), atrial fibrillation (OR, 14.0; 95% CI, 4.8–40.8), and active neoplasm (OR, 7.1; 95% CI, 1.4–36.2) were associated with cardioembolic stroke. Conclusions. Although a cohort of young and healthy men with cardioembolic and large vessel occlusions can be distinguished using both clinical sub-grouping and unsupervised clustering, stroke in other patients may be explained based on the existing comorbidities.

Keywords: cerebrovascular disorders; stroke; SARS-CoV-2; COVID-19; cluster analysis; risk factors; comorbidity

1. Introduction

Since the emergence of the Coronavirus Disease 2019 (COVID-19) pandemic, many cerebrovascular events have been reported among patients with SARS-CoV-2 infection. Some reports have highlighted strokes in critically ill and older patients with a higher number of comorbidities, while others have suggested a higher risk in younger and healthy individuals [1–5]. Studies have suggested that stroke patients with SARS-CoV-2 present with multiple cerebral infarcts [2,4,6], systemic coagulopathies [7], uncommon thrombotic events such as aortic [8] or common carotid artery thrombosis [9], and simultaneous arterial and venous thrombus formation [10].

Considering the hypercoagulable state as one of the main etiologies of stroke among the SARS-CoV-2 infected patients, we would expect a similar increased rate for cardiovascular thrombotic events and acute coronary syndrome after the pandemic. However, higher acute coronary syndrome case fatality rate and other adverse outcomes among cardiac patients compared with the pre-pandemic era have been attributed to public fear and reluctance to call for medical aid and increased pre-hospital delay. A dramatic decline in the guideline-indicated care, hospitalization rate, and revascularization procedures are other possible factors attributing to adverse outcomes in patients with acute coronary syndrome [11–15]. Studies have failed to show any difference among cardiovascular patients in terms of age, sex, comorbidities, clinical presentation, and diagnosis pre- and post-pandemic era [14,16]. Similarly, a higher rate of coronary stent thrombosis in comparison with the pre-pandemic era [17,18] was reported among the patients with multiple comorbidities (about 44% with at least four vascular risk factors) and a median age of 65 years [18]. Acute myocardial injury (defined as a substantial increase in cardiac troponin level) is associated with the underlying cardiac pathology in the majority of the SARS-CoV-2 infected patients [19] rather than a thrombotic event.

The first report from our Multinational COVID-19 Stroke Study Group and recent meta-analyses on reported infected patients presented a stroke incidence rate of 0.5–1.4% [20–22]. The odds of stroke after SARS-CoV-2 may not be greater than in non-infected patients [23]. In addition, meta-analyses of the reported patients presented that SARS-CoV-2 infected patients who experienced a stroke had a mean age of over 65 years, carried a load of comorbidities, and were affected by more severe infections [21,22]. Thereby, in some patients, stroke may be a coincidence or an indirect consequence of critical illness [24,25] and not a direct complication of the SARS-CoV-2 infection. As an example, there is an increased risk of ischemic stroke (odds ratio (OR) > 28) and hemorrhagic stroke (OR > 12) within two weeks of sepsis [26]. This might be due to new-onset atrial fibrillation (6%) that put the patient at risk of in-hospital stroke (2.6%) [24].

Understanding the population at risk for having a stroke after SARS-CoV-2 infection can promote timely diagnosis and proper management of these patients.

We designed this study to explore the pattern of traditional vascular risk factors and stroke etiology among stroke patients with prior SARS-CoV-2 infection. We leveraged unsupervised hierarchical and spectral model-based clustering in addition to clinical risk scoring models to decipher patterns of comorbidity among stroke patients with prior

SARS-CoV-2 infection. We further expanded our analysis to corroborate whether the comorbidities under each subclass of TOAST (the Trial of Org 10172 in Acute Stroke Treatment [27]) were similar to the AIS population studies prior to the pandemic.

2. Methods

This report presents a multicenter prospective and observational study from our Multinational COVID-19 Stroke Study Group [20] and a cohort of patients extracted from the literature.

2.1. Original Dataset

Collaborators from 71 centers of 17 countries (Brazil, Canada, Croatia, Egypt, France, Germany, Greece, Iran, Israel, Italy, Portugal, Republic of Korea, Singapore, Spain, Switzerland, Turkey, and the United States) reported data on their patients for this study. We included consecutive SARS-CoV-2 infected adult patients who had imaging confirmed subsequent acute ischemic stroke.

The study protocol, details of eligibility criteria, data elements, and neurological investigations have been previously published [20]. The demographics, vascular risk factors, and comorbidities—i.e., hypertension, diabetes, ischemic heart disease, atrial fibrillation, carotid stenosis, chronic kidney disease, congestive heart failure with cardiac ejection fraction <40%, active neoplasms, rheumatological diseases, smoking status, and history of transient ischemic attack (TIA) or stroke—were recorded for the stroke patients [28–31]. We also recorded the neurological examinations, the National Institute of Health Stroke Scale (NIHSS), TOAST [27] subclasses, presence of large-vessel occlusions (LVOs), and brain imaging findings.

The study protocol was designed at the Neuroscience Institute of Geisinger Health System, Pennsylvania, United States, and received approval by the Institutional Review Board of Geisinger Health System and participating institutions, as needed. The study was conducted and reported according to the Strengthening the Reporting of Observational Studies in Epidemiology (STROBE) [32], and Preferred Reporting Items for Systematic Reviews and Meta-Analyses (PRISMA) [33].

2.2. Systematic Literature Review

To compare our results with the available literature, we searched PubMed for reports of patients with subsequent stroke after SARS-CoV-2 infection. Different terms in addition to Medical Subject Headings (MeSH) were utilized to build the search protocol (Document S1). The search was last updated on 15 October 2020, with no limitation to study design, language, or document type. The search was augmented by forward and backward citation tracking in PubMed and Google Scholar. We additionally searched medRxiv to track the documents ahead of publication and communicated with the corresponding authors to include them under peer review or in press studies prior to publication. Two reviewers (EK and SS) independently evaluated the titles/abstracts of the retrieved results and reviewed the full texts of candidate articles. Data available from the literature were extracted per the same datasheet as the data collected in our original multicenter case series when possible. The extracted data were further reviewed by two neurologists (G.F. and R.Z.).

2.3. Comorbidity-Based Subgrouping: Expert Opinion

The details of the subgroups are available in Document S2. In the risk scoring models based on the EXpert opinion (EX), we considered the number of present stroke-related comorbidities—either All the 11 collected comorbidities (EX-A) as mentioned above, or eight Selected comorbidities (EX-S, excluding congestive heart failure, active neoplasm, and rheumatological disorders) [27–30]. We considered equal weights for all comorbidities. We divided the patients based on EX-A and EX-S scores into two subgroups (EX-A_2 and EX-S_2); Subgroup "a" included patients who had a history of zero or one stroke-related comorbidity, and subgroup "b" included the patients with >1 comorbidity. In addition, we divided the patients based on EX-A and EX-S scores into three subgroups (EX-A_3 and EX-S_3). In this second classification, subgroup "a" represented the patients without any known comorbidity, subgroup "b" with one or two comorbidities, and subgroup "c" included the patients with more than two comorbidities.

2.4. Comorbidity-Based Subgrouping: Unsupervised Modeling

We explore the probable similarities among the patients based on the presence of comorbidities in a data-driven approach. These patterns might have been remained hidden by clinical risk scores to the experts. For this purpose, we leveraged unsupervised algorithms and Machine Learning models (ML) (Document S2). We applied hierarchical (complete linkage method) and K-means (Hartigan-Wong algorithm) clustering (ML-K models) to group the patients into 2 (ML-K_2) and 3 (ML-K_3) subgroups. We also used Spectral clustering [34] (ML-S models) and clustered the patients into two (ML-S_2) and three subgroups (ML-S_3). Tables S1 and S2 present the clustering of the patients into four and five subgroups. Patients from the original dataset and literature review were clustered independently.

We used the contingency matrix (also known as a contingency table) [35] to demonstrate the subgroups of each model versus other models. The average similarity of the models in clustering the patients was calculated as $Sim = \frac{\sum_1^i Maximum\ Value\ in\ Column\ i}{\sum_1^k Value\ in\ Cell\ k}$; where i is the number of columns and k is the total number of cells in the contingency matrix. Similarities among the models were considered as mild (50–65%), moderate (65–80%), and strong (80–100%). The packages *stat* [36] and *gplots* [37] in R version 3.6.3, and the scikit-learn package [38] in Python version 3.7 were used.

2.5. Statistical Analysis

We used descriptive statistics to summarize the data. Demographic data, comorbidities, laboratory findings, and neurological investigations were reported as medians (interquartile range (IQR)) and mean (standard deviations (SD)). Categorical variables were reported as absolute frequencies and percentages. The comparison between categorical variables was conducted with the Pearson chi-square test, while the differences among continuous variables were assessed by an independent *t*-test. We explored the association of comorbidities with each subclass of TOAST criteria by binary logistic regression. A *p*-value < 0.05 was considered significant in all analyses.

3. Results

3.1. Patients Characteristics

This study included 323 AIS patients from our original prospective multicenter case series, with a mean age of 67 ± 15 years and 60% men (Table S3). The most prevalent comorbidities were hypertension (63%), diabetes (35%), and ischemic heart disease (24%). In addition, through our systematic review of the literature, we retrieved data from an additional 412 stroke patients (including dural sinus thrombosis) post-SARS-CoV-2 infection (Figure 1). The data from the 412 patients were extracted from 81 articles (in 18 countries). Among the 412 patients, individual-level data of 145 AIS patients were reported from 36 centers in nine countries. The mean age of the retrieved AIS patients was 63 ± 14 years, and 57% were men (Table S3).

In comparison with our original multicenter dataset, patients reported in the literature were younger (mean age of 63 versus 67 years, $p < 0.01$), with a higher proportion of LVOs (83% versus 45%, $p < 0.0001$), and strokes of undetermined (38% versus 22%, $p < 0.01$) or other determined etiologies (31% versus 8%, $p < 0.001$). Although not statistically significant, reported patients in the literature had more severe strokes (median NIHSS of 15 versus nine, $p = 0.11$). Fewer patients of this cohort were reported to have had vascular risk factors; however, hypertension (55%), diabetes (37%), and atrial fibrillation (12%) were the most prevalent reported comorbidities among the patients from the published reports.

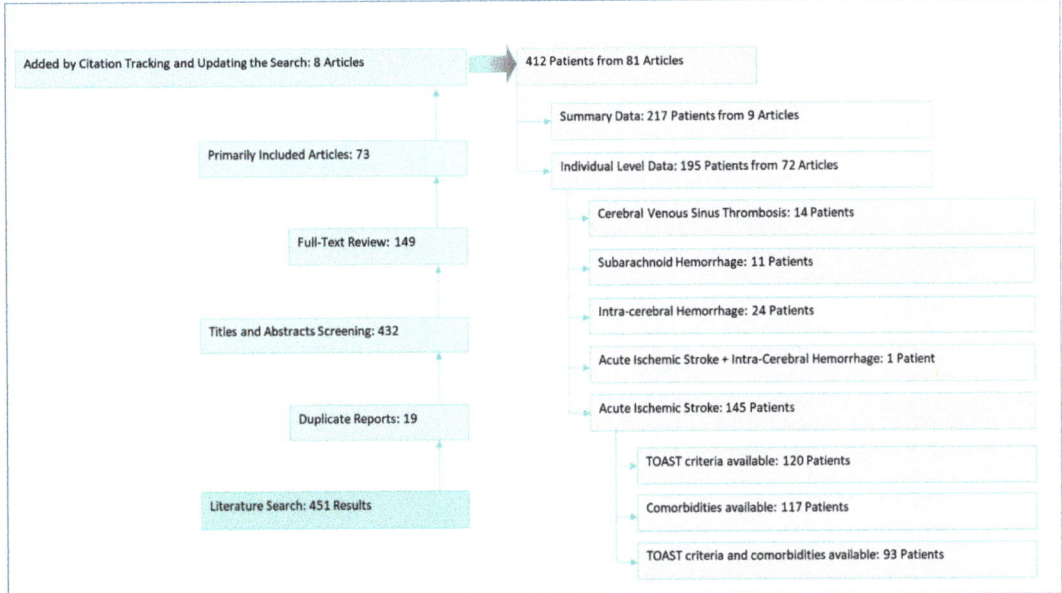

Figure 1. The process of literature review and main results.

3.2. Clinical Risk Scoring Models Revealed a Large Cohort of Young Men with No Comorbidities Who Suffered from Large Vessel Occlusions (LVOs)

Among the 323 AIS patients from the original dataset, 65 (22%) patients reported no known comorbidities, and 115 (39%) had at most one known comorbidity (Table 1). Among the 117 patients from the literature review who had a completed comorbidity panel, 33 (28%) reported no known comorbidity, and 71 (61%) had at most one known comorbidity (Table S4).

In both datasets, we identified a cohort of patients with no vascular risk factors with distinct features—subgroup "a" in all clinical risk scoring models; original dataset, EX-A_3a: 22% and EX-S_3a: 25% (Table 1); literature review, EX-A_3a = EX-S_3a: 28% (Table S4). These cohorts included patients with (1) younger age (over 8 years in comparison with other subgroups of the original dataset), (2) male predominance (original dataset, EX-A_3a: 55% and EX-S_3a: 54%; literature review, EX-A_3a = EX-S_3a: 59%), and (3) a higher proportion of embolic-appearing imaging stroke pattern (original dataset, 82%; literature review dataset 67%). About half of patients in the original dataset had LVOs (EX-A_3a: 48% and EX-S_3a: 49%), as did the majority of patients reported in the literature (EX-A_3a = EX-S_3a: 80%). In comparison with patients who carried a high load of comorbidities (subgroup "c"), the cohorts of patients without comorbidities (subgroup "a") had a longer length of hospital stay (original dataset EX-S_3a, 16 days versus 11 days in EX-S_3c, $p = 0.03$). Although not statistically significant, patients in the subgroup "a" also had less severe strokes (median NIHSS in the original dataset, eight versus 12 in subgroup "c"; median NIHSS in review dataset, six versus nine in subgroup "c"), but a higher chance of a need for mechanical ventilation (original dataset EX-A_3a: 34% versus 28%, $p = 0.39$; EX-S_3a: 37% versus 28%, $p = 0.16$).

Table 1. Characteristics of the patients grouped by clinical risk scoring models.

Parameters	EX-A₂ (All Comorbidities)				EX-S₂ (Selected Comorbidities)				EX-A₃ (All Comorbidities)				EX-S₃ (Selected Comorbidities)			
	a n = 115 (38.9%)	b n = 181 (61.1%)		p-Value	a n = 137 (46.3%)	b n = 159 (53.7%)		p-Value	a n = 65 (22.0%)	b n = 140 (47.3%)	c n = 91 (30.7%)	p-Value	a n = 74 (25.0%)	b n = 147 (49.7%)	c n = 75 (25.3%)	p-Value
Age; Mean (SD); Years	61 ± 18	69 ± 14		<0.001	62 ± 17	69 ± 14		<0.001	60 ± 18	68 ± 14	70 ± 14	<0.001	59 ± 18	69 ± 13	71 ± 13	<0.001
Sex; Male; n (%)	66 (57.4)	113 (62.4)		0.29	72 (56.3)	107 (63.7)		0.61	36 (55.4)	87 (62.1)	56 (61.5)	0.63	36 (54.5)	98 (64.9)	45 (57.0)	0.46
Large Vessel Occlusion; n (%)	43 (43.9)	76 (44.4)		0.93	49 (41.2)	70 (46.7)		0.37	26 (48.1)	50 (39.4)	43 (50.0)	0.26	31 (49.2)	52 (39.1)	36 (50.7)	0.20
Intravenous Thrombolysis; n (%)	13 (7.4)	26 (12.4)		0.11	16 (8.0)	23 (12.3)		0.17	6 (9.2)	14 (10.0)	19 (20.9)	0.03	7 (9.5)	17 (9.5)	15 (20.0)	0.12
Mechanical Thrombectomy; n (%)	9 (5.1)	15 (7.1)		0.41	10 (5.0)	14 (7.5)		0.32	5 (7.7)	9 (6.4)	10 (11.0)	0.46	6 (8.1)	9 (6.1)	9 (12.0)	0.32
National Institutes of Health Stroke Scale (NIHSS); Median (IQR)	11.0 ± 9.0	12.0 ± 9.0		0.95	11.0 ± 9.0	12.0 ± 8.0		0.87	8 (4–22)	9 (4–16)	12 (6–20)	0.18	9 (4–22)	8 (4–16)	12 (6–19)	0.21
TOAST Criteria				<0.001				<0.001				<0.001				<0.001
2003 Large-Artery Atherosclerosis; n (%)	21 (30.4)	35 (34.7)			21 (27.3)	35 (37.6)			16 (43.2)	21 (26.9)	19 (34.5)		16 (42.1)	24 (27.3)	16 (36.4)	
Cardio-Embolism; n (%)	10 (14.5)	36 (35.6)			12 (15.6)	34 (36.6)			5 (13.5)	13 (16.7)	28 (50.9)		5 (13.2)	20 (22.7)	21 (47.7)	
Small-Vessel Occlusion; n (%)	7 (10.1)	10 (9.9)			8 (10.4)	9 (9.7)			1 (2.7)	12 (15.4)	4 (7.3)		1 (2.6)	12 (13.6)	4 (9.1)	
Stroke of Other Determined Etiology; n (%)	11 (15.9)	2 (2.0)			11 (14.3)	2 (2.2)			6 (16.2)	2 (2.6)	0.0 (0.0)		7 (18.4)	6 (6.8)	0 (0.0)	
Stroke of Undetermined Etiology; n (%)	20 (29.0)	18 (17.8)			25 (32.5)	13 (14.0)			9 (24.3)	25 (32.1)	4 (7.3)		9 (23.7)	25 (29.5)	3 (6.5)	
Imaging Patterns																
Embolic-Appearing; n (%)	76 (83.5)	195 (92.9)			189 (95.0)	173 (92.5)			41 (82.0)	97 (79.5)	67 (80.7)		42 (82.4)	106 (80.3)	57 (79.2)	
Lacune; n (%)	10 (11.0)	16 (9.8)		0.43	14 (12.5)	12 (8.4)		0.56	4 (8.0)	17 (13.9)	5 (6.0)	0.31	4 (7.8)	17 (12.9)	5 (6.9)	0.72
Borderzone; n (%)	5 (5.5)	18 (11.0)			9 (8.0)	14 (9.8)			5 (10.0)	8 (6.6)	10 (12.0)		5 (9.8)	9 (6.8)	9 (12.5)	
Vasculitis Pattern; n (%)	0 (0.0)	1 (0.6)			0 (0.0)	1 (0.7)			0 (0.0)	0 (0.0)	1 (1.2)		0 (0.0)	0 (0.0)	1 (1.4)	
Interval Between Infection Onset to Stroke; Median (IQR); Days	7.0 ± 8.0	5.0 ± 6.0		0.07	7.0 ± 7.0	5.0 ± 6.0		0.15	7.0 ± 8.0	5.0 ± 6.0	5.0 ± 7.0	0.19	7.0 ± 7.0	5.0 ± 6.0	6.0 ± 7.0	0.27
Mechanical Ventilation; n (%)	22 (33.8)	63 (27.3)		0.30	27 (36.5)	58 (26.1)		0.09	22 (33.8)	38 (27.1)	25 (27.5)	0.39	27 (36.5)	37 (25.2)	21 (28.0)	0.16
Disposition																
Discharged Home; n (%)	66 (42.0)	77 (36.7)		0.46	75 (41.7)	68 (36.4)		0.44	31 (50.8)	60 (43.2)	36 (39.6)	0.39	32 (51.6)	62 (41.3)	33 (41.8)	0.16
In Hospital Mortality; n (%)	45 (28.7)	72 (34.3)			52 (28.9)	65 (34.8)			14 (23.0)	33 (23.7)	30 (33.0)		14 (22.6)	35 (23.3)	28 (35.4)	
Still in Hospital/Subacute Care; n (%)	46 (29.3)	61 (29.0)			53 (29.4)	54 (28.9)			16 (26.2)	46 (33.1)	25 (27.5)		16 (25.8)	53 (35.3)	18 922.8)	
Length of Hospital Stay; Median (IQR); Days	14.0 ± 15.0	11.0 ± 11.0		0.46	16.0 ± 17.0	11.0 ± 9.0		0.04	14.0 ± 15.0	12.0 ± 12.0	10.0 ± 8.0	0.28	16.0 ± 17.0	11.0 ± 9.0	11.0 ± 8.0	0.03
Comorbidities																
Hypertension; n (%)	22 (19.1)	158 (87.3)		<0.001	30 (23.4)	150 (89.3)		<0.001	0 (0.0)	95 (67.9)	85 (93.4)	<0.001	0 (0.0)	104 (68.9)	76 (96.2)	<0.001
Diabetes Mellitus; n (%)	5 (4.3)	93 (51.4)		<0.001	8 (6.3)	90 (53.6)		<0.001	0 (0.0)	37 (26.4)	61 (67.0)	<0.001	0 (0.0)	41 (27.2)	57 (72.2)	<0.001
Ischemic Heart Disease; n (%)	4 (3.5)	68 (37.6)		<0.001	4 (3.1)	68 (40.5)		<0.001	0 (0.0)	19 (13.6)	53 (58.2)	<0.001	0 (0.0)	24 (15.9)	48 (60.8)	<0.001
Atrial Fibrillation; n (%)	4 (3.5)	38 (21.0)		<0.001	6 (4.7)	36 (21.4)		<0.001	0 (0.0)	12 (8.6)	30 (33.0)	<0.001	0 (0.0)	15 (9.9)	27 (34.2)	<0.001
Carotid Stenosis; n (%)	1 (0.9)	37 (20.4)		<0.001	1 (0.8)	37 (20.4)		<0.001	0 (0.0)	11 (7.9)	27 (29.7)	<0.001	0 (0.0)	11 (7.3)	27 (34.2)	<0.001
Chronic Kidney Disease; n (%)	9 (7.8)	23 (12.7)		0.02	9 (7.0)	32 (19.0)		0.003	0 (0.0)	23 (16.4)	18 (19.8)	<0.001	0 (0.0)	24 (15.9)	17 (21.5)	<0.001
Cardiac Ejection Fraction <40%; n (%)	1 (0.9)	17 (10.1)		<0.001	7 (5.5)	17 (10.1)		0.15	0 (0.0)	6 (4.3)	18 (19.8)	<0.001	0 (0.0)	10 (6.6)	13 (16.5)	0.003
Active Neoplasm; n (%)	0 (0.0)	21 (11.6)		<0.001	6 (4.7)	15 (8.9)		0.16	0 (0.0)	5 (3.6)	16 (17.6)	<0.001	0 (0.0)	12 (7.9)	9 (11.4)	0.02
Rheumatological Disease; n (%)	0 (0.0)	5 (2.8)		0.07	3 (2.3)	2 (1.2)		0.45	0 (0.0)	3 (2.1)	3 (3.3)	0.27	0 (0.0)	4 (2.6)	1 (1.3)	0.35
Prior Stroke or Transient Ischemic Attack; n (%)	1 (0.9)	4 (2.2)		0.38	1 (0.8)	4 (2.4)		0.29	0 (0.0)	2 (1.4)	3 (3.3)	0.27	0 (0.0)	2 (1.3)	3 (3.8)	0.18
Smoking; n (%)	3 (2.6)	45 (24.9)		<0.001	3 (2.3)	45 (26.8)		<0.001	0 (0.0)	18 (12.9)	30 (33.0)	<0.001	0 (0.0)	19 (12.6)	29 (36.7)	<0.001

EX-A₂: clinical risk-scoring (expert opinion) model including all comorbidities; a, 0–1 comorbidity; b, >1 comorbidity; EX-S₂: clinical risk-scoring model including selected comorbidities; a, 0–1 comorbidity; b, >1 comorbidity; EX-A₃: clinical risk scoring model including all comorbidities; a, 0 comorbidity; b, 1–2 comorbidities, c, >2 comorbidities; EX-S₃: clinical risk scoring model including selected comorbidities; a, 0 comorbidities, b, 1–2 comorbidities, c, >2 comorbidities. Due to missingness, we provided the valid percentages in this table.

3.3. Unsupervised Clustering Revealed Three Subgroups of Stroke Patients

In addition to clinical risk scoring, we used unsupervised algorithms to potentially identify hidden comorbidity patterns among AIS patients. There were strong similarities (Sim > 80%) among the models in grouping the patients, except two sets that were moderately similar (Figure S1). Clustering the patients from the original dataset (Table 2) demonstrated a subgroup of patients with no or few comorbidities—subgroup "a" in all ML models (ML-K_3a: 36% and ML-S_3a: 42% of patients, Table 2). The latter is similar to subgroup "a" in all EX models (22–46% of patients, Table 1). The patients in these groups were (1) mainly men (ML-K_3a: 59% and ML-S_3a: 60%), (2) more than six years younger than other subgroups, (3) had a higher risk of embolic-appearing stroke on imaging (ML-K_3a: 83% and ML-S_3a: 85%), and (4) had about 50% risk of LVOs (ML-K_3a: 50% and ML-S_3a: 53%). Patients in the second subgroup (ML-K_3b: 30% and ML-S_3b: 43%; similar to EX-A_3b: 47% and EX-S_3b: 50%) presented with a high proportion of hypertension, diabetes, chronic kidney disease, and smoking. These patients had a higher risk of large artery atherosclerosis (ML-K_3b: 40%, and ML-S_3b: 31%). The third subgroup (ML-K_3c: 34% and ML-S_3c: 15% similar to EX-A_3c: 31% and EX-S_3c: 25%) presented mostly with hypertension, diabetes, ischemic heart disease, atrial fibrillation, congestive heart failure, carotid stenosis, neoplasm, and smoking. The majority of these patients (ML-K_3c: 34% and ML-S_3c: 60%) had cardioembolic strokes based on TOAST and imaging patterns consistent with an embolic ischemic stroke.

Similar patterns were observed among patients reported in the literature (Tables S4 and S5). The first group (subgroup "a" in all models, 28–61%) included the patients with no or few comorbidities. These patients were more likely men (63–100%), with over 80% LVOs, about 65% strokes of undetermined or other determined etiologies, and over 60% embolic-appearing strokes. In the second subgroup identified by unsupervised clustering (ML-K_3b: 41% and ML-S_3b: 66%, similar to EX-A_3b: 33% and EX-S_3b: 33%), the majority of the patients presented with hypertension and diabetes. Strokes of undetermined (ML-K_3b: 39% and ML-S_3b: 33%) and other determined (ML-K_3b: 33% and ML-S_3b: 37%) etiologies were more prevalent in these subgroups. The third subgroup (ML-K_3c: 16% and ML-S_3c: 26%, similar to EX-A_3c: 39% and EX-S_3c: 39%) included the patients with hypertension, diabetes, ischemic heart disease, atrial fibrillation, smoking, and prior stroke or TIA. The majority of the patients in the third subgroup of the literature review dataset had strokes of undetermined (ML-K_3c, 46% and ML-S_3c, 50%) or other determined etiologies (ML-K_3c: 27% and ML-S_3c: 18%).

3.4. The TOAST Subtype Classification Was Consistent with the Patients' Risk Profile

We observed significantly different proportions of hypertension, ischemic heart disease, atrial fibrillation, carotid stenosis, chronic kidney disease, and active neoplasms among subclasses of TOAST (Table 3). Binominal logistic regression models demonstrated that atrial fibrillation (OR: 0.2; 95% CI: 0.04–0.8) and carotid stenosis (OR: 6.9; 95% CI: 2.2–21.4) were associated with large-artery atherosclerosis; ischemic heart disease (OR: 4.9; 95% CI: 1.6–14.7), atrial fibrillation (OR: 14.0; 95% CI: 4.8–40.8), and active neoplasm (OR: 7.1; 95% CI: 1.4–36.2) with cardioembolic stroke; chronic kidney disease (OR: 6.23; 95% CI: 1.8–21.5) with small-vessel occlusion; and ischemic heart disease (OR: 0.1; 95% CI: 0.01–0.5), carotid stenosis (OR: 0.1; 95% CI: 0.01–0.8), and chronic kidney disease (OR: 0.2; 95% CI: 0.04–0.9) with strokes of other determined etiology.

Among the AIS patients reported in the literature, 120 patients had available TOAST criteria, 109 patients had available comorbidity panel, and 93 patients had data regarding both the TOAST criteria and the comorbidities. Because of the small sample size under each subgroup of TOAST, further analysis of the association of TOAST and comorbidities among these patients was not performed.

Table 2. Characteristics of the patients clustered with unsupervised machine learning algorithms.

Parameters	ML-K₂ (K-Mean)			ML-S₂ (Spectral)			ML-K₃ (K-Mean)				ML-S₃ (Spectral)			
	a $n=112$ (38.4%)	b $n=180$ (61.6%)	p-Value	a $n=173$ (60.3%)	b $n=114$ (39.7%)	p-Value	a $n=106$ (36.3%)	b $n=87$ (29.8%)	c $n=99$ (33.9%)	p-Value	a $n=120$ (41.8%)	b $n=123$ (42.9%)	c $n=44$ (15.3%)	p-Value
Age; Mean (SD); Years	62 ± 17	70 ± 13	<0.001	66 ± 17	68 ± 13	0.02	62 ± 17	68 ± 13	72 ± 13	<0.001	63 ± 17	70 ± 14	70 ± 14	<0.001
Sex; Male; n (%)	67 (59.8)	110 (61.1)	0.08	107 (61.8)	66 (57.4)	0.05	63 (59.4)	51 (58.6)	63 (63.6)	0.75	72 (60.0)	77 (62.6)	24 (53.3)	<0.001
Large Vessel Occlusion; n (%)	46 (48.4)	73 (42.7)	0.37	64 (42.1)	54 (50.0)	0.21	46 (49.5)	36 (44.4)	38 (40.4)	0.47	55 (53.4)	41 (35.3)	22 (53.7)	0.64
Intravenous Thrombolysis; n (%)	16 (14.3)	23 (12.8)	0.71	17 (9.8)	23 (17.5)	0.06	14 (13.2)	15 (17.2)	10 (10.1)	0.36	15 (12.5)	10 (8.1)	12 (27.3)	0.01
Mechanical Thrombectomy; n (%)	10 (8.9)	14 (7.8)	0.73	12 (6.9)	12 (10.5)	0.28	10 (9.4)	8 (9.2)	6 (6.1)	0.63	13 (10.8)	7 (5.7)	4 (9.1)	0.34
National Institutes of Health Stroke Scale (NIHSS); Median (IQR)	12.0 ± 9.0	11.0 ± 8.0	0.52	11.0 ± 8.0	13.0 ± 8.0	0.11	10 (5–19)	12 (6–18)	8 (4–16)	0.28	11 (5–19)	8 (4.16)	13 (7–20)	0.03
TOAST Criteria														
Large-Artery Atherosclerosis; n (%)	25 (38.5)	31 (29.8)	0.03	32 (31.1)	24 (35.8)	0.002	23 (36.5)	19 (40.4)	14 (23.7)	0.08	27 (38.6)	23 (30.7)	6 (24.0)	0.003
Cardio-Embolism; n (%)	11 (16.9)	35 (33.7)		19 (18.4)	27 (40.3)		11 (17.5)	15 (31.9)	20 (33.9)		14 (20.0)	17 (22.7)	15 (60.0)	
Small-Vessel Occlusion; n (%)	7 (10.8)	9 (8.7)		11 (10.7)	6 (9.0)		7 (11.1)	4 (8.5)	5 (8.5)		7 (10.0)	8 (10.7)	2 (8.0)	
Stroke of Other Determined Etiology; n (%)	9 (13.8)	4 (3.8)		12 (11.7)	1 (1.5)		9 (14.3)	1 (2.1)	3 (5.1)		9 (12.9)	4 (5.3)	0 (0.0)	
Stroke of Undetermined Etiology; n (%)	13 (20.0)	25 (24.0)		29 (28.2)	9 (13.4)		13 (20.6)	8 (17.0)	17 (28.8)		13 (18.6)	23 (30.7)	2 (8.0)	
Imaging Patterns														
Embolic-Appearing; n (%)	74 (83.1)	131 (79.4)	0.44	115 (79.3)	84 (80.8)	0.38	71 (82.6)	59 (77.6)	75 (81.5)	0.49	83 (84.7)	81 (73.6)	35 (85.4)	0.22
Lacune; n (%)	10 (11.2)	15 (9.1)		18 (12.4)	8 (7.7)		10 (11.6)	6 (7.9)	9 (9.8)		10 (10.2)	12 (10.9)	4 (9.8)	
Borderzone; n (%)	5 (5.6)	18 (10.9)		12 (8.3)	11 (10.6)		5 (5.8)	10 (13.2)	8 (8.7)		5 (5.1)	16 (14.5)	2 (4.9)	
Vasculitis Pattern; n (%)	0 (0.0)	1 (0.6)		0 (0.0)	1 (1.0)		0 (0.0)	1 (1.3)	0 (0.0)		0 (0.0)	1 (0.9)	0 (0.0)	
Interval Between Infection Onset to Stroke; Median (IQR); Days	6.0 ± 7.0	5.0 ± 6.0	0.19	6.0 ± 7.0	5.0 ± 7.0	0.38	7.0 ± 7.0	5.0 ± 7.0	5.0 ± 6.0	0.28	6.0 ± 7.0	5.0 ± 6.0	6.0 ± 8.0	0.37
Mechanical Ventilation; n (%)	36 (32.1)	47 (26.1)	0.27	51 (29.5)	32 (28.1)	0.80	34 (32.1)	24 (27.6)	25 (25.3)	0.55	39 (32.5)	31 (25.2)	13 (25.9)	0.27
Disposition														
Discharged Home; n (%)	53 (48.6)	72 (40.2)	0.36	81 (47.4)	43 (37.7)	0.27	50 (48.5)	38 (43.7)	37 (37.8)	0.57	56 (47.1)	51 (41.8)	17 (38.6)	0.27
In Hospital Mortality; n (%)	27 (24.8)	49 (27.4)		41 (24.0)	33 (28.9)		24 (23.3)	25 (28.7)	27 (27.6)		27 (22.7)	30 (24.6)	17 (38.6)	
Still in Hospital/Subacute Care; n (%)	29 (26.6)	58 (32.4)		49 (28.7)	38 (33.3)		29 (28.2)	24 (27.6)	34 (34.7)		36 (30.3)	41 (33.6)	10 (22.7)	
Length of Hospital Stay; Median (IQR); Days	14.0 ± 15.0	11 ± 9.0	0.14	13.0 ± 14.0	11.0 ± 9.0	0.23	14.0 ± 15.0	12.0 ± 9.0	10.0 ± 8.0	0.11	13.0 ± 15.0	12.0 ± 9.0	10.0 ± 7.0	0.56
Comorbidities														
Hypertension; n (%)	0 (0.0)	179 (99.4)	<0.001	65 (37.6)	109 (94.8)	<0.001	0 (0.0)	80 (92.0)	99 (100.0)	<0.001	13 (10.8)	121 (98.4)	40 (88.9)	<0.001
Diabetes Mellitus; n (%)	16 (14.3)	81 (45.0)	<0.001	13 (7.5)	83 (72.2)	<0.001	10 (9.4)	87 (100.0)	0 (0.0)	<0.001	11 (9.2)	51 (41.5)	34 (75.6)	<0.001
Ischemic Heart Disease; n (%)	16 (14.3)	55 (30.6)	0.002	13 (7.5)	58 (50.4)	<0.001	10 (9.4)	36 (41.4)	25 (25.3)	<0.001	26 (21.7)	1 (0.8)	44 (97.8)	<0.001
Atrial Fibrillation; n (%)	10 (8.9)	31 (17.2)	0.05	14 (8.1)	28 (24.3)	<0.001	9 (8.5)	14 (16.1)	18 (18.2)	0.11	9 (7.5)	16 (13.0)	17 (37.8)	<0.001
Carotid Stenosis; n (%)	4 (3.6)	34 (18.9)	<0.001	10 (5.8)	27 (23.5)	<0.001	4 (3.8)	21 (24.1)	13 (13.1)	<0.001	5 (4.2)	15 (12.2)	17 (37.8)	<0.001
Chronic Kidney Disease; n (%)	14 (12.5)	27 (15.0)	0.55	28 (16.2)	13 (11.3)	0.25	14 (13.2)	10 (11.5)	17 (17.2)	0.51	12 (10.0)	26 (21.1)	3 (6.7)	0.01
Cardiac Ejection Fraction <40%; n (%)	2 (1.8)	22 (12.2)	0.002	7 (4.0)	17 (14.8)	<0.001	2 (1.9)	10 (11.5)	12 (12.1)	0.01	3 (2.5)	10 (10.6)	8 (17.8)	0.003
Active Neoplasm; n (%)	6 (5.4)	15 (8.3)	0.34	7 (4.0)	14 (12.2)	0.009	4 (3.8)	9 (10.3)	8 (8.1)	0.19	6 (5.0)	5 (4.1)	10 (22.2)	<0.001
Rheumatological Disease; n (%)	1 (0.9)	4 (2.2)	0.39	4 (2.3)	1 (0.9)	0.36	1 (0.9)	1 (1.1)	3 (3.0)	0.46	1 (0.8)	4 (3.3)	0 (0.0)	0.22
Prior Stroke or Transient Ischemic Attack; n (%)	2 (1.8)	3 (1.7)	0.94	2 (1.2)	3 (2.6)	0.36	1 (0.9)	3 (3.4)	1 (1.0)	0.33	1 (0.8)	2 (4.3)	2 (4.4)	0.28
Smoking; n (%)	7 (6.3)	41 (22.8)	<0.001	19 (11.0)	27 (23.5)	0.005	7 (6.6)	17 (19.5)	24 (24.2)	0.002	10 (8.3)	24 (19.5)	12 (26.7)	0.006

ML-K₂: machine learning model using K-mean, dividing the patients into two subgroups; ML-S₂: machine learning model using spectral, dividing the patients into two subgroups; ML-K₃: machine learning model using K-mean, dividing the patients into three subgroups; ML-S₃: machine learning model using spectral, dividing the patients into three subgroups. Please note a, b, and c in this table are not based on the number of comorbidities and just indicated a distinct subgroup detected by unsupervised algorithms. Due to missingness, we provided the valid percentages in this table.

Table 3. The proportion of comorbidities under each subgroup of TOAST in original dataset and literature review dataset. Due to missingness, the valid percentages are reported in this table.

Parameter	Original Data from Multicenter Study						Literature Review				
	Large Artery Atherosclerosis $n = 56$ (32.9%)	Cardio-Embolic $n = 46$ (27.1%)	Small Artery Occlusion $n = 17$ (10.0%)	Other Determined Etiologies $n = 13$ (7.6%)	Undetermined Etiology $n = 38$ (22.4%)	p-Value	Large Artery Atherosclerosis $n = 12$ (10.0%)	Cardio-Embolic $n = 17$ (14.2%)	Small Artery Occlusion $n = 8$ (6.7%)	Other Determined Etiologies $n = 37$ (30.8%)	Undetermined Etiology $n = 46$ (38.3%)	p-Value
Hypertension n (%)	30 (53.6)	35 (76.1)	10 (58.8)	4 (30.8)	25 (65.8)	0.025	6 (66.7)	7 (50.0)	2 (33.3)	15 (48.4)	19 (54.3)	0.762
Diabetes Mellitus n (%)	20 (35.7)	15 (32.6)	6 (35.3)	1 (7.7)	12 (31.6)	0.407	3 (33.3)	1 (7.1)	2 (33.3)	12 (38.7)	17 (48.6)	0.112
Ischemic Heart Disease n (%)	11 (19.6)	21 (45.7)	3 (17.6)	1 (7.7)	2 (5.3)	<0.001	3 (33.3)	1 (7.1)	0 (0.0)	1 (3.2)	3 (8.6)	0.063
Atrial Fibrillation n (%)	2 (3.6)	23 (50.0)	4 (23.5)	1 (7.7)	1 (2.6)	<0.001	1 (11.1)	2 (14.3)	0 (0.0)	3 (9.7)	7 (20.0)	0.625
Carotid stenosis n (%)	16 (28.6)	6 (13.0)	1 (5.9)	0 (0)	2 (5.3)	0.005	0 (0.0)	0 (0.0)	0 (0.0)	1 (3.2)	1 (2.9)	0.923
Chronic Kidney Disease n (%)	8 (14.3)	3 (6.5)	6 (35.3)	1 (7.7)	3 (7.9)	0.028	1 (11.1)	0 (0.0)	0 (0.0)	1 (3.2)	0 (0.0)	0.296
Congestive Heart Failure with Cardiac Ejection Fraction < 40% n (%)	5 (8.9)	8 (17.4)	1 (5.9)	1 (7.7)	5 (13.2)	0.612	0 (0.0)	0 (0.0)	0 (0.0)	0 (0.0)	1 (2.90)	0.785
Active Neoplasm n (%)	2 (3.6)	9 (19.6)	1 (5.9)	0 (0)	0 (0)	0.003	0 (0.0)	0 (0.0)	0 (0.0)	0 (0.0)	0 (0.0)	*
Rheumatological Disease n (%)	0 (0)	3 (6.5)	1 (5.9)	0 (0)	1 (2.6)	0.321	0 (0.0)	0 (0.0)	0 (0.0)	0 (0.0)	0 (0.0)	*
Previous stroke/Transient Ischemic Attack n (%)	0 (0)	0 (0)	0 (0)	0 (0)	1 (2.6)	0.479	2 (22.2)	0 (0.0)	0 (0.0)	2 (6.5)	3 (8.6)	0.315
Current Smoker n (%)	11 (19.6)	5 (10.9)	2 (11.8)	0 (0)	4 (10.5)	0.336	1 (11.1)	2 (14.3)	1 (16.7)	2 (6.3)	3 (8.6)	0.878

* Due to missingness, this value could not be computed. We provided the valid percentages in this table.

4. Discussion

The results of our study indicated that SARS-CoV-2 infection could cause AIS among a considerable number of young and majority male patients who did not have vascular risk factors. The majority of these young patients had embolic-appearing stroke on their neuroimaging. Stroke in older patients can be attributed to the existing vascular risk factors.

4.1. Unsupervised Clustering Identified Three Subgroups of SARS-CoV-2 Infected AIS Patients

Despite several reports of special features and probable underlying coagulopathy in AIS with prior SARS-CoV-2 infection [2,4,6–10], similar reports are lacking in the literature regarding acute coronary syndrome and cardiovascular thromboembolic events. The majority of adverse outcomes among patients with stroke [39,40] or acute coronary syndrome [11–15] were related to the declining trend in seeking urgent care, hospitalization, and receiving guideline indicated measures. On the other hand, the meta-analyses of AIS infected patients presented a mean age of over 65 years and a high load of comorbidities [21,22]. Thereby, there might be a specific group of AIS patients with prior SARS-CoV-2 infection that can be attributed to the virus, while the incidence of stroke among other patients, especially older patients, might be related to their vascular risk factors or critical illness. On this basis, we analyzed the data from our Multinational COVID-19 Stroke Study Group [20] and a dataset of reported patients in the literature. The two cohorts facilitated the identification of three main subgroups. The first group includes patients with no or very few comorbidities—EX-A_3a, EX-S_3a, ML-K_3a, and ML-S_3a. The majority of these patients are young men who had an embolic-appearing stroke. The second subgroup was distinguishable by having a high proportion of hypertension, diabetes, chronic kidney disease, and carotid stenosis, large-artery atherosclerosis origin of stroke, and embolic-appearing stroke on imaging—ML-K_3b, ML-S_3b, EX-A_3b, and EX-S_3b. The third group presented with hypertension, diabetes, ischemic heart disease, atrial fibrillation, congestive heart failure, smoking, and prior TIA or stroke—ML-K_3c, ML-S_3c, EX-A_3c, and EX-S_3c. The majority of the patients in the third group had cardioembolic strokes based on the TOAST classification and had a consistent imaging pattern. Subgroups of patients identified by clinical risk scoring and unsupervised clustering based on the comorbidity panels were similar in the original and literature review datasets. However, unlike the original dataset, the etiology of the stroke in the majority of patients in the second and third subgroups of the review datasets were reported as "strokes of undetermined etiology". Overall, the identified pattern demonstrated by all models may indicate that AIS in only a subgroup of patients can be attributed to the SARS-CoV-2 infection (subgroup a in all models), while AIS in the second and third group of patients may be explained by the existing comorbidities.

4.2. Higher Proportion of AIS Showed Lack of Comorbidities among SARS-CoV-2 Infected Patients

Our study indicated a subgroup of patients with no known comorbidities among the SARS-CoV-2 infected patients (22.0%). The result of our systematic literature review on SARS-CoV-2 infected stroke patients reported from 36 centers in nine countries similarly demonstrated that 24% of the patients had no prior comorbidities. The proportion of the patients without known comorbidities was not available from large-scale studies on SARS-CoV-2 infected stroke patients reported from the UK [5] and the Global COVID-19 Stroke Registry [41]. However, a case series from New York presented that among 32 infected AIS patients, seven (22%) did not report hypertension, diabetes, dyslipidemia, coronary artery disease, congestive heart failure, atrial fibrillation, prior stroke or transient ischemic stroke, or active smoking [42]. A series of 22 AIS patients with SARS-CoV-2 infection from the US demonstrated that 12 out of 22 (54%) of the patients did not report any comorbidities (i.e., hypertension, congestive heart failure, chronic lung disease, chronic kidney disease, diabetes, or atrial fibrillation) [43]. In a report of six consecutive SARS-CoV-2 infected AIS patients from the UK, one patient (16%) had no prior medical history [44]. All of these patients had LVO strokes and elevated D-dimer levels. Similarly, among the five young patients in the US who had LVO stroke after SARS-CoV-2, 2 (40%) reported no prior comorbidities [1]. These findings may suggest that after SARS-CoV-2 infection, higher percentages of patients without comorbidities are having a stroke.

4.3. The Proportion of Comorbidities under Each Subclass of TOAST Is Similar to Population Studies Prior to the Pandemic

The second report from our Multinational COVID-19 Stroke Study Group [20] indicated a lower rate of small-vessel occlusion and lacunar infarcts and a higher risk of embolic-appearing stroke in patients with SARS-CoV-2 infection in comparison with population studies conducted prior to the pandemic. These findings were valid even after considering the geographical regions and countries' health expenditure. The results of subgroup analyses and binary logistic regression in the current study presented that the comorbidity panel of the patients from the original dataset is consistent with the stroke subtypes. To see if the comorbidity panel of AIS patients infected with SARS-CoV-2 was consistent with the large-scale population studies, we further investigated the proportion of comorbidities under each subclass of TOAST (Table 3). We observed that in comparison with population studies, AIS patients infected with SARS-CoV-2 have an almost similar rate of comorbidities under each subclass of TOAST [45–48]. Among patients with large-artery atherosclerosis in our study, 54% had hypertension (versus 54–85%), 36% had diabetes (versus 13–32%), and 20% were smokers (versus 17–50%). Among patients with cardioembolism, hypertension was recorded in 76% (versus 59–86%), diabetes in 33% (versus 13–32%), ischemic heart disease in 46% (versus 20–32%), and atrial fibrillation in 50% (versus 79–86%). Similarly, patients with small-vessel occlusion had 59% hypertension (versus 54–58%), 35% diabetes (versus 12–35%), and 18% ischemic heart disease (versus 15–20%) [45–48]. The result of the literature review presented similar findings, although we recognized a selective report of patients with a lower comorbidity panel (Table 3). These findings suggest that the comorbidities under each stroke etiology are not highly different from the population studies prior to the pandemic, and we should still consider the possibility of bias in reporting the patients with SARS-CoV-2 infection and stroke before concluding the role of the virus as an absolute direct cause of stroke.

5. Study Limitations

To build up the database of SARS-CoV-2 infected patients with stroke, several attempts have been made in collaboration with multiple centers around the world. In addition, we reviewed all available reports to present a comprehensive overview of the topic. Despite this effort, these findings could largely be affected by selection and low sample size bias as well as bias due to incomplete diagnostic workups. In addition, we could not include dyslipidemia in the comorbidity list because data regarding lipid profile could not pass the quality control phase. For instance, some of the included patients were reported before comprehensive diagnostic tests, which may cause a bias in determining the subclasses of TOAST criteria. We also detected publication bias among the reported patients in the literature (significantly lower age, higher LVOs, more severe strokes, and strokes with undetermined and other determined etiologies). In addition, clustering the patients in this study is limited to the vascular risk factors, and we did not include the laboratory findings. Lastly, the unsupervised algorithms tend to be susceptible to the presence of outliers, especially when used for data with a small sample size.

6. Conclusions

Among patients with SARS-CoV-2 and acute ischemic stroke, there is a considerable number of young and majority male patients who did not report vascular risk factors. Therefore, young patients with SARS-CoV-2 infection should be monitors for the sign and symptoms of vascular events, including ischemic stroke. It is reasonable to ensure that these patients and their families are aware of early signs of stroke (BE-FAST) [49]. Stroke in other patients can be attributed to the existing comorbidity panel. We also observed that the proportions of comorbidities under each subclass of TOAST criteria were not different from the population studies prior to the SARS-CoV-2 pandemic.

Supplementary Materials: The following are available online at https://www.mdpi.com/2077-0383/10/5/931/s1. 1. Document S1. Search Strategy in PubMed. 2. Document S2. Detailed Description of the Clustering. 3. Table S1. Dividing the SARS-CoV-2 infected acute ischemic stroke patients into 4 and 5 subgroups based on K-Mean clustering. 4. Table S2. Dividing the SARS-CoV-2 infected acute ischemic stroke patients into 4 and 5 subgroups by Spectral clustering. 5. Table S3. The characteristics of SARS-CoV-2 infected stroke patients in original dataset and literature review. 6. Table S4. The characteristics of the patients from the literature review dataset divided based on clinical risk scoring models. 7. Table S5. The characteristics of the patients from the literature review dataset divided based on unsupervised machine learning models. 8. Figure S1. Contingency Matrices. 9. The COVID-19 Stroke Study Group collaborators affiliations

Author Contributions: Conceptualization, R.Z., V.A. C.G., J.L. and S.S.; methodology, R.Z., V.A. (Venkatesh Avula), S.S., G.T., A.V.S., V.A. (Venkatesh Avula); software, V.A. (Vida Abedi), V.A. (Venkatesh Avula), D.M. and A.V.S.; validation, R.Z., A.M, G.T., S.N., S.S. and M.R.A.; formal analysis, S.S., E.K., J.L. and D.M.; investigation, S.S., M.A., E.K., D.C., C.G. and G.F.; resources, G.T., S.N., A.M., G.F., M.R.A. and the Multinational COVID-19 Stroke Study Group; data curation, S.S., G.F., S.N., V.A. (Venkatesh Avula) and D.M.; writing—original draft preparation, S.S., M.A., E.K., G.F. and D.C.; writing—review and editing, G.T., S.N., A.M., C.G., M.R.A., J.L., R.Z. and the Multinational COVID-19 Stroke Study Group; visualization, A.V.S., V.A. (Venkatesh Avula), D.M. and V.A. (Vida Abedi); supervision, R.Z., V.A. (Vida Abedi) and C.G.; project administration, S.S.; funding acquisition, None. All authors have read and agreed to the published version of the manuscript.

Funding: This research received no external funding.

Institutional Review Board Statement: The study was conducted according to the guidelines of the Declaration of Helsinki and approved by Geisinger Institutional Review Board (IRB ID: 2020-0321, date of approval: 31 March 2020) and other participating institutions, as needed.

Informed Consent Statement: Informed consent wad obtained from majority of subjects involved in this study. Some centers waived the need for informed consent for studies regarding SARS-CoV-2 as a rapid response to COVID-19 pandemic.

Data Availability Statement: The data presented in this study are available in the manuscript and supplemental materials. Additional data are available on request from the corresponding author. The data are not publicly available due to health information privacy.

Conflicts of Interest: The authors declare no conflict of interest.

References

1. Oxley, T.J.; Mocco, J.; Majidi, S.; Kellner, C.P.; Shoirah, H.; Singh, I.P.; De Leacy, R.A.; Shigematsu, T.; Ladner, T.R.; Yaeger, K.A.; et al. Large-Vessel Stroke as a Presenting Feature of Covid-19 in the Young. *N. Engl. J. Med.* **2020**, *382*, e60. [CrossRef]
2. Escalard, S.; Maïer, B.; Redjem, H.; Delvoye, F.; Hébert, S.; Smajda, S.; Ciccio, G.; Desilles, J.-P.; Mazighi, M.; Blanc, R.; et al. Treatment of Acute Ischemic Stroke due to Large Vessel Occlusion With COVID-19. *Stroke* **2020**, *120*, 1–4. [CrossRef]
3. Morassi, M.; Bagatto, D.; Cobelli, M.; D'Agostini, S.; Gigli, G.L.; Bnà, C.; Vogrig, A. Stroke in patients with SARS-CoV-2 infection: Case series. *J. Neurol.* **2020**, *267*, 1–8. [CrossRef] [PubMed]
4. Zhang, Y.; Xiao, M.; Zhang, S.; Xia, P.; Cao, W.; Jiang, W.; Chen, H.; Ding, X.; Zhao, H.; Zhang, H.; et al. Coagulopathy and Antiphospholipid Antibodies in Patients with Covid-19. *N. Engl. J. Med.* **2020**, *382*, e38. [CrossRef] [PubMed]
5. Varatharaj, A.; Thomas, N.; Ellul, M.A.; Davies, N.W.S.; Pollak, T.A.; Tenorio, E.L.; Sultan, M.; Easton, A.; Breen, G.; Zandi, M.; et al. Neurological and neuropsychiatric complications of COVID-19 in 153 patients: A UK-wide surveillance study. *Lancet Psychiatry* **2020**, *2*, 1–8. [CrossRef]
6. D'Anna, L.; Kwan, J.; Brown, Z.; Halse, O.; Jamil, S.; Kalladka, D.; Venter, M.; Banerjee, S. Characteristics and clinical course of Covid-19 patients admitted with acute stroke. *J. Neurol.* **2020**, *11*, 3161–3165. [CrossRef]
7. García Espinosa, J.; Moya Sánchez, E.; Martínez Martínez, A. Severe COVID-19 with debut as bilateral pneumonia, ischemic stroke, and acute myocardial infarction. *Med. Clin.* **2020**, *155*, 188–189. [CrossRef] [PubMed]
8. Gomez-Arbelaez, D.; Ibarra-Sanchez, G.; Garcia-Gutierrez, A.; Comanges-Yeboles, A.; Ansuategui-Vicente, M.; Gonzalez-Fajardo, J.A. Covid-19-Related Aortic Thrombosis: A Report of Four Cases. *Ann. Vasc. Surg.* **2020**, *67*, 10–13. [CrossRef] [PubMed]
9. Viguier, A.; Delamarre, L.; Duplantier, J.; Olivot, J.M.; Bonneville, F. Acute ischemic stroke complicating common carotid artery thrombosis during a severe COVID-19 infection. *J. Neuroradiol.* **2020**, *47*, 393–394. [CrossRef]
10. Malentacchi, M.; Gned, D.; Angelino, V.; Demichelis, S.; Perboni, A.; Veltri, A.; Bertolotto, A.; Capobianco, M. Concomitant brain arterial and venous thrombosis in a COVID-19 patient. *Eur. J. Neurol.* **2020**, *27*, e38–e39. [CrossRef] [PubMed]

11. Solomon, M.D.; McNulty, E.J.; Rana, J.S.; Leong, T.K.; Lee, C.; Sung, S.-H.; Ambrosy, A.P.; Sidney, S.; Go, A.S. The Covid-19 Pandemic and the Incidence of Acute Myocardial Infarction. *N. Engl. J. Med.* **2020**, *383*, 689–691. [CrossRef]
12. Shekhar, A.C.; Effiong, A.; Ruskin, K.J.; Blumen, I.; Mann, N.C.; Narula, J. COVID-19 and the Prehospital Incidence of Acute Cardiovascular Events (from the Nationwide US EMS). *Am. J. Cardiol.* **2020**, *134*, 152–153. [CrossRef]
13. Rashid Hons, M.; Gale Hons, C.P.; Curzen Hons, N.; Ludman Hons, P.; De Belder Hons, M.; Timmis Hons, A.; Mohamed Hons, M.O.; Lüscher Hons, T.F.; Hains Hons, J.; Wu, J.; et al. Impact of Coronavirus Disease 2019 Pandemic on the Incidence and Management of Out-of-Hospital Cardiac Arrest in Patients Presenting With Acute Myocardial Infarction in England. *J. Am. Heart Assoc.* **2020**, *9*, e018579. [CrossRef]
14. Chan, D.Z.; Stewart, R.A.; Kerr, A.J.; Dicker, B.; Kyle, C.V.; Adamson, P.D.; Devlin, G.; Edmond, J.; El-Jack, S.; Elliott, J.M.; et al. The impact of a national COVID-19 lockdown on acute coronary syndrome hospitalisations in New Zealand (ANZACS-QI 55). *Lancet Reg. Health West. Pacific* **2020**, *5*, 100056. [CrossRef]
15. Mesnier, J.; Cottin, Y.; Coste, P.; Ferrari, E.; Schiele, F.; Lemesle, G.; Thuaire, C.; Angoulvant, D.; Cayla, G.; Bouleti, C.; et al. Hospital admissions for acute myocardial infarction before and after lockdown according to regional prevalence of COVID-19 and patient profile in France: A registry study. *Lancet Public Health* **2020**, *5*, e536–e542. [CrossRef]
16. Primessnig, U.; Pieske, B.M.; Sherif, M. Increased mortality and worse cardiac outcome of acute myocardial infarction during the early COVID-19 pandemic. *ESC Heart Fail.* **2020**. [CrossRef]
17. Prieto-Lobato, A.; Ramos-Martínez, R.; Vallejo-Calcerrada, N.; Corbí-Pascual, M.; Córdoba-Soriano, J.G. A Case Series of Stent Thrombosis During the COVID-19 Pandemic. *JACC Case Rep.* **2020**, *2*, 1291–1296. [CrossRef] [PubMed]
18. Hamadeh, A.; Aldujeli, A.; Briedis, K.; Tecson, K.M.; Sanz-Sánchez, J.; Al dujeili, M.; Al-Obeidi, A.; Diez, J.L.; Žaliūnas, R.; Stoler, R.C.; et al. Characteristics and Outcomes in Patients Presenting With COVID-19 and ST-Segment Elevation Myocardial Infarction. *Am. J. Cardiol.* **2020**, *131*, 1–6. [CrossRef] [PubMed]
19. Anupama, B.K.; Chaudhuri, D. A Review of Acute Myocardial Injury in Coronavirus Disease 2019. *Cureus* **2020**, *12*. [CrossRef]
20. Shahjouei, S.; Naderi, S.; Li, J.; Khan, A.; Chaudhary, D.; Farahmand, G.; Male, S.; Griessenauer, C.; Sabra, M.; Mondello, S.; et al. Risk of Cerebrovascular Events in Hospitalized Patients with SARS-CoV-2 Infection. *Ebiomedicine* **2020**, *59*, 102939. [CrossRef]
21. Nannoni, S.; de Groot, R.; Bell, S.; Markus, H.S. Stroke in COVID-19: A systematic review and meta-analysis. *Int. J. Stroke* **2020**, 1–13. [CrossRef] [PubMed]
22. Yamakawa, M.; Kuno, T.; Mikami, T. Clinical Characteristics of Stroke with COVID-19: A Systematic Review and Meta-Analysis. *J. Stroke Cerebrovasc. Dis.* **2020**, *29*, 105288. [CrossRef] [PubMed]
23. Bekelis, K.; Missios, S.; Ahmad, J.; Labropoulos, N.; Schirmer, C.M.; Calnan, D.R.; Skinner, J.; MacKenzie, T.A. Ischemic Stroke Occurs Less Frequently in Patients with COVID-19: A Multicenter Cross-Sectional Study. *Stroke* **2020**, 3570–3576. [CrossRef] [PubMed]
24. Walkey, A.J.; Wiener, R.S.; Ghobrial, J.M.; Curtis, L.H.; Benjamin, E.J. Incident stroke and mortality associated with new-onset atrial fibrillation in patients hospitalized with severe sepsis. *JAMA* **2011**, *306*, 2248–2255. [CrossRef] [PubMed]
25. Moss, T.J.; Calland, J.F.; Enfield, K.B.; Gomez-Manjarres, D.C.; Ruminski, C.; Dimarco, J.P.; Lake, D.E.; Moorman, J.R. New-onset atrial fibrillation in the critically ill. *Crit. Care Med.* **2017**, *45*, 790–797. [CrossRef]
26. Boehme, A.K.; Ranawat, P.; Luna, J.; Kamel, H.; Elkind, M.S.V. Risk of Acute Stroke after Hospitalization for Sepsis: A Case-Crossover Study. *Stroke* **2017**, *48*, 574–580. [CrossRef] [PubMed]
27. Zaki, N.; Alashwal, H.; Ibrahim, S. Association of hypertension, diabetes, stroke, cancer, kidney disease, and high-cholesterol with COVID-19 disease severity and fatality: A systematic review. *Diabetes Metab. Syndr. Clin. Res. Rev.* **2020**, *14*, 1133–1142. [CrossRef]
28. Boehme, A.K.; Esenwa, C.; Elkind, M.S.V. Stroke Risk Factors, Genetics, and Prevention. *Circ. Res.* **2017**, *120*, 472–495. [CrossRef]
29. Wiseman, S.J.; Ralston, S.H.; Wardlaw, J.M. Cerebrovascular disease in rheumatic diseases a systematic review and meta-analysis. *Stroke* **2016**, *47*, 943–950. [CrossRef] [PubMed]
30. Ghoshal, S.; Freedman, B.I. Mechanisms of Stroke in Patients with Chronic Kidney Disease. *Am. J. Nephrol.* **2019**, *50*, 229–239. [CrossRef]
31. Adams, H.; Bendixen, B.; Kappelle, L.; Biller, J.; Love, B.; Gordon, D.; Marsh, E. Classification of Subtype of Acute Ischemic Stroke. *Stroke* **1993**, *23*, 35–41. [CrossRef] [PubMed]
32. Von Elm, E.; Altman, D.G.; Egger, M.; Pocock, S.J.; Gøtzsche, P.C.; Vandenbroucke, J.P. The strengthening the reporting of observational studies in epidemiology (STROBE) statement: Guidelines for reporting observational studies. *Int. J. Surg.* **2014**, *12*, 1495–1499. [CrossRef]
33. Moher, D.; Shamseer, L.; Clarke, M.; Ghersi, D.; Liberati, A.; Petticrew, M.; Shekelle, P.; Stewart, L.A. PRISMA-P Group Preferred reporting items for systematic review and meta-analysis protocols (PRISMA-P) 2015 statement. *Syst. Rev.* **2015**, *4*, 1. [CrossRef]
34. Von Luxburg, U. A tutorial on spectral clustering. *Stat. Comput.* **2007**, *17*, 395–416. [CrossRef]
35. Palacio-Niño, J.-O.; Berzal, F. Evaluation Metrics for Unsupervised Learning Algorithms. *arXiv* **2019**, arXiv:1905.05667.
36. Andy Bunn, M.K. An Introduction to dplR. *Ind. Commer. Train.* **2008**, *10*, 11–18. [CrossRef]
37. Warnes, G.R.; Bolker, B.; Bonebakker, L.; Gentleman, R.; Huber, W.; Liaw, A.; Lumley, T.; Maechler, M.; Magnusson, A.; Moeller, S. Gplots: Various R programming tools for plotting data. *R Packag. Version* **2009**, *2*, 1.
38. Pedregosa, F.; Varoquaux, G.; Gramfort, A.; Michel, V.; Thirion, B.; Grisel, O.; Blondel, M.; Prettenhofer, P.; Weiss, R.; Dubourg, V.; et al. Scikit-learn: Machine Learning in Python. *J. Mach. Learn. Res.* **2011**, *12*, 2825–2830.

39. Richter, D.; Eyding, J.; Weber, R.; Bartig, D.; Grau, A.; Hacke, W.; Krogias, C. Analysis of Nationwide Stroke Patient Care in Times of COVID-19 Pandemic in Germany. *Stroke* **2020**, *18*, 1756286420971895. [CrossRef]
40. Ghoreishi, A.; Arsang-Jang, S.; Sabaa-Ayoun, Z.; Yassi, N.; Sylaja, P.N.; Akbari, Y.; Divani, A.A.; Biller, J.; Phan, T.; Steinwender, S.; et al. Stroke Care Trends During COVID-19 Pandemic in Zanjan Province, Iran. From the CASCADE Initiative: Statistical Analysis Plan and Preliminary Results. *J. Stroke Cerebrovasc. Dis.* **2020**, *29*, 105321. [CrossRef]
41. Ntaios, G.; Michel, P.; Georgiopoulos, G.; Guo, Y.; Li, W.; Xiong, J.; Calleja, P.; Ostos, F.; González-Ortega, G.; Fuentes, B.; et al. Characteristics and Outcomes in Patients With COVID-19 and Acute Ischemic Stroke The Global COVID-19 Stroke Registry. *Stroke* **2020**, *51*, e254–e258. [CrossRef] [PubMed]
42. Yaghi, S.; Ishida, K.; Torres, J.; Mac Grory, B.; Raz, E.; Humbert, K.; Henninger, N.; Trivedi, T.; Lillemoe, K.; Alam, S.; et al. SARS2-CoV-2 and Stroke in a New York Healthcare System. *Stroke* **2020**, *120*, 1–10.
43. Sweid, A.; Hammoud, B.; Bekelis, K.; Missios, S.; Tjoumakaris, S.I.; Gooch, M.R.; Herial, N.A.; Zarzour, H.; Romo, V.; DePrince, M.; et al. Cerebral ischemic and hemorrhagic complications of coronavirus disease 2019. *Int. J. Stroke* **2020**, *15*, 733–742. [CrossRef]
44. Beyrouti, R.; Adams, M.E.; Benjamin, L.; Cohen, H.; Farmer, S.F.; Goh, Y.Y.; Humphries, F.; Jäger, H.R.; Losseff, N.A.; Perry, R.J.; et al. Characteristics of ischaemic stroke associated with COVID-19. *J. Neurol. Neurosurg. Psychiatry* **2020**, *91*, 889–891. [CrossRef]
45. Porcello Marrone, L.C.; Diogo, L.P.; De Oliveira, F.M.; Trentin, S.; Scalco, R.S.; De Almeida, A.G.; Gutierres, L.D.C.V.; Marrone, A.C.H.; Da Costa, J.C. Risk factors among stroke subtypes in Brazil. *J. Stroke Cerebrovasc. Dis.* **2013**, *22*, 32–35. [CrossRef]
46. Jackova, J.; Sedova, P.; Brown, R.D.; Zvolsky, M.; Volna, M.; Baluchova, J.; Belaskova, S.; Bednarik, J.; Mikulik, R. Risk Factors in Ischemic Stroke Subtypes: A Community-Based Study in Brno, Czech Republic. *J. Stroke Cerebrovasc. Dis.* **2020**, *29*, 104503. [CrossRef]
47. Bejot, Y.; Catteau, A.; Caillier, M.; Rouaud, O.; Durier, J.; Marie, C.; Di Carlo, A.; Osseby, G.V.; Moreau, T.; Giroud, M. Trends in incidence, risk factors, and survival in symptomatic lacunar stroke in dijon, france, from 1989 to 2006: A population-based study. *Stroke* **2008**, *39*, 1945–1951. [CrossRef]
48. Ihle-Hansen, H.; Thommessen, B.; Wyller, T.B.; Engedal, K.; Fure, B. Risk factors for and incidence of subtypes of ischemic stroke. *Funct. Neurol.* **2012**, *27*, 35–40. [PubMed]
49. Aroor, S.; Singh, R.; Goldstein, L.B. BE-FAST (Balance, Eyes, Face, Arm, Speech, Time): Reducing the Proportion of Strokes Missed Using the FAST Mnemonic. *Stroke* **2017**, *48*, 479–481. [CrossRef] [PubMed]

Article

Usefulness of Respiratory Mechanics and Laboratory Parameter Trends as Markers of Early Treatment Success in Mechanically Ventilated Severe Coronavirus Disease: A Single-Center Pilot Study

Daisuke Kasugai [1,*], Masayuki Ozaki [1], Kazuki Nishida [2], Hiroaki Hiraiwa [1], Naruhiro Jingushi [1], Atsushi Numaguchi [1], Norihito Omote [3], Yuichiro Shindo [3] and Yukari Goto [1]

1. Department of Emergency and Critical Care Medicine, Nagoya University Graduate School of Medicine, Tsurumai-cho 65, Syowa-ku, Nagoya, Aichi 466-8550, Japan; mozaki@med.nagoya-u.ac.jp (M.O.); hiraiwa.hiroaki@med.nagoya-u.ac.jp (H.H.); jinjin435@yahoo.co.jp (N.J.); nummer0116@gmail.com (A.N.); gotoyu@med.nagoya-u.ac.jp (Y.G.)
2. Department of Biostatistics Section, Center for Advanced Medicine and Clinical Research, Nagoya University Graduate School of Medicine, 65, Tsurumaicho, Showa, Nagoya, Aichi 466-8550, Japan; nishida@med.nagoya-u.ac.jp
3. Department of Respiratory Medicine, Nagoya University Graduate School of Medicine, Tsurumai-cho 65, Syowa-ku, Nagoya, Aichi 466-8550, Japan; nori920@med.nagoya-u.ac.jp (N.O.); yshindo@med.nagoya-u.ac.jp (Y.S.)
* Correspondence: dkasugai@med.nagoya-u.ac.jp; Tel./Fax: +81-52-744-2659

Citation: Kasugai, D.; Ozaki, M.; Nishida, K.; Hiraiwa, H.; Jingushi, N.; Numaguchi, A.; Omote, N.; Shindo, Y.; Goto, Y. Usefulness of Respiratory Mechanics and Laboratory Parameter Trends as Markers of Early Treatment Success in Mechanically Ventilated Severe Coronavirus Disease: A Single-Center Pilot Study. *J. Clin. Med.* 2021, *10*, 2513. https://doi.org/10.3390/jcm10112513

Academic Editors: Vida Abedi and Michela Sabbatucci

Received: 24 April 2021
Accepted: 4 June 2021
Published: 6 June 2021

Publisher's Note: MDPI stays neutral with regard to jurisdictional claims in published maps and institutional affiliations.

Copyright: © 2021 by the authors. Licensee MDPI, Basel, Switzerland. This article is an open access article distributed under the terms and conditions of the Creative Commons Attribution (CC BY) license (https://creativecommons.org/licenses/by/4.0/).

Abstract: Whether a patient with severe coronavirus disease (COVID-19) will be successfully liberated from mechanical ventilation (MV) early is important in the COVID-19 pandemic. This study aimed to characterize the time course of parameters and outcomes of severe COVID-19 in relation to the timing of liberation from MV. This retrospective, single-center, observational study was performed using data from mechanically ventilated COVID-19 patients admitted to the ICU between 1 March 2020 and 15 December 2020. Early liberation from ventilation (EL group) was defined as successful extubation within 10 days of MV. The trends of respiratory mechanics and laboratory data were visualized and compared between the EL and prolonged MV (PMV) groups using smoothing spline and linear mixed effect models. Of 52 admitted patients, 31 mechanically ventilated COVID-19 patients were included (EL group, 20 (69%); PMV group, 11 (31%)). The patients' median age was 71 years. While in-hospital mortality was low (6%), activities of daily living (ADL) at the time of hospital discharge were significantly impaired in the PMV group compared to the EL group (mean Barthel index (range): 30 (7.5–95) versus 2.5 (0–22.5), $p = 0.048$). The trends in respiratory compliance were different between patients in the EL and PMV groups. An increasing trend in the ventilatory ratio during MV until approximately 2 weeks was observed in both groups. The interaction between daily change and earlier liberation was significant in the trajectory of the thrombin–antithrombin complex, antithrombin 3, fibrinogen, C-reactive protein, lymphocyte, and positive end-expiratory pressure (PEEP) values. The indicator of physiological dead space increases during MV. The trajectory of markers of the hypercoagulation status, inflammation, and PEEP were significantly different depending on the timing of liberation from MV. These findings may provide insight into the pathophysiology of COVID-19 during treatment in the critical care setting.

Keywords: COVID-19; mechanical ventilation; respiratory failure

1. Introduction

The number of patients with coronavirus disease (COVID-19) is increasing worldwide, including in Japan. In Japan, 8.1% of all COVID-19 cases require mechanical ventilation (MV), and the 30-day mortality rate has been reported to be 30% [1–3]. COVID-19 requires a longer treatment duration than other causes of viral pneumonia, with a median length of stay in the intensive care unit (ICU) of 10 days [4]. Once the capacity of ICU services for COVID-19 is overwhelmed, a significant increase in mortality and excess mortality from any cause may be expected [3,5]. Furthermore, prolonged MV is a risk factor for ICU-acquired weakness [6]. In this context, whether the patient with severe COVID-19 will be liberated from MV is of particular interest for improving patients' outcomes.

Thus far, little is known about the time course of COVID-19-related respiratory failure during ICU treatment. Previous studies have suggested that severe COVID-19 is characterized by excessive inflammation and hypercoagulation [7–9]. In addition to the conventional acute respiratory distress syndrome phenotype, there is another phenotype of high pulmonary compliance and increased physiologic dead space, which is thought to be due to pulmonary microthrombosis [10]. Meanwhile, lower compliance was reported to be associated with prolonged MV, which is similar to findings in other causes of acute respiratory distress syndrome [11]. Considering the complexity of the pathophysiology of severe COVID-19, knowledge of how time series data of clinical parameter changes is needed to assess the response to treatment and to make clinical decisions. However, it is poorly documented how respiratory and laboratory findings—including respiratory compliance, physiologic dead space, and inflammatory and coagulation biomarkers of severe COVID-19—change in response to empirical treatment, including anti-viral medication usage, anti-coagulation, or corticosteroid administration.

The aim of this study was to characterize the time course of the parameters and outcomes of severe COVID-19 in relation to the timing of liberation from MV.

2. Materials and Methods

2.1. Ethics Statements

The Nagoya University Hospital Institutional Review Board approved this study (registration number: 2020-0519), and informed consent of the participants was waived but the opt-out method was adopted according to the ethics guidelines.

2.2. Study Design, Setting, and Population

To characterize the time course of the parameters and outcomes of severe COVID-19 in relation to the timing of liberation from MV, we conducted a retrospective observational study at Nagoya University Hospital from 1 March 2020 to 15 December 2020. Nagoya University Hospital is a quaternary academic medical center with 1035 beds, including 10 emergency and medical ICU (EMICU) beds and 30 surgical ICU beds, located in the Aichi Prefecture, one of the epicenters of COVID-19 from the first wave of the pandemic in Japan. The EMICU usually treats 10–20 patients with extracorporeal membrane oxygenation (ECMO) annually for the management of severe respiratory failure or cardiogenic shock. All severe COVID-19 cases in the hospital and transfers from other hospitals, which are coordinated by the Infectious Disease Control Office in Nagoya City, were admitted to the air-isolated beds of the EMICU. Patients requiring less than 4 L of oxygen were transferred to another COVID-19 ward.

Eligible patients in this study had COVID-19 that required MV. Exclusion criteria were patients introduced to venovenous (VV)-ECMO. The diagnosis of COVID-19 was confirmed by real-time polymerase chain reaction test of severe acute respiratory syndrome coronavirus 2 (SARS-CoV-2) from any specimen. Patients were categorized into the early liberation from ventilation group (EL group) or prolonged MV group (PMV group). Early liberation from MV was defined as successful extubation within 10 days of MV, since 10 days is the widely adopted duration of antiviral and steroid treatment [12,13].

2.3. Management of Coronavirus Disease

All mechanically ventilated patients with COVID-19 were initially managed with pressure-controlled ventilation. Placement in the prone position was considered when the PaO_2/FiO_2 ratio was less than 150, and was performed at the physicians' discretion.

Neuromuscular blockade was administered for less than 48 h when significant patient ventilator desynchrony was observed. All patients received favipiravir or remdesivir as antiviral medications, depending on clinical availability. A 10-day course of intravenous dexamethasone (6.6 mg) once daily was initially started [12]. Antibiotics were administered to patients with suspected bacterial co-infections. Unfractured heparin was administered and titrated to maintain the activated prothrombin time ratio between 1.5 and 2.5 after MV in all patients [14]. Tracheostomy was considered if patients could not be extubated within 10 days [15]. Because of inadequate personal protective equipment and concerns about nosocomial infections, physiotherapists were unable to be directly involved in bedside rehabilitation [16]. The bedside rehabilitation was performed by a physiotherapist after negative conversion of the SARS-CoV-2 PCR test result, or it was performed by doctors and nurses under the supervision of a physiotherapist after the patient was liberated from MV.

2.4. Data Collection

Demographic information was extracted from patients' electronic medical records. The details of the parameters during ICU management were extracted from the ICU patient information system (Fortec ACSYS, Phillips Japan). Ventilator parameters were recorded minutely by the IntelliVue MX800 (Philips Japan). Static compliance was calculated using the tidal volume and driving pressure. As an indicator of physiologic dead space, the ventilatory ratio was calculated using the following formula: [minute ventilation (mL/min) × partial pressure of carbon dioxide (mm Hg)]/(predicted body weight × 100 × 37.5) [17,18]. The following laboratory parameters were routinely monitored daily during MV and extracted from the database: coagulation markers (D-dimer, thrombin-antithrombin complex (TAT), plasmin-alpha2-plasmininhibitor-complex, fibrin degradation products (FDP), antithrombin 3 (AT3), fibrinogen, activated partial thromboplastin time ratio, and platelet count), biomarkers of inflammation and lung injury (C-reactive protein level, procalcitonin (PCT) level, ferritin level, white blood cell count, neutrophil count, lymphocyte count, 50% hemolytic complement activity (CH50), and Krebs von den Lungen-6 (KL-6)). Activities of daily living (ADL) before admission and at the time of hospital discharge were measured using the Barthel index, which was routinely evaluated by the nurses and recorded in the nursing summary [19,20].

2.5. Statistical Analysis

Continuous data are summarized as median and interquartile range (25th–75th percentiles). Categorical variables are expressed as numbers (%). Non-parametric variables were compared between the EL and PMV groups using the Mann–Whitney U test. The Barthel index at hospital discharge was compared between the groups, and the median Barthel index of each component in both groups was visualized using a Rader chart. Non-parametric trending changes in each parameter in both groups were fitted by smoothing splines. Additionally, multivariable mixed effect linear regression models were used to evaluate the longitudinal associations between daily changes in each parameter during initial 5 days and the EL group [21]. Variables were excluded from this evaluation when the linearity assumption seems to be inappropriate, by judging from the spline regression analysis. Within-subject changes were included in the model as random effects to adjust for patient factors. Early liberation, days after MV, and their interaction were assumed as fixed effects in the model. When the interaction term was statistically significant, we considered that the trajectory of the parameter was different between the two groups. Using the parameters that showed significant differences in daily changes that interacted with early liberation in the linear mixed effect model, the trajectory of each parameter was converted into the coefficient using linear regression model, and finally converted into the EL prediction score. The cutoff of each coefficient was determined by the results of the linear mixed effect model. Receiver operating characteristic (ROC) curve analysis was subsequently used to evaluate the performance of the predictive score. For missing data, the number of missing values were reported and complete-case analysis was performed. All analyses were performed using R software (version 4.0.2; The R Foundation).

3. Results

3.1. Patient Characteristics and Outcomes

Of the 52 patients with COVID-19 admitted to the EMICU during the study period, 31 of 32 mechanically ventilated patients were included in this study; one patient required VV-ECMO and was excluded (Supplementary Figure S1: additional file S1). The details of the baseline characteristics are shown in Table 1. The median age of the patients was 71 years. Most patients did not require nursing care before admission (median Barthel index: 100) and were more likely to be male (86%). Common comorbidities included diabetes mellitus (58%) and hypertension (38%). Twenty cases were successful in early liberation from MV (69%). The median worst partial pressure of oxygen/fraction of inspired oxygen (P/F) ratio was found to be 96. The initial ventilatory parameters did not differ between the groups. D-dimer levels were slightly elevated in the PMV group compared to the MV group. Overall, in-hospital mortality was low (6%), and one patient developed massive ischemic stroke after extubation and was withdrawn from care. Figure 1A,B shows the Barthel indexes of both groups at hospital discharge. ADL at the time of hospital discharge was significantly impaired in the PMV group compared to the EL group (median Barthel index (range): 30 (7.5–95) versus 2.5 (0–22.5), $p = 0.048$).

Table 1. Patient characteristics.

Characteristic	Total Patients (31)	Early Liberation from MV		p Value
		Success (20)	Failure (11)	
Age, years, median (IQR)	71 (64–76)	71 (64–77)	70 (56–73)	0.535
Male sex, n (%)	25 (81)	17 (85)	8 (73)	0.546
BMI (kg/m^2), median (IQR)	24.5 (21.8–28.5)	25.2 (21.5–28.5)	23.2 (22.4–30.2)	0.67
Comorbidities, n, median (IQR)	1 (1–2)	1 (1–2)	2 (1–2)	0.118
HT, n (%)	11 (35)	6 (30)	5 (45)	0.452
DM, n (%)	18 (58)	10 (50)	8 (73)	0.275
Chronic heart failure, n (%)	3 (9.6)	1 (5)	2 (18)	0.281
End-stage renal disease, n (%)	5 (16)	2 (10)	3 (27)	0.317
Cancer, n (%)	2 (6.4)	1 (5)	1 (9.1)	>0.99
Chronic pulmonary disease, n (%)	2 (6.4)	1 (5)	1 (9.1)	>0.99
Dementia, n (%)	3 (9.6)	3 (15)	0 (0)	0.535
4C mortality score, median (IQR)	12 (11–14)	12 (11–13)	12 (11–14)	0.707
SOFA score, median (IQR)	7 (6–10)	7 (5–10)	7 (6–10)	0.802
APACHE II score, median (IQR)	13 (11–19)	13 (11–19)	15 (11–19)	0.521
Parameters at the time of MV				
PaO$_2$/FiO$_2$ ratio	96 (82–114)	85 (81–114)	101 (89–113)	0.47
Static compliance, mL/cmH$_2$O, median (IQR)	38 (33–42)	38 (34–43)	38 (33–39)	0.614
Ventilatory ratio, median (IQR)	1.26 (1.17–1.41)	1.24 (1.17–1.32)	1.38 (1.18–1.58)	0.119
PEEP, cmH$_2$O	11 (10–14)	10 (10–12)	14 (10–15)	
NMB, n (%)	5 (16)	4 (20)	1 (9.1)	
Prone positioning, n (%)	13 (42)	7 (35)	6 (55)	0.477

Table 1. Cont.

Characteristic	Total Patients (31)	Early Liberation from MV		p Value
		Success (20)	Failure (11)	
D-dimer level, µg/mL, median (IQR)	2.31 (1.52–4.54)	1.63 (1.09–4.18)	3.36 (2.35–10.1)	0.132
Treatment				
Anti-viral, n (%)				
Favipiravir	15 (48)	8 (40)	7 (64)	
Remdesivir	16 (52)	13 (65)	3 (27)	
Steroid, n (%)	26 (84)	19 (95)	7 (64)	0.0416
Initial antibacterial drug, n (%)	21 (68)	14 (70)	7 (64)	>0.99
Tracheostomy, n (%)	7 (23)	0 (0)	7 (64)	<0.001
Duration of mechanical ventilation (days), median (IQR)	10 (5–20)	6 (4–9)	24 (20–30)	<0.001
ICU stay, median (IQR)	12 (10–20)	11 (8–12)	27 (21–36)	<0.001
In-hospital mortality, n (%)	2 (6.5)	1 (5)	1 (9.1)	>0.99
Barthel index at discharge, median (IQR)	20 (0–65)	30 (7.5–95)	2.5 (0–22.5)	0.048

BMI, body mass index; HT, hypertension; DM, diabetes mellitus; SOFA, Sequential Organ Failure Assessment; APACHE II, acute physiology and chronic health evaluation II; MV, mechanical ventilation; PaO_2/FiO_2, partial pressure of oxygen/fraction of inspired oxygen; PEEP, positive end-expiratory pressure; NMB, neuromuscular blockade; ICU, intensive care unit.

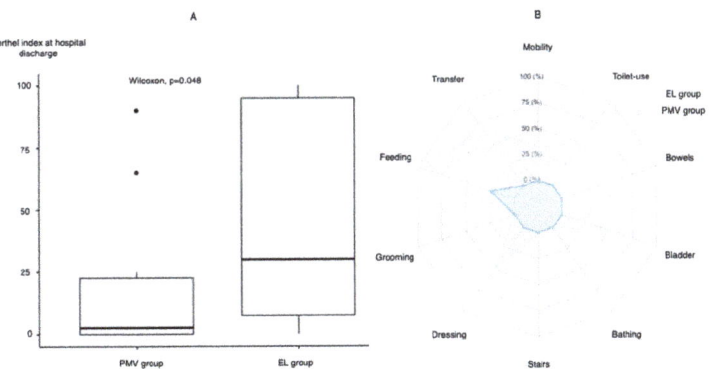

Figure 1. Comparison of the Barthel index at hospital discharge between the early liberation and prolonged mechanical ventilation groups. (**A**) Comparison between the two groups. (**B**) Radar chart of each component of the Barthel index. EL group, early liberation from ventilation group; PMV group, prolonged mechanical ventilation group.

3.2. Ventilatory and Laboratory Parameters and Liberation from Mechanical Ventilation

Figure 2 shows the trends in ventilatory parameters in each group. The EL group was managed with a lower PEEP throughout the period. Trends of compliance and the P/F ratio were different between the EL and PMV groups with an inflection point on day 5 of MV. The ventilatory ratio was higher in the PMV group than in the EL group. Of note, an increasing trend in the ventilatory ratio during MV until approximately 2 weeks was observed in both groups.

Figures 3 and 4 show each trend of laboratory parameters according to the duration of MV. Despite appropriate therapeutic anticoagulation, D-dimer and FDP levels were gradually increased and the AT3 level was decreased until day 14 in the PMV group. A decrease in the platelet count was not observed. In terms of inflammatory biomarkers, CRP levels were continuously high in the PMV group. PCT levels were initially high in patients with successful early liberation, and then they immediately became negative. The ferritin levels increased in both groups at about 2 weeks, but a significant difference in their trajectory was not observed. While the CH50 level was decreased within the normal range, it increased in the EL group. KL-6 levels were significantly high initially in the PMV group, but elevation of KL-6 levels was observed in both groups.

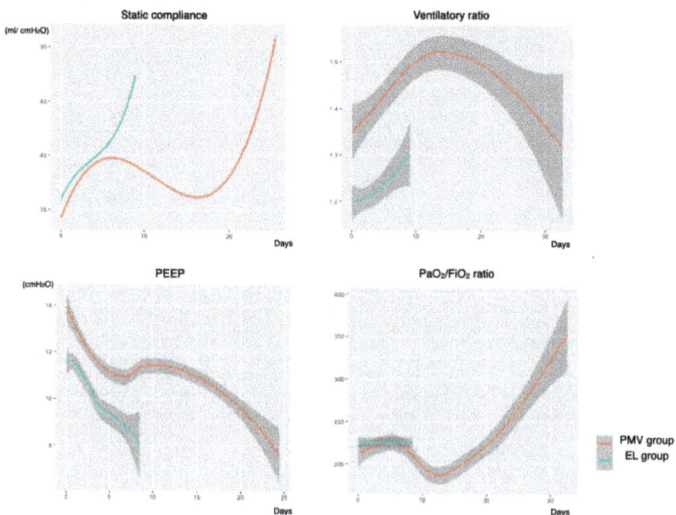

Figure 2. Trend of respiratory mechanic parameters in relation to the timing of liberation from mechanical ventilation. PEEP, positive end-expiratory pressure; EL group, early liberation from ventilation group; PMV group, prolonged mechanical ventilation group. The number of study timepoint: static compliance, 474,429; ventilatory ratio, 1813; PEEP, 474,941; PaO_2/FiO_2 ratio, 1778.

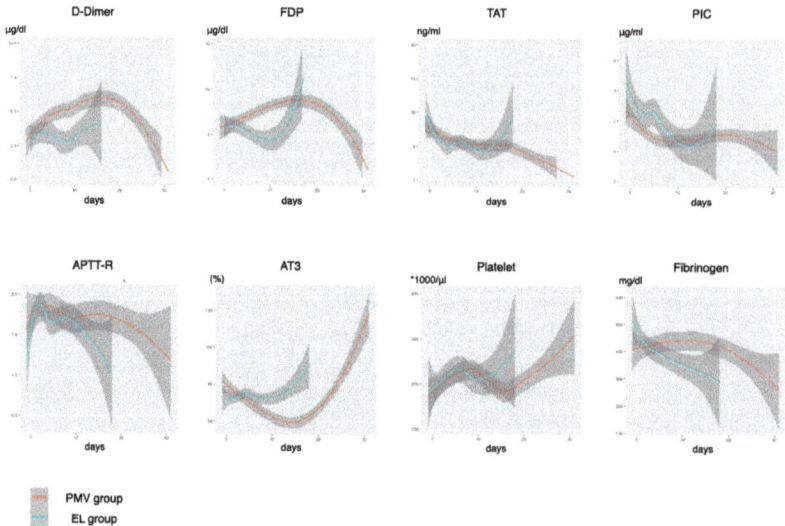

Figure 3. Trends of the coagulation parameters. FDP, fibrin degradation products; TAT, thrombin-antithrombin complex; PIC, plasmin-alpha2-plasmininhibitor-complex; APTT-R, activated partial thromboplastin time ratio; AT3, antithrombin 3; EL group, early liberation from ventilation group; PMV group, prolonged mechanical ventilation group. The number of study timepoint: D-dimer, 393; FDP, 392; TAT, 355; PIC, 354; APTT-R, 394; AT3, 392; platelet, 394; FG, 394.

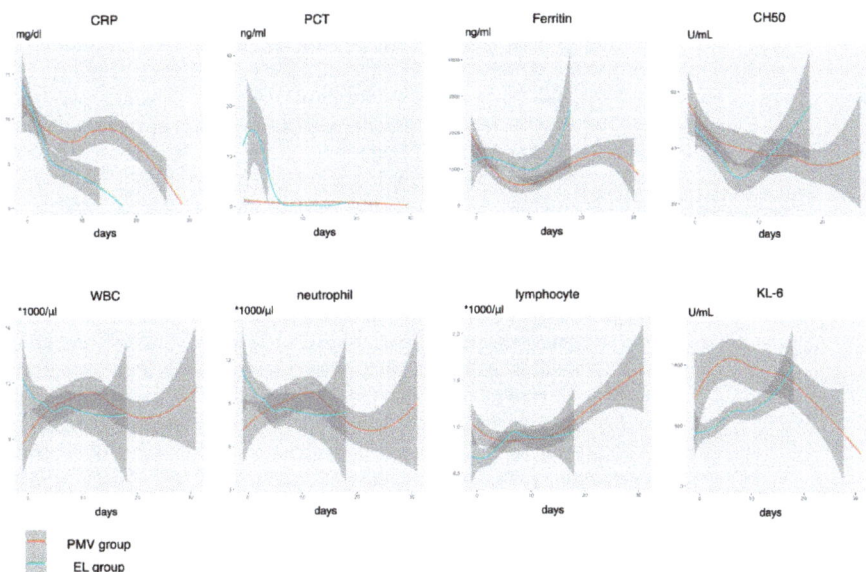

Figure 4. Trends of the laboratory parameters of inflammation. CH50, 50% hemolytic complement activity; CRP, C-reactive protein; PCT, procalcitonin; WBC, white blood cell; KL6, Krebs von den Lungen-6; EL group, early liberation from ventilation group; PMV group, prolonged mechanical ventilation group. The number of study timepoint: CRP, 394; PCT, 392; Ferritin, 349; CH50, 198; WBC, 396; neutrophil, 393; lymphocyte, 393; KL6, 370.

The results of the longitudinal association between daily changes in each parameter during the initial 5 days and early liberation from MV are shown in Supplementary Figure S2 (Additional file S2). We found that CRP ($p = 0.048$), TAT ($p = 0.019$), fibrinogen ($p = 0.002$), AT3 ($p < 0.001$), lymphocyte ($p = 0.009$), and PEEP ($p < 0.001$) values showed significantly different daily changes that interacted with early liberation. An EL prediction score was developed using the trajectory of these variables (Supplementary Figure S3: Additional file S3). The area under ROC for the prediction of early liberation (95 %CI) was 0.913 (0.823–1), which was significantly higher than other severity scales (0.573 (0.34–0.802), 0.47 (0.262–0.679), and 0.457 (0.225–0.689) for the APACHEII, SOFA, and 4C mortality scores, respectively).

4. Discussion

The main findings of this study are as follows: (1) prolonged MV was significantly associated with poor ADL at discharge in the setting of rehabilitation-limiting situations; (2) the trajectory of ventilator and laboratory data were characterized between patients with early liberation and prolonged MV; and (3) early-phase differences in the trajectories of hypercoagulability, inflammatory, and PEEP markers were observed depending on the timing of liberation from MV, which can potentially be useful in identifying patients with early treatment success.

In this single-center observational study, the mortality rate was low compared to that in previous reports [1–3]. However, patients with prolonged MV showed significantly poor ADL. The relationship between the length of MV and ADL is well-known [22]. The ADL impairment may be due to clinical setting characteristics in the management of severe COVID-19, i.e., bedside interventions of rehabilitation were significantly impaired in our hospital because of physiotherapists' concerns of exhaustion of personal protective equipment and nosocomial infection. Although we could not evaluate the long-term outcome of quality of life, our findings indicate that post-intensive care syndrome is particularly important in COVID-19 patients with prolonged MV. This finding may aid in future clinical decision-making and policymaking in terms of staffing and resource allocation in critical care settings during ongoing pandemics. Our findings indicate the importance of direct intervention by physiotherapists in the management of COVID-19. The duration of MV may be used as a surrogate marker for ADL impairment after treatment.

We observed a decreasing trend in respiratory static compliance despite the higher PEEP setting after day 5 and a higher ventilatory ratio in patients with prolonged MV than in those with early liberation. In patients with worsening COVID-19, two types of pathophysiologies may explain this change: pulmonary micro-thromboembolism and organizing pneumonia [23]. Our findings were consistent with those of previous reports in that therapeutic anticoagulation was not fully controlled coagulopathy in COVID-19 [24]. The decrease in the AT3 level and continuous elevation of the TAT suggests poorly controlled thrombin activity during the treatment. The role of complement activation in thrombotic tendency uncontrolled by heparin has been previously documented [25]. In this study, complements were gradually consumed during the treatment phase, which is consistent with previous findings [26]. Meanwhile, the combination of the elevation of the KL-6 level, a marker of interstitial lung injury, worsening respiratory compliance with poor recruitment, and increased physiologic dead space may be explained by the ongoing fibrin deposition of organizing pneumonia [27,28]. This is consistent with the pathologic findings of acute fibrinous and organizing pneumonia-predominant histology in the later phase of treatment, and this may explain the downward trend in compliance despite the higher PEEP setting [29,30]. To further understand the underlying mechanism in the exacerbating conditions, prospective studies with computed tomography pulmonary angiography and/or bronchoalveolar lavage evaluation may be warranted.

Notably, an increasing trend in the ventilatory ratio was also observed in patients with early liberation and in patients with prolonged ventilation. Taken together, these findings may indicate that empirical therapeutic anticoagulation and a 10-day course of dexamethasone (6.6 mg) were not enough to manage the underlying mechanisms. Recently, the CoDEX trial showed that administration of a higher dose of dexamethasone for severe COVID-19 shortened the duration of MV [31]. Further evaluation of anticoagulation and more intensive anti-inflammatory management may be warranted in patients with prolonged ventilation. The trajectory of respiratory compliance and oxygenation was different between the two groups after day 5 of MV. Early tracheostomy was associated with early liberation from MV and preserved ADL [32,33]. It may be reasonable to make a clinical decision for additional treatment or earlier tracheostomy by reviewing the clinical time course until about day 5 of MV.

This study has several limitations. Firstly, because of the nature of the single-center observational study with a small sample size, we mainly focused on descriptive analysis. Furthermore, selection bias might have occurred in inter-hospital transfers, which may limit the external validity of our study. The prognostic value of each parameter and the predictive score should be evaluated in further multicenter studies. Secondly, the titration of PEEP was not protocolized and carried out according to bedside clinicians' preferences. Although a higher PEEP setting was used in patients with prolonged MV, it is unclear whether these patients require a higher PEEP setting because of poor oxygenation or if an unnecessarily high PEEP setting was prescribed, as this may worsen the ventilation perfusion mismatch [34–36].

5. Conclusions

Prolonged MV was associated with poor ADL at hospital discharge during COVID-19 infection. The indicator of physiological dead space increases during MV. The trajectory of markers of the hypercoagulation status, inflammation, and PEEP were significantly different depending on the timing of liberation from MV. These findings may provide insight into the pathophysiology of COVID-19 during treatment in a critical care setting.

Supplementary Materials: The following are available online at https://www.mdpi.com/article/10.3390/jcm10112513/s1, Supplementary Figure S1: Flow diagram of patient selection, Supplementary Figure S2: Association between daily change in each parameter during the initial 5 days and early liberation from mechanical ventilation. CRP, C-reactive protein; FDP, fibrin degradation products; TAT, thrombin-antithrombin complex; PIC, plasmin-alpha2-plasmininhibitor-complex; AT3, antirhombin3; KL6, Krebs von den lungen-6; CH50, 50% hemolytic complement activity; EL group, early liberation from ventilation group; PMV group, prolonged mechanical ventilation group. The number of missing values were following: KL6, 13; _TAT, 16; PIC, 16; ferritin, 16; CH50, 63, Supplementary Figure S3: The components of the EL prediction score and its performance. The cutoff coefficient of each component was determined by the estimated effect of daily change and its interaction with early liberation (A). The area under the receiver operating characteristic curve of the EL prediction score was significantly high compared to other severity scales (B). PEEP, positive end-expiratory pressure; TAT, thrombin-antithrombin complex; AT3, antirhombin3; CRP, C-reactive protein; EL, early liberation; APACHE II, acute physiology and chronic health evaluation II; SOFA, Sequential Organ Failure Assessment.

Author Contributions: D.K. and M.O. were responsible for conceptualization and design of the study and data extraction. D.K. and K.N. were responsible for data analyses. D.K. drafted the manuscript. K.N., M.O., H.H., N.J., A.N., N.O., Y.S. and Y.G. critically analyzed and reviewed the draft analyses. All authors have read and agreed to the published version of the manuscript.

Funding: This research was funded by Nakatani Foundation for Advancement of Measuring Technologies in Biomedical Engineering.

Institutional Review Board Statement: This study was conducted according to the guidelines of the declaration of Helsinki, and approved by The Nagoya University Hospital Institutional Review Board (registration number: 2020-0519).

Informed Consent Statement: Patient consent was waived due to the retrospective nature of this study.

Data Availability Statement: The dataset supporting the conclusions of this article is available from the corresponding author on reasonable request.

Acknowledgments: We thank all staff for treating coronavirus disease in our intensive care unit. Data extraction was supported by Philips.

Conflicts of Interest: The authors declare no conflict of interests.

Abbreviations

COVID-19, coronavirus disease; MV, mechanical ventilation; ICU, intensive care unit; EMICU, emergency and medical intensive care unit; ECMO, extracorporeal membrane oxygenation; VV, venovenous; SARS-CoV-2, severe acute respiratory syndrome coronavirus 2; EL group, early liberation from ventilation group; PMV group, prolonged mechanical ventilation group; CH50, 50% hemolytic complement activity; ADL, activities of daily living; P/F, partial pressure of oxygen/fraction of inspired oxygen; TAT, thrombin-antithrombin complex; FDP, fibrin degradation products; AT3, antithrombin 3; PCT, procalcitonin; KL-6, Krebs von den Lungen-6.

References

1. Matsunaga, N.; Hayakawa, K.; Terada, M.; Ohtsu, H.; Asai, Y.; Tsuzuki, S.; Suzuki, S.; Toyoda, A.; Suzuki, K.; Endo, M.; et al. Clinical epidemiology of hospitalized patients with COVID-19 in Japan: Report of the COVID-19 Registry Japan. *Clin. Infect. Dis.* **2020**, ciaa1470. [CrossRef] [PubMed]
2. Miike, S.; Sakamoto, N.; Washino, T.; Kosaka, A.; Kuwahara, Y.; Ishida, T.; Hikone, M.; Oyabu, T.; Kojima, H.; Iwabuchi, S.; et al. Critically ill patients with COVID-19 in Tokyo, Japan: A single-center case series. *J. Infect. Chemother.* **2020**, *27*, 291–295. [CrossRef] [PubMed]
3. Japan ECMOnet for COVID-19; Shime, N. Save the ICU and save lives during the COVID-19 pandemic. *J. Intensive Care* **2020**, *8*, 40. [CrossRef] [PubMed]

4. Piroth, L.; Cottenet, J.; Mariet, A.S.; Bonniaud, P.; Blot, M.; Tubert-Bitter, P.; Quantin, C. Comparison of the characteristics, morbidity, and mortality of COVID-19 and seasonal influenza: A nationwide, population-based retrospective cohort study. *Lancet Respir. Med.* **2020**, *9*, 251–259. [CrossRef]
5. Alicandro, G.; Remuzzi, G.; La Vecchia, C. Italy's first wave of the COVID-19 pandemic has ended: No excess mortality in May, 2020. *Lancet* **2020**, *396*, e27–e28. [CrossRef]
6. Vanhorebeek, I.; Latronico, N.; Van den Berghe, G. ICU-acquired weakness. *Intensive Care Med.* **2020**, *46*, 637–653. [CrossRef] [PubMed]
7. Ferrando, C.; Suarez-Sipmann, F.; Mellado-Artigas, R.; Hernández, M.; Gea, A.; Arruti, E.; Aldecoa, S.; Martinez-Palli, G.; Marintez-Gonzalez, M.A.; Slutsky, A.S.; et al. Clinical features, ventilatory management, and outcome of ARDS caused by COVID-19 are similar to other causes of ARDS. *Intensive Care Med.* **2020**, *46*, 2200–2211. [CrossRef]
8. Grasselli, G.; Tonetti, T.; Protti, A.; Langer, T.; Girardis, M.; Bellani, G.; Laffey, J.; Carrafiello, G.; Carsana, L.; Rizzuto, C.; et al. Pathophysiology of COVID-19-associated acute respiratory distress syndrome: A multicentre prospective observational study. *Lancet Respir. Med.* **2020**, *8*, 1201–1208. [CrossRef]
9. Wiersinga, W.J.; Rhodes, A.; Cheng, A.C.; Peacock, S.J.; Prescott, H.C. Pathophysiology, Transmission, Diagnosis, and Treatment of Coronavirus Disease 2019 (COVID-19): A Review. *JAMA* **2020**, *324*, 782–793. [CrossRef] [PubMed]
10. Beenen, L.F.M.; Bos, L.D.; Scheerder, M.J.; Lobé, N.H.J.; Muller, M.C.A.; Schultz, M.J.; van den Aardweg, J.G.; Goorhuis, A.; Bonta, P.I.; Middledorp, S.; et al. Extensive pulmonary perfusion defects compatible with microthrombosis and thromboembolic disease in severe Covid-19 pneumonia. *Thromb. Res.* **2020**, *196*, 135–137. [CrossRef] [PubMed]
11. Gamberini, L.; Tonetti, T.; Spadaro, S.; Zani, G.; Mazzoli, C.A.; Capozzi, C.; Giampalma, E.; Bacchi Reggiani, M.L.; Bertellini, E.; Castelli, A.; et al. Factors influencing liberation from mechanical ventilation in coronavirus disease 2019: Multicenter observational study in fifteen Italian ICUs. *J. Intensive Care* **2020**, *8*, 80. [CrossRef] [PubMed]
12. RECOVERY Collaborative Group; Horby, P.; Lim, W.S.; Emberson, J.R.; Mafham, M.; Bell, J.L.; Linsell, L.; Staplin, N.; Brightling, C.; Ustianowski, A.; et al. Dexamethasone in Hospitalized Patients with Covid-19—Preliminary Report. *N. Engl. J. Med.* **2020**, *384*, 693–704. [CrossRef]
13. Wang, Y.; Zhang, D.; Du, G.; Du, R.; Zhao, J.; Jin, Y.; Fu, S.; Gao, L.; Cheng, Z.; Lu, Q.; et al. Remdesivir in adults with severe COVID-19: A randomised, double-blind, placebo-controlled, multicentre trial. *Lancet* **2020**, *395*, 1569–1578; Erratum in **2020**, *395*, 1694. [CrossRef]
14. Sato, R.; Ishikane, M.; Kinoshita, N.; Suzuki, T.; Nakamoto, T.; Hayakawa, K.; Bekki, N.; Hara, H.; Ohmagari, N. A new challenge of unfractionated heparin anticoagulation treatment for moderate to severe COVID-19 in Japan. *Glob. Health Med.* **2020**, *2*, 190–192. [CrossRef] [PubMed]
15. Nishio, N.; Hiramatsu, M.; Goto, Y.; Shindo, Y.; Yamamoto, T.; Jingushi, N.; Wakahara, K.; Sone, M. Surgical strategy and optimal timing of tracheostomy in patients with COVID-19: Early experiences in Japan. *Auris Nasus Larynx* **2020**, *48*, 518–524. [CrossRef]
16. Iida, Y.; Iwata, K.; Uchiyama, Y.; Utsunomiya, A.; Endo, S.; Kasai, F.; Kato, M.; Kubo, T.; Kojima, N.; Sasanuma, N.; et al. Q&A on Rehabilitation Medicine for COVID-19 Patients in ICU. The Japanese Society of Intensive Care Medicine. Available online: https://www.jsicm.org/news/upload/COVID-19_rehab_qa_v1.pdf (accessed on 10 January 2021).
17. Liu, X.; Liu, X.; Xu, Y.; Xu, Z.; Huang, Y.; Chen, S.; Li, S.; Liu, D.; Lin, Z.; Li, Y. Ventilatory Ratio in Hypercapnic Mechanically Ventilated Patients with COVID-19-associated Acute Respiratory Distress Syndrome. *Am. J. Respir. Crit. Care Med.* **2020**, *201*, 1297–1299. [CrossRef] [PubMed]
18. Sinha, P.; Singh, S.; Hardman, J.G.; Bersten, A.D.; Soni, N.; Australia and New Zealand Intensive Care Society Clinical Trials Group. Evaluation of the physiological properties of ventilatory ratio in a computational cardiopulmonary model and its clinical application in an acute respiratory distress syndrome population. *Br. J. Anaesth.* **2014**, *112*, 96–101. [CrossRef]
19. Doiron, K.A.; Hoffmann, T.C.; Beller, E.M. Early intervention (mobilization or active exercise) for critically ill adults in the intensive care unit. *Cochrane Database Syst. Rev.* **2018**, *3*, CD010754. [CrossRef] [PubMed]
20. Martínez-Velilla, N.; Casas-Herrero, A.; Zambom-Ferraresi, F.; Saez de Asteasu, M.L.; Lucia, A.; Galbete, A.; Garcia-Baztan, A.; Alonso-Remedo, J.; Gonzalez-Glaria, B.; Gonzalo-Lozaro, M.; et al. Effect of Exercise Intervention on Functional Decline in Very Elderly Patients During Acute Hospitalization: A Randomized Clinical Trial. *JAMA Intern. Med.* **2019**, *179*, 28–36; Erratum in **2019**, *179*, 127. [CrossRef]
21. Davis, S.D.; Rosenfeld, M.; Lee, H.S.; Ferkol, T.W.; Sagel, S.D.; Dell, S.D.; Milla, C.; Pittman, J.E.; Shapiro, A.J.; Sullivan, K.M.; et al. Primary Ciliary Dyskinesia: Longitudinal Study of Lung Disease by Ultrastructure Defect and Genotype. *Am. J. Respir. Crit. Care Med.* **2019**, *199*, 190–198. [CrossRef]
22. Yang, T.; Li, Z.; Jiang, L.; Wang, Y.; Xi, X. Risk factors for intensive care unit-acquired weakness: A systematic review and meta-analysis. *Acta Neurol. Scand.* **2018**, *138*, 104–114. [CrossRef]
23. Martini, K.; Blüthgen, C.; Walter, J.E.; Nguyen-Kim, T.D.L.; Thienemann, F.; Frauenfelder, T. Patterns of organizing pneumonia and microinfarcts as surrogate for endothelial disruption and microangiopathic thromboembolic events in patients with coronavirus disease 2019. *PLoS ONE* **2020**, *15*, e0240078. [CrossRef]
24. Hasan, S.S.; Radford, S.; Know, C.S.; Zaidi, S.T.R. Venous thromboembolism in critically ill COVID-19 patients receiving prophylactic or therapeutic anticoagulation: A systematic review and meta-analysis. *J. Thromb. Thrombolysis* **2020**, *50*, 814–821. [CrossRef] [PubMed]

25. Risitano, A.M.; Mastellos, D.C.; Huber-Lang, M.; Yancopoulou, D.; Garlanda, C.; Ciceri, F.; Lambris, J.D. Complement as a target in COVID-19? *Nat. Rev. Immunol.* **2020**, *20*, 343–344; Erratum in **2020**, *20*, 448. [CrossRef] [PubMed]
26. Skendros, P.; Mitsios, A.; Chrysanthopoulou, A.; Mastellos, D.C.; Metallidis, S.; Rafailidis, P.; Nitinopoulou, M.; Sertaridou, E.; Tsironidou, V.; Tsigalou, C.; et al. Complement and tissue factor-enriched neutrophil extracellular traps are key drivers in COVID-19 immunothrombosis. *J. Clin. Investig.* **2020**, *130*, 6151–6157. [CrossRef] [PubMed]
27. d'Alessandro, M.; Cameli, P.; Refini, R.M.; Bergantini, L.; Alonzi, V.; Lanzarone, N.; Bennett, D.; Rana, G.D.; Montagnani, F.; Scolletta, S.; et al. Serum KL-6 concentrations as a novel biomarker of severe COVID-19. *J. Med. Virol.* **2020**, *92*, 2216–2220. [CrossRef]
28. Kory, P.; Kanne, J.P. SARS-CoV-2 organising pneumonia: 'Has there been a widespread failure to identify and treat this prevalent condition in COVID-19?'. *BMJ Open Respir. Res.* **2020**, *7*, e000724. [CrossRef] [PubMed]
29. Copin, M.C.; Parmentier, E.; Duburcq, T.; Poissy, J.; Mathieu, D.; Lille COVID-19 ICU and Anatomopathology Group. Time to consider histologic pattern of lung injury to treat critically ill patients with COVID-19 infection. *Intensive Care Med.* **2020**, *46*, 1124–1126. [CrossRef]
30. Flikweert, A.W.; Grootenboers, M.J.J.H.; Yick, D.C.Y.; du Mée, A.W.F.; van der Meer, N.J.M.; Rettig, T.C.D.; Kant, M.K.M. Late histopathologic characteristics of critically ill COVID-19 patients: Different phenotypes without evidence of invasive aspergillosis, a case series. *J. Crit. Care* **2020**, *59*, 149–155. [CrossRef]
31. Tomazini, B.M.; Maia, I.S.; Cavalcanti, A.B.; Berwanger, O.; Rosa, R.G.; Veiga, V.C.; Avezum, A.; Lopes, R.D.; Bueno, F.R.; Silva, M.V.A.O.; et al. Effect of Dexamethasone on Days Alive and Ventilator-Free in Patients With Moderate or Severe Acute Respiratory Distress Syndrome and COVID-19: The CoDEX Randomized Clinical Trial. *JAMA* **2020**, *324*, 1307–1316. [CrossRef]
32. Avilés-Jurado, F.X.; Prieto-Alhambra, D.; González-Sánchez, N.; de Ossó, J.; Arancibia, C.; Rojas-Lechuga, M.J.; Ruiz-Sevilla, L.; Remacha, R.; Sanchez, I.; Lehrer-Coriat, E.; et al. Timing, Complications, and Safety of Tracheotomy in Critically Ill Patients With COVID-19. *JAMA Otolaryngol. Head Neck Surg.* **2020**, *147*, 1–8. [CrossRef]
33. Sutt, A.L.; Tronstad, O.; Barnett, A.G.; Kitchenman, S.; Fraser, J.F. Earlier tracheostomy is associated with an earlier return to walking, talking, and eating. *Aust. Crit. Care* **2020**, *33*, 213–218. [CrossRef] [PubMed]
34. Tsolaki, V.; Siempos, I.; Magira, E.; Kokkoris, S.; Zakynthinos, G.E.; Zakynthinos, S. PEEP levels in COVID-19 pneumonia. *Crit. Care* **2020**, *24*, 303. [CrossRef]
35. Roesthuis, L.; van den Berg, M.; van der Hoeven, H. Advanced respiratory monitoring in COVID-19 patients: Use less PEEP! *Crit. Care* **2020**, *24*, 230. [CrossRef] [PubMed]
36. Beloncle, F.M.; Pavlovsky, B.; Desprez, C.; Fage, N.; Olivier, P.Y.; Asfar, P.; Richard, J.C.; Mercat, A. Recruitability and effect of PEEP in SARS-Cov-2-associated acute respiratory distress syndrome. *Ann. Intensive Care* **2020**, *10*, 55. [CrossRef] [PubMed]

Article

Artificial Neural Network for Predicting the Safe Temporary Artery Occlusion Time in Intracranial Aneurysmal Surgery

Shima Shahjouei [1,2,*], Seyed Mohammad Ghodsi [2], Morteza Zangeneh Soroush [3,4], Saeed Ansari [5] and Shahab Kamali-Ardakani [2]

[1] Neurology Department, Neuroscience Institute, Geisinger Health System, Danville, PA 17822, USA
[2] Department of Neurosurgery, Tehran University of Medical Sciences, Tehran 14155-6559, Iran; ghodsism@sina.tums.ac.ir (S.M.G.); kamalishahab30@yahoo.com (S.K.-A.)
[3] Bio-Intelligence Research Unit, Electrical Engeneering Department, Sharif University of Technology, Tehran 14588-89694, Iran; morteza.soroush@sharif.edu
[4] Department of Biomedical Engineering, Science and Research Branch, Islamic Azad University, Tehran 14778-93855, Iran
[5] National Institute of Neurological Disorders and Stroke, National Institute of Health, Bethesda, MD 20892, USA; saeed.ansarisadrabadi@nih.gov
* Correspondence: sshahjouei@geisinger.edu or sshimashah@gmail.com

Abstract: Background. Temporary artery clipping facilitates safe cerebral aneurysm management, besides a risk for cerebral ischemia. We developed an artificial neural network (ANN) to predict the safe clipping time of temporary artery occlusion (TAO) during intracranial aneurysm surgery. Method. We devised a three-layer model to predict the safe clipping time for TAO. We considered age, the diameter of the right and left middle cerebral arteries (MCAs), the diameter of the right and left A1 segment of anterior cerebral arteries (ACAs), the diameter of the anterior communicating artery, mean velocity of flow at the right and left MCAs, and the mean velocity of flow at the right and left ACAs, as well as the Fisher grading scale of brain CT scans as the input values for the model. Results. This study included 125 patients: 105 patients from a retrospective cohort for training the model and 20 patients from a prospective cohort for validating the model. The output of the neural network yielded up to 960 s overall safe clipping time for TAO. The input values with the greatest impact on safe TAO were mean velocity of blood at left MCA and left ACA, and Fisher grading scale of brain CT scan. Conclusion. This study presents an axillary framework to improve the accuracy of the estimated safe clipping time interval of temporary artery occlusion in intracranial aneurysm surgery.

Keywords: aneurysm surgery; temporary artery occlusion; clipping time; artificial neural network

1. Introduction

Intracranial aneurysms have a prevalence of 3.2% in the general population [1]. Although the majority of patients can remain asymptomatic, cerebral aneurysms have a significant risk of rupture. Temporary artery occlusion (TAO) is an indispensable technique to facilitate aneurysm dissection and clipping and to reduce the risk of intra-operative rupture [2]. However, TAO may be complicated with detrimental consequences such as cerebral ischemia and postoperative neurological deficits [3]. Thereby, estimating a safe clipping time (SCT) for TAO is essential to give the surgeons the maximum window to perform the surgery, and keep the patients safe from the complications of the surgery. Although several intra-operative neurophysiologic monitoring and imaging methods have been proposed for determining safe occlusion time [4,5], SCT is mostly estimated based on clinicians' expertise in real practice. The purpose of this study is to leverage machine learning to identify the prominent clinical features determining the outcome of TAO and to predict the SCT for intracranial aneurysm surgeries.

Machine learning can be used to extract meaningful relationships and patterns from a set of features (model inputs) for estimating the future values of a phenomenon (model outcome). An artificial neural network (ANN) is a type of data mining and pattern recognition method which reveals complex nonlinear relationships in addition to linear correlations. ANNs have been widely used in a variety of neurosurgical applications, such as predicting the occurrence of symptomatic cerebral vasospasm after aneurysmal subarachnoid hemorrhage [6], traumatic brain injury outcome and survival [7,8], recurrent lumbar disk herniation [9], and endoscopic third ventriculostomy success in childhood hydrocephalus [10]. Regarding cerebral aneurysm surgeries, the majority of the studies deployed these techniques to predict the aneurysm rupture [11,12], or for automated detection of the aneurysms on imaging [13]. In this study, we aimed to evaluate the feasibility and validity of ANN modeling in predicting the SCT and for determining the prominent clinical features of cerebral aneurysm surgeries.

2. Methods

This study was conducted in Shariati Hospital, Tehran, Iran. To develop the ANN, we used two separate datasets.

2.1. Retrospective Cohort, Training, and Testing Set of the Model

We retrospectively reviewed the medical records of all patients who underwent craniotomy and clipping for aneurysm management between 2004 and 2011. Clinical data, including demographic information, comorbidities, pre- and post-neurological examination, Fisher grading scale of computerized tomography (CT) scan imaging, pre- and post-operative trans cranial doppler (TCD), location and diameter of the aneurysm(s), and temporary artery clipping time and number(s), were extracted. The presence or absence of flow-through vessels of the circle of Willis and possible anatomic variations were indicated by either digital subtraction angiography (DSA), computed tomography angiography (CTA), magnetic resonance angiography (MRA), or T2 weighted magnetic resonance imaging (MRI). The mean velocity of flow in cerebral arteries was measured from pre-operative TCD.

The information from the patients in the retrospective cohort was used to train the model. To obtain the SCT, we excluded all patients with unfavorable outcomes or any signs of ischemia. Patients with Glasgow coma scale (GCS) less than 11, presence of a neurologic deficit in the pre-operative examination, post-operative decline in either motor or sensory function, or any pathologic finding in neuroimaging other than the presence of aneurysm were excluded from the training set.

2.2. Prospective Cohort and Validation Set of the Model

Between 2011 and 2013, we devised a protocol to prospectively include the patients with surgical clipping of cerebral aneurysms (ruptured and un-ruptured). We only included those with aneurysms of the anterior communicating artery (AcomA) or middle cerebral arteries (MCA). Data were collected using the same protocol as the retrospective cohort. In addition, all patients of the prospective cohort underwent diffusion weighted imaging (DWI) MRI within 6 h and 24 h of the surgery to rule out cerebral ischemia. We also measured the diameter of arteries in the circle of Willis (anterior cerebral arteries (ACA), AcomA, and MCA) from CTA images. Image-J software (Image J 1.42q software, U.S. National Institutes of Health, Bethesda, MA, USA) was used for this purpose. The information obtained from the prospective cohort was used to test and validate the model.

2.3. Surgical Techniques

The surgical procedure for clipping of the aneurysms was either a standard pterional craniotomy (MCA location) or frontotemporal craniotomy (AcomA location). For AcomA aneurysms, the ipsilateral and contralateral A1 segments were exposed and temporarily clipped. When the AcomA segment aneurysm was dissected and permanently clipped, the temporal clipping of the A1 segments was subsequently removed. In MCA aneurysms, the MCA was exposed from proximal to distal to identify the location of the aneurysm.

Temporal clipping of the proximal MCA at the M1 segment was applied and then the aneurysm was dissected. Subsequently, the temporal clip of the MCA was removed. The duration of temporary vascular obstruction following clipping was measured in seconds.

2.4. Feature Selection for ANN Model

Through a comprehensive literature review and consultation with clinicians, a wide variety of related clinical and physiological parameters with a possible impact on the SCT were proposed. Based on the anatomical distribution of intracranial aneurysms and the importance of compensatory blood flow mechanisms in each segment of the circle of Willis, 11 features were selected as the input for the ANN model.

Age, the diameter of the right and left MCAs, the diameter of the right and left A1 segment of ACAs, the diameter of AcomA, mean velocity of flow at the right and left MCAs, mean velocity of flow at the right and left ACAs, and Fisher grading scale of brain CT scan were considered as the input values for the model. The diameter of the P1 segment of the right and left posterior cerebral arteries (PCAs) and flow in the posterior circulation were excluded in our final model due to the low prevalence of posterior aneurysms.

2.5. Structure of the ANN Model

A three-layer structure neural network was used in this study: an input layer, one hidden layer, and an output layer (Figure 1). The number of input values (units) in the first layer of the model was equal to 11, the same as the number of selected features that was proposed to affect the outcome of clipping and subsequent ischemia. For determining the number and structure of the hidden layer, we considered the training accuracy and generalization. The presence of too many hidden layers (which is needed for accuracy) may cause overtraining, and this will result in a decline in generalization. To apply the optimum number of neurons in the hidden layer, the model was run with different counts. The architecture with five units on the hidden layer was accompanied by the lowest error. The output layer consisted of only one neuron, representing the SCT as the outcome of the model.

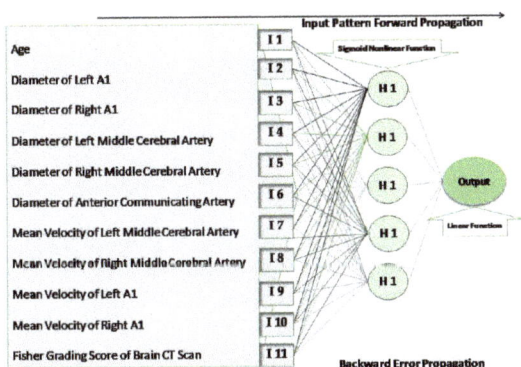

Figure 1. The structure of the artificial neural network. I, input unit; H, hidden unit.

The units within each layer of the model were connected with the units of the adjacent layers through directed edges (weights). There were no connections between the units within the same layer [14]. A nonlinear Sigmoid function was applied to the hidden layer, and a linear function was applied to the output layer.

2.6. Training and Validating of the ANN Model

Five-fold cross-validation was used for this model. In each run of the modeling, 80% of the retrospective cohort was randomly selected to train the ANN model. The remaining 20% of the dataset was used to test the performance of the model. During the training phase, the weights and interactions of the input variables were gradually determined during each run. For this purpose, each set of input features was broadcast to every unit in the hidden layer. After computing its activation, each unit in the hidden layer transferred the signal to the unit of the adjacent output layer. In this way, the response of the network was computed for a specific set of input values (feed-forward propagation phase). In the backward propagation phase, the computed activation in the output layer (predicted SCT) was compared with the observed SCT value (obtained from the patient's medical record), and the training error was calculated. The error was then propagated back to each unit of the hidden layer and updated the weights between the output layer and the hidden units. Correspondingly, the computed error in this layer was distributed to the input layer and the weights between the hidden layer and input layer were updated as well. This process was repeated several times, using different random sets of patients for training and testing the ANN model.

Data from the prospective cohort of the patients were used to validate the model and provide the performance metrics for the model. We used the trained ANN model (based on data from the retrospective cohort) to predict the SCT for patients in the prospective cohort. This cohort was kept unseen from the ANN algorithms in the training phase to prevent bias and overfitting.

2.7. Importance of Each Clinical Feature in Predicting the SCT

To evaluate the importance of the input parameters in predicting the SCT, a model sensitivity test was implemented. For this purpose, we considered a fixed weight of 1 for all the input variables. In each turn, we increased the weight of one variable up to 10% and evaluated the variation in the output value. After repeating this process for each input parameter, we ranked the obtained sensitivity values.

2.8. Estimating the Errors

To evaluate the proposed pattern recognition model performance, two types of error were proposed. The mean absolute deviation (Equation (1)) calculated the difference between the clinical assigned SCT values in real practice and those predicted by the model.

$$Mean\ Absolute\ Deviation = \frac{\sum_{i=1}^{N_{tr}} |SCT_i - S\hat{C}T_i|}{N_{te}} \% \qquad (1)$$

where N is the total number of patients, $N_{tr} = \frac{4N}{K}$ the total number of training samples, $N_{te} = \frac{N}{K}$ the total number of test samples, $K = 5$ the realization of the K-fold validation algorithm in our model, SCT stands for safe clipping time, and $S\hat{C}T_i$ is the predicted value as the outcome of the model.

For relative error (Equation (2)), the mean absolute deviation was adjusted by the greatness of the error according to each value of the observed outcome. This criterion resulted in a better perception of the bias on the model. The relative error was considered to report the bias of the model in this study.

$$Relative\ Error = \frac{1}{N_{te}} \sum_{i=1}^{N_{tr}} \left| \frac{SCT_i - S\hat{C}T_i}{SCT_i} \right| \% \qquad (2)$$

where the parameters are as above.

MATLAB software was used for mathematical modeling and designing the ANN. The confidence interval of 95% was assigned to the outputs. We used a T-test to assess the independence of the outputs by considering a p value less than 5% as significant.

3. Results

A total of 131 patients were evaluated for this study (105 patients from the retrospective cohort and 26 patients from the prospective cohort). Six patients were excluded from the prospective cohort due to low GCS (4 patients) and positive DWI MRI indicating postoperative cerebral ischemia (2 patients, none could be directly related to temporary clipping). Demographic data of the included patients, location of the aneurysms, and also details of the Fisher grading scale of each cohort are available in Table 1.

Table 1. Demographic and surgical characteristics of the patients in retrospective and prospective datasets.

Parameter	Retrospective Dataset (n = 105)	Prospective Dataset (n = 20)
Age; Mean (Range); Years	48.7 (30–72)	50.2 (30–76)
Men; n (%)	32 (30.4%)	9 (45%)
Location of Aneurysm		
Middle Cerebral Artery; n (%)	80 (76.1%)	14 (70%)
Anterior Communicating Artery; n (%)	25 (23.9%)	6 (30%)
Fisher Grading Scale of CT Scan Images		
One; n (%)	28 (26.66%)	1 (5%)
Two; n (%)	46 (43.8%)	9 (45%)
Three; n (%)	23 (21.9%)	4 (20%)
Four; n (%)	8 (7.61%)	6 (30%)

The overall predicted TAO based on the prospective cohort was 90–960 s; 120–932 s in AcomA, 240–960 s in right MCA, and 90–950 s in left MCA (Table 2). The average deviation of predicted SCT by the ANN model in this study from the clinical observed SCT of the unseen prospective cohort was 12%, leaving an 88% accuracy of the model.

Table 2. Output values. The safe clipping time interval is based on the aneurysm location.

Site of Obstruction	Safe Time Interval (Seconds)
Overall	90–960
Right Middle Cerebral Artery	240–960
Left Middle Cerebral Artery	90–950
Anterior Communicating Artery	120–932

A sensitivity analysis of the input values showed that mean velocity of the left M1, mean velocity of the left A1, and Fisher grading scale had the greatest impact on SCT (Table 3).

Table 3. Ranked output of the sensitivity analysis.

Rank	Input Value	Sensitivity (%)
1	Mean velocity of flow at left MCA (middle cerebral arteries)	73.82 ± 1.95
2	Mean velocity of flow at left ACA (anterior cerebral arteries)	67.23 ± 2.74
3	Fisher grading scale of brain CT scan	65.71 ± 5.31
4	Mean velocity of flow at right ACA	63.87 ± 4.82
5	Diameter of right MCA	59.22 ± 5.24
6	Diameter of AcomA (anterior communicating artery)	57.56 ± 3.13
7	Diameter of left MCA	55.59 ± 3.13
8	Diameter of left A1	45.74 ± 2.47
9	Age	41.35 ± 1.78
10	Mean velocity of flow at right MCA	32.19 ± 3.62
11	Diameter of right A1	23.45 ± 2.15

4. Discussion

Surgical management of aneurysms is among the most critical procedures in neurosurgery. Temporary artery occlusion (TAO) is a fundamental component in facilitating aneurysm dissection. The main purpose of this study was to introduce an alternative intelligent predictive tool besides the commonly accepted clinical experience, rather than providing an absolute value for SCT. However, the ANN model in this study demonstrated that the clipping time might be considered as safe for intervals longer than those practiced in the clinic. We observed that mean velocity of flow at the left MCA and left ACA, in addition to the Fisher grading scale of brain CT scans have the greatest impact on the outcome of the TAO.

Although a detrimental consequence of clipping is ischemia, several mechanisms such as redirection of blood flow from the contralateral side through communicating arteries of the Willis circle, leptomeningeal and collateral vessels, and cortical anastomosis can compensate for the hypo-perfusion and eliminate the cerebral ischemia [15–18]. Aging has been shown to reduce the efficacy of collateral flow and cortical anastomosis capacity by decreasing the collateral number and diameter, increasing tortuosity, and impairment of remodeling capacity [19–21].

In addition, the difference in predicted SCT for different vessels might have a biological basis. Predicted SCTs were higher in the left hemisphere. The difference in the origin of right and left common carotid arteries (aortic arc versus the brachiocephalic artery on the right side), the curvature of the vessels, carotid intima-media thickness (CIMT), and other hemodynamic characteristics of the vessels in the right and left side may result in variation between flow in the right and left circulation [22,23]. Blood flow in each vascular section is a function of the velocity of blood and diameter of the vessel at that section (Flow = Velocity × Diameter). Accordingly, by considering the similar diameter of vessels on both sides, the higher velocity of the blood on the left side might be representative of the greater flow in the left circulation. This might be the underlying reason why the velocity of the left ACA and MCA has a major impact on the outcome. The higher incidence rate of aneurysm formation and greater wall shear stress (WSS) and wall shear stress gradient (WSSG) on the left side in comparison with the right in our study (not presented in this draft), may verify this assumption. Additionally, the difference in blood flow may produce a higher compensatory potential for the dominant side in case of vessel occlusion, by redirecting the blood flow through the Willis circle toward the site of obstruction. Consequently, the extra ten seconds of safe occlusion time in the right MCA TAO (960 s versus 950 s for left MCA TAO), although clinically insignificant, may demonstrate this bonus reperfusion provided by the contralateral dominant side.

4.1. Selected Features as Input of the Model

WSS and WSSG can affect the SCT by promoting aneurysm formation. Permanent pathologic alteration of vasculature, such as disruption of the internal elastic lamina or thinning of the media along with increasing the number and tortuosity of collateral vessels, were introduced as complications of WSS and WSSG [19,24–27]. Alteration in hemodynamic parameters such as the diameter of vessels and velocity of blood flow can change WSS and WSSG [28–30]. Thereby, we considered the diameter of ACAs, MCAs, and AcomA, and the mean velocity of ACAs and MCAs as an indirect measure of WSS and WSSG.

Primarily, we considered the diameter of the P1 segment of right and left PCA and flow in posterior circulation as other predictors of SCT. Previous studies suggested that AcomA is more prominent in maintaining the blood flow after obstruction than the posterior communicating arteries [25,31]. Besides this, aneurysms are not uniformly distributed [32]. Less than 1% of intracranial aneurysms occur at the vertebra–basilar junction, basilar artery, and superior cerebellar artery bifurcation. ACA and MCA bifurcations together account for more than 50% of intracranial aneurysms [33]. Consequently, we did not include the diameter of right and left P1 and flow in the posterior circulation in our final model.

4.2. Limitations and Error Estimation

The strength of this study was to include information of the patients from two different cohorts in model training, using cross-validation from a retrospective cohort, and model testing using a prospective cohort. Using a very select number of features with clinical value was important to ensure our study did not suffer from missingness, which could have introduced selection bias. We considered a comprehensive panel of clinical and imaging features as the input to assess the feasibility of our approach. However, the Institutional Review Board (IRB) prevented us from including sex as an input variable in the validation cohort due to the deidentification process for datasets including less common pathologies with fewer than 100 patients. Despite considering various imaging modalities to monitor the possible post-operative ischemia, determining the exact underlying cause of ischemia (e.g., impact of final clipping rather than temporary clipping, vasospasm, and other intra- or post-operative complications) was challenging, and we did not include patients with cerebral ischemia in our models. Adding intraoperative variables and patients with adverse outcome could improve the predictive value of our ANN model.

The average deviation of predicted SCT from clinically assigned SCT (relative error of our ANN) was equal to 12%. In the training phase, we used five-fold cross validation, which resulted in average relative regression errors of 4.3% (training set) and 11.3% (test set). This training error can be considered quite low and acceptable for training process. After finalizing our regression model, we employed our final model to estimate SCT for the validation set (prospective cohort). This result indicates that our model does not suffer from overfitting or underfitting or unequal distribution over different subsets. Although, an 88% accuracy is a promising result for our pilot study with a total of 131 patients, the model would benefit from validation and justification over larger datasets. However, considering the prevalence of cerebral aneurysms which need surgical intervention, including a large cohort of patients is not simple. Furthermore, in this pilot feasibility study, we used ANN as our machine learning framework, however; comparative analysis with other modeling tools and deep learning methods may provide better performance. We will employ commonly used regression models in our future study to better visualize the power of our model compared to previously used linear models in the medical literature.

5. Conclusions

The main goal of this study was to present an axillary framework to improve the accuracy of the estimated safe clipping time interval of temporary artery occlusion during intracranial aneurysm surgery. The proposed method was an offline approach that can provide a prediction for the SCT in TAO before the surgery. However, to provide an accurate and precise SCT during the surgery, integration of online measurements and frequent updates of the predicted clipping time is required. To design a model with higher generalization, further studies with more clinical variables, larger sample size, and more diverse demographics are recommended.

Author Contributions: Conceptualization, S.K.-A., S.M.G., and S.A.; methodology, S.S., M.Z.S., S.A., S.K.-A.; software, M.Z.S.; validation, S.S., S.M.G., S.K.-A., and S.A.; formal analysis, S.S. and S.K.-A.; investigation, S.S., S.K.-A., and S.A.; resources, S.M.G.; data curation, S.S., and M.Z.S.; writing—original draft preparation, S.S. and S.K.-A.; writing—review and editing, S.M.G., S.A.; visualization, S.S. and M.Z.S.; supervision, S.M.G. and S.A.; project administration, S.K.-A., S.S.; funding acquisition, None. All authors have read and agreed to the published version of the manuscript.

Funding: This research received no external funding.

Institutional Review Board Statement: The study was conducted according to the guidelines of the Declaration of Helsinki, and approved by the Institutional Review Board and Medical Ethics and History of Medicine Research Center at Tehran University of Medical Sciences (no. 2011-00611012N).

Informed Consent Statement: Informed consent was obtained from all subjects involved in the study.

Conflicts of Interest: The authors declare no conflict of interest.

References

1. Zhao, J.; Lin, H.; Summers, R.; Yang, M.; Cousins, B.G.; Tsui, J. Current Treatment Strategies for Intracranial Aneurysms: An Overview. *Angiology* **2018**, *69*, 17–30. [CrossRef]
2. Schramm, J.; Cornelia Cedzich, C. Outcome and management of intraoperative aneurysm rupture. *Surg. Neurol.* **1993**, *40*, 26–30. [CrossRef]
3. Taylor, C.L.; Selman, W.R. Temporary vascular occlusion during cerebral aneurysm surgery. *Neurosurg. Clin. N. Am.* **1998**, *9*, 673–679. [CrossRef]
4. Kameda, M.; Hishikawa, T.; Hiramatsu, M.; Yasuhara, T.; Kurozumi, K.; Date, I. Precise MEP monitoring with a reduced interval is safe and useful for detecting permissive duration for temporary clipping. *Sci. Rep.* **2020**, *10*. [CrossRef] [PubMed]
5. Staarmann, B.; O'Neal, K.; Magner, M.; Zuccarello, M. Sensitivity and Specificity of Intraoperative Neuromonitoring for Identifying Safety and Duration of Temporary Aneurysm Clipping Based on Vascular Territory, a Multimodal Strategy. *World Neurosurg.* **2017**, *100*, 522–530. [CrossRef]
6. Dumont, T.M.; Rughani, A.I.; Tranmer, B.I. Prediction of symptomatic cerebral vasospasm after aneurysmal subarachnoid hemorrhage with an artificial neural network: Feasibility and comparison with logistic regression models. *World Neurosurg.* **2011**, *75*, 57–63. [CrossRef]
7. Hsu, M.-H.; Li, Y.-C.; Chiu, W.-T.; Yen, J.-C. Outcome prediction after moderate and severe head injury using an artificial neural network. *Stud. Health Technol. Inform.* **2005**, *116*, 241–246. [PubMed]
8. Rughani, A.I.; Dumont, T.M.; Lu, Z.; Bongard, J.; Horgan, M.A.; Penar, P.L.; Tranmer, B.I. Use of an artificial neural network to predict head injury outcome. *J. Neurosurg.* **2010**, *113*, 585–590. [CrossRef] [PubMed]
9. Azimi, P.; Mohammadi, H.R.; Benzel, E.C.; Shahzadi, S.; Azhari, S. Use of artificial neural networks to predict recurrent lumbar disk herniation. *Clin. Spine Surg.* **2015**, *28*, E161–E165. [CrossRef]
10. Azimi, P.; Mohammadi, H.R. Predicting endoscopic third ventriculostomy success in childhood hydrocephalus: An artificial neural network analysis. *J. Neurosurg. Pediatr.* **2014**, *13*, 426–432. [CrossRef]
11. Tanioka, S.; Ishida, F.; Yamamoto, A.; Shimizu, S.; Sakaida, H.; Toyoda, M.; Kashiwagi, N.; Suzuki, H. Machine Learning Classification of Cerebral Aneurysm Rupture Status with Morphologic Variables and Hemodynamic Parameters. *Radiol. Artif. Intell.* **2020**, *2*, e190077. [CrossRef]
12. Detmer, F.J.; Lückehe, D.; Mut, F.; Slawski, M.; Hirsch, S.; Bijlenga, P.; von Voigt, G.; Cebral, J.R. Comparison of statistical learning approaches for cerebral aneurysm rupture assessment. *Int. J. Comput. Assist. Radiol. Surg.* **2020**, *15*, 141–150. [CrossRef] [PubMed]
13. Dai, X.; Huang, L.; Qian, Y.; Xia, S.; Chong, W.; Liu, J.; Di Ieva, A.; Hou, X.; Ou, C. Deep learning for automated cerebral aneurysm detection on computed tomography images. *Int. J. Comput. Assist. Radiol. Surg.* **2020**, *15*, 715–723. [CrossRef]
14. Dorronsoro, J.R.; López, V.; Cruz, C.S.; Siguenza, J.A. Autoassociative neural networks and noise filtering. *IEEE Trans. Signal Process.* **2003**, *51*, 1431–1438. [CrossRef]
15. Long, Q.; Luppi, L.; König, C.S.; Rinaldo, V.; Das, S.K. Study of the collateral capacity of the circle of Willis of patients with severe carotid artery stenosis by 3D computational modeling. *J. Biomech.* **2008**, *41*, 2735–2742. [CrossRef] [PubMed]
16. Sacca, A.; Pedrini, L.; Vitacchiano, G.; Pisano, E.; Zagni, P.; Bellanova, B.; Dondi, M.; Monetti, N. Cerebral SPECT with 99mTc-HMPAO in extracranial carotid pathology: Evaluation of changes in the ischemic area after carotid endarterectomy. *Int. Angiol. J. Int. Union Angiol.* **1992**, *11*, 117–121.
17. Vanninen, R.; Koivisto, K.; Tulla, H.; Manninen, H.; Partanen, K. Hemodynamic effects of carotid endarterectomy by magnetic resonance flow quantification. *Stroke* **1995**, *26*, 84–89. [CrossRef] [PubMed]
18. Vernieri, F.; Pasqualetti, P.; Matteis, M.; Passarelli, F.; Troisi, E.; Rossini, P.M.; Caltagirone, C.; Silvestrini, M. Effect of collateral blood flow and cerebral vasomotor reactivity on the outcome of carotid artery occlusion. *Stroke* **2001**, *32*, 1552–1558. [CrossRef]
19. Faber, J.E.; Zhang, H.; Lassance-Soares, R.M.; Prabhakar, P.; Najafi, A.H.; Burnett, M.S.; Epstein, S.E. Aging causes collateral rarefaction and increased severity of ischemic injury in multiple tissues. *Arterioscler. Thromb. Vasc. Biol.* **2011**, *31*, 1748–1756. [CrossRef]
20. Liebeskind, D.S. Collateral circulation. *Stroke* **2003**, *34*, 2279–2284. [CrossRef] [PubMed]
21. Wang, J.; Peng, X.; Lassance-Soares, R.M.; Najafi, A.H.; Alderman, L.O.; Sood, S.; Xue, Z.; Chan, R.; Faber, J.E.; Epstein, S.E. Aging-induced collateral dysfunction: Impaired responsiveness of collaterals and susceptibility to apoptosis via dysfunctional eNOS signaling. *J. Cardiovasc. Transl. Res.* **2011**, *4*, 779–789. [CrossRef] [PubMed]
22. Luo, X.; Yang, Y.; Cao, T.; Li, Z. Differences in left and right carotid intima–media thickness and the associated risk factors. *Clin. Radiol.* **2011**, *66*, 393–398. [CrossRef] [PubMed]
23. Manbachi, A.; Hoi, Y.; Wasserman, B.A.; Lakatta, E.G.; Steinman, D.A. On the shape of the common carotid artery with implications for blood velocity profiles. *Physiol. Meas.* **2011**, *32*, 1885. [CrossRef] [PubMed]
24. Alnæs, M.S.; Isaksen, J.; Mardal, K.-A.; Romner, B.; Morgan, M.K.; Ingebrigtsen, T. Computation of hemodynamics in the circle of Willis. *Stroke* **2007**, *38*, 2500–2505. [CrossRef] [PubMed]
25. Kulcsár, Z.; Ugron, A.; Marosfői, M.; Berentei, Z.; Paal, G.; Szikora, I. Hemodynamics of cerebral aneurysm initiation: The role of wall shear stress and spatial wall shear stress gradient. *Am. J. Neuroradiol.* **2011**, *32*, 587–594. [CrossRef]
26. Metaxa, E.; Tremmel, M.; Natarajan, S.K.; Xiang, J.; Paluch, R.A.; Mandelbaum, M.; Siddiqui, A.H.; Kolega, J.; Mocco, J.; Meng, H. Characterization of critical hemodynamics contributing to aneurysmal remodeling at the basilar terminus in a rabbit model. *Stroke* **2010**, *41*, 1774–1782. [CrossRef]

27. Valencia, A.; Morales, H.; Rivera, R.; Bravo, E.; Galvez, M. Blood flow dynamics in patient-specific cerebral aneurysm models: The relationship between wall shear stress and aneurysm area index. *Med. Eng. Phys.* **2008**, *30*, 329–340. [CrossRef]
28. Farnoush, A.; Qian, Y.; Avolio, A. Effect of inflow on computational fluid dynamic simulation of cerebral bifurcation aneurysms. In Proceedings of the 2011 Annual International Conference of the IEEE Engineering in Medicine and Biology Society, Boston, MA, USA, 30 August–3 September 2011; pp. 1025–1028.
29. Hassan, T.; Hassan, A.A.; Ahmed, Y.M. Influence of parent vessel dominancy on fluid dynamics of anterior communicating artery aneurysms. *Acta Neurochir.* **2011**, *153*, 305–310. [CrossRef]
30. Jou, L.-D.; Lee, D.H.; Mawad, M.E. Cross-flow at the anterior communicating artery and its implication in cerebral aneurysm formation. *J. Biomech.* **2010**, *43*, 2189–2195. [CrossRef]
31. Silva, P.A.; Cerejo, A.; Vilarinho, A.; Dias, C.; Vaz, R. Regional variations in brain oxygenation during temporary clipping in aneurysm surgery. *Neurol. Res.* **2012**, *34*, 971–976. [CrossRef]
32. Nixon, A.M.; Gunel, M.; Sumpio, B.E. The critical role of hemodynamics in the development of cerebral vascular disease: A review. *J. Neurosurg.* **2010**, *112*, 1240–1253. [CrossRef] [PubMed]
33. Alfano, J.M.; Kolega, J.; Natarajan, S.K.; Xiang, J.; Paluch, R.A.; Levy, E.I.; Siddiqui, A.H.; Meng, H. Intracranial aneurysms occur more frequently at bifurcation sites that typically experience higher hemodynamic stresses. *Neurosurgery* **2013**, *73*, 497–505. [CrossRef] [PubMed]

Article

Areas of Interest and Attitudes towards the Pharmacological Treatment of Attention Deficit Hyperactivity Disorder: Thematic and Quantitative Analysis Using Twitter

Miguel Angel Alvarez-Mon [1,2,*], Laura de Anta [1], Maria Llavero-Valero [3], Guillermo Lahera [2,4,5], Miguel A. Ortega [2,6], Cesar Soutullo [7], Javier Quintero [1,8], Angel Asunsolo del Barco [6,9] and Melchor Alvarez-Mon [2,6,10,11]

Citation: Alvarez-Mon, M.A.; de Anta, L.; Llavero-Valero, M.; Lahera, G.; Ortega, M.A.; Soutullo, C.; Quintero, J.; Asunsolo del Barco, A.; Alvarez-Mon, M. Areas of Interest and Attitudes towards the Pharmacological Treatment of Attention Deficit Hyperactivity Disorder: Thematic and Quantitative Analysis Using Twitter. *J. Clin. Med.* 2021, *10*, 2668. https://doi.org/10.3390/jcm10122668

Academic Editor: Vida Abedi

Received: 15 March 2021
Accepted: 13 June 2021
Published: 17 June 2021

Publisher's Note: MDPI stays neutral with regard to jurisdictional claims in published maps and institutional affiliations.

Copyright: © 2021 by the authors. Licensee MDPI, Basel, Switzerland. This article is an open access article distributed under the terms and conditions of the Creative Commons Attribution (CC BY) license (https://creativecommons.org/licenses/by/4.0/).

1. Service of Psychiatry and Mental Health, Hospital Universitario Infanta Leonor, 28031 Madrid, Spain; lanta.79@gmail.com (L.d.A.); fjquinterog@salud.madrid.org (J.Q.)
2. Department of Medicine and Medical Specialities, University of Alcala, 28805 Alcala de Henares, Spain; guillermo.lahera@gmail.com (G.L.); miguel.angel.ortega92@gmail.com (M.A.O.); mademons@gmail.com (M.A.-M.)
3. Department of Endocrinology and Clinical Nutrition, Hospital Universitario Infanta Leonor, 28031 Madrid, Spain; maria.llavero@salud.madrid.org
4. Department of Psychiatry, University Hospital "Principe de Asturias", 28805 Alcala de Henares, Spain
5. CIBERSAM (Biomedical Research Networking Centre in Mental Health), 22807 Madrid, Spain
6. Institute Ramon y Cajal for Health Research (IRYCIS), 28034 Madrid, Spain; angel.asunsolo@uah.es
7. Louis A Faillace Department of Psychiatry and Behavioral Science, The University of Texas Health Science Centre at Houston, Houston, TX 77054, USA; Cesar.A.Soutullo@uth.tmc.edu
8. Department of Legal Medicine, Psychiatry and Pathology, Complutense University, 28040 Madrid, Spain
9. Department of Surgery, Medical and Social Sciences, Faculty of Medicine and Health Sciences, University of Alcalá, 28805 Alcala de Henares, Spain
10. Biomedical Institute for Liver and Gut Diseases (CIBEREHD), Instituto de Salud Carlos III, Av. Monforte de Lemos, 3-5, 28029 Madrid, Spain
11. Service of Internal Medicine and Rheumatology, Autoimmune Diseases University Hospital "Principe de Asturias", 28805 Alcala de Henares, Spain
* Correspondence: maalvarezdemon@icloud.com; Tel.: +34-918854505

Abstract: We focused on tweets containing hashtags related to ADHD pharmacotherapy between 20 September and 31 October 2019. Tweets were classified as to whether they described medical issues or not. Tweets with medical content were classified according to the topic they referred to: side effects, efficacy, or adherence. Furthermore, we classified any links included within a tweet as either scientific or non-scientific. We created a dataset of 6568 tweets: 4949 (75.4%) related to stimulants, 605 (9.2%) to non-stimulants and 1014 (15.4%) to alpha-2 agonists. Next, we manually analyzed 1810 tweets. In the end, 481 (48%) of the tweets in the stimulant group, 218 (71.9%) in the non-stimulant group and 162 (31.9%) in the alpha agonist group were considered classifiable. Stimulants accumulated the majority of tweets. Notably, the content that generated the highest frequency of tweets was that related to treatment efficacy, with alpha-2 agonist-related tweets accumulating the highest proportion of positive consideration. We found the highest percentages of tweets with scientific links in those posts related to alpha-2 agonists. Stimulant-related tweets obtained the highest proportion of likes and were the most disseminated within the Twitter community. Understanding the public view of these medications is necessary to design promotional strategies aimed at the appropriate population.

Keywords: ADHD; social media; Twitter; pharmacotherapy; stimulants; alpha-2 adrenergic agonists; non-stimulants

1. Introduction

Attention deficit hyperactivity disorder (ADHD) is one of the most common neuropsychiatric disorders of childhood and adolescence, often persisting into adulthood [1]. The reported prevalence of ADHD in children varies from 2 to 18 percent [2,3]. ADHD is associated with negative health outcomes and marked impairment in academic, occupational and social functioning [4,5].

The treatment of ADHD is complex and may involve behavioral, psychological and educational interventions, as well as medication [6]. Different pharmacological treatments have shown efficacy in reducing ADHD symptoms and improving daily functioning [6]. As has been reported, however, the efficacy of these treatments is not homogenous, nor is the frequency and pattern of associated side effects [6]. The choice of the initial medication depends upon a number of factors, including the individual preferences of the clinician, patient and family [6]. Furthermore, adherence to the treatment regimen is critical for the efficacy of the medical intervention [7,8]. Determinants of patient behavior, including adherence to medication and one's own lifestyle habits, are influenced by patients' experiences, attitudes and opinions with regard to their treatment [7,8]. In order to better optimize medical treatments for the management of ADHD, analyses of the opinions of patients and their families are therefore required.

Social media platforms are increasingly being leveraged by researchers for public health surveillance, intervention delivery, the study of attitudes toward health behaviors and diseases, predictions on diseases, and insight into the medical experiences of patients [9–12]. In particular, Twitter is the most commonly used social media platform within health research, and content analysis is the most common approach [13,14]. In this context, the exploration of tweets discussing perceptions of medications for better understanding, compliance and therapeutic decision making has been sufficiently established [15,16].

Moreover, research on patients' beliefs and attitudes has traditionally relied on surveys, interviews and clinical trials [17,18]. However, social media may also allow for a wider range of patients' voices to be heard, including those perspectives from patients reluctant to participate in surveys or research. In addition, since social media posts are spontaneous in nature, they may be more reflective of what patients truly experience than surveys conducted by researchers, which rely on structured, formal interviews [19–21]. Moreover, postings can be collected nearly in real time, thereby avoiding recall bias. Consequently, platforms such as Twitter may provide a useful insight into patients' beliefs.

Finally, the analysis of tweets on psychiatric disorders is a recently significant area of study for understanding the sentiments of society, patients and health professionals [22–24]. That being said, topics of medical and non-medical interest among Twitter users with relation to ADHD treatment have not yet been established, with the dissemination of ADHD-related tweets remaining unknown.

In this study, we have hypothesized that, firstly, the pharmacological treatment for ADHD is an area of interest for Twitter users and that, secondly, a diverse perception towards the different drug treatments available can be observed. More specifically, the aims of this multidisciplinary research were to investigate the interest and social considerations of Twitter users towards approved pharmacological treatments for ADHD. In addition, we investigated the dissemination of these tweets.

2. Materials and Methods
2.1. Data Collection

In this observational quantitative and qualitative study, we focused on searching for tweets that referred to medications approved for the treatment of ADHD: Adderall, Dexedrina, Dextrostat, Focalin, Metilin, Ritalin, Metadate CD (methylphenidate), Ritalin LA (methylphenidate), Adderal-XR, Vyvanse (Lisdexamfetamine), Concerta, Daytrana, Focalin XR, Quillivant XR (methylphenidate), Intuniv (guanfacine), Kapvay (clonidine) and Strattera (Atomoxetine). The inclusion criteria for tweets were: (1) being posted publicly; (2) using any of the previously mentioned hashtags; (3) being posted between 20 September and 31 October 2019; (4) being written in English or Spanish. The six-week period was chosen to avoid any potential bias in the content of the tweets. We collected the number of likes each tweet generated, the date and time of each tweet, a permanent link to the tweet and each user's profile description. In addition, we obtained a list of the ten hashtags most frequently associated with the hashtags of our study.

2.2. Search Tool

We used the Twitter Firehose data stream, which is managed by Gnip and allows access to 100% of all public tweets that match a certain criteria (query). In our study, the search criteria were the previously mentioned hashtags.

2.3. Content Analysis Process

All 118,388 retrieved tweets were included in the dataset (Figure 1). First, we excluded those tweets mentioning any of the aforementioned medications in an unrelated context. For example, Concerta is also the name of a political party in Chile. In this case, any tweets referring to the political party were omitted. Secondly, we excluded all tweets, including hashtags and keywords, not related to health (e.g., political issues). Specifically, Concerta and Ritalin generated 10,773 and 13,987 tweets, respectively, but 10,127 (94%) and 13,567 (97%), respectively, were not related to health. Indeed, most of them included hashtags (#mesacentral, #apoyofirmado, #tumbamadre, #lamarchamasgrande, #Pinerarenuncia) or keywords related to political conflict occurring in Chile. Similarly, Adderall generated 87,808 tweets, of which 86,052 (98.7%) included hashtags or keywords related to political issues (e.g., Trump, impeachment).

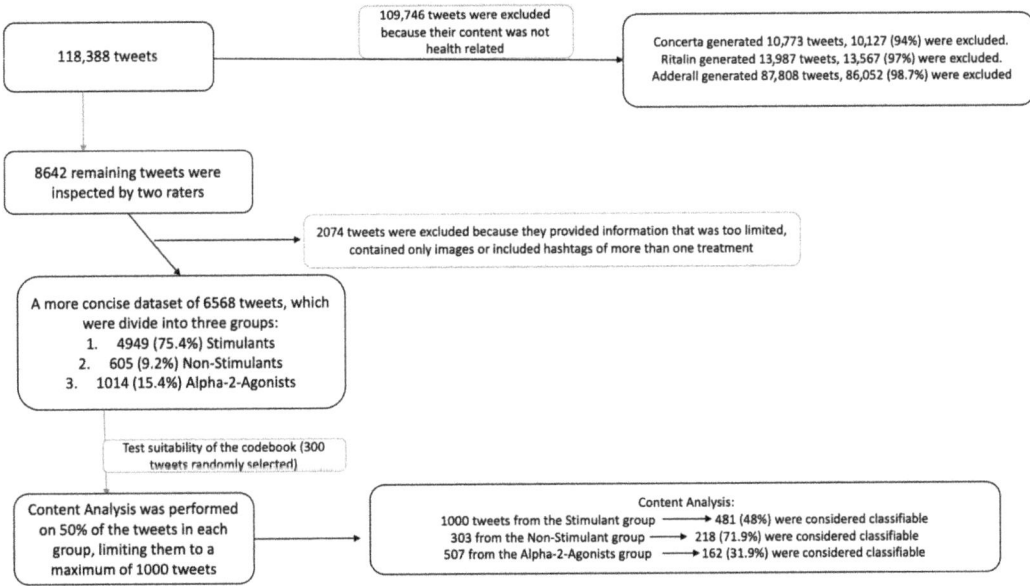

Figure 1. Flowchart of data management.

All 8642 remaining tweets were inspected by two raters (M.A.A.-M. and L.d.A.). First, we scanned all of the tweets and excluded 2074 that provided information that was too limited, contained only images or included hashtags of more than one treatment. This process led to the creation of a more concise dataset of 6568 tweets, which we divided into three groups: 4949 (75.4%) stimulants, 605 (9.2%) non-stimulants and 1014 (15.4%) alpha-2-adrenergic agonists.

Next, we created a codebook based on our research questions, our previous experience in analyzing tweets and what we determined to be the most common themes. M.A.A.-M.

and L.d.A. analyzed 300 tweets separately to test the suitability of the codebook. Discrepancies were discussed between the raters and with another author (M.L.-V.). After revising the codebook, the raters then proceeded to perform a content analysis of 50% of the tweets in each group, limiting them to a maximum of 1000 tweets randomly selected. Thus, we manually analyzed 1000 tweets from the stimulant group, 303 from the non-stimulant group and 507 from the alpha-2 agonist group (Figure 1). Classification criteria and examples of tweets are shown in Table 1.

Table 1. Category, definitions and examples of classification. Usernames and personal names were removed.

Category	Examples of Tweets
EFFICACY (refers to the ability or inability of a treatment to provide a beneficial effect)	• I like to talk about meds. been on ADHD meds almost consistently from 8 yrs old to now (19). im on Concerta right now and it's working wonders for me. people are very strung out about medicating kids and i get that but, i really needed it as a kid and need it more as an adult. • Unfortunately concerta didn't work for me: (but everybody's different! it was so long ago i can't remember what my problem with it was haha...i think it just wasn't strong enough for me. but it's not a bad drug i know some ppl that take it! make sure you're eating ok?
SIDE EFFECTS (refers to any effect that is secondary to the one intended either adverse or beneficial; we also included tweets discussing tolerability of the drug)	• I just vividly remember going off Concerta as a kid because it killed my appetite and I have a hard enough time keeping weight on as it is (this 3-week depressive low has already ate away [haha] at 2 or 3 lbs) and I'm afraid of that happening again • Concerta makes me want to eat three leaves of lettuce a day and id still feel bloated. • I was diagnosed at an early age and was put on a few medications. I had some medications that made me very emotional. The last medication I remember being on was concerta and it flattened my mood waaay too much • I was really thirsty, not eating, and super paranoid when I tried vyvanse. • I remember taking my first concerta, it was the 18 mg and I was in matric. Stayed up all night like a maniac
ADHERENCE (refers to the degree of conformity to the recommendations about the treatment with respect to the timing, dosage or frequency)	• I love the way you explained it! I was diagnosed in 2012, five years into my serving in the military. I took concerta for the first 3 months after my diagnosis and then stopped. I struggled with accepting this diagnosis. Now in 2019 I've accepted it & want to get help. • Uhm I'm not doing this willingly. I'm all for medicine. I'm not taking my meds rn because I need to do a new examination of my diagnosis and I need to have 0 trace of concerta in my body by then. I legit can't wait to get to take meds again. • I have 72 mg Concerta, ive been on it for years but i dont take it every single day.

2.4. Measuring Influence and Interest on Twitter

We analyzed the number of likes generated by each tweet as an indicator of user interest on a given topic. We also measured the potential reach and impact of all analyzed hashtags. Impact is defined as a numerical value representing the potential views a tweet may receive, while reach is defined as a numerical value measuring the potential audience of the hashtag.

In addition, we measured how positive or negative a hashtag was on a scale from 1 (negative) to 100 (positive). Sentiment analysis tools analyze all words contained in a tweet, and each word has its own score that can vary depending on the context. The average score of all the tweets with a certain hashtag determines that hashtag's overall sentiment score.

2.5. Ethical Considerations

This study was approved by the Research Ethics Committee of the University of Alcala (OE 14_2020).

2.6. Statistical Analysis

A descriptive study of the sample was performed, describing the variables by their absolute and relative frequencies. The percentages found were compared using the chi-square test. In the case of quantitative variables, it was checked whether they followed a normal distribution using the Kolmogorof–Smirnof test. As this was not the case, non-parametric tests were used. The Kruskal–Wallis test was used for comparisons of median values among three groups, followed by post hoc testing using a Bonferroni-adjusted alpha level.

3. Results

3.1. Stimulants Accumulated the Most Interest among Twitter Users

According to the codebook, 521 (52%) of the stimulant tweets, 85 (28.1%) of the non-stimulant tweets and 345 (68.1%) of the alpha-2 agonist tweets were considered unclassifiable. These tweets shared information or news either about the commercialization of the medication, business-related information, or mentions of treatments for other disorders apart from ADHD. In the end, 481 (48%) of the tweets in the stimulant group, 218 (71.9%) in the non-stimulant group and 162 (31.9%) in the alpha agonist group were considered classifiable (Figure 1). In terms of the content of these tweets, the mention of the specific medications was related to their efficacy, side effects or adherence to treatment for ADHD (Table 1). Moreover, these coding categories were not mutually exclusive in the sense that a generated tweet could be listed under more than one category.

There were significant differences in the percentage of tweets with medical efficacy content between the three groups of drugs (Table 2). The percentage of tweets related to the efficacy of the alpha-2 agonist group was higher than that found in the stimulant and non-stimulant groups. Furthermore, the alpha-2 agonist group also had the highest percentage of tweets containing a positive description of the efficacy of their use (74.1%). Similar results were observed in the percentage of tweets addressing efficacy, as well as the valuation of that efficacy among the stimulant and non-stimulant groups.

Table 2. Descriptive characteristics of the tweets considered classifiable in the content analysis, categorized by total amount per drug and category.

N		ALPHA-2 AGONIST	NON-STIMULANT	STIMULANT	p-Value
		162	218	481	
EFFICACY	No Mention	36 (22.2%)	84 (38.5%)	176 (36.6%)	
	Positive	120 (74.1%)	118 (54.1%)	270 (56.1%)	
	Negative	6 (3.7%)	16 (7.3%)	35 (7.3%)	
					$p < 0.001$
SIDE EFFECTS	No Mention	40 (24.7%)	77 (35.3%)	239 (49.7%)	
	Positive	4 (2.5%)	3 (1.4%)	6 (1.2%)	
	Negative	118 (72.8%)	138 (63.3%)	236 (49.1%)	
					$p < 0.001$

Table 2. Cont.

N		ALPHA-2 AGONIST	NON-STIMULANT	STIMULANT	p-Value
		162	218	481	
ADHERENCE	No Mention	148 (91.4%)	196 (89.9%)	451 (93.8%)	
	Positive	8 (4.9%)	12 (5.5%)	9 (1.9%)	
	Negative	6 (3.7%)	10 (4.6%)	21 (4.4%)	
					$p = 0.1$
LINK	No Mention	65 (40.1%)	145 (66.5%)	466 (96.9%)	
	Scientific	94 (58.0%)	68 (31.2%)	13 (2.7%)	
	Non-Scientific	3 (1.9%)	5 (2.3%)	2 (0.4%)	
					$p < 0.001$

For each category, total number of tweets (n) and relative proportions (%) are provided. Chi-square tests were conducted to assess for statistical differences.

The analysis of the content related to the side effects of the treatments also showed significant differences between the three groups of drugs (Table 2). The alpha-2 agonist group had the highest percentage of tweets with content related to side effects and accumulated the highest percentage of those tweets with a negative valuation (72.8%). In contrast, the stimulant group had the lowest percentage of negative valuations towards side effects (49.1%). There were not any significant differences in the percentages of those tweets mentioning treatment adherence between the three groups of drugs, being that they were all low.

3.2. Scientific Links Were Mainly Found in Alpha-2 Agonist-Related Tweets

We investigated the use of sources defined by the inclusion of links within the tweet. The links were categorized as scientific or non-scientific sources. Of the tweets related to ADHD, 185 out of the 861 (21.5%) included a reference source, the majority of which were scientific in nature (94.6%). We found significant differences between the percentages of tweets containing a reference link between the three groups of drugs ($p < 0.001$) (Table 2). Those tweets related to alpha-2 agonists had the highest percentage of links, of which most were scientific. In contrast, tweets related to the stimulant drug group had the lowest percentage of links (3.1%).

We observed that the percentages of tweets with negative or positive content related to the efficacy of treatments were different among those tweets both including and not including a link ($p < 0.001$) (Table 3). The negative opinion of treatment efficacy was higher in those without a link (8.1%). In contrast, the percentage of tweets related to side effects was higher among those with a link than in those without one included ($p < 0.001$). Interestingly, the use of links in tweets with adherence content was very low (0.5%).

We studied the use of links in the three groups of treatments. We found a different pattern of distribution of links within the different categories. Within the group of alpha-2 agonist tweets, we observed that the majority of the tweets with a link were focused on efficacy and side effects (Table 4). In contrast, within the non-stimulant group, references to efficacy were mainly posted without a link. Lastly, within the stimulant drug group, efficacy was mainly addressed using a link, whereas side effects were mainly addressed without one.

Table 3. Descriptive characteristics of the tweets considered classifiable in the content analysis, categorized by either including or not including a link.

Total		WITHOUT LINK	WITH LINK	p-Value
		676	185	
EFFICACY	No Mention	238 (35.4%)	57 (30.8%)	
	Positive	382 (56.5%)	126 (68.1%)	
	Negative	55 (8.1%)	2 (1.1%)	
				$p < 0.001$
SIDE EFFECTS	No Mention	320 (47.3%)	36 (19.5%)	
	Positive	10 (1.5%)	3 (1.6%)	
	Negative	346 (51.2%)	146 (78.9%)	
				$p < 0.001$
ADHERENCE	No Mention	611 (90.4%)	184 (99.5%)	
	Positive	29 (4.3%)	0	
	Negative	36 (5.3%)	1 (0.5%)	
				$p < 0.001$

For each category, total number of tweets (n) and relative proportions (%) are provided. Chi-square tests were conducted to assess for statistical differences.

Table 4. Use of links in the different content categories of the tweets related to the three different groups of pharmacological treatments.

		ALPHA-2 AGONIST		NON-STIMULANTS		STIMULANTS	
		WITHOUT LINK	WITH LINK	WITHOUT LINK	WITH LINK	WITHOUT LINK	WITH LINK
Total		65	97	145	73	466	15
SIDE EFFECTS	NM	26 (40%)	14 (14%)	66 (45.5%)	11 (15.1%)	288 (48.9%)	11 (73.3%)
	+	1 (2%)	3 (3%)	3 (2.1%)	0	6 (1.3%)	0
	−	38 (58%)	80 (82%)	76 (52.4%)	62 (84.9%)	232 (49.8%)	4 (26.7%)
		$p = 0.001$		$p < 0.001$		$p = 0.17$	
EFFICACY	NM	24 (37%)	12 (12%)	42 (29%)	42 (57.5%)	173 (37.1%)	3 (20%)
	+	36 (55%)	84 (87%)	87 (60%)	31 (42.5%)	259 (55.6%)	11 (73.3%)
	−	5 (8%)	1 (1%)	16 (11%)	0	34 (7.3%)	1 (6.7%)
		$p < 0.001$		$p < 0.001$		$p = 0.37$	

Table 4. Cont.

		ALPHA-2 AGONIST		NON-STIMULANTS		STIMULANTS	
		WITHOUT LINK	WITH LINK	WITHOUT LINK	WITH LINK	WITHOUT LINK	WITH LINK
ADHERENCE	NM	52 (80%)	96 (99%)	123 (84.8%)	73 (100%)	436 (93.6%)	15 (100%)
	+	8 (12%)	0	12 (8.3%)	0	9 (1.9%)	0
	−	5 (8%)	1 (1%)	10 (6.9%)	0	21 (4.5%)	0
		$p < 0.001$		$p = 0.002$		$p = 0.60$	

Percentages (%) were calculated with respect to the total number of tweets generated without or with links in each group of treatments and content category. NM = no mention. + = positive. − = negative.

3.3. Stimulant Related Tweets Were the Most Disseminated within the Twitter Community

We found that the probabilities of a tweet being liked among the three groups were significantly different ($p < 0.001$). Alpha-2 agonists showed a statistically significantly lower number of likes than both non-stimulant ($p = 0.024$) and stimulant ($p < 0.001$). Stimulant-related tweets accumulated the highest median of likes per tweet. In addition, we analyzed the number of likes received per tweet as classified by the inclusion or absence of a link. We found that tweets not including a link had a significantly higher median of likes per tweet than those tweets including a link ($p = 0.041$).

Furthermore, we found that stimulant-related tweets had the highest potential reach and impact (Figure 2). Both parameters were markedly lower for non-stimulant and alpha-2 agonist-related tweets. Regarding the sentiment analyses of the content of the tweets, we found that it was positive for all three groups (Figure 3).

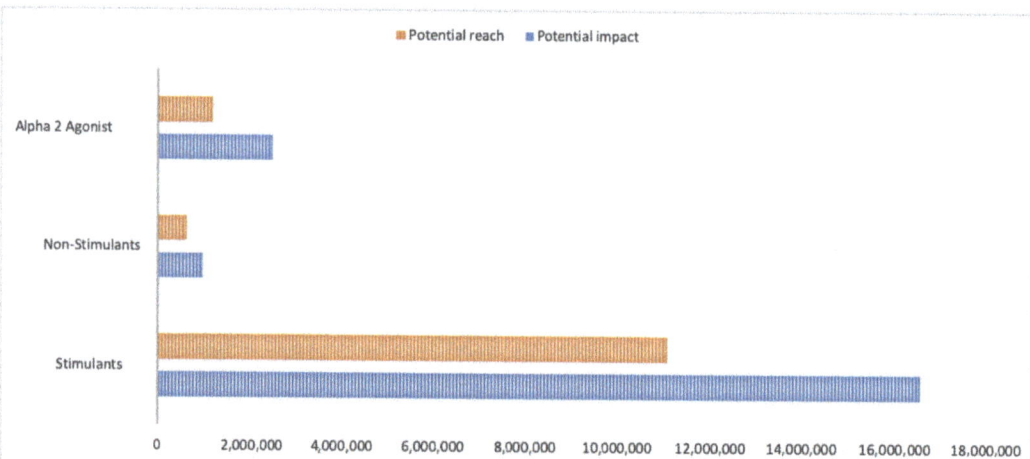

Figure 2. Potential reach and potential impact.

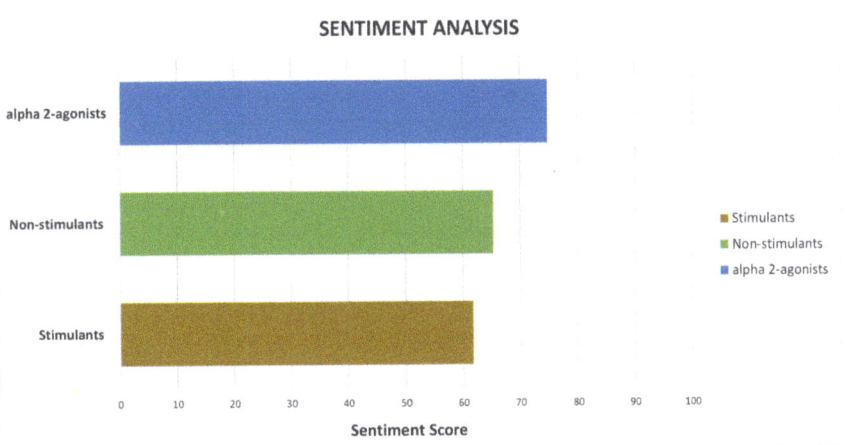

Figure 3. Sentiment score comparisons between alpha-2 agonists, non-stimulants and stimulants. Sentiment analysis is classifying the polarity of the tweet on a scale of 0 (very negative) to 100 (very positive).

4. Discussion

4.1. Principal Findings

In this study, we have found that Twitter users show a great interest in ADHD drugs, mainly focusing on stimulants. These tweets are centered on the efficacy and side effects of ADHD treatment. Tweets containing a positive consideration of efficacy were mainly observed in those posts related to alpha-2 agonists. The frequency of tweets with content related to adherence to treatment was marginal. The highest percentages of tweets with scientific links were observed in those related to alpha-2 agonists. Furthermore, those tweets referencing stimulants obtained the highest potential reach and impact.

The treatment of ADHD is complex, involving both the use of non-pharmacological tools and the prescription of drugs [6]. Regarding pharmacological treatments, different variables condition their clinical results. For instance, the efficacy of a drug for controlling disease symptoms and the frequency and intensity of side effects are considered to be critical for a treatment's success [6]. Nevertheless, the subjective experience of a drug being used by a patient is pivotal too in terms of adherence to treatment [7,8]. Furthermore, a patient's experience when consuming a drug is conditioned by any information or social valuations received [25]. Thus, the study of patients' experiences with regard to the efficacy and side effects of, as well as adherence to, ADHD treatments is an area of intense focus, having been previously assessed mainly through the use of qualitative studies such as surveys and interviews [26,27]. However, contradictory results have also been reported on the different drugs employed in ADHD treatment [28].

Currently, Twitter serves as one of the predominant social platforms for disseminating perspectives publicly, giving anonymity to user testimonies and encouraging communication by people with real or perceived personal and social restrictions [29]. This anonymity also prevents the potential stigmatization of a Twitter user for his/her attitudes towards a disease, or for any physical or mental conditions they choose to disclose [30]. Thus, Twitter has become a relevant tool for the dissemination of medical information and an interesting resource for the study of individual experiences and opinions [31]. Furthermore, it has been shown that young people tend to hide information from their doctors, especially that information related to behaviors of which health care providers do not usually approve [32]. As a result, Twitter gives them the opportunity to express their experiences anonymously [33].

In this study, we have demonstrated that the use of Twitter for sharing information on patient experiences regarding ADHD treatment is significant, with tweets of this type maintaining a high frequency among those containing content more generally related to medical treatment. Nevertheless, Twitter users tend to be younger than the population at large; likewise, ADHD tends to affect a mostly younger demographic [1]. Moreover, the majority of the tweets with medical content on ADHD drug treatments were related to the stimulant group. Interestingly, these data uphold the elevated frequency of the use of these drugs in the treatment of ADHD patients globally [34].

The high frequency of tweets with content related to the efficacy and side effects of pharmacological treatments supports their significance to ADHD patients. Several studies have also examined the efficacy of each treatment on ADHD symptoms; however, with contradictory results [28]. Various reasons might explain such a discrepancy, yet this strategy for obtaining patient information is critical regardless. Additionally, it has been proposed that infodemiology may overcome the Hawthorne Effect as well as any memory recall biases common to cross-sectional surveys and questionnaire-based studies [19,35]. In terms of medical efficacy, our findings show that the alpha-2 agonist group of drugs accumulated the highest frequency of tweets with a positive valuation, even though frequency levels observed for both stimulants and non-stimulants ranked similarly. However, the alpha-2 agonist group of drugs received the highest frequency of tweets related to their side effects; interestingly, stimulants received the lowest frequency of tweets with regard to tolerability. It has been previously shown that some of the side effects of stimulant drugs have even been considered positive and actively pursued by patients [36]. These results might support the designation of stimulant drugs as the first pharmacological option for treating ADHD, as evidenced by several guidelines [6,37].

Our data also show that adherence to a pharmacological treatment is not a relevant consideration for ADHD patients who are Twitter users. Additional to this point is the fact that a similarly low frequency of tweets related to treatment adherence was found within all three groups of drugs, with a positive valuation towards adherence uncommon but slightly higher in the non-stimulant and alpha-2 agonist groups. Furthermore, the limited interest for treatment adherence found among Twitter users confirms previous studies carried out that employed other strategies [38,39].

Correct medical information is considered to be a cornerstone for the understanding of disease and subsequent patient treatments [40,41]. Currently, access to medical information has been generalized across the internet. For instance, we have found that one fifth of the content related to medical treatment included a link, a majority of which was deemed scientific in nature. This low frequency of the inclusion of links in tweets related to ADHD pharmacological treatment contrasted with those found in a study on statins [19]. Moreover, tweets including a link were twenty times more frequent in those posts referring to alpha-2 agonists than in those related to stimulants.

Different patterns in the use of links were also found between the different groups of drugs analyzed. Within the group of alpha-2 agonist tweets, for instance, the majority of tweets with a link were focused on efficacy and side effects. In contrast, among the non-stimulant group, the majority of tweets mentioning efficacy did not include a link. These results indicate the significant relevance of scientific information and medical research for ADHD patients who are Twitter users. As an example, most alpha-2 agonist medications have been approved for ADHD treatment over the last ten years, while stimulants have been used for decades. This finding therefore supports Twitter's value as a means of communicating scientific content. However, it is worrying that only a limited number of tweets referring to ADHD treatment adherence included a scientific link, especially considering that adherence is pivotal to treatment success [7,8]. That being said, trends in information exchanged over Twitter may still be important as studies have identified that certain health behaviors can be affected [42,43].

Our study also shows that the names of those drugs used for ADHD treatment coincided with tweets referencing political, social and other non-medical content. Furthermore, we observed pejorative uses of these names by Twitter users. These findings suggest that social stigmatization towards mental health, as previously described, still persists, producing deleterious effects in the lives of people suffering from mental health conditions [44,45]. As well, the non-medical use of psychostimulant drugs, which has not always been uncovered via traditional surveys, has nevertheless been revealed through the analysis of Twitter content [46].

Clinicians themselves should therefore take into consideration information posted over social media with regard to pharmacological treatment that otherwise may not be spontaneously reported during a patient interview. This is particularly important for medications commonly abused or consumed over the counter, behaviors commonly hidden by patients from doctors [47]. In this context, social media may be deemed a friendlier place to discuss the effects of medications, especially those usually rejected by doctors. As relates to this study, an increase in the dissemination of scientific information on ADHD treatment and, in particular, the importance of the adherence to said treatment appears to be a primary objective for the medical community at large.

4.2. Limitations

First, Twitter may not be reflective of the general population. Secondly, researchers cannot directly measure clinical outcomes from tweets. Third, the codebook design and text analysis imply a degree of subjectivity. However, this methodology is consistent with previous medical research studies using Twitter. Furthermore, to address this last issue, our study comprised a series of countermeasures including an initial review, design of the codebook, and an agreement between coders. Although computerized machine learning methods have been tested to automatically identify and classify topics in medical research over social media, we used an analytical strategy based on raters' clinical expertise in psychiatry, which constituted a qualitative advantage compared to other automated strategies [48]. Finally, we did not determine whether the date of FDA approval affected Twitter activity differently when comparing more recent medication to older medication.

5. Conclusions

This study identified interesting beliefs and opinions regarding the pharmacological treatment of ADHD that may affect patient behavior. Moreover, social media may be useful for investigating the public's prevailing attitudes when investigating particular medications, as well as when patients report on adverse events and efficacy since both issues can affect their choice of and adherence to treatment. Public perceptions about medications could in turn help inform clinicians, particularly when developing treatment guidelines. Specific to ADHD, public opinions elucidated by this study could be used to help update guidelines, improve communication between health care professionals and patients and ultimately help to build more viable bridges between both parties.

Author Contributions: Material preparation, data collection and analysis were performed by M.A.A.-M., L.d.A., M.L.-V., A.A.d.B. conducted and reported statistical analysis. The first draft of the manuscript was written by M.A.A.-M. Interpretation of data and revision of the manuscript for important intellectual content was carried out by M.A.O., G.L., C.S. and J.Q. M.A.-M. contributed as supervisor of all the stages. All authors have read and agreed to the published version of the manuscript.

Funding: This work was partially supported by grants from the Fondo de Investigación de la Seguridad Social, Instituto de Salud Carlos III (PI18/01726), Spain, and the Programa de Actividades de I+D de la Comunidad de Madrid en Biomedicina (B2017/BMD-3804), Madrid, Spain.

Institutional Review Board Statement: The study was conducted according to the guidelines of the Declaration of Helsinki, and approved by the Research Ethics Committee of the University of Alcala (OE 14_2020).

Informed Consent Statement: Not applicable.

Data Availability Statement: The data that support the findings of this study are available from the corresponding author upon reasonable request.

Conflicts of Interest: The authors declare no conflict of interest.

References

1. Fayyad, J.; De Graaf, R.; Kessler, R.; Alonso, J.; Angermeyer, M.; Demyttenaere, K.; De Girolamo, G.; Haro, J.M.; Karam, E.G.; Lara, C.; et al. Cross-national prevalence and correlates of adult attention-deficit hyperactivity disorder. *Br. J. Psychiatry* **2007**, *190*, 402–409. [CrossRef]
2. Danielson, M.L.; Bitsko, R.H.; Ghandour, R.M.; Holbrook, J.R.; Kogan, M.D.; Blumberg, S.J. Prevalence of Parent-Reported ADHD Diagnosis and Associated Treatment Among U.S. Children and Adolescents, 2016. *J. Clin. Child Adolesc. Psychol.* **2018**, *47*, 199–212. [CrossRef]
3. Merikangas, K.R.; He, J.-P.; Brody, D.; Fisher, P.W.; Bourdon, K.; Koretz, D.S. Prevalence and treatment of mental disorders among US children in the 2001–2004 NHANES. *Pediatrics* **2010**, *125*, 75–81. [CrossRef]
4. Hechtman, L.; Swanson, J.M.; Sibley, M.H.; Stehli, A.; Owens, E.B.; Mitchell, J.T.; Arnold, L.E.; Molina, B.S.G.; Hinshaw, S.P.; Jensen, P.S.; et al. Functional Adult Outcomes 16 Years After Childhood Diagnosis of Attention-Deficit/Hyperactivity Disorder: MTA Results. *J. Am. Acad. Child Adolesc. Psychiatry* **2016**, *55*, 945–952.e2. [CrossRef]
5. Roy, A.; Hechtman, L.; Arnold, L.E.; Swanson, J.M.; Molina, B.S.G.; Sibley, M.H.; Howard, A.L.; MTA Cooperative Group. Childhood Predictors of Adult Functional Outcomes in the Multimodal Treatment Study of Attention-Deficit/Hyperactivity Disorder (MTA). *J. Am. Acad. Child Adolesc. Psychiatry* **2017**, *56*, 687–695.e7. [CrossRef]
6. Wolraich, M.L.; Hagan, J.F.; Allan, C.; Chan, E.; Davison, D.; Earls, M.; Evans, S.W.; Flinn, S.K.; Froehlich, T.; Frost, J.; et al. Clinical Practice Guideline for the Diagnosis, Evaluation, and Treatment of Attention-Deficit/Hyperactivity Disorder in Children and Adolescents. *Pediatrics* **2019**, *144*, e20192528. [CrossRef]
7. Pappadopulos, E.; Jensen, P.S.; Chait, A.R.; Arnold, L.E.; Swanson, J.M.; Greenhill, L.L.; Hechtman, L.; Chuang, S.; Wells, K.C.; Pelham, W.; et al. Medication adherence in the MTA: Saliva methylphenidate samples versus parent report and mediating effect of concomitant behavioral treatment. *J. Am. Acad. Child Adolesc. Psychiatry* **2009**, *48*, 501–510. [CrossRef]
8. Schaefer, M.R.; Wagoner, S.T.; Young, M.E.; Rawlinson, A.R.; Kavookjian, J.; Shapiro, S.K.; Gray, W.N. Subjective Versus Objective Measures of Medication Adherence in Adolescents/Young Adults with Attention-Deficit Hyperactivity Disorder. *J. Dev. Behav. Pediatr.* **2019**, *40*, 54–59. [CrossRef]
9. Alvarez-Mon, M.A.; Asunsolo del Barco, A.; Lahera, G.; Quintero, J.; Ferre, F.; Pereira-Sanchez, V.; Ortuño, F.; Alvarez-Mon, M. Increasing Interest of Mass Communication Media and the General Public in the Distribution of Tweets About Mental Disorders: Observational Study. *J. Med. Internet Res.* **2018**, *20*, e205. [CrossRef] [PubMed]
10. Saha, K.; Torous, J.; Kiciman, E.; De Choudhury, M. Understanding Side Effects of Antidepressants: Large-scale Longitudinal Study on Social Media Data. *JMIR Ment. Health* **2021**, *8*, e26589. [CrossRef]
11. Colditz, J.B.; Chu, K.-H.; Emery, S.L.; Larkin, C.R.; James, A.E.; Welling, J.; Primack, B.A. Toward Real-Time Infoveillance of Twitter Health Messages. *Am. J. Public Health* **2018**, *108*, 1009–1014. [CrossRef]
12. Teo, A.R.; Strange, W.; Bui, R.; Dobscha, S.K.; Ono, S.S. Responses to Concerning Posts on Social Media and Their Implications for Suicide Prevention Training for Military Veterans: Qualitative Study. *J. Med. Internet Res.* **2020**, *22*, e22076. [CrossRef]
13. Sinnenberg, L.; Buttenheim, A.M.; Padrez, K.; Mancheno, C.; Ungar, L.; Merchant, R.M. Twitter as a Tool for Health Research: A Systematic Review. *Am. J. Public Health* **2017**, *107*, e1–e8. [CrossRef]
14. Dol, J.; Tutelman, P.R.; Chambers, C.T.; Barwick, M.; Drake, E.K.; Parker, J.A.; Parker, R.; Benchimol, E.I.; George, R.B.; Witteman, H.O. Health Researchers' Use of Social Media: Scoping Review. *J. Med. Internet Res.* **2019**, *21*, e13687. [CrossRef]
15. Martinez, B.; Dailey, F.; Almario, C.V.; Keller, M.S.; Desai, M.; Dupuy, T.; Mosadeghi, S.; Whitman, C.; Lasch, K.; Ursos, L.; et al. Patient Understanding of the Risks and Benefits of Biologic Therapies in Inflammatory Bowel Disease. *Inflamm. Bowel Dis.* **2017**, *23*, 1057–1064. [CrossRef]
16. Golder, S.; Bach, M.; O'Connor, K.; Gross, R.; Hennessy, S.; Gonzalez Hernandez, G. Public Perspectives on Anti-Diabetic Drugs: Exploratory Analysis of Twitter Posts. *JMIR Diabetes* **2021**, *6*, e24681. [CrossRef]
17. Nanna, M.G.; Navar, A.M.; Zakroysky, P.; Xiang, Q.; Goldberg, A.C.; Robinson, J.; Roger, V.L.; Virani, S.S.; Wilson, P.W.F.; Elassal, J.; et al. Association of Patient Perceptions of Cardiovascular Risk and Beliefs on Statin Drugs With Racial Differences in Statin Use: Insights From the Patient and Provider Assessment of Lipid Management Registry. *JAMA Cardiol.* **2018**, *3*, 739–748. [CrossRef]
18. Wei, M.Y.; Ito, M.K.; Cohen, J.D.; Brinton, E.A.; Jacobson, T.A. Predictors of statin adherence, switching, and discontinuation in the USAGE survey: Understanding the use of statins in America and gaps in patient education. *J. Clin. Lipidol.* **2013**, *7*, 472–483. [CrossRef] [PubMed]
19. Golder, S.; O'Connor, K.; Hennessy, S.; Gross, R.; Gonzalez-Hernandez, G. Assessment of Beliefs and Attitudes About Statins Posted on Twitter. *JAMA Netw. Open* **2020**, *3*, e208953. [CrossRef]
20. Lachmar, E.M.; Wittenborn, A.K.; Bogen, K.W.; McCauley, H.L. #MyDepressionLooksLike: Examining Public Discourse about Depression on Twitter. *JMIR Ment. Health* **2017**, *4*, e43.
21. Berry, N.; Lobban, F.; Belousov, M.; Emsley, R.; Nenadic, G.; Bucci, S. #WhyWeTweetMH: Understanding Why People Use Twitter to Discuss Mental Health Problems. *J. Med. Internet Res.* **2017**, *19*, e107.
22. Viguria, I.; Alvarez-Mon, M.A.; Llavero-Valero, M.; Asunsolo Del Barco, A.; Ortuño, F.; Alvarez-Mon, M. Eating Disorder Awareness Campaigns: Thematic and Quantitative Analysis Using Twitter. *J. Med. Internet Res.* **2020**, *22*, e17626. [CrossRef]

23. Alvarez-Mon, M.A.; Llavero-Valero, M.; Sánchez-Bayona, R.; Pereira-Sanchez, V.; Vallejo-Valdivielso, M.; Monserrat, J.; Lahera, G.; Asunsolo del Barco, A.; Alvarez-Mon, M. Areas of Interest and Stigmatic Attitudes of the General Public in Five Relevant Medical Conditions: Thematic and Quantitative Analysis Using Twitter. *J. Med. Internet Res.* **2019**, *21*, e14110. [CrossRef]
24. Pereira-Sanchez, V.; Alvarez-Mon, M.A.; Asunsolo del Barco, A.; Alvarez-Mon, M.; Teo, A. Exploring the Extent of the Hikikomori Phenomenon on Twitter: Mixed Methods Study of Western Language Tweets. *J. Med. Internet Res.* **2019**, *21*, e14167. [CrossRef]
25. Mohammed, M.A.; Moles, R.J.; Chen, T.F. Medication-related burden and patients' lived experience with medicine: A systematic review and metasynthesis of qualitative studies. *BMJ Open* **2016**, *6*, e010035. [CrossRef]
26. Loewen, O.K.; Maximova, K.; Ekwaru, J.P.; Asbridge, M.; Ohinmaa, A.; Veugelers, P.J. Adherence to Life-Style Recommendations and Attention-Deficit/Hyperactivity Disorder. *Psychosom. Med.* **2020**, *82*, 305–315. [CrossRef]
27. Pringsheim, T.; Stewart, D.G.; Chan, P.; Tehrani, A.; Patten, S.B. The Pharmacoepidemiology of Psychotropic Medication Use in Canadian Children from 2012 to 2016. *J. Child Adolesc. Psychopharmacol.* **2019**, *29*, 740–745. [CrossRef]
28. Cortese, S.; Adamo, N.; Del Giovane, C.; Mohr-Jensen, C.; Hayes, A.J.; Carucci, S.; Atkinson, L.Z.; Tessari, L.; Banaschewski, T.; Coghill, D.; et al. Comparative efficacy and tolerability of medications for attention-deficit hyperactivity disorder in children, adolescents, and adults: A systematic review and network meta-analysis. *Lancet Psychiatry* **2018**, *5*, 727–738. [CrossRef]
29. Gillespie-Lynch, K.; Kapp, S.K.; Shane-Simpson, C.; Smith, D.S.; Hutman, T. Intersections between the autism spectrum and the internet: Perceived benefits and preferred functions of computer-mediated communication. *Intellect. Dev. Disabil.* **2014**, *52*, 456–469. [CrossRef] [PubMed]
30. Birnbaum, M.L.; Rizvi, A.F.; Correll, C.U.; Kane, J.M.; Confino, J. Role of social media and the Internet in pathways to care for adolescents and young adults with psychotic disorders and non-psychotic mood disorders. *Early Interv. Psychiatry* **2017**, *11*, 290–295. [CrossRef] [PubMed]
31. Passerello, G.L.; Hazelwood, J.E.; Lawrie, S. Using Twitter to assess attitudes to schizophrenia and psychosis. *BJPsych Bull.* **2019**, *43*, 158–166. [CrossRef] [PubMed]
32. Gray, W.N.; Kavookjian, J.; Shapiro, S.K.; Wagoner, S.T.; Schaefer, M.R.; Resmini Rawlinson, A.; Hinnant, J.B. Transition to College and Adherence to Prescribed Attention Deficit Hyperactivity Disorder Medication. *J. Dev. Behav. Pediatr.* **2017**, *39*, 1–9. [CrossRef] [PubMed]
33. Guntuku, S.C.; Ramsay, J.R.; Merchant, R.M.; Ungar, L.H. Language of ADHD in Adults on Social Media. *J. Atten. Disord.* **2019**, *23*, 1475–1485. [CrossRef] [PubMed]
34. Charach, A. Editorial: Time for a New Conversation on Stimulant Use. *J. Am. Acad. Child Adolesc. Psychiatry* **2020**, *59*, 929–930. [CrossRef]
35. Eysenbach, G. Infodemiology and Infoveillance: Framework for an Emerging Set of Public Health Informatics Methods to Analyze Search, Communication and Publication Behavior on the Internet. *J. Med. Internet Res.* **2009**, *11*, e11. [CrossRef] [PubMed]
36. Teter, C.J.; McCabe, S.E.; Cranford, J.A.; Boyd, C.J.; Guthrie, S.K. Prevalence and motives for illicit use of prescription stimulants in an undergraduate student sample. *J. Am. Coll. Health* **2005**, *53*, 253–262. [CrossRef] [PubMed]
37. Pliszka, S.R.; Crismon, M.L.; Hughes, C.W.; Corners, C.K.; Emslie, G.J.; Jensen, P.S.; McCRACKEN, J.T.; Swanson, J.M.; Lopez, M.; Texas Consensus Conference Panel on Pharmacotherapy of Childhood Attention Deficit Hyperactivity Disorder. The Texas Children's Medication Algorithm Project: Revision of the algorithm for pharmacotherapy of attention-deficit/hyperactivity disorder. *J. Am. Acad. Child Adolesc. Psychiatry* **2006**, *45*, 642–657. [CrossRef]
38. Emilsson, M.; Gustafsson, P.; Öhnström, G.; Marteinsdottir, I. Impact of personality on adherence to and beliefs about ADHD medication, and perceptions of ADHD in adolescents. *BMC Psychiatry* **2020**, *20*, 139. [CrossRef]
39. Biederman, J.; Fried, R.; DiSalvo, M.; Woodworth, K.Y.; Biederman, I.; Driscoll, H.; Noyes, E.; Faraone, S.V.; Perlis, R.H. Further evidence of low adherence to stimulant treatment in adult ADHD: An electronic medical record study examining timely renewal of a stimulant prescription. *Psychopharmacology* **2020**, *237*, 2835–2843. [CrossRef]
40. Felnhofer, A.; Bussek, T.; Goreis, A.; Kafka, J.X.; König, D.; Klier, C.; Zesch, H.; Kothgassner, O.D. Mothers' and Fathers' Perspectives on the Causes of Their Child's Disorder. *J. Pediatr. Psychol.* **2020**, *45*, 803–811. [CrossRef]
41. Oerbeck, B.; Furu, K.; Zeiner, P.; Aase, H.; Reichborn-Kjennerud, T.; Pripp, A.H.; Overgaard, K.R. Child and Parental Characteristics of Medication Use for Attention-Deficit/Hyperactivity Disorder. *J. Child Adolesc. Psychopharmacol.* **2020**, *30*, 456–464. [CrossRef]
42. Turner-McGrievy, G.M.; Beets, M.W. Tweet for health: Using an online social network to examine temporal trends in weight loss-related posts. *Transl. Behav. Med.* **2015**, *5*, 160–166. [CrossRef] [PubMed]
43. Booth, R.G.; Allen, B.N.; Bray Jenkyn, K.M.; Li, L.; Shariff, S.Z. Youth Mental Health Services Utilization Rates After a Large-Scale Social Media Campaign: Population-Based Interrupted Time-Series Analysis. *JMIR Ment. Health* **2018**, *5*, e27. [CrossRef] [PubMed]
44. Robinson, P.; Turk, D.; Jilka, S.; Cella, M. Measuring attitudes towards mental health using social media: Investigating stigma and trivialisation. *Soc. Psychiatry Psychiatr. Epidemiol.* **2019**, *54*, 51–58. [CrossRef] [PubMed]
45. Joseph, A.J.; Tandon, N.; Yang, L.H.; Duckworth, K.; Torous, J.; Seidman, L.J.; Keshavan, M.S. #Schizophrenia: Use and misuse on Twitter. *Schizophr. Res.* **2015**, *165*, 111–115.
46. Hanson, C.L.; Burton, S.H.; Giraud-Carrier, C.; West, J.H.; Barnes, M.D.; Hansen, B. Tweaking and Tweeting: Exploring Twitter for Nonmedical Use of a Psychostimulant Drug (Adderall) Among College Students. *J. Med. Internet Res.* **2013**, *15*, e62. [CrossRef]

47. Cassidy, T.A.; McNaughton, E.C.; Varughese, S.; Russo, L.; Zulueta, M.; Butler, S.F. Nonmedical Use of Prescription ADHD Stimulant Medications Among Adults in a Substance Abuse Treatment Population. *J. Atten. Disord.* **2015**, *19*, 275–283. [CrossRef] [PubMed]
48. Saha, K.; Torous, J.; Ernala, S.K.; Rizuto, C.; Stafford, A.; De Choudhury, M. A computational study of mental health awareness campaigns on social media. *Transl. Behav. Med.* **2019**, *9*, 1197–1207. [CrossRef]

Article

Attitudes towards Trusting Artificial Intelligence Insights and Factors to Prevent the Passive Adherence of GPs: A Pilot Study

Massimo Micocci [1,2,*], Simone Borsci [1,2,3], Viral Thakerar [4], Simon Walne [1,2], Yasmine Manshadi [5], Finlay Edridge [5], Daniel Mullarkey [5], Peter Buckle [1,2] and George B. Hanna [1,2]

1 NIHR London In-Vitro Diagnostics Cooperative, London W2 1PE, UK; s.borsci@imperial.ac.uk (S.B.); s.walne@imperial.ac.uk (S.W.); p.buckle@imperial.ac.uk (P.B.); g.hanna@imperial.ac.uk (G.B.H.)
2 Department of Surgery and Cancer, Imperial College London, London W2 1PE, UK
3 Faculty of Behavioural, Management and Social Sciences (BMS), University of Twente, 7522 NB Enschede, The Netherlands
4 Department of Primary Care and Public Health, Imperial College London, London W6 8RP, UK; v.thakerar@imperial.ac.uk
5 Skin Analytics Limited, London EC2A 4PS, UK; yasmine@skinanalytics.co.uk (Y.M.); finlay@skinanalytics.co.uk (F.E.); dan@skinanalytics.co.uk (D.M.)
* Correspondence: m.micocci@imperial.ac.uk; Tel.: +44-(0)20-3312-6532

Abstract: Artificial Intelligence (AI) systems could improve system efficiency by supporting clinicians in making appropriate referrals. However, they are imperfect by nature and misdiagnoses, if not correctly identified, can have consequences for patient care. In this paper, findings from an online survey are presented to understand the aptitude of GPs ($n = 50$) in appropriately trusting or not trusting the output of a fictitious AI-based decision support tool when assessing skin lesions, and to identify which individual characteristics could make GPs less prone to adhere to erroneous diagnostics results. The findings suggest that, when the AI was correct, the GPs' ability to correctly diagnose a skin lesion significantly improved after receiving correct AI information, from 73.6% to 86.8% ($X^2 (1, N = 50) = 21.787, p < 0.001$), with significant effects for both the benign ($X^2 (1, N = 50) = 21, p < 0.001$) and malignant cases ($X^2 (1, N = 50) = 4.654, p = 0.031$). However, when the AI provided erroneous information, only 10% of the GPs were able to correctly disagree with the indication of the AI in terms of diagnosis (d-AIW M: 0.12, SD: 0.37), and only 14% of participants were able to correctly decide the management plan despite the AI insights (d-AIW M:0.12, SD: 0.32). The analysis of the difference between groups in terms of individual characteristics suggested that GPs with domain knowledge in dermatology were better at rejecting the wrong insights from AI.

Keywords: artificial intelligence; trust; passive adherence; human factors

1. Introduction

Artificial Intelligence (AI)-based technologies used for medical purposes may have the ability to change the healthcare landscape, providing opportunities for the prioritization of patients who are most at risk [1] and for the support of clinicians making diagnostic conclusions [2].

A growing field of development of AI systems is dermatology, in which early detection of melanoma may benefit patients [3–5]. Every year in the UK, General Practitioners (GPs) see over 13 million patients for dermatological concerns [6]; melanoma is one of the most dangerous forms of skin cancer, with the potential to metastasise to other parts of the body via the lymphatic system and bloodstream. The current standard of care for skin cancer is set by the National Institute for Health and Care Excellence (NICE) [7], which adopt a 'risk threshold' value of 3% positive predictive value (PPV) in primary care to underpin recommendations for suspected skin cancer pathway referrals and urgent direct access investigations in cancer. GPs are expected to refer under the 2WW if the probability of cancer is 3% or higher. Referral rates are also influenced by factors beyond clinical suspicion of the lesion, such as a clinician's individual risk tolerance and perceived patient expectations or concerns [8]. Dermatology is the speciality with the highest referral rate in the NHS [9]; however, of the half a million cases referred on this pathway, melanoma and squamous cell carcinoma (SCC) only made up 6.5% of referrals in 2019/20 [10]. This reflects the accepted behaviour amongst clinicians of referring with a very low threshold to facilitate detection in the early stages of the disease. The same data from the National Cancer Registration and Analysis Service (NCRAS) also indicate that only 64% of cancers are detected through 2WW referrals, suggesting that considerable numbers of skin cancer cases are detected through alternative pathways, potentially representing missed diagnoses by GPs and risking delays in diagnosis. These professionals, given their role as generalists rather than specialist dermatologists [11], represent the first line of defence against skin cancer, and they might benefit from the support of an accurate AI solution for the early detection of skin cancer and the identification of atypical presentations, with an overall beneficial impact for patients and the NHS [12].

The number of studies assessing the efficacy of intelligent systems for dermatology applications [13–18] is significant. However, to date, only a few of these AI-enabled medical devices have made it through to real-world deployment. This is also a result of a lack of randomized trials [18] and the absence of AI assessments for lesions with abnormal presentation and clinical features similar to melanoma that may produce erroneous diagnoses [19]. These tools are dependent on the quantity and quality of training data [12,20]. The introduction of algorithm-based tools into a complex socio-technical system may create friction and conflict in decision making; this is due to the intrinsic tendency of artificial intelligence to reach a certain 'conclusion' that may not be transparent to human decision-makers and the consequent alterations in practices.

Ultimately, the key issue with AI is how much decision makers will trust these medical devices once deployed in the market. The inclusion of AI systems in the healthcare field should be supported by the awareness that these systems, like the existing workforce, are imperfect. For decision support tools, the resilience of the diagnostic process is in the hands of the clinicians, even when an AI is involved, as they are the only ones who have a holistic view of each clinical scenario, and they can decide to agree or disagree with an AI [21]. Beyond the issue associated with having a 'black box' AI or a fully transparent tool to support decisions [22], the main risk could also be that professionals might over-trust the insights provided by these tools due to a lack of expertise in the use of the technology or the complexity around the cases [4,23,24].

In this paper, we present results from an online survey conducted on a pool of GPs who were presented with a combination of accurate and inaccurate results from a hypothetical AI-enabled diagnostic tool for the early detection of skin cancer. This study aimed to explore the attitudes of GPs when asked to trust (or not to trust) the AI diagnosis as appropriate. We also explore 'predicting factors to trust' that would make GPs resilient enough to prioritise their clinical opinion when an AI produces erroneous diagnoses.

2. Materials and Methods

A total of 73 GPs participated in the study. Among them, 23 were excluded because they were not able to finalise or correctly complete the test. The final sample of 50 GPs (mean age: 34.4, min = 26, max = 53; 76% female) completed the test online via Qualtrics^{XM} between the 10 April 2020 and the 10 May 2020. Participants were directly informed of this study and recruited by email through a clinical lead in primary care research at the NIHR LIVD; also, the link to the survey was posted on social media (Twitter and LinkedIn) and in a private WhatsApp group used by GPs and GPs with special interests working in the Greater London area.

The online test was composed of the following sections:
- Demographics. This section was composed of 15 items. It included qualitative questions regarding individual characteristics (age, gender, years of practice etc.) and

questions regarding the respondent's interest in dermatology and attendance at dermatology courses in the past three years, as well as their perceived confidence in dermatology and familiarity with tools for early skin cancer diagnosis. Three questions considered the GPs overall trust attitude toward innovations in medical devices [25].
- Main test. This was composed of questions on 10 lesions (See Appendix A) purposively selected to be representative of commonly encountered lesions. The cases presented are realistic. Cases of misclassification were modified to explore GPs' attitudes when their diagnosis conflicted with those from the AI.

Each lesion was accompanied by vignettes of hypothetical patient details likely to be asked after in a routine GP consultation (age, gender, duration of the skin lesion, evolution/changes of the lesion, sensory changes, bleeding, risk factors, body location). Each lesion was associated with three questions pertaining to:

- The diagnosis, with a range of seven options (melanoma; squamous cell carcinoma; basal cell carcinoma; intra-epidermal carcinoma; actinic keratosis; benign, other);
- The management plan, with a range of four options (two-week 2WW referral; routine, but not 2WW; discharge with safety net advice; other);
- The confidence in their decision making, on a five-point Likert scale.

The 10 skin lesions were divided in terms of the type of decision making and type of case (benign and malignant) as follows:

- Everyday cases (EC-5 lesions), including lesions whose features are commonly observed in routine consultations and considered easy to interpret [26]; two of these were benign and three were malignant skin lesions (cases 2–6);
- Cases with uncertainties (CU-3 lesions); i.e., cases in which the picture of the skin lesion is hard to interpret or it contains a bias (marked for biopsy) and for which GPs might be expected to ask for a second opinion. One of these CU cases was malignant and two were benign (cases 1, 7 and 8). For all the cases from 1 to 8 (EC and CU), the scenario was set up with the AI system presenting the correct diagnosis to the GPs;
- Dangerous scenarios (DS-2 lesions), including one benign case misclassified as malignant and one malignant case misclassified as benign.

2.1. Procedure

The study was presented to participants as a simulation—with fictitious patients' details—to assess their agreement with an AI system to better report diagnostic test results. Once the study was completed, a disclaimer email was sent to each participant clarifying that the provided combinations of lesions/diagnoses in the study were not always accurate; the study aim of assessing GPs' performance and attitudes with both accurate and inaccurate AI diagnoses was fully explained. After the demographic survey, each participant received ten blocks of questions (each related to one lesion) in a fully randomised order. Participants completed these questions regarding the diagnosis, the management plan and their confidence twice:

1. When they had access only to patient information and images of the skin lesions (Figure 1);
2. When they had access to the AI insights, as shown in Figure 2, in addition to this information;

GPs were then asked to decide whether to change or to maintain their answers regarding the diagnosis, management plan and their confidence in their decision.

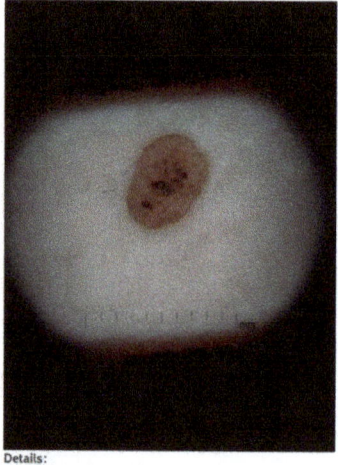

Details:
Age of the patient: 78
Gender: female
Duration of lesion: years
Evolution/changes: none
Sensory changes: none
Bleeds: none
Risk factors: none
Body location: back

Figure 1. Example of one lesion with only patient information (fictitious).

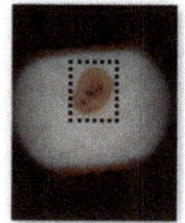

Lesion #1 - Head
Benign Lesion
Reassure Patient

Reassure patient, recommend self-monitoring and further GP review if particular clinical concern. If you are clinically concerned despite this result consider referral.

Probablity of Diagnosis

Melanoma	0.0%
SCC	0.0%
BCC	0.0%
IEC	0.1%
AK	0.0%
Benign	99.9%

Figure 2. Example of one lesion with a fictitious AI assessment.

2.2. *Data Analysis*

Descriptive statistics were used to observe participants' characteristics, the frequency of correct diagnoses and management plans, and the GPs' confidence in their decision making before and after receiving the AI-enabled information. The pre-and post-AI performance levels of the GPs, in terms of their diagnoses and management plans, were dichotomised (correct/incorrect) and McNemar's Chi-square test was used to analyse the effect of AI information in each decision-making group (EC, UC, DS) by also accounting for the type of case (benign and malignant). The percentage of confidence was tested using a generalized linear mixed model.

The hit and false rates of the GPs for the diagnostic and management decision making before and after the wrong AI insights were used to model GPs' resilience when dealing with erroneous AI information (i.e., DS cases). In line with signal detection theory [27], a computation was used to compose a sensitivity index for when AI was wrong (d-AIW, see Appendix B); the higher the index compared to zero, the better the GP's ability to ignore the wrong indication of the AI. The index was used to distinguish two groups: one included GPs who had a d-AIW over zero (hereafter called the 'resilient group') and the other included GPs with an index below or equal to zero (hereafter called the 'non-resilient group') for the management and diagnostics of patients with skin lesions. A Kruskal–Wallis test was performed to check if resilient and non-resilient GPs performed significantly differently when AI provided them with correct and incorrect answers and to observe the differences between the two groups in terms of individual characteristics.

3. Results

3.1. Individual Characteristics

In total, 76% of the participants had less than 5 years of experience, 16% from 5 to 10 years and 8% had more than 10 years of experience. Overall, the GPs in our cohort declared an average level of confidence in dermatology of 51.5 out of 100 (SD: 16.2), although 34% of them had attended specialisation courses on the topic in the previous three years. Seventy per cent of the participants stated that they had not used a dermatoscope in the previous 12 months, with only 4% of the GPs declaring weekly use of such an instrument. Thirty-eight per cent never used digital systems for skin lesions (e.g., taking pictures of patients' skin lesions to be uploaded into the system), while among those who used such digital systems for diagnostic purposes, 2% declared daily usage, 10% weekly and 50% stated that they used them at least once per month. The level of trust toward AI support systems declared by GPs for this application domain was sufficient (M: 61.2%; SD: 14.5%).

3.2. General Practitioners' Correct Decision Making before and after AI Insights

Table 1 shows the statistics of GPs' performances before and after receiving the fictitious AI-enabled information, which suggests that GPs tended to adhere to the indications of the AI. Specifically, when the AI was correct (EC and CU cases), there was a positive effect on GPs' performance and confidence. Correct diagnosis, supported by a trustworthy AI, went up by 13.2 points for EC cases and 16.5 points for CU cases. Similarly, the selection of the correct management plan went up by 7.6 points (EC) and 18.5 points (CU). GPs' confidence in their decision making went up of 12.7 for EC cases after the insights of the AI, while this aspect only increased by 1.5 points when dealing with CU cases. Conversely, when the AI provided incorrect insights (DS cases), the correctness of diagnoses and management went down by 24 and 29 points respectively, with a positive boost of 5.7 points in the GPs' confidence in their decision making after receiving AI insights.

McNemar's Chi-square test clarified how the AI insights affected the GPs' decision making for each group.

Table 1. Statistics for GP performance before and after receiving the fictitious AI assessment.

Decision Making Groups	Before AI			After AI		
	Correct Diagnosis (%)	Correct Management (%)	GP Confidence (%)	Correct Diagnosis (%)	Correct Management (%)	GP Confidence (%)
EC	73.6	82.4	66.8	86.8	90	79.5
Only benign	68	62	63.5	89	84	82.7
Only malignant	77.4	96	69.1	85.4	96	76.5
CU	37.5	44	61.8	54	62.5	63.3
Only benign	9	8	61.7	42	41	62.5
Only malignant	66	80	62.5	66	84	65
DS	46	54	60	22	25	65.7
Only benign	32	32	58.5	10	4	67
Only malignant	60	76	62.5	34	46	64

Everyday cases: GPs' ability to correctly diagnose a skin lesion significantly improved after receiving the AI information from 73.6% to 86.8% (X^2 (1, N = 50) = 21.787, $p < 0.001$), with significant effects for both the benign (X^2 (1, N = 50) = 21, $p < 0.001$) and malignant (X^2 (1, N = 50) = 4.654, $p = 0.031$) cases. The selection of the correct management plan was also positively affected by the AI information, going from 82.4% to 90% (X^2 (1, N = 50) = 3.78, $p < 0.001$), and it was particularly relevant for the plans regarding benign cases (X^2 (1, N = 50) = 22, $p < 0.001$), while no major improvement was observed for malignant cases. Confidence about decision making, independent of the type of skin lesion, significantly improved from 66.8% to 79.5% after receiving the AI information (X^2 (1, N = 48) = 107.2, $p < 0.001$).

Cases with uncertainties (CU): GPs' correct diagnosis improved significantly from 37.5% to 54% correct decision making when supported by the AI (X^2 (1, N = 50) = 24.9, $p < 0.001$). This difference was significant for benign cases (X^2 (1, N = 50) = 31.03, $p < 0.001$), while no significant differences emerged in malignant cases before and after receiving AI information. Concurrently, the ability to correctly define a management plan significantly increased from 44% to 62.5% thanks to the AI (X^2 (1, N = 50) = 28.195, $p < 0.001$), and this effect was significant for begin cases (X^2 (1, N = 50) = 31, $p < 0.001$). GPs' confidence was not significantly affected by the AI information.

Dangerous situations (DS): When erroneous information was provided by the AI, it seems that GPs were significantly pushed to adhere to the erroneous suggestions of the AI. Correct diagnosis of the skin lesions significantly decreased from 46% to 22% (X^2 (1, N = 50) = 22.04, $p < 0.001$). Adherence to the wrong AI insights was significant for both benign (X^2 (1, N = 50) = 9.08, $p = 0.026$) and malignant (X^2 (1, N = 50) = 11.7, $p = 0.009$) cases. Similarly, decision making about management was significantly affected by wrong AI insights, decreasing the ability of GPs to correctly decide the plan for the patient from 54% to 25% (X^2 (1, N = 50) = 25.290, $p < 0.001$). This significantly affected GPs' decision making regarding both benign (X^2 (1, N = 50) = 12.07, $p = 0.005$) and malignant (X^2 (1, N = 50) = 11.52, $p = 0.007$) cases. Confidence was not affected by the information provided by the AI.

3.3. Resilience to the Erroneous Insights of the Artificial Agent

When the AI provided erroneous information (DS cases), only 10% of the GPs were able to correctly disagree with the indication of the AI in terms of diagnosis (d-AIW M: 0.12, SD: 0.37), and only 14% of participants were able to correctly decide the management plan despite the AI insights (d-AIW M: 0.12, SD: 0.32). These GPs were categorized as the resilient ones (i.e., the ones able to correctly reject the AI insights), as opposed to all the others, who were categorized as less resilient to the wrong indications of the AI.

The Kruskal–Wallis test, when carried out on EC and CU cases (when the AI provided correct results), suggested that the performance of the GPs in the resilient group was not significantly different to the performance of the less resilient group. Conversely, when the AI provided erroneous diagnoses (DS cases), a significant difference was found between the two groups in terms of diagnostic decision making (X^2 = 12.4, $p < 0.001$) and the correct management plan (X^2 = 6.8, $p = 0.009$).

The analysis of the differences between the groups in terms of individual characteristics suggested that GPs who declared regular usage of the dermatoscope were better at rejecting the wrong insights from the AI and making correct diagnoses (X^2 = 7.8, $p = 0.005$) and at managing patients (X^2 = 5.1, $p = 0.023$) compared to less resilient GPs. Some moderate but still significant effects also emerged concerning GPs' overall confidence in dermatology, indicating that resilient GPs were more confident than non-resilient doctors, and this may have played a role in their ability to correctly diagnose (X^2 = 3.8, $p = 0.049$) and define a management plan (X^2 = 5, $p = 0.024$) even when the AI provided erroneous insights. The other individual factors (e.g., age, sex, training, predisposition to trust, etc.) only showed some moderate tendencies.

4. Discussion

The results demonstrate high levels of trust among GPs towards results attributed to a fictitious AI system, a finding which has both positive and negative implications for the healthcare system. Whilst an accurate clinical decision support tool may support GPs in correctly identifying benign lesions, thus reducing the number of false positives referred to 2WW clinics, there is also a possibility that an erroneous result from the AI system could lead to a patient's case being under-triaged.

Adherence to an AI system that can provide correct insights about cases, even when there are uncertainties, can significantly improve the decision making (diagnosis and plan) of GPs. The correctness and confidence of GPs in their decision making were significantly improved by using the AI when a case presented no uncertainties. Given the pressure on the 2WW pathway, this result may be convenient for ruling out negative cases at the triage stage, with benefits on patient flow and for the individual patients who will avoid unnecessary anxiety associated with a suspected cancer referral. However, when dealing with some uncertainties (CU cases) or when the AI was wrong (DS cases), the confidence of the GPs in the final decision was not affected by the AI insights. This might suggest that when GPs had doubts on how to treat a case (CU cases) or when they were not convinced by the insights of the AI (DS cases), they were not completely reassured by the use of the AI; however, a large majority of the GPs continued to adhere to the indications of the AI. These findings are in alignment with previous studies [28] suggesting that over-reliance on automated systems may be triggered by confirmatory bias when participants direct their attention towards features consistent with the (inaccurate) advice. We also considered the variability of personal expertise and attitudes towards automated systems as having an influence by reducing passive adherence. The results suggest that the tendency to adhere, even when the AI is inaccurate, may be due to a lack of experience with the specific tasks or domain knowledge that may bring GPs to overestimate the insights of the intelligent systems. The small number of resilient GPs who were able to critically interpret the results of the AI declared significantly higher usage of essential dermatological tools (i.e., dermatoscope) and confidence in the specific domain of dermatology compared to the GPs who adhered to the suggestions of the mistaken AI.

The present pilot study is intended as an initial step in the understanding of the future relationship between AI and clinicians in the domain of dermatology.

Limitations and Future Work

Three main limitations of the present work should be considered for future studies.

First, the small sample surveyed may not be representative of the variety of expertise, exposure to dermatology cases and experience with similar technologies that GPs may have. A power analysis using SAS revealed a 95.9% power to detect the difference in correctness with and without AI support. Our sample size could have detected a minimum difference of 6.5% with 80% power.

Secondly, the participants of the present study were aware that the test was a simulation and that no real AI technology was involved; therefore, we cannot rule out that they may have changed their behaviour because of the attention they received [29] and because of the absence of implications for patients. This effect may have implications for the generalisability of our findings.

Finally, how information from an AI system is presented may impact the end-user. In future studies, we advocate a larger group of GPs, with different expertise, varying familiarity with AI systems, and different cultural backgrounds to expand the current results. Concurrently, a larger number of cases should be tested with equal numbers of different types of lesions in each group. This may bring further insights into the mechanism that leads to adherence to information provided by AI. Mixed-methods studies [30] could help in mitigating the effects of bias and changes in the behaviour of research participants under the influence of observation and measurement. The risk of a passive adherence to AI in the real world could also emerge due to the complexity of the healthcare system [21] and future longitudinal studies on real cases should be implemented to monitor such a possibility. As well as the user interface, the role of training and documentation, such as the 'Instructions for Use' (IFU), should be considered in future research, both academically and from the perspective of regulatory applications.

5. Conclusions

Well-designed, accurate and intelligent systems may be able to support GPs in managing patients in primary care with suspicious skin lesions confidently and appropriately, helping them to not only refer suspicious lesions but also manage other lesions in primary care, thus relieving pressure on busy dermatology departments and saving patients from the anxiety of an unnecessary 2WW referral.

Whilst standards of clinical evidence for AI systems should continue to improve, with more emphasis on prospective clinical trials, it is fair to assume that, much like the existing clinical workforce, no AI system will be 100% sensitive in a real-world deployment. Human expertise can be amplified by AI systems, but human decision-makers need to have the domain knowledge and confidence to disagree with such systems when it is necessary.

This counter-intuitively suggests that AI tools are better suited in the hands of clinicians with certain domain knowledge (senior or specialist clinicians) rather than less expert professionals, and this should perhaps be reflected in early deployments. For the specific case of skin cancer, the results suggested that the more clinicians practised dermatological skills, the more they were able to maximize the benefit of the AI systems.

How the new relationship between healthcare professionals and AI systems will be regulated in the future requires further exploration [31]. The risk of under-or overestimating the usefulness of AI tools during clinical decision making might lead to severe consequences for patients.

Designing safe, explainable, reliable and trustworthy AI systems based on fair, inclusive and unbiased data is a key element supporting the diffusion of such tools in the medical field. However, medical professionals will need to adapt, learn and put in place behaviour and strategies to accommodate the unavoidable uncertainties around the interaction with intelligent systems. In this sense, the diffusion and adoption of AI in clinical practice will inevitably impact the training and education of clinicians, who should learn how to interact with these systems, establish a practice to minimise and prevent system failure and learn how to operate when the system fails, misbehaves or malfunctions.

Author Contributions: Conceptualization, M.M., S.B., V.T. and S.W.; methodology, M.M., S.B. and P.B.; formal analysis, M.M. and S.B.; investigation, M.M.; resources, Y.M., F.E., D.M. and V.T.; writing—original draft preparation, M.M.; writing—review and editing, M.M., S.B., V.T. and S.W.; supervision, G.B.H. All authors have read and agreed to the published version of the manuscript.

Funding: This research was funded by Biomedical Catalyst 2018 round 2: late stage; project no.: 25763.

Institutional Review Board Statement: Local approval for Service Evaluation was sought and obtained from Imperial College Healthcare NHS Trust (ICHNT)—registration no. 373.

Informed Consent Statement: Participants who consented to complete the survey were asked to read the Participants Information Sheet and to sign the Consent Form, by which they agreed to take part in the study and to have their personal opinions reflected, anonymously, in reports and academic publications.

Data Availability Statement: The data are not publicly available to protect the privacy and confidentiality of study participant.

Acknowledgments: The authors would like to thank the study participants for their input in this study and Anna McLister for her assistance in editing the paper.

Conflicts of Interest: Y.M., D.M. and F.E. declare non-financial competing interests. The other authors declare no conflicts of interest.

Appendix A

Table A1 shows the ten lesions used in the simulation study and their classification.

Table A1. The ten cases used in the simulation study.

Lesions	Classification
Case 2, Case 3	Correct benign
Case 4, Case 5, Case 6	Correct malignant
Case 1	Borderline—correct benign
Case 7	Borderline—correct malignant
Case 8	Borderline—correct benign
Case 9	Melanoma misclassified as benign

Table A1. *Cont.*

Lesions	Classification
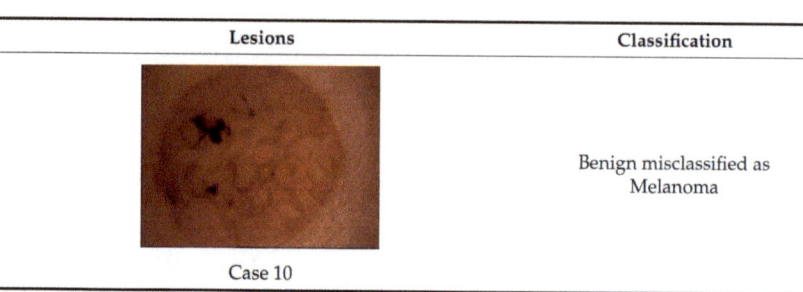 Case 10	Benign misclassified as Melanoma

Appendix B

Computation used to compose the sensitivity indexes:

$$d' = z^8 - z(\text{False})$$

- Decision wrong before and correct after AI insights = Hit rate
- Decision correct before and wrong after AI insights = False rate
- Decision correct before and correct after AI insights = Correct rejection
- Decision wrong before and wrong after AI insights = Miss

References

1. The AHSN Network. Accelerating Artificial Intelligence in Health and Care: Results from a State of the Nation Survey. Available online: https://wessexahsn.org.uk/img/news/AHSN%20Network%20AI%20Report-1536078823.pdf (accessed on 23 May 2019).
2. NHSx. Artificial Intelligence: How to Get it Right. Putting Policy into Practice for Safe Data-Driven Innovation in Health and Care. Available online: https://www.nhsx.nhs.uk/media/documents/NHSX_AI_report.pdf (accessed on 31 October 2019).
3. Petrie, T.; Samatham, R.; Witkowski, A.M.; Esteva, A.; Leachman, S.A. Melanoma Early Detection: Big Data, Bigger Picture. *J. Investig. Dermatol.* **2019**, *139*, 25–30. [CrossRef] [PubMed]
4. Mar, V.J.; Soyer, H.P. Artificial Intelligence for Melanoma Diagnosis: How Can We Deliver on the Promise? *Ann. Oncol.* **2018**, *29*, 1625–1628. [CrossRef] [PubMed]
5. Kromenacker, B.; Maarouf, M.; Shi, V.Y. Augmented Intelligence in Dermatology: Fantasy or Future? *Dermatology* **2019**, *235*, 250–252. [CrossRef] [PubMed]
6. British Associations of Dermatologists. How Can Dermatology Services Meet Current and Future Patient Needs, While Ensuring Quality of Care Is Not Compromised and Access Is Equitable Across the UK? Available online: https://www.bad.org.uk/shared/get-file.ashx?id=2348&itemtype=document (accessed on 12 April 2021).
7. NICE. Suspected Cancer: Recognition and Referral. Available online: https://www.nice.org.uk/guidance/ng12/chapter/Introduction (accessed on 21 December 2020).
8. Foot, C.; Naylor, C.; Imison, C. *The Quality of GP Diagnosis and Referral*; The King's Fund: London, UK, 2010.
9. NHS England. Waiting Times for Suspected and Diagnosed Cancer Patients. Available online: https://www.england.nhs.uk/statistics/wp-content/uploads/sites/2/2020/07/Cancer-Waiting-Times-Annual-Report-201920-Final.pdf (accessed on 12 April 2021).
10. National Cancer Registration and Analysis Service-NCRAS. Urgent Suspected Cancer Referrals: Conversion and Detection Rates. Available online: http://www.ncin.org.uk/cancer_type_and_topic_specific_work/topic_specific_work/tww_conversion_and_detection (accessed on 12 April 2021).
11. British Association of Dermatologists. GP Trainees. Available online: https://www.bad.org.uk/healthcare-professionals/education/gps/gp-trainees (accessed on 21 December 2020).
12. Yu, K.-H.; Beam, A.L.; Kohane, I.S. Artificial intelligence in healthcare. *Nat. Biomed. Eng.* **2018**, *2*, 719–731. [CrossRef] [PubMed]
13. Phillips, M.; Marsden, H.; Jaffe, W.; Matin, R.N.; Wali, G.N.; Greenhalgh, J.; McGrath, E.; James, R.; Ladoyanni, E.; Bewley, A.; et al. Assessment of Accuracy of an Artificial Intelligence Algorithm to Detect Melanoma in Images of Skin Lesions. *JAMA Netw. Open* **2019**, *2*, e1913436. [CrossRef] [PubMed]
14. Esteva, A.; Kuprel, B.; Novoa, R.A.; Ko, J.; Swetter, S.M.; Blau, H.M.; Thrun, S. Dermatologist-level classification of skin cancer with deep neural networks. *Nature* **2017**, *542*, 115–118. [CrossRef] [PubMed]
15. Haenssle, H.A.; Fink, C.; Schneiderbauer, R.; Toberer, F.; Buhl, T.; Blum, A.; Kalloo, A.; Hassen, A.B.H.; Thomas, L.; Enk, A.; et al. Man against machine: Diagnostic performance of a deep learning convolutional neural network for dermoscopic melanoma recognition in comparison to 58 dermatologists. *Ann. Oncol.* **2018**, *29*, 1836–1842. [CrossRef] [PubMed]

16. Phillips, M.; Greenhalgh, J.; Marsden, H.; Palamaras, I. Detection of Malignant Melanoma Using Artificial Intelligence: An Observational Study of Diagnostic Accuracy. *Dermatol. Pr. Concept.* **2019**, *10*, e2020011. [CrossRef] [PubMed]
17. Chuchu, N.; Takwoingi, Y.; Dinnes, J.; Matin, R.N.; Bassett, O.; Moreau, J.F.; Bayliss, S.; Davenport, C.; Godfrey, K.; O'Connell, S.; et al. Smartphone applications for triaging adults with skin lesions that are suspicious for melanoma. *Cochrane Database Syst. Rev.* **2018**, *12*, CD013192. [CrossRef] [PubMed]
18. Topol, E.J. Welcoming new guidelines for AI clinical research. *Nat. Med.* **2020**, *26*, 1318–1320. [CrossRef] [PubMed]
19. Freeman, K.; Dinnes, J.; Chuchu, N.; Takwoingi, Y.; Bayliss, S.; Matin, R.N.; Jain, A.; Walter, F.M.; Williams, H.C.; Deeks, J.J. Algorithm based smartphone apps to assess risk of skin cancer in adults: Systematic review of diagnostic accuracy studies. *BMJ* **2020**, *368*, m127. [CrossRef] [PubMed]
20. Academy of Medical Royal Colleges. Artificial Intelligence in Healthcare. Available online: https://www.aomrc.org.uk/reports-guidance/artificial-intelligence-in-healthcare/ (accessed on 30 June 2020).
21. Lynn, L.A. Artificial intelligence systems for complex decision-making in acute care medicine: A review. *Patient Saf. Surg.* **2019**, *13*, 1–8. [CrossRef] [PubMed]
22. Alufaisan, Y.; Marusich, L.R.; Bakdash, J.Z.; Zhou, Y.; Kantarcioglu, M. Does Explainable Artificial Intelligence Improve Human Decision-Making? *arXiv* **2020**, arXiv:2006.11194 2020.
23. Gilmore, S.J. Automated decision support in melanocytic lesion management. *PLoS ONE* **2018**, *13*, e0203459. [CrossRef] [PubMed]
24. Farmer, E.R.; Gonin, R.; Hanna, M.P. Discordance in the histopathologic diagnosis of melanoma and melanocytic nevi between expert pathologists. *Hum. Pathol.* **1996**, *27*, 528–531. [CrossRef]
25. McKnight, D.H.; Choudhury, V.; Kacmar, C. Developing and Validating Trust Measures for e-Commerce: An Integrative Typology. *Inf. Syst. Res.* **2002**, *13*, 334–359. [CrossRef]
26. Erdmann, F.; Lortet-Tieulent, J.; Schüz, J.; Zeeb, H.; Grenert, R.; Breitbart, E.W.; Bray, F. International trends in the incidence of malignant melanoma 1953–2008—are recent generations at higher or lower risk? *Int. J. Cancer* **2013**, *132*, 385–400. [CrossRef] [PubMed]
27. Macmillan, N.A.; Creelman, C.D. *Detection Theory: A User's Guide*; Psychology Press: Hove, UK, 2004.
28. Gaube, S.; Suresh, H.; Raue, M.; Merritt, A.; Berkowitz, S.J.; Lermer, E.; Coughlin, J.F.; Guttag, J.V.; Colak, E.; Ghassemi, M. Do as AI say: Susceptibility in deployment of clinical decision-aids. *NPJ Digit. Med.* **2021**, *4*, 1–8. [CrossRef]
29. Sedgwick, P.; Greenwood, N. Understanding the Hawthorne effect. *BMJ* **2015**, *351*, h4672. [CrossRef] [PubMed]
30. O'Cathain, A.; Murphy, E.; Nicholl, J. Three techniques for integrating data in mixed methods studies. *BMJ* **2010**, *341*, c4587. [CrossRef] [PubMed]
31. European Commission. White Paper: On Artificial Intelligence-A European Approach to Excellence and Trust. Available online: https://ec.europa.eu/info/sites/info/files/commission-white-paper-artificial-intelligence-feb2020_en.pdf (accessed on 21 December 2020).

Review

Artificial Intelligence (AI)-Empowered Echocardiography Interpretation: A State-of-the-Art Review

Zeynettin Akkus *, Yousof H. Aly, Itzhak Z. Attia, Francisco Lopez-Jimenez, Adelaide M. Arruda-Olson, Patricia A. Pellikka, Sorin V. Pislaru, Garvan C. Kane, Paul A. Friedman and Jae K. Oh

Department of Cardiovascular Medicine, Mayo Clinic, Rochester, MN 55905, USA; Aly.Yousof@mayo.edu (Y.H.A.); attia.itzhak@mayo.edu (I.Z.A.); lopez@mayo.edu (F.L.-J.); ArrudaOlson.Adelaide@mayo.edu (A.M.A.-O.); Pellikka.Patricia@mayo.edu (P.A.P.); Pislaru.Sorin@mayo.edu (S.V.P.); Kane.Garvan@mayo.edu (G.C.K.); Friedman.Paul@mayo.edu (P.A.F.); Oh.Jae@mayo.edu (J.K.O.)
* Correspondence: akkus.zeynettin@mayo.edu

Abstract: Echocardiography (Echo), a widely available, noninvasive, and portable bedside imaging tool, is the most frequently used imaging modality in assessing cardiac anatomy and function in clinical practice. On the other hand, its operator dependability introduces variability in image acquisition, measurements, and interpretation. To reduce these variabilities, there is an increasing demand for an operator- and interpreter-independent Echo system empowered with artificial intelligence (AI), which has been incorporated into diverse areas of clinical medicine. Recent advances in AI applications in computer vision have enabled us to identify conceptual and complex imaging features with the self-learning ability of AI models and efficient parallel computing power. This has resulted in vast opportunities such as providing AI models that are robust to variations with generalizability for instantaneous image quality control, aiding in the acquisition of optimal images and diagnosis of complex diseases, and improving the clinical workflow of cardiac ultrasound. In this review, we provide a state-of-the art overview of AI-empowered Echo applications in cardiology and future trends for AI-powered Echo technology that standardize measurements, aid physicians in diagnosing cardiac diseases, optimize Echo workflow in clinics, and ultimately, reduce healthcare costs.

Keywords: cardiac ultrasound; echocardiography; artificial intelligence; portable ultrasound

1. Introduction

Echocardiography (Echo), also known as cardiac ultrasound (CUS), is currently the most widely used noninvasive imaging modality for assessing patients with various cardiovascular disorders. It plays a vital role in evaluation of patients with symptoms of heart disease by identifying structural as well as functional abnormalities and assessing intracardiac hemodynamics. However, accurate echo measurements can be hampered by variability between interpreters, patients, and operators and image quality. Therefore, there is a clinical need for standardized methods of echo measurements and interpretation to reduce these variabilities. Artificial-intelligence-empowered echo (AI-Echo) can potentially reduce inter-interpreter variability and indeterminate assessment and improve the detection of unique conditions as well as the management of various cardiac disorders.

In this state-of-the-art review, we will provide a brief background on transthoracic echocardiography (TTE) and artificial intelligence (AI) followed by a summary of the advances in echo interpretation using deep learning (DL) with its self-learning ability. Since DL approaches have shown superior performance compared to machine-learning (ML) approaches based on hand-crafted features, we focus on DL progress in this review and refer the readers to other reviews [1,2] for ML approaches used to interpret echo. The AI advances could potentially allow objective evaluation of echocardiography, improving clinical workflow, and reducing healthcare costs. Subsequently, we will present currently available AI-Echo applications, delve into challenges of current AI applications using DL, and share our view on future trends in AI-Echo.

1.1. Transthoracic Echocardiogram

Transthoracic echocardiogram transmits and receives sound waves with frequencies higher than human hearing using an ultrasound transducer. It generates ultrasound waves and transmits to the tissue and listens to receive the reflected sound wave (echo). The reflected echo signal is recorded to construct an image of the interrogated region. The sound waves travel through soft tissue medium with a speed of approximately 1540 m/s. The time of flight between the transmitted and received sound waves is used to locate objects and construct an image of the probed area. The recorded echo data can be either a single still image or a movie/cine clip over multiple cardiac cycles. CUS has several advantages compared to cardiac magnetic resonance, cardiac computed tomography, and cardiac positron emission tomography imaging modalities. CUS does not use ionizing radiation, is less expensive, portable for point-of-care (POCUS) applications, and provides actual real-time imaging. It can be carried to a patient's bedside for examining patients and monitoring changes over time. Disadvantages of TTE include its dependence on operator and interpreter skill, with variability in data acquisition and interpretation. In addition to operator variability, it includes patient specific variability (e.g., signal-to-noise ratio and limited acoustic window due to anatomical or body mass differences) and machine specific variability (e.g., electronic noise and post-processing filters applied to acquired images). Image quality plays an important factor for accurate measurements. Suboptimal image quality can affect all measurements and can result in misdiagnosis.

Diverse image types are formed by using cardiac ultrasound (Figure 1). The most common types used in clinics are:

B-mode: It is also called brightness mode (B-mode), which is the most well-known US image type. An ultrasound beam is scanned across the tissue to construct a 2D cross section image of the tissue.

M-mode: Motion mode (M-mode) is used to examine motion over time. For example, it provides a single scan line of the heart, and all of the reflectors along this line are shown along the time axis to measure temporal resolution of the cardiac structures.

Doppler ultrasound: A change in the frequency of a wave occurs when the source and observer are moving relative to each other, this is called the Doppler effect. An US wave is transmitted with a specific frequency through an ultrasound probe (the observer). The US waves that are reflected from moving objects (e.g., red blood cells in vessels) return to the probe with a frequency shift. This frequency shift is used to estimate the velocity of the moving object. In blood flow, the velocity of red blood cells moving towards and away from the probe is recorded to construct Doppler signals. The velocity of information overlaid on top of a B-mode anatomical image to show color Doppler images of blood flow.

Contrast enhanced ultrasound (CEUS): CEUS is a functional imaging that suppresses anatomical details but visualizes blood pool information. It exploits the non-linear response of ultrasound contrast agents (lipid coated gas bubbles). Generally, two consecutive US signals are propagated through the same medium, and their echo response is subtracted to obtain contrast signal. Since the tissue generates linear echo response, the subtraction cancels out the tissue signal, and only the difference signal from non-linear responses of bubbles remains. This imaging technique is used to enhance cardiac chamber cavities when B-mode US provides poor quality images. It is useful to detect perfusion abnormalities in tissues and enhance the visibility of tissue boundaries.

Strain imaging: This technique detects myocardial deformation patterns such as longitudinal, radial, and circumferential deformations, and early functional abnormalities before they become noticeable as regional wall motion abnormalities or reduced ejection fraction on B-mode cardiac images.

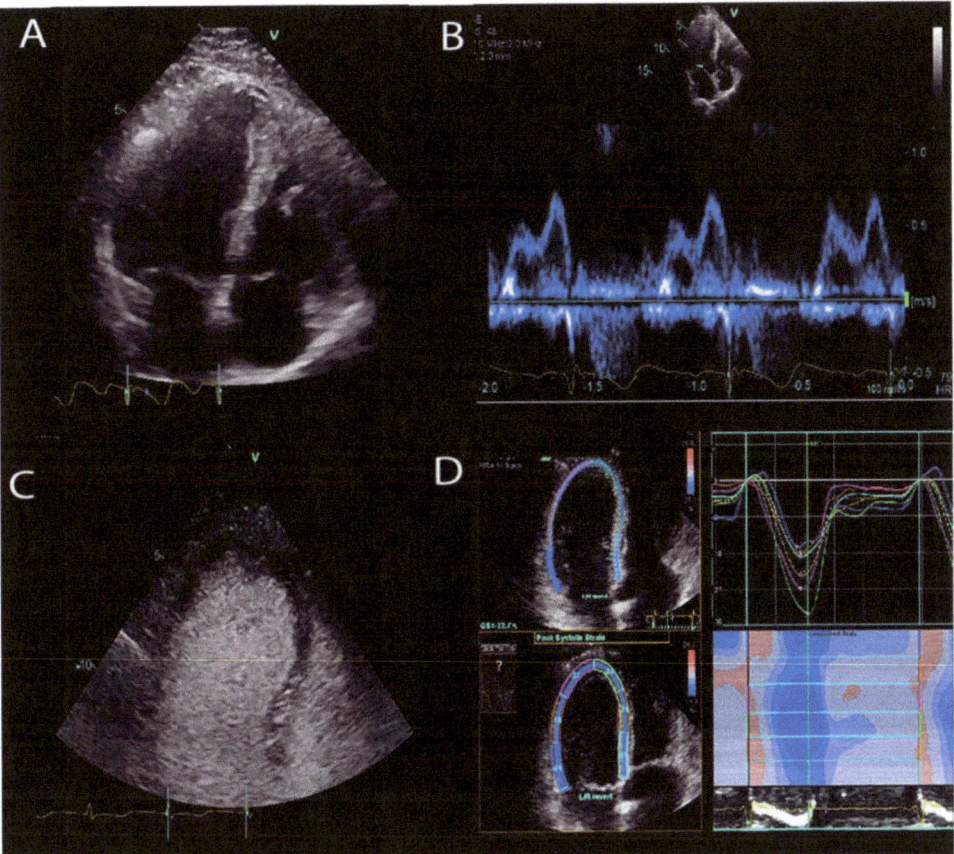

Figure 1. Sample US images showing different US modes. (**A**) B-mode image of the apical 4 chamber view of a heart. (**B**) Doppler image of mitral inflow. (**C**) Contrast enhanced ultrasound image of left ventricle. (**D**) Strain imaging of the left ventricle.

1.2. Artificial Intelligence

Artificial intelligence (AI) is considered to be a computer-based system that can observe an environment and takes actions to maximize the success of achieving its goals. Some examples include a system that has the ability of sensing, reasoning, engaging, and learning, are computer vision for understanding digital images, natural language processing for interaction between human and computer languages, voice recognition for detection and translation of spoken languages, robotics and motion, planning and organization, and knowledge capture. ML is a subsection of AI that covers the ability of a system to learn about data using supervised or unsupervised statistical and ML methods such as regression, support vector machines, decision trees, and neural networks. Deep learning (DL), which is a subclass of ML, learns a sequential chain of pivotal features from input data that maximizes the success of the learning process with its self-learning ability. This is different from statistical ML algorithms that require handcrafted feature selection [3] (Figure 2).

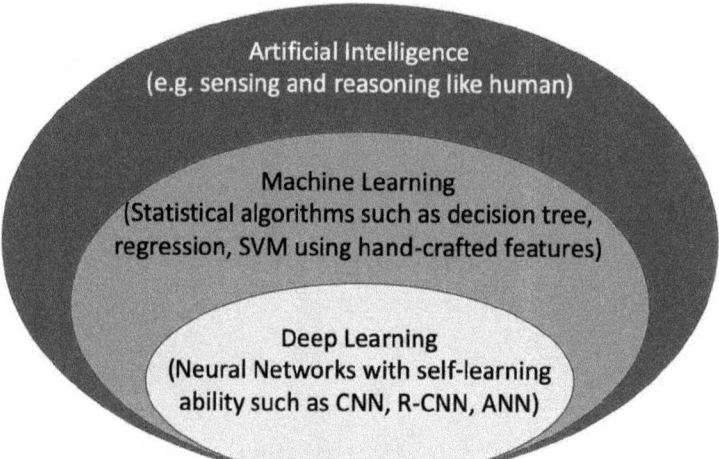

Figure 2. The context of artificial intelligence, machine learning, and deep learning. SVM: Support Vector Machine. CNN: convolutional neural networks, R-CNN: recurrent CNN, ANN: artificial neural networks.

Artificial neural networks (ANN) are the first DL network design where all nodes are fully connected to each other. It mimics biological neurons for creating representation from an input signal, including many consecutive layers that learn a hierarchy of features from an input signal. ANN and the advance in graphics processing units (GPU) processing power have enabled the development of deep and complex DL models with simultaneous multitasking at the same time. DL models can be trained with thousands or millions of samples to gain robustness to variations in data. The representation power of DL models is massive and can create representation for any given variation of a signal. Recent accomplishments of DL, especially in image classification and segmentation applications, made it very popular in the data science community. Traditional ML methods use hand-crafted features extracted from data and process them in decomposable pipelines. This makes them more comprehensible as each component is explainable. On the other hand, they tend to be less generalizable and robust to variations in data. With DL models, we give up interpretability in exchange for obtaining robustness and greater generalization ability, while generating complex and abstract features.

State-of-the-art DL models have been developed for a variety of tasks such as object detection and segmentation in computer vision, voice recognition, and genotype/phenotype prediction. There are different types of models that include convolutional neural networks (CNNs), deep Boltzmann machines, stacked auto-encoders [4], and deep belief neural networks [5]. The most commonly used DL method for processing images that are CNNs as fully connected ANN is computationally heavy for 2D/3D images and requires extensive GPU memory. CNNs share weights across each feature map or convolutional layers to mitigate this. CNN approaches have gained enormous awareness, achieving impressive results in the ImageNet [6–8] competition in 2012 [8], which includes natural photographic images. They were utilized to classify a dataset of around a million images that comprise a thousand diverse classes, achieving half the error rates of the most popular traditional ML approaches [8]. CNNs have been widely utilized for medical image classification and segmentation tasks with great success [3,9–12]. Since DL algorithms outperform ML algorithms in general and exploit the GPU processing power, it allows real-time processing of US images. We will only focus on DL applications of AI-powered US cardiology in this review.

To assess the performance of ML models, data are generally split into training, validation, and test sets. The training set is used for learning about the data. The validation set is employed to establish the reliability of learning results, and the test set is used to assess the generalizability of a trained model on the data that are never seen by the model. When training samples are limited, k-fold cross validation approaches (e.g., leave-one-out, five-fold, or ten-fold cross validation) are utilized. In cross-validation, the data are divided randomly into k equal sized pieces. One piece is reserved for assessing the performance of a model, and the remaining pieces (k-1) are utilized for training models. The training process is typically performed in a supervised way, which involves ground truth labels for each input data and minimizes a loss function over training samples iteratively, as shown in Figure 3. Supervised learning is the most common training approach for ML, but it requires a laborious ground truth label generation. In medical imaging, ground truth labels are generally obtained from clinical notes for diagnosis or quantification. Furthermore, manual outlining of structures by experts are used to train ML models for segmentation tasks.

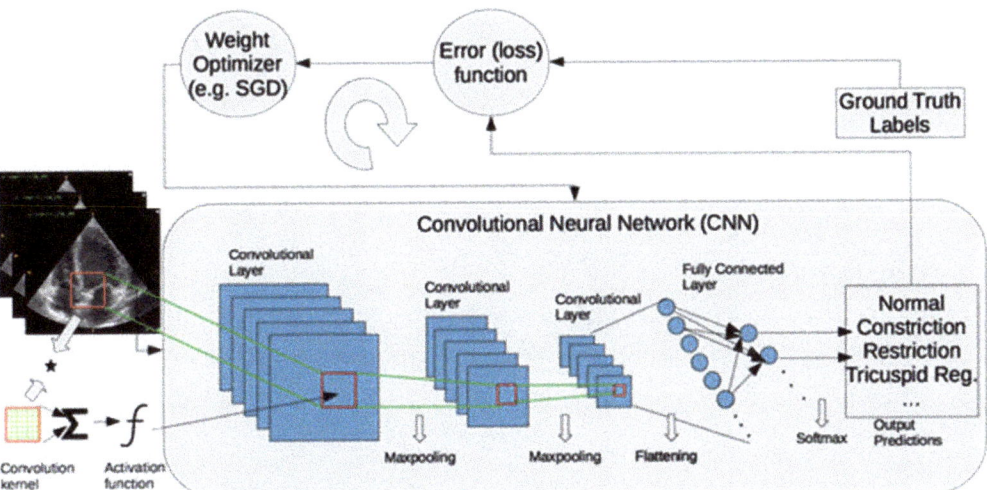

Figure 3. A framework of training a deep-learning model for classification of myocardial diseases. Operations between layers are shown with arrows. SGD: Stochastic Gradient Descent.

2. Methods and Results: Automated Echo Interpretation

We performed a thorough analysis of the literature using Google Scholar and PubMed search engines. We included peer-reviewed journal publications and conference proceedings in this field (IEEE Transactions on Medical Imaging, IEEE Journal of Biomedical and Health Informatics, Circulation, Nature, and conference proceedings from SPIE, the Medical Image Computing and Computer Assisted Intervention Society, the Institute of Electrical and Electronics Engineers, and others) that describe the application of DL to cardiac ultrasound images before 15 January 2021. We included a total of 14 journal papers and three conference proceedings that are relevant to the scope of this review (see Figure 4 for the detailed flowchart for the identification, screening, eligibility, and inclusion). We divided reports into three groups on the basis of the task performed: view identification and quality control, image segmentation and quantification, and disease diagnosis.

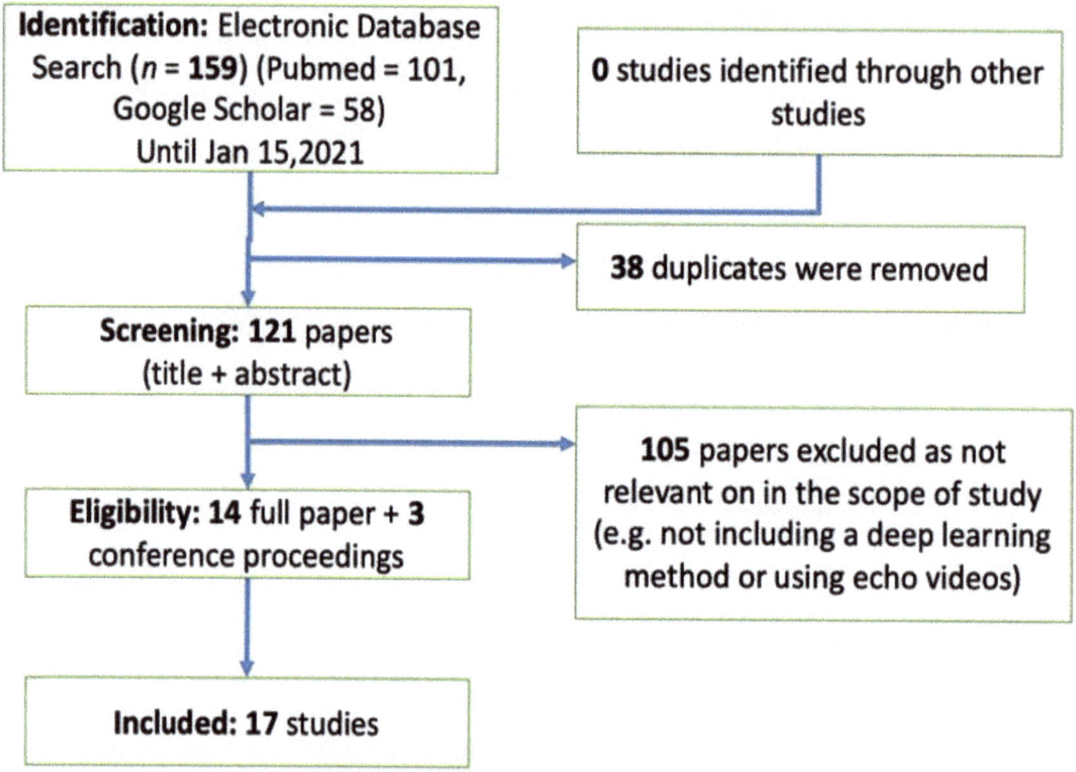

Figure 4. The flowchart of systematic review that includes identification, screening, eligibility, and inclusion.

Current Echo-AI applications require several successive processing steps such as view labelling and quality control, segmentation of cardiac structures, echo measurements, and disease diagnosis (Figure 5). AI-Echo can be used for low-cost, serial, and automated evaluation of cardiac structures and function by experts and non-experts in cardiology, primary care, and emergency clinics. This would also allow triaging incoming patients with chest pain in an emergency department by providing preliminary diagnosis and longitudinally monitoring patients with cardiovascular risk factors in a personalized manner.

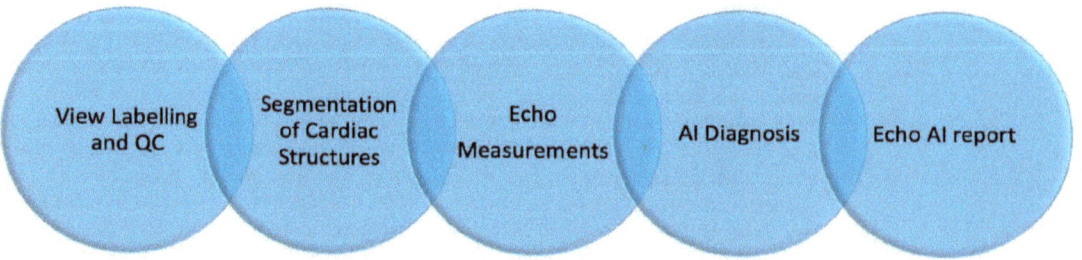

Figure 5. The flowchart of automated artificial-intelligence-empowered echo (AI-Echo) interpretation pipeline using a chain approach. QC: Quality Control.

With the advancing ultrasound technology, the current clinical cart-based ultrasound systems could be replaced with portable point-of-care ultrasound (POCUS) systems or could be used together. GE Vscan, Butterfly IQ, and Philips Lumify are popular POCUS devices. A single Butterfly IQ probe contains 9000 micro-machined semiconductor sensors and emulates linear, phased, and curved array probes. While the Butterfly IQ probe using ultrasound-on-chip technology could be used for imaging the whole body, Philips Lumify provides different probes for each organ (e.g., s4-1 phased array probe for cardiac applications). GE Vscan comes with two transducers placed in one probe and can be used for scanning deep and superficial structures. Using POCUS devices powered with cloud-based AI-Echo interpretation at point of care locations could significantly reduce the US cost and increase the utility of AI-Echo by non-experts in primary and emergency departments (see Figure 6). A number of promising studies using DL approaches have been published for classification of standard echo views (e.g., apical and parasternal views), segmentation of heart structures (e.g., ventricle, atrium, septum, myocardium, and pericardium), and prediction of cardiac diseases (e.g., heart failure, hypertrophic cardiomyopathy, cardiac amyloidosis, and pulmonary hypertension) in recent years [13–16]. In addition, several companies such as TOMTEC IMAGING SYSTEMS GMBH, Munich, Germany and Ultromics, Oxford, United Kingdom have already obtained premarket FDA clearance on auto ejection fraction (EF) and echo strain packages using artificial intelligence. The list of companies and their provided AI tools is shown in Table 1.

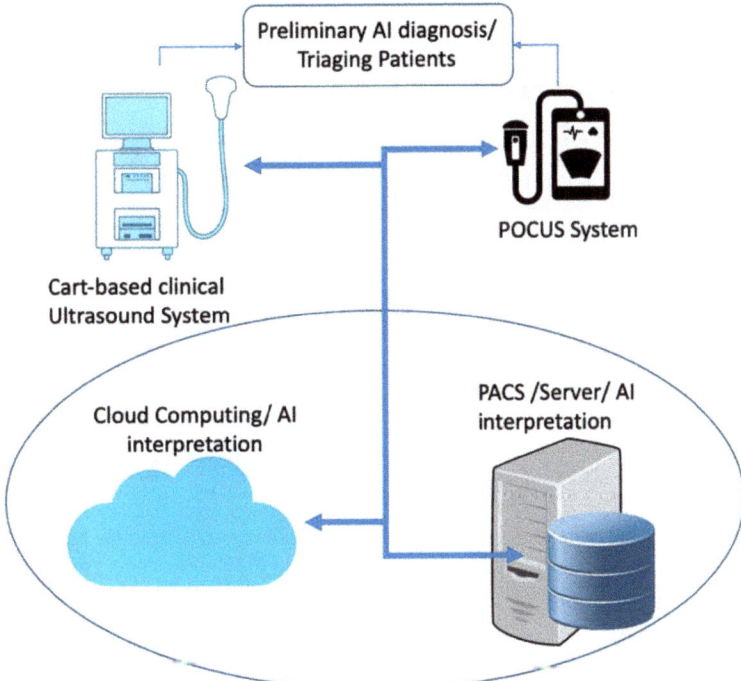

Figure 6. A schematic diagram of AI (artificial intelligence) interpretation of echocardiography images for preliminary diagnosis and triaging patients in emergency and primary care clinics. POCUS: point of care ultrasound.

Table 1. The list of commercial software packages that provides automated measurements or diagnosis.

Company	Software Package	AI-Empowered Tools
Siemens Medical Solutions Inc., USA	syngo Auto Left Heart, Acuson S2000 US system.	Auto EF, Auto LV and LA volumes, Auto Strain for manually selected views.
GE Healthcare, Inc., USA	Ultra Edition Package, Vivid Ultrasound Systems	Auto EF, Auto LV and LA volumes, Auto Strain for manually selected views
TOMTEC Imaging Systems GmbH, Germany	Tomtec-Arena/ Tomtec-Zero	Auto EF, Auto LV and LA volumes, Auto Strain for manually selected views
Ultromics Ltd., United Kingdom	Echo Go/Echo Go Pro	Auto EF, Auto LV and LA volumes, Auto Strain, Auto identification of CHD (Fully automated)
Dia Imaging Analysis Ltd., Israel	DiaCardio's LVivoEF Software/LVivo Seamless	Auto EF and Auto standard echo view identification (Fully automated)
Caption Health, Inc., USA	The Caption Guidance software	AI tool for assisting to capture images of a patient's heart

EF: ejection fraction. CHD: coronary heart disease.

2.1. View Identification and Quality Control

A typical TTE study includes the acquisition of multiple cine clips of the heart's chambers from five standardized windows that are left parasternal window (i.e., parasternal long and short axis views), apical window (i.e., two, three, four, five chamber views), subcostal window (i.e., four chamber view, long axis inferior vena cava view), and suprasternal notch window (i.e., aortic arch view), right parasternal window (i.e., ascending aorta view). In addition to these, the study includes several other cine clips of color Doppler, strain imaging, and 3D ultrasound and still images of valves, walls, and the blood vessels (e.g., aorta and pulmonary veins). View identification and quality control are essential prerequisite steps for a fully automated echo interpretation.

Zhang et al. [16,17] presented a fully automated echo interpretation pipeline that includes 23 view classifications. They trained a 13-layer CNN model with 7168 labelled cine clips and used five-fold cross validation to assess the performance of their model. In evaluation, they selected 10 random frames per clip and averaged the resulting probabilities. The overall accuracy of their model was 84% at an individual image level. They also reported that distinguishing the various apical views was the greatest challenge in the setting of partially obscured left ventricles. They made their source code and model weights publicly available at [18]. Mandani et al. [19] presented the classification of 15 standard echo views using DL. They trained a VGG CNN network with 180,294 images of 213 studies and tested their model on 21,747 images of 27 studies. They obtained 91.7% overall accuracy on the test dataset at a single image level and 97.8% overall accuracy when considering the model's top two guesses. Akkus et al. [20] trained a CNN inception model with residual connections on 5544 images of 140 patients for predicting 24 Doppler image classes and automating Doppler mitral inflow analysis. They obtained overall accuracy of 97% on the test set that included 1737 images of 40 patients.

Abdi et al. [21,22] trained a fully connected CNN with 6196 apical four chamber (A4C) images that were scored between 0 to 5 to assess the A4C quality of echo images. They used three-fold cross validation and reported an error comparable to intra-rater reliability (mean absolute error: 0.71 ± 0.58). Abdi et al. [23] later extended their previous work and trained a CNN regression architecture that includes five regression models with the same weights in the first few layers for assessing the quality of cine loops across five standard view planes (i.e., apical 2, 3, and 4 chamber views and parasternal short axis views at papillary muscle and aortic valve levels). Their dataset included 2435 cine clips, and they achieved an average of 85% accuracy compared to gold standard scores assigned by experienced echo sonographers on 20% of the dataset. Zhang et al. [16,17] calculated the averaged probability score of views classification across all videos in their study to define an image quality score for each view. They assumed that poor quality cine clips tended to have a more ambiguous view assignment, and the view classification probability could be used for quality assessment. Dong et al. [24] presented a generic quality control framework for fetal ultrasound cardiac four chamber planes (CFPs). Their proposed framework consists of three networks that roughly classify four-chamber views from the raw data, determine the gain and zoom of images, and detect the key anatomical structures on a plane. The overall quantitative score of each CFP was achieved based on the output of the three networks. They used five-fold cross validation to assess their model across 2032 CFPs and 5000 non-CFPs and obtained a mean average precision of 93.52%. Labs et al. [25] trained a hybrid model including CNN and LSTM layers to assess the quality of apical four-chamber view images for three proposed attributes (i.e., foreshortening, gain/contrast, and axial target). They split a dataset of 1039 unique apical four-chamber views into 60:20:20% ratio for training, validation, and testing, respectively, and achieved an average accuracy of 86% on the test set.

View identification and quality assessment of cine clips are the most important pieces of a fully automated echo interpretation pipeline. As shown in Table 2, there is an error range of 3–16% in the current studies for both view identification and quality control. The proposed models were generally trained with a dataset from a single or a few vendors or a single center. Apart from the study of Zhang et al. [16,17], none of the studies shared their source code and model weights for comparisons. In some studies, customized CNN models were used, but not enough evidence or comparisons were shown to support that their choices perform better than the state-of-the-art CNN models such as Resnet, Inception, and Densenet.

Table 2. Deep-learning-based AI studies for view identification and quality assessment. MAE: mean absolute error.

	Task	DL Model	Data/Validation	Performance
Zhang et al. [16,17]	23 standard echo view classification	Customized 13-layer CNN model	5-fold cross validation/7168 cine clips of 277 studies	Overall accuracy: 84% at individual image level
Mandani et al. [19]	15 standard echo view classification	VGG [26]	Training: 180,294 images of 213 studies Testing: 21,747 images of 27 studies	Overall accuracy: 97.8% at individual image level and 91.7% at cine-lip level
Akkus et al. [20]	24 Doppler image classes	Inception_resnet [27]	Training: 5544 images of 140 studies Testing: 1737 images of 40 studies	Overall accuracy of 97%
Abdi et al. [21,22]	Rating quality of apical 4 chamber views (0–5 scores)	A customized fully connected CNN	3-fold cross validation/6196 images	MAE: 0.71 ± 0.58
Abdi et al. [23]	Quality assessment for five standard view planes	CNN regression architecture	Total dataset: 2435 cine clips Training: 80% Testing: 20%	Average of 85% accuracy
Dong et al. [24]	QC for fetal ultrasound cardiac four chamber planes	Ensembled three CNN model	5-fold cross validation (7032 images)	Mean average precision of 93.52%.
Labs et al. [25]	Assessing quality of apical 4 chamber view	Hybrid model including CNN and LSTM layers	Training/validation/testing (60/20/20%) of in total of 1039 images	Average accuracy of 86% on the test set

2.2. Image Segmentation and Quantification

Partitioning of an identified view into the region of interests such as left/right ventricle or atrium, ventricular septum, and mitral/tricuspid valves is necessary to quantify certain biomarkers such as ejection fraction, volume changes, and velocity of septal or distal annulus. Several studies have used DL methods to segment left ventricles from apical four and two chamber views.

Zhang et al. [16,17] presented a fully automated echo interpretation pipeline that includes segmentation of cardiac chambers in five common views and quantification of structure and function. They used five-fold cross validation on 791 images that have manual segmentation of left ventricle and reported the intersection over union metric ranging from 0.72 to 0.90 for the performance of their U-Net-based segmentation model. In addition, they produced automated measurements such as LV ejection fraction (LVEF), LV volumes, LV mass, and global longitudinal strain from the resulting segmentations. Compared to manual measurements, median absolute deviation of 9.7% (n = 6407 studies) was achieved for LVEF; median absolute deviation of 15–17% was obtained for LV volume and mass measurements; median absolute deviation of 7.5% (n = 419) and 9.0% (n = 110) was obtained for strain. They concluded that they obtained cardiac structure measurements comparable with values in study reports. Leclerc et al. [13] studied the state-of-art encoder–decoder type DL methods (e.g., U-Net [28]) for segmenting cardiac structures and made a large dataset (500 patients) publicly available with segmentation labels of end diastole and systole frames. The full dataset is available for download at [29]. They showed that their U-Net-based model outperformed the state-of-the-art non-deep-learning methods for measurements of end-diastolic and end-systolic left ventricular volumes and LVEF. They achieved a mean correlation of 0.95 and an absolute mean error of 9.5 mL for LV volumes and a mean correlation coefficient of 0.80 and an absolute mean error of 5.6% for LVEF. Jafari et al. [30] presented a recurrent CNN and optical flow for segmentation of the left ventricle in echo images. Jafari et al. [14] also presented biplane ejection fraction estimation with POCUS using multi-task and learning and adversarial training. The performance of the proposed model for the segmentation of LV was an average Dice score of 0.92 and, for the automated ejection fraction, was shown to be around an absolute error of 6.2%. Chen et al. [31] proposed an encoder–decoder type CNN with multi-view regularization to improve LV segmentation. The method was evaluated on 566 patients and achieved an average Dice score of 0.88. Oktay et al. [32] incorporated anatomical prior knowledge in their CNN model that allows following the global anatomical properties of the underlying anatomy. Ghorbani et al. [33] used a custom CNN model, named EchoNet, to predict left ventricular end systolic and diastolic volumes ($R2$ = 0.74 and $R2$ = 0.70), and ejection fraction ($R2$ = 0.50). Ouyang et al. [15] trained a semantic segmentation model using atrous convolutions on echocardiogram videos. Their model obtained Dice similarity coefficient of 0.92 for left ventricle segmentation of apical four-chamber view and used a spatiotemporal 3D CNN model with residual connections and predicted ejection fraction with mean absolute errors of 4.1 and 6% for internal and external datasets, respectively. Ouyang et al. [15] de-identified 10,030 echocardiogram videos, resized them into 112 × 112 pixels, and made their dataset publicly available at [34].

U-Net is the most common DL model used for echo image segmentation. As shown in Table 3, the error range for LVEF is ranging between 4 and 10%, while it ranges between 10 and 20% for LV and LA volume measurements.

2.3. Disease Diagnosis

Several studies have shown that DL models can be used to assess cardiac diseases (see Table 4). Zhang et al. [16,17] presented a fully automated echo interpretation pipeline for disease detection. They trained a VGG [26] network using three random images per video as an input and provided two prediction outputs (i.e., diseased or normal). The ROC curve performance of their model for prediction of hypertrophic cardiomyopathy, cardiac amyloidosis, and pulmonary hypertension were 0.93, 0.87, and 0.85, respectively. Ghorbani et al. [33] trained a customized CNN model that includes inception connections, named EchoNet, on a dataset of more than 1.6 million echocardiogram images from 2850 patients to identify local cardiac structures, estimate cardiac function, and predict systemic risk factors. The proposed CNN model identified the presence of pacemaker leads with AUC = 0.89, enlarged left atrium with AUC = 0.86, and left ventricular hypertrophy with AUC = 0.75. Ouyang et al. [15] trained a custom model that includes spatiotemporal 3D convolutions with a residual connection network together with semantic segmentation of the left ventricle to predict the presence of heart failure with reduced ejection fraction.

The output of the spatiotemporal network and semantic segmentation were combined to classify heart failure with reduced ejection fraction. Their model achieved an area under the curve of 0.97 for predicting heart failure with reduced ejection fraction. Omar et al. [35] trained a modified VGG-16 CNN model on a 3D Dobutamine stress echo dataset to detect wall motion abnormalities and compared its performance to hand-crafted approaches: support vector machines (SVM) and random forests (RF). They achieved slightly better accuracy with the CNN model: RF (72.1%), SVM (70.5%), and CNN (75.0%). In another study, Kusunose et al. [36] investigated whether a CNN model could provide improved detection of wall motion abnormalities. They presented that the area under the AUC produced by the deep-learning algorithm was comparable to that produced by the cardiologists and sonographer readers (0.99 vs. 0.98, respectively) and significantly higher than the AUC result of the resident readers (0.99 vs. 0.90, respectively). Narula et al. [37] trained SVM, RF, and artificial neural network (ANN) with hand-crafted echo measurements (i.e., LV wall thickness, end-diastolic volume, end-systolic volume, and ejection fraction, pulsed-wave Doppler-derived transmitral early diastolic velocity (E), the late diastolic atrial contraction wave velocity (A), and the ratio E/A to differentiate hypertrophic cardiomyopathy (HCM) from physiological hypertrophy seen in athletes (ATH). They reported overall sensitivity and specificity of 87 and 82%, respectively.

Unlike other hand-crafted feature-based ML approaches, the DL approaches may extract features from data beyond human perception. DL-based AI approaches have the potential to support accurate diagnosis and discovering crucial features from echo images. In the near future, these tools may aid physicians in diagnosis and decision making and reduce the misdiagnosis rate.

Table 3. Deep-learning-based AI studies for image segmentation and quantification. MAD: mean absolute difference. LVEF: left ventricle ejection fraction.

	Task	DL Model	Data/Validation	Performance
Zhang et al. [16,17]	LV/LA segmentation; LVEF, LV and LA volumes, LV mass, global longitudinal strain	U-Net [28]	LV segmentation: 5-fold cross validation on 791 images; LV volumes: 4748 measurements; LV mass: 4012 measurements; strain: 526 studies	IOU: 0.72–0.90 for LV segmentation; MAD of 9.7% for LVEF; MAD of 15–17% for LV/LA volumes and LV mass; MAD of 9% for strain.
Leclerc et al. [13]	LVEF, LV volumes	U-Net [28]	500 patients	LVEF: AME of 5.6% LV volumes: AME of 9.7 mL
Jafari et al. [14]	LV segmentation and bi-plane LVEF	A shallow U-Net with multi-task learning and adversarial training	854 studies split into 80% training and 20% testing sets	DICE of 0.92 for LV segmentation; MAE of 6.2% for LVEF
Chen et al. [31]	LV segmentation in apical 2, 3, 4, or 5 chamber views	An encoder–decoder type CNN with multi-view regularization	Training set: 33,058 images; test set: 8204 images	Average DICE of 0.88
Oktay et al. [32]	LV segmentation; LVEF	Anatomically constrained CNN model	CETUS'14 3D US challenge dataset. (training set: 15 studies; test set: 30 studies)	DICE of 0.91 ± 0.23 for LV segmentation; correlation of 0.91 for LVEF
Ghorbani et al. [33]	LV systolic and diastolic volumes; LVEF	A customized CNN model (EchoNet) for semantic segmentation	Training set: 1.6 million images from 2850 patients; test set: 169,000 images from 373 studies	Systolic and diastolic volumes (R^2 = 0.74 and R^2 = 0.70); R^2 = 0.50 for LVEF
Ouyang et al. [15]	LVEF	3D CNN model with residual connections	Training set: 7465 echo videos; internal test dataset (n = 1277); external test dataset (n = 2895)	MAE of 4.1% and 6% for internal and external datasets

Table 4. Deep-learning-based AI studies for disease diagnosis. AUC: area under the curve.

	Task	DL Model	Data/Validation	Performance
Zhang et al. [16,17]	Diagnosis of hypertrophic cardiomyopathy (HCM), cardiac amyloidosis (amyloid), and pulmonary hypertension (PAH)	VGG [26]	HCM: 495/2244 Amyloid:179/804 PAH:584/2487 (Diseased/Control) 5-fold cross validation	Hypertrophic cardiomyopathy: AUC of 0.93; cardiac amyloidosis: AUC of 0.87; pulmonary hypertension: AUC of 0.85
Ghorbani et al. [33]	Diagnose presence of pacemaker leads; enlarged left atrium; LV hypertrophy	A customized CNN model	Training set: 1.6 million images from 2850 patients; test set: 169,000 images from 373 studies	Presence of pacemaker leads with AUC = 0.89; enlarged left atrium with AUC = 0.86, left ventricular hypertrophy with AUC = 0.75.
Ouyang et al. [15]	Predict presence of HF with reduced EF	3D convolutions with residual connection	Training set: 7465 echo videos; internal test dataset (n = 1277); external test dataset (n = 2895)	AUC of 0.97
Omar et al. [35]	Detecting wall motion abnormalities	Modified VGG-16 [26]	120 echo studies. One-leave-out cross validation	Accuracy: RF = 72.1%, SVM = 70.5% CNN = 75.0%
Kusunose et al. [36]	Detecting wall motion abnormalities (WMA)	Resnet [38]	300 patients with WMA +100 normal control. Training = 64% Validation:16% Test: 20%	AUC of 0.99
Narula et al. [37]	Differentiate HCM from ATH	A customized ANN	77 ATH and 62 HCM patients. Ten-fold cross validation	Sensitivity: 87% Specificity: 82%

3. Discussion and Outlook

Automated image interpretation that mimics human vision with traditional machine learning has existed for a long time. Recent advances in parallel processing with GPUs and deep-learning algorithms, which extract patterns in images with their self-learning ability, have changed the entire automated image interpretation practice with respect to computation speed, generalizability, and transferability of these algorithms. AI-empowered echocardiography has been advancing and moving closer to be used in routine clinical workflow in cardiology due to the increased demand for standardizing acquisition and interpretation of cardiac US images. Even though DL-based methods for echocardiography provide promising results in diagnosis and quantification of diseases, AI-Echo still needs to be validated with larger study populations including multi-center and multi-vendor datasets. High intra-/inter-variability in echocardiography makes standardization of image acquisition and interpretation challenging. However, AI-Echo will provide solutions to mitigate operator-dependent variability and interpretability. AI applications in cardiac US are more challenging than those in cardiac CT and MR imaging modalities due to patient-dependent factors (e.g., obesity, limited acoustic window, artifacts, and signal drops) and natural US speckle noise pattern. These factors that affect US image quality will remain as challenges with cardiac ultrasound.

Applications of DL in echocardiography are rapidly advancing as evidenced by the growing number of studies recently. DL models have enormous representation power and are hungry for large amounts of data in order to obtain generalization ability and stability. Creating databases with large datasets that are curated and have good quality data and labels is the most challenging and time-consuming part of the whole AI model development process. Although it has been shown that AI-echo applications have superb performance compared to classical ML methods, most of the models were trained and evaluated on small datasets. It is important to train AI models on large multi-vendor and multi-center datasets to obtain generalization and validate on large multi-vendor datasets to increase reliability of a proposed model. An alternative way to overcome the limitation of having small training datasets would be augmenting the dataset with realistic transformations (e.g., scaling, horizontal flipping, translations, adding noise, tissue deformation, and adjusting image contrast) that could help improve generalizability of AI models. On the other hand, realistic transformations need to be used to genuinely simulate variations in cardiac ultrasound images, and transformations-applied images should not create artifacts. Alternatively, generative adversarial networks, which include a generator and a discriminator model, are trained until the model generates images that are not separable by the discriminator. This could be used to generate realistic cardiac ultrasound B-mode images of the heart. Introducing such transformations during the training process will make AI models more robust to small perturbations in input data space.

Making predictions and measurements based on only 2D echo images could be considered as a limitation of AI-powered US systems. Two-dimensional cross section images include limited information and do not constitute the complete myocardium. Training AI models on 3D cardiac ultrasound data that include the entire heart or the structure of interest would potentially improve the diagnostic accuracy of an AI model.

It is important to design AI models that are transparent for the prediction of any disease from medical images. The AI models developed for diagnosis of a disease must elucidate the reasons and motivations behind their predictions in order to build trust in them. Comprehension of the inner mechanism of an AI model necessitates interpreting the activity of feature maps in each layer [39–41]. However, the extracted features are a combination of sequential layers and become complicated and conceptual with more layers. Therefore, the interpretation of these features become difficult compared to handcrafted imaging features in traditional ML methods. Traditional ML methods are designed for separable components that are more understandable, since each component of ML methods has an explanation but usually is not very accurate or robust. With DL-based AI models, the interpretability is given up for the robustness and complex imaging features with greater generalizability. Recently, a number of methods have been introduced about what DL models see and how to make their predictions. Several CNN architectures [26,28,38,42,43] employed techniques such as deconvolutional networks [44], gradient back-propagation [45], class activation maps (CAM) [41], gradient-weighted CAM [46], and saliency maps [47,48] to make CNN understandable. With these techniques, gradients of a model have been projected back to the input image space, which shows what parts in the input image contribute the most to the prediction outcome that maximizes the classification accuracy. Although making AI models understandable has been an active research topic in the DL community, there is still much further research needed in the area. Despite the fact that high prediction performances were achieved and reported in the studies discussed in this review, none of the studies have provided an insight on which heart regions play an important role in any disease prediction.

Developing AI models that standardize image acquisition and interpretation with less variability is essential considering that echocardiography is an operator- and interpreter-dependent imaging modality. AI guidance during data acquisition for the optimal angle, view, and measurements would make echocardiography less operator-dependent and smarter, while standardizing data acquisition. Cost-effective and easy access of POCUS systems with AI capability would help clinicians and non-experts perform swift initial examinations on patients and progress with vital and urgent decisions in emergency and primary care clinics. In the near future, POCUS systems with AI capability could replace the stethoscopes that doctors use in their daily practice to listen to patients' hearts. Clinical cardiac ultrasound or POCUS systems empowered with AI, which can assess multi-mode data, steer sonographers during acquisition, and deliver objective qualifications, measurements, and diagnoses, will assist with decision making for diagnosis and treatments, improve echocardiography workflow in clinics, and lower healthcare cost.

Author Contributions: Conceptualization, Z.A., J.K.O. and F.L.-J.; methodology, Z.A. writing—original draft preparation, Z.A., J.K.O. and F.L.-J.; writing—review and editing, Y.H.A., I.Z.A., A.M.A.-O., P.A.P., S.V.P., G.C.K., P.A.F., F.L.-J., and J.K.O.; visualization, Z.A. and Y.H.A.; supervision, J.K.O. and F.L.-J.; project administration, J.K.O. and F.L.-J. All authors have read and agreed to the published version of the manuscript.

Funding: This research received no external funding.

Conflicts of Interest: The authors declare no conflict of interest.

References

1. Zamzmi, G.; Hsu, L.-Y.; Li, W.; Sachdev, V.; Antani, S. Harnessing Machine Intelligence in Automatic Echocardiogram Analysis: Current Status, Limitations, and Future Directions. *IEEE Rev. Biomed. Eng.* **2020**. [CrossRef] [PubMed]
2. Alsharqi, M.; Woodward, W.J.; Mumith, J.A.; Markham, D.C.; Upton, R.; Leeson, P. Artificial intelligence and echocardiography. *Echo Res. Pract.* **2018**, *5*, R115–R125. [CrossRef]
3. Akkus, Z.; Galimzianova, A.; Hoogi, A.; Rubin, D.L.; Erickson, B.J. Deep Learning for Brain MRI Segmentation: State of The Art and Future Directions. *J. Digit. Imaging* **2017**, *30*, 449–459. [CrossRef] [PubMed]
4. Vincent, P.; Larochelle, H.; Lajoie, I.; Bengio, Y.; Manzagol, P.-A. Stacked Denoising Autoencoders: Learning Useful Representations in a Deep Network with a Local Denoising Criterion. *J. Mach. Learn. Res.* **2010**, *11*, 3371–3408.
5. Hinton, G.E.; Osindero, S.; Teh, Y.-W. A Fast Learning Algorithm for Deep Belief Nets. *Neural Comput.* **2006**, *18*, 1527–1554. [CrossRef]
6. Deng, J.; Dong, W.; Socher, R.; Li, L.-J.; Li, K.; Li, F.-F. ImageNet: A large-scale hierarchical image database. In *Proceedings of the 2009 IEEE Conference on Computer Vision and Pattern Recognition*; IEEE: Piscataway, NJ, USA, 2009.
7. Russakovsky, O.; Deng, J.; Su, H.; Krause, J.; Satheesh, S.; Ma, S.; Huang, Z.; Karpathy, A.; Khosla, A.; Bernstein, M.; et al. ImageNet Large Scale Visual Recognition Challenge. *Int. J. Comput. Vis.* **2015**, *115*, 211–252. [CrossRef]
8. Krizhevsky, A.; Sutskever, I.; Hinton, G.E. ImageNet Classification with Deep Convolutional Neural Networks. In *Advances in Neural Information Processing Systems 25*; Pereira, F., Burges, C.J.C., Bottou, L., Weinberger, K.Q., Eds.; Curran Associates, Inc.: Hong Kong, China, 2012; pp. 1097–1105.
9. Akkus, Z.; Kostandy, P.; Philbrick, K.A.; Erickson, B.J. Robust brain extraction tool for CT head images. *Neurocomputing* **2020**, *392*, 189–195. [CrossRef]
10. Akkus, Z.; Ali, I.; Sedlář, J.; Agrawal, J.P.; Parney, I.F.; Giannini, C.; Erickson, B.J. Predicting Deletion of Chromosomal Arms 1p/19q in Low-Grade Gliomas from MR Images Using Machine Intelligence. *J. Digit. Imaging* **2017**, *30*, 469–476. [CrossRef]
11. Cai, J.C.; Akkus, Z.; Philbrick, K.A.; Boonrod, A.; Hoodeshenas, S.; Weston, A.D.; Rouzrokh, P.; Conte, G.M.; Zeinoddini, A.; Vogelsang, D.C.; et al. Fully Automated Segmentation of Head CT Neuroanatomy Using Deep Learning. *Radiol. Artif. Intell.* **2020**, *2*, e190183. [CrossRef]
12. Akkus, Z.; Cai, J.; Boonrod, A.; Zeinoddini, A.; Weston, A.D.; Philbrick, K.A.; Erickson, B.J. A Survey of Deep-Learning Applications in Ultrasound: Artificial Intelligence-Powered Ultrasound for Improving Clinical Workflow. *J. Am. Coll. Radiol.* **2019**, *16*, 1318–1328. [CrossRef]
13. Leclerc, S.; Smistad, E.; Pedrosa, J.; Ostvik, A.; Cervenansky, F.; Espinosa, F.; Espeland, T.; Berg, E.A.R.; Jodoin, P.-M.; Grenier, T.; et al. Deep Learning for Segmentation using an Open Large-Scale Dataset in 2D Echocardiography. *IEEE Trans. Med. Imaging* **2019**. [CrossRef] [PubMed]
14. Jafari, M.H.; Girgis, H.; Van Woudenberg, N.; Liao, Z.; Rohling, R.; Gin, K.; Abolmaesumi, P.; Tsang, T. Automatic biplane left ventricular ejection fraction estimation with mobile point-of-care ultrasound using multi-task learning and adversarial training. *Int. J. Comput. Assist. Radiol. Surg.* **2019**, *14*, 1027–1037. [CrossRef]
15. Ouyang, D.; He, B.; Ghorbani, A.; Yuan, N.; Ebinger, J.; Langlotz, C.P.; Heidenreich, P.A.; Harrington, R.A.; Liang, D.H.; Ashley, E.A.; et al. Video-based AI for beat-to-beat assessment of cardiac function. *Nature* **2020**, *580*, 252–256. [CrossRef] [PubMed]
16. Zhang, J.; Gajjala, S.; Agrawal, P.; Tison, G.H.; Hallock, L.A.; Beussink-Nelson, L.; Lassen, M.H.; Fan, E.; Aras, M.A.; Jordan, C.; et al. Fully automated echocardiogram interpretation in clinical practice: Feasibility and diagnostic accuracy. *Circulation* **2018**, *138*, 1623–1635. [CrossRef] [PubMed]
17. Zhang, J.; Gajjala, S.; Agrawal, P.; Tison, G.H.; Hallock, L.A.; Beussink-Nelson, L.; Fan, E.; Aras, M.A.; Jordan, C.; Fleischmann, K.E.; et al. A web-deployed computer vision pipeline for automated determination of cardiac structure and function and detection of disease by two-dimensional echocardiography. *arXiv* **2017**, arXiv:1706.07342.
18. Deo, R. Echocv. Available online: https://bitbucket.org/rahuldeo/echocv (accessed on 26 March 2021).
19. Madani, A.; Arnaout, R.; Mofrad, M.; Arnaout, R. Fast and accurate view classification of echocardiograms using deep learning. *NPJ Digit. Med.* **2018**, *1*. [CrossRef]
20. Elwazir, M.Y.; Akkus, Z.; Oguz, D.; Ye, Z.; Oh, J.K. Fully Automated Mitral Inflow Doppler Analysis Using Deep Learning. In *Proceedings of the 2020 IEEE 20th International Conference on Bioinformatics and Bioengineering (BIBE)*; IEEE: Piscataway, NJ, USA, 2020; pp. 691–696.
21. Abdi, A.H.; Luong, C.; Tsang, T.; Allan, G.; Nouranian, S.; Jue, J.; Hawley, D.; Fleming, S.; Gin, K.; Swift, J.; et al. Automatic quality assessment of apical four-chamber echocardiograms using deep convolutional neural networks. In *Proceedings of the Medical Imaging 2017: Image Processing; International Society for Optics and Photonics*; IEEE: Piscataway, NJ, USA, 2017; Volume 10133, p. 101330S.
22. Abdi, A.H.; Luong, C.; Tsang, T.; Allan, G.; Nouranian, S.; Jue, J.; Hawley, D.; Fleming, S.; Gin, K.; Swift, J.; et al. Automatic Quality Assessment of Echocardiograms Using Convolutional Neural Networks: Feasibility on the Apical Four-Chamber View. *IEEE Trans. Med. Imaging* **2017**, *36*, 1221–1230. [CrossRef] [PubMed]

23. Abdi, A.H.; Luong, C.; Tsang, T.; Jue, J.; Gin, K.; Yeung, D.; Hawley, D.; Rohling, R.; Abolmaesumi, P. Quality Assessment of Echocardiographic Cine Using Recurrent Neural Networks: Feasibility on Five Standard View Planes. In *Proceedings of the Medical Image Computing and Computer Assisted Intervention–MICCAI 2017*; Springer International Publishing: Berlin/Heidelberg, Germany, 2017; pp. 302–310.
24. Dong, J.; Liu, S.; Liao, Y.; Wen, H.; Lei, B.; Li, S.; Wang, T. A Generic Quality Control Framework for Fetal Ultrasound Cardiac Four-Chamber Planes. *IEEE J. Biomed. Health Inform.* **2020**, *24*, 931–942. [CrossRef]
25. Labs, R.B.; Vrettos, A.; Azarmehr, N.; Howard, J.P.; Shun-shin, M.J.; Cole, G.D.; Francis, D.P.; Zolgharni, M. Automated Assessment of Image Quality in 2D Echocardiography Using Deep Learning. In Proceedings of the International Conference on Radiology, Medical Imaging and Radiation Oncology, Paris, France, 25–26 June 2020.
26. Simonyan, K.; Zisserman, A. Very Deep Convolutional Networks for Large-Scale Image Recognition. *arXiv* **2014**, arXiv:1409.1556.
27. Szegedy, C.; Ioffe, S.; Vanhoucke, V.; Alemi, A.A. Inception-v4, inception-resnet and the impact of residual connections on learning. In Proceedings of the Thirty-First AAAI Conference on Artificial Intelligence, San Francisco, CA, USA, 4–6 February 2017.
28. Ronneberger, O.; Fischer, P.; Brox, T. U-Net: Convolutional Networks for Biomedical Image Segmentation. In *Medical Image Computing and Computer-Assisted Intervention–MICCAI 2015*; Lecture Notes in Computer Science; Navab, N., Hornegger, J., Wells, W.M., Frangi, A.F., Eds.; Springer International Publishing: Munich, Germany, 2015; Volume 9351, pp. 234–241, ISBN 9783319245737.
29. Leclerc, S.; Smistad, E.; Pedrosa, J.; Ostvik, A. Cardiac Acquisitions for Multi-Structure Ultrasound Segmentation. Available online: https://camus.creatis.insa-lyon.fr/challenge/ (accessed on 26 March 2021).
30. Jafari, M.H.; Girgis, H.; Liao, Z.; Behnami, D.; Abdi, A.; Vaseli, H.; Luong, C.; Rohling, R.; Gin, K.; Tsang, T.; et al. A Unified Framework Integrating Recurrent Fully-Convolutional Networks and Optical Flow for Segmentation of the Left Ventricle in Echocardiography Data. In *Proceedings of the Deep Learning in Medical Image Analysis and Multimodal Learning for Clinical Decision Support*; Springer International Publishing: Granada, Spain, 2018; pp. 29–37.
31. Chen, H.; Zheng, Y.; Park, J.-H.; Heng, P.-A.; Zhou, S.K. Iterative Multi-domain Regularized Deep Learning for Anatomical Structure Detection and Segmentation from Ultrasound Images. In Proceedings of the Medical Image Computing and Computer-Assisted Intervention–MICCAI 2016, Athens, Greece, 17–21 October 2016; pp. 487–495.
32. Oktay, O.; Ferrante, E.; Kamnitsas, K.; Heinrich, M.; Bai, W.; Caballero, J.; Cook, S.A.; de Marvao, A.; Dawes, T.; O'Regan, D.P.; et al. Anatomically Constrained Neural Networks (ACNNs): Application to Cardiac Image Enhancement and Segmentation. *IEEE Trans. Med. Imaging* **2018**, *37*, 384–395. [CrossRef]
33. Ghorbani, A.; Ouyang, D.; Abid, A.; He, B.; Chen, J.H.; Harrington, R.A.; Liang, D.H.; Ashley, E.A.; Zou, J.Y. Deep learning interpretation of echocardiograms. *NPJ Digit. Med.* **2020**, *3*, 10. [CrossRef]
34. Ouyang, D. EchoNet-Dynamic. Available online: https://echonet.github.io/dynamic/ (accessed on 26 March 2021).
35. Omar, H.A.; Domingos, J.S.; Patra, A.; Upton, R.; Leeson, P.; Noble, J.A. Quantification of cardiac bull's-eye map based on principal strain analysis for myocardial wall motion assessment in stress echocardiography. In Proceedings of the 2018 IEEE 15th International Symposium on Biomedical Imaging (ISBI 2018), Washington, DC, USA, 4–7 April 2018; pp. 1195–1198.
36. Kusunose, K.; Abe, T.; Haga, A.; Fukuda, D.; Yamada, H.; Harada, M.; Sata, M. A Deep Learning Approach for Assessment of Regional Wall Motion Abnormality from Echocardiographic Images. *JACC Cardiovasc. Imaging* **2020**, *13*, 374–381. [CrossRef] [PubMed]
37. Narula, S.; Shameer, K.; Salem Omar, A.M.; Dudley, J.T.; Sengupta, P.P. Machine-Learning Algorithms to Automate Morphological and Functional Assessments in 2D Echocardiography. *J. Am. Coll. Cardiol.* **2016**, *68*, 2287–2295. [CrossRef]
38. He, K.; Zhang, X.; Ren, S.; Sun, J. Deep Residual Learning for Image Recognition. *arXiv* **2015**, arXiv:1512.03385.
39. Zeiler, M.D.; Fergus, R. Visualizing and Understanding Convolutional Networks. In Proceedings of the Lecture Notes in Computer Science, Zurich, Switzerland, 6–12 September 2014; pp. 818–833.
40. Zeiler, M.D.; Taylor, G.W.; Fergus, R. Adaptive deconvolutional networks for mid and high level feature learning. In Proceedings of the 2011 International Conference on Computer Vision, Washington, DC, USA, 6–13 November 2011.
41. Zhou, B.; Khosla, A.; Lapedriza, A.; Oliva, A.; Torralba, A. Learning Deep Features for Discriminative Localization. In Proceedings of the 2016 IEEE Conference on Computer Vision and Pattern Recognition (CVPR), Las Vegas, NV, USA, 27–30 June 2016.
42. Szegedy, C.; Vanhoucke, V.; Ioffe, S.; Shlens, J.; Wojna, Z. Rethinking the inception architecture for computer vision. In Proceedings of the IEEE Conference on Computer Vision and Pattern Recognition, Las Vegas, NV, USA, 27–30 June 2016; pp. 2818–2826.
43. Badrinarayanan, V.; Kendall, A.; Cipolla, R. SegNet: A Deep Convolutional Encoder-Decoder Architecture for Image Segmentation. *IEEE Trans. Pattern Anal. Mach. Intell.* **2017**, *39*, 2481–2495. [CrossRef] [PubMed]
44. Zeiler, M.D.; Krishnan, D.; Taylor, G.W.; Fergus, R. *Deconvolutional Networks*; IEEE Computer Society: San Francisco, CA, USA, 2010; pp. 2528–2535. ISBN 9781424469840.
45. Springenberg, J.T.; Dosovitskiy, A.; Brox, T.; Riedmiller, M. Striving for Simplicity: The All Convolutional Net. *arXiv* **2014**, arXiv:1412.6806.

46. Chattopadhay, A.; Sarkar, A.; Howlader, P.; Balasubramanian, V.N. Grad-CAM++: Generalized Gradient-Based Visual Explanations for Deep Convolutional Networks. In Proceedings of the 2018 IEEE Winter Conference on Applications of Computer Vision (WACV), Lake Tahoe, NV, USA, 12–15 March 2018; pp. 839–847.
47. Li, G.; Yu, Y. Visual Saliency Detection Based on Multiscale Deep CNN Features. *IEEE Trans. Image Process.* **2016**, *25*, 5012–5024. [CrossRef] [PubMed]
48. Philbrick, K.A.; Yoshida, K.; Inoue, D.; Akkus, Z.; Kline, T.L.; Weston, A.D.; Korfiatis, P.; Takahashi, N.; Erickson, B.J. What Does Deep Learning See? Insights from a Classifier Trained to Predict Contrast Enhancement Phase from CT Images. *AJR Am. J. Roentgenol.* **2018**, *211*, 1184–1193. [CrossRef] [PubMed]

MDPI
St. Alban-Anlage 66
4052 Basel
Switzerland
Tel. +41 61 683 77 34
Fax +41 61 302 89 18
www.mdpi.com

Journal of Clinical Medicine Editorial Office
E-mail: jcm@mdpi.com
www.mdpi.com/journal/jcm

www.ingramcontent.com/pod-product-compliance
Lightning Source LLC
LaVergne TN
LVHW070705100526
838202LV00013B/1036